CW00678076

A HISTORY
OF THE
TOWNSHIP
OF
TIMPERLEY, CHESHIRE
1070-1988

by

Ronald Broadhurst

First published in 1996 by
Ronald Broadhurst, 13 Ridgeway Road, Timperley, Altrincham, Cheshire WA15
7HA

© Ronald Broadhurst
ISBN 0 9527188 0 4

Typeset by Northern Writers Advisory Services, 77 Marford Crescent, Sale,
Cheshire M33 4DN

Computer graphics by Roger N. Broadhurst

Printed by Intype London Ltd, Woodman Works, Durnsford Road, Wimbledon
Park, London SW19 8DR

All rights reserved. No part of this publication may be reproduced in any form
without the prior written permission of the author.

Cover illustration
The seal of Thomas de Mascy, younger brother of Edward Mascy, Lord of
Bacford and Tymperlegh. It is engraved with the arms of the Mascy of Bacford
and Tymperlegh family:

'Quarterly Argent and Gules a Bendlet Azure, a fleur de lys in second quarter.'
(NB. This last probably a mark of cadency.)

It appeared on a label of a Grant of Lands in Aston by John Leycester dated 37
Edward III (i.e. 1364). The cover illustration is an enlarged version of the original.

CONTENTS

CHARTS

DOCUMENTS

DRAWINGS OF
CHRIST CHURCH, TIMPERLEY

MAPS

PHOTOGRAPHS

PLANS

To
Marjorie

PREFACE

I hold that the principal function of a local history is to provide the reader with an appreciation of the factors which, down the centuries, have impinged upon and caused change in a local community. In this book I have endeavoured to develop that tenet in the particular case of Timperley township.

My research, which was sporadic, spanned much of the 1980s and included, in addition to the essential archive research, a survey of the boundaries and 'nooks and crannies' (on foot and equipped with camera) of the township.

Once launched on the project I rapidly discovered that the extant archive material (apropos particular facets of the township's history) was limited, especially for the time preceding the nineteenth century. This paucity of documentary evidence inhibited my development of the chapters dealing with Timperley Hall, the Bridgewater Canal, and, to a lesser extent, Licensed Houses and Education.

My enquiries indicate that following amalgamation with Altrincham (1936) Timperley's Parish Council records were dispersed and in the process much, if not all, of the archive was either 'lost' or 'destroyed'. Additionally, I suspect that when the Altrincham Divisional Education Executive (inter-alia it administered Timperley's schools) was disbanded after the Local Government re-organisation of 1974, its archive suffered a similar fate. I have ascertained that neither archive has been deposited at Trafford Local Studies Centre nor Cheshire County Record Office in Chester.

In one respect, I have transgressed the conventional mores for the writing of local history by supplementing the text with apposite demographic statistics. I have also included a detailed description (with illustrations) of the architecture of the Parish Church. Purists advocate the avoidance of what they are pleased to call minutiae. I beg to demur. Such material 'fleshes out the skeleton', as the metaphor has it.

There is an adage which states: 'A History is outdated on the day following its completion'. It is certainly true of the post-1950 decades in the township during which the pace of change, when compared with the early years of the twentieth century, has been phenomenal. Post-1950s new development has been continuous and predominantly residential. This continuing urbanisation of Timperley acres has radically transformed the topography of the township as compared with its 1920 aspect.

On completion of the text at the end of 1989 the typescript lay fallow until the autumn of 1994 when I decided to publish this history. At that juncture I decided to update certain items by recording changes which had occurred in the interim. Such additions are concerned principally with the photographs and associated captions, articles appearing in local free newspapers and – where applicable – amplifying footnotes.

Within these pages I have striven to ensure the accuracy of the material contained therein. Whenever possible I have quoted documentary sources and/or other evidences in support of my conclusions. However, if errors of fact have occurred the fault is entirely mine and I offer, in advance, my sincere apologies to the reader.

R. Broadhurst
Timperley, Altrincham, Cheshire
1996

ACKNOWLEDGEMENTS

My grateful thanks are conveyed to all the people whose generous co-operation and helpful suggestions facilitated my research. In particular I wish to mention by name the Revd. D. Probets, for kindly allowing me to research the documentary material deposited in the Parish Chest at Christ Church; Mr S.C. Pillar, a church member, for his assistance on many occasions whilst I was engaged on researching the Church archive; the Revd. M. Braddy for his permission to consult the Baptism and Marriage Registers of Timperley Methodist Church; Mrs G. Fitzpatrick for her advice and expertise in the retrieval of relevant material then deposited at Altrincham Reference Library; the archivists at Cheshire County Record Office and Manchester Central Library; also members of staff at Trafford Local Studies Centre, Sale, all of whom invariably extended their assistance to me on the numerous occasions I visited each of those depositories.

R. Broadhurst

Timperley,
Altrincham,
Cheshire

ABBREVIATIONS USED IN THE TEXT

A	–	Acre(s)	N.R.C.	–	Nuisance Removal Committee
A.D.	–	*Anno Domini*			
Aet.	–	*Aetatis* (Of (or) At age of)	O.E.	–	Old English
A.P.L.U.	–	Altrincham Poor Law Union	O.N.	–	Old Norse (to 1150)
Appdx.(s)	–	Appendix/Appendices	O. of P.	–	Overseer(s) of the Poor
A. of P.	–	Act of Parliament	O.S.	–	Ordnance Survey
A.S.	–	Anglo Saxon			
A.U.D.C.	–	Altrincham Urban District Council	Pam.	–	Pamphlet
			Ped.	–	Pedigree
A.B.C.	–	Altrincham Borough Council	P.	–	Perch (a unit of measurement)
			P.C.	–	Parish Council
B.M.	–	Bastardy Money(ies)	p.a.	–	Per Annum
B. of G.	–	Board of Guardians	P.L.	–	Poor Law
B.R.D.C.	–	Bucklow Rural District	P.N.	–	Place Name
			Popln.	–	Population
C.	–	Circa (About/Around)	Prop.	–	Proprietor
Ch.	–	Chapter	Pub.	–	Publisher (or) Published
C.C.C.	–	Cheshire County Council			
Ccl(r)	–	Council/Councillor	Q.S.	–	Quarter Sessions
Clk.	–	Clerk			
C.P.S.	–	County Primary School	R.	–	Rood (a unit of measurement)
C.C.R.O.	–	Cheshire County Record Office	R.D.C.	–	Rural District Council
			Ref.	–	Reference
d.	–	daughter (or) died	R.V.	–	Rateable Value
D.B.	–	Domesday Book	R.S.D.	–	Rural Sanitary District
dd.	–	dated			
dj.	–	*de jure* (By right or (or) rightfully)	S.A.C.	–	School Attendance Committee
			Sec.	–	Secretary
Dir.	–	Directory	S.V.	–	Select Vestry
			sic	–	Thus used (or) spelt
Fac.	–	Faculty	S.L.A.	–	School Leaving Age
			S.M.	–	Southern Moiety
G. of P.	–	Guardians of the Poor	s. & h.	–	son and heir
			S. of H.	–	Surveyor of Highways
h.	–	heir/heiress	*supra*	–	above
infra	–	below or under	s.p.	–	*sine prole* (without issue)
Inq. P.M.	–	Inquisition Post Mortem	s.p.m.	–	*sine prole mort* (died without issue)
J.P.	–	Justice of the Peace			
			T.A.	–	Tithe Assessments
L.D.	–	Local Directory(ies)	T.P.C.	–	Timperley Parish Council
L.E.A.	–	Local Education Authority			
L.G.B.	–	Local Government Board	U.D.C.	–	Urban District Council
Ltr.	–	Letter	Ux.	–	*Uxoris* (wife or spouse)
m.	–	married	V	–	Vide
M.E.	–	Middle English (1150-1500)	VCH	–	Victorian County Histories
Mod. Eng.	–	Modern English (1500 onwards)	Vistn.	–	Visitation
Mtg.	–	Meeting	Viz.	–	*Videlicet* (that is)
			V.S.	–	Voluntary Subscription(s)
N.E.T.	–	North East Transept			
N.M.	–	Northern Moiety	W.T.	–	West Transept
Nr.	–	Near			

Timperley Village looking east. The block of modern shop property (left foreground) originally contained large Victorian residential housing. Note the original garden gate pillars still in situ. Adjacent to the white car (centre-ground) stood an ancient beech tree (about one hundred years plus old) which was blown down in a freak gale at the end of May 1992. (Photograph taken by author, February 1993.)

Timperley Village looking west. (Photograph taken by author, February 1993.)

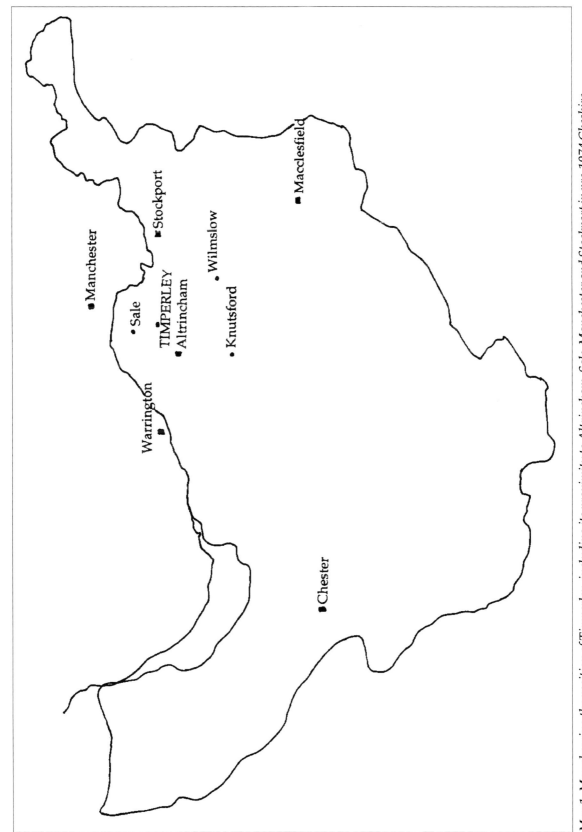

Map 1. Map showing the position of Timperley, including its proximity to Altrincham, Sale, Manchester and Stockport in pre-1974 Cheshire.

THE ORIGIN AND MEANING OF THE PLACE NAME 'TIMPERLEY'
OR
The Game of the Name

'Yet leaving here a name I trust that will not perish in the dust.'

R. Southey

History may be defined thus:

'A study of Change in Society and the Factors which have occasioned it.'

The pace of change is variable – as a general rule it has evolved slowly but during certain periods it has been rapid (for example, the twentieth century). Local history epitomises this truism.

Of the many facets which, taken collectively, chart the history of a township, its place name, as a general rule, is the facet exhibiting the least change down the centuries. Its spelling form and/or pronunciation may vary over the years yet its contemporary form, in many cases, is comparable and identifiable with spelling forms inscribed in documents of the Middle English period. By contrast, its contemporary topography and the socio-economic lifestyle of its inhabitants exhibit fundamental changes.

This chapter investigates and endeavours to answer the questions posed below.

- When did the place name *Timperley* originate?
- What is its *Original Meaning*?
- What factors have influenced the *Form* of the name?

For some townships the overwhelming weight of factual evidence extant enables a researcher to establish conclusively the original meaning of a particular P.N. On the other hand, for many P.N.s one is constrained to conclude that a definitive answer to the questions posed above is, due to the paucity and/or conflicting evidences available, impossible. In such cases one can only present the evidences considered and give reasons for accepting, or rejecting, all or any of them. A subjective definition, based on the balance of probability, indicated by those evidences, may then be ventured.

The author's research suggests that the P.N. 'Timperley' falls into the latter category. The material considered embraces the undermentioned evidences.

Documentary
The most important source of place name spelling forms. (NB. The cardinal requisite for an absolute definition of a P.N. is an early spelling form.)

Language Development
Our original Celtic language was first superseded by Old English (i.e. Anglo-Saxon), its vocabulary being extended subsequently by the assimilation of words of Scandinavian and French origin.

Dialectical and Phonological
Down the centuries original sounds have often undergone subtle modifications due to variations in dialectical pronunciation influencing the spelling form of a name.

Topographical and Habitational
These are the two principal types of P.N. *Topographical* – P.N. identifies with a prominent natural feature (for example, river, ford, hill). *Habitational* – P.N. identifies with a dwelling (for example, farm, homestead, castle).

Prof. K. Cameron[1] states that:

'The vast majority of our old P.N.s were in existence by the time of the Norman Conquest; names of Celtic origin... were already in use before the coming of the Anglo-Saxons (fifth century) and others were given by the Anglo-Saxons (mid-fifth to eleventh century) whilst P.N. of Scandinavian origin date from late ninth to eleventh centuries' *and also* '... since many of our old P.N.s date from the Anglo-Saxon period the original forms of them are in O.E...' *and* '... the Anglo-Saxons adopted some existing P.N.s from the British (Celtic) inhabitants and assimilated the P.N.s as far as possible to O.E. – vowels and consonants being represented by the nearest O.E. equivalent...' *also* '... that though many English P.N.s originated before 1066 A.D. few spellings of them, from pre-Conquest times, have survived because of the loss of many of the early documents and thus most of the early spelling forms extant come from the M.E. period... but the vast majority of village and parish names, however old, are not recorded from the Anglo-Saxon period. For most P.N.s the earliest spelling form is that found in D.B. 1086 A.D.'

Prof. E. Ekwall[2] states that:

'If good name forms from D.B. or texts of the twelfth or early thirteenth centuries are available a fairly safe etymology can generally be attained, but even then the etymology of many names remains more or less doubtful.'

He also stresses the importance of the local topography on the origin of many P.N.s.

Bearing in mind the quotations above, the factors above-mentioned are considered with regard to the P.N. *Timperley*.

Documentary Evidence
It occurs frequently in documents of the M.E. period.

Spelling Form	Date	Reference
Timperleie	1211-1225	Barraclough (p)
Timperleigh	1211-1272	Henry III (Pudsey)
Tympirleg	1285	Court (p)
Ti & Tymperleg(h)	c.1290-1293	Mid. Ch. (Ormerod)
Ti & Tymperlegh(e)	1293	Ch.
Ti & Tymperle(e)	1296-1300	Plea
Ti & Tymperleg(e)	1304	Chamb.
Ti & Tymperleigh	1349-1350	Earwaker & Chamb.
Tymporlegh(-ley)	1367 & 1389	Ch. R.R.
Tympurlegh	1371	A.D.
Tympalegh	1375	Tab.
Tympurley	1419	B.J.R.L.
Tympyrleg	1503	Plea
Templey	1549	Pat.
Timporley	1724	Not. Cestr.

(For explanations of these abbreviations see list at the end of the chapter.)

A close study of these spelling forms reveals two salient points.

- Excluding the form 'Templey', each spelling form gives the same, or practically the same, pronunciation as the contemporary spelling form. Thus the *sound* form and the *spelling* form of Timperley have both remained most consistent for over 750 years.

- The variations in the spelling forms are understandable for three cardinal reasons:
  They preceded, for the most part, the introduction of printing.

Prior to the introduction of printing spelling was either *traditional* or *phonetical*.

The stabilisation of the spelling form only became essential following the introduction of printing and even then took many decades to establish.

Practically all of the above spelling forms are recorded in documents of the M.E. period by Anglo-French clerks when Latin was the principal vehicle for their written work. Following the Norman Conquest many English P.N.s were recorded for the first time by these Norman scribes (or English clerks educated in Norman schools); these scribes, in the absence of an established system of spelling, relied on a phonetical spelling form which represented the pronunciation of local speakers, or else wrote a document from the dictation of others who were not necessarily local people.[3] In some cases a scribe would use a traditional P.N. form found in a document he was copy-ing, making no change. Such a spelling form often persists from the A.S. or early M.E. period down to the present day.

The variations in the spelling form are, in the first syllable TIM, 'i' or 'y' for the sound 'i' as in P*I*N. This is of no consequence. It arises because O.E. had seven vowels (i.e. a, æ, e, i, o, u, y) and during the course of time 'æ' and 'y' have ceased to be included.

In the M.E. period 'i' and 'y' were obviously used vicariously to represent the short vowel sound of 'i'; 'y' is still used for the short 'i' sound in many contemporary words (for example, sympathy, cynic, etc.) and also the 'i' sound (for example, rhyme, cry, dry, etc.).

In the second syllable PER is rendered vicariously as 'per', 'por', 'pyr', 'pur', 'pir', 'pa'. Here again we notice the interchangeability of the 'i' and 'y' in the digraphs '*ir*' and '*yr*'. These, together with '*er*' and '*ur*' are variously used to represent the one phonetic sound '*er*' (as in 'fern'). The digraph '*or*' is the only one of the group representing a different phonetic sound (for example, '*or*' as in 'born'). I have formed the opinion that '*or*', along with the form '*pa*', represents a slightly different dialectical pronunciation of the medial syllable which the scribe has denoted with symbols he considered correctly represented the particular pronunciation of the person dictating to him. We can still see today the use variously of '*ir*', '*yr*', '*er*', '*ur*' to represent the digraph sound '*er*' as in 'fern' (for example, f*ir*m, sat*yr*, s*er*ve, b*ur*n). Thus they merely reflect the idiosyncratic spelling of individual Anglo-French clerks when required to represent an A.S. word phonetically.

In the final syllable LEY is rendered in a number of spelling forms, but basically they can be reduced to two pronunciations:

LEE – as in '*lee*k' – represented by 'legh', 'leigh', 'leie' and 'lee';
LI – as in '*li*p' – represented by 'ley' and 'le'.

These also reflect dialectical variations in pronunciation. Over the years the sound '*lee*' (as in 'leek') has metamorphosed to the contemporary pronunciation '*ly*' (as in 'lip'). It is interesting to note that the sound pronounced '*lee*' as in 'leek' still persists in a number of Cheshire P.N.s such as High Leigh and Little Leigh and the spelling form conforms with the spelling form extant in the thirteen and fourteenth century. This would appear to lend weight to the theory that in the case of Timperley, the change in pronunciation stems from dialectical variations due to 'sloppiness' in enunciation resulting in the clipping of the final syllable.

It is also interesting to note that the spelling forms ending in 'legh' and 'leghe' are largely from documentary sources originating in London; whereas most of the other spelling forms are found in Cheshire documents. This suggests that London clerks relied on a P.N. spelling found in another document, whilst the spelling forms of local origin were written down from dictation and reflect differing dialectical pronunciations.

What is the original meaning of the Place Name 'Timperley'?
It splits naturally into three syllables:

Tim – per – ley or alternatively *Timp – er – ley*.

The latter fragmentation may be significant as will be appreciated subsequently.

It is accepted that P.N.s whose origins preceded the Norman Conquest may be divided into two main groups: *Habitative* and *Topographical*. In the particular case of Timperley, and discussing the last syllable first, we find that the terminal '*ley*' is a derivative of the O.E. '*lēah*' (dative: '*lēa*', '*lēage*',

3

'*līeg*'). It corresponds to the old High German '*lōh*' = 'grove'; Low German '*lōh*' = thin wood; Old Norman '*lō*' = low lying meadow; Dutch '*loo*' = wood and the Latin '*lucus*' = grove.

It is only found in O.E. charter material, but there it is very common. This must be A.S. in origin. The original meaning of '*lēah*' was '*an open place in a wood*' or '*a part in a wood with the trees scattered so that grass could grow*'. In English P.N.s two senses are to be reckoned with: the more common one is '*open place in a wood*' (or glade) and probably defined a naturally open space. If the rendering *clearing* is used it should be taken in the sense *glade*. P.N.s with this element were originally topographical but it is possible that the meaning of the element changed. As a '*ham*' or '*lēah*' often coincided with the (cultivated) area of a settlement the original meaning of the words could easily change into '*land belonging to a homestead or village*'.

The other main sense is '*wood*' or '*forest*'. Such open spaces would lend themselves to agricultural use for pasture or arable cultivation. Some P.N.s ending in *ley* suggest this:

Arable Use – *Wheatley, Flaxley*	Cattle Grazing – *Calverley*
Type of Wood – *Ashley, Hazeley*	Timber Product – *Staveley*

P.N.s ending in *ley* proliferate in Cheshire; an O.S. map reveals scores of them within a few miles' radius of Timperley. In this connection it is interesting to note that the oldest roads in the township all have an affinity with woodland (for example, Thorley, Wood and Grove Lanes and also Woodlands Parkway). Even today the county is well wooded – one has only to view the landscape from a vantage point (for example, Bowdon Church) to appreciate the fact.

On the basis of the evidence above one can confidently assert that in pre-Conquest times this area of Cheshire was densely wooded; further more it suggests that such P.N.s ending in '*ley*' probably originated in the same historical period; also that P.N.s were much influenced by some topographical feature or land use.

Reverting to the first element of *Timper*ley, what kind of a '*lēah*' is denoted by the element '*Timper*'? Prima facie it does not suggest a land use *or* topographical connotation. Hypotheses, indicated by research, are listed below.

It may denote:

- *A Timber building in a '*lēah*' (C.O.D.). From P.N. '*Timperon*' (defined as 'timber building' presumably from '*Timber – ærn*') (n.b. '*Ærn*' from O.E. a 'dwelling house' or 'storehouse')

- A '*Timber – wood*' or '*Timber – glade*' (C.O.D.) (derived from '*Timber – lēah*)

- *A sandstone outcrop in a wood* (or *glade*) (Pamphlet. 171 – Alt. Ref.)

Each of these hypotheses is now considered.

- Can '*Timper*' be equated with '*Timber*' and '*ley*' with '*ærn*'? There is a Cumberland P.N. '*Timperon Hall*'. Could this be a modified spelling form of '*Timper – ærn*' due to dialectical modifications? Alas *no*. Research reveals that the P.N. derives from an old Irish/Scandinavian compound '*tiompan*' (a 'small abrupt hill' *or* 'standing stone') and the M.E. '*ron*' (from the O.N. '*runnr*' – a 'brake' *or* 'thicket'). Also the spelling of Timper-ley does not allow of the old Irish word and this '*tiompan*' cannot be equated with '*timper*' and '*Timber*' cannot be equated with '*Tiompan*'.[4]

- Can '*Timper*' be equated with '*Timber*' and '*ley*' with '*lēah*'? From the spelling forms '*Timper – leigh*' (Henry III – Pudsey 1211-1272) and '*Tymperleg*' (1285 Court and later) it denotes a '*Timber – wood*' or '*Timber – glade*'. The word '*Timber – lunt*' (D.B.) and also '*Timber – lund*' (1155 D.M.) denotes 'Grove where timber was got of' (V.C.H. – (K) III). The O.E. '*lund*'; O.N. '*lunder*' denoting grove *or* copse is the source of '*lunt*' and '*lund*'. The O.E. '*Timber*'; O.N. – '*Timbr*'; denotes '*Timber – wood*'. It usually takes the meaning 'grove' *or* 'copse' when the *first* element of a P.N. (for example, *Lond – esboro: Lond – on*) whereas when it forms the last element takes the meaning 'land' (for example *Sinder – land, Kirk – land*). Thus '*Timber – lunt*' seems to indicate '*Timber – land*' and cannot be equated with '*Timper – leigh*' because '*lunt*' is NOT the second element of Timperley. Furthermore, unless it can be proved that 'p' has been substituted for 'b', '*Timber*'[5] cannot be equated with '*Timper*'.

Can Timperley be equated with the definition 'Township sited at a stone outcrop in a woodland clearing',[6] which is advanced by a life-long Timperley resident writing in a m.s. letter (c.1933/4)? The relevant points from that letter are quoted on below. The brackets are his.

'O.E. – Tymp – "A huge block of quarried sandstone": "Teutonic – burgh – A town".'
'A.S. – ley – "A woodland clearing".'

The letter continues:

'... Timperley rests on solid sandstone, possesses large stone quarries (now disused)... Great blocks of stone were quarried from time immemorial at Timperley (Tymperley). These were called "tymps" (see W.D. Whitney for confirmation)[7] and in almost every farmyard in the township one may be seen, hollowed and used as cisterns or drinking troughs. They exist in the houses themselves as hearthstones, millstones, grindstones, smithy hearths and at Ironfounders' works, all evidence of a "tymp"...'

Observations on the etymology advanced by Mr H. Hulme

- The terms 'O.E.', 'Teutonic' and 'A.S.' are synonymous (i.e. the English language as spoken and written up to 1150A.D.).
- No sources are quoted in support of his definition of the name as Anglo-Saxon.
- States correctly the existence of stone quarries in the township but presents no evidence to support his statement '... blocks of stone quarried from time immemorial...'.
- States that the element 'tymp' connotes a 'huge block of sandstone...' and adds '... see W.D. Whitney...'. That publication defines 'Tymp' as '... arch of masonry "*tymp arch*"' or 'a block of stone *tymp – stone*...' and continues '... appears in documents from 1645...'.
  Thus his thesis has *not proved* that *in the thirteenth century* the term 'tymp' connoted 'a huge block of sandstone...'.
- States that '... '"burgh" means a "town"' and appears to equate it with the 'er' in Timperley. 'Burgh' is O.E. for *'fortified place'* in its primary sense and has other meanings (for example, 'fortified house').

None of the three hypotheses above determine, conclusively, a *positive* original meaning and/or the *precise date* of origin of the P.N. 'Timperley'. Accordingly, it cannot be definitively classified as Celtic, Anglo-Saxon, Scandinavian, or Norman; thus any assessment of the relative merit of a particular hypothesis must be drawn from the established facts. What are the facts?

1. Numerous spelling forms extant from the early thirteenth century – all remarkably consistent in form and mostly in M.E.

2. P.N. a compound name of typical O.E. form.

3. All the spelling forms possess a first element 'Timper' spelt with a 'p'; *NOT ONE* spelling form substitutes a 'b' for a 'p'.

4. Final syllable a derivative of the O.E. 'lēah' whose original meaning was 'an open space in a wood' *or* 'a part in a wood where trees scattered so that grass can grow'. With the passage of time it developed alternative interpretations (for example, 'grove' *or* 'glade'.

5. It has a very common P.N. suffix – *'ley'* (manifested in many Cheshire P.N.s)

6. County still well wooded.

7. Most P.N.s Habitational *or* Topographical in origin.

8. Not mentioned in D.B. – but evidence of strip farming in the parish.[8]

9. Most P.N.s extant, but few were recorded, pre-1066. Most had original spelling forms in O.E.

10. Spelling forms vary because of dialectical pronunciation and phonetical interpretation by clerks.

11. O.E. assimilated many words of Scandinavian origin. Usually the first element of a Scandinavian P.N. is a personal name.

12. With the passage of time the pronunciation of P.N.s has changed due to variations of syllable stress and long and short vowel rules in O.E. (for example, child – children; south – southern).

13. It is extremely difficult to determine names of Celtic origin.

14. Stone quarries (now abandoned) sited in centre of township.

15. Village wholly agricultural until c.1850.

16. Certain field names in township suggest they were in cultivation pre-1066 (see 8 above).

From the facts listed above the P.N. Timperley is, in the opinion of the author:

- A *Topographical* name of O.E. form and origin (see 1 and 2 above).
- It was *extant*, but not recorded, pre-1066 (see 9 above).
- Its first element denotes a *'STONE OUTCROP'* (see 14 above).
- Its final element denotes an *'OPEN PLACE IN A WOOD'* (see 4 above).
- The available evidence is insufficient to establish a precise date of origin.

These deductions indicate that the P.N. means:

'A sandstone outcrop'	(at)	*'An open place in a wood'*
TIMPER	–	LEY

The etymologies which equate Timperley with a *'Timber – lēah'* and *'Timber – ærn'* are rejected for the reasons listed below:

- No extant spelling form incorporates a 'b'.
- If, during the course of time, 'p' replaced an original 'b' for dialectical or phonological reasons, it would be reasonable to expect at *least one* of those earlier spelling form to exhibit a 'b' in its spelling.
- A wood was important economically to communities in the Middle Ages, if only for the timber it provided; yet amongst the many Cheshire P.N.s ending in 'ley' none apparently incorporates the element 'Timber' in its name. If *Timper*ley connotes 'Timber' surely it would be spelt with a 'b' in M.E.
- O.E. 'ærn' has the meaning 'dwelling house' *or* 'storehouse' whereas all the evidence indicates that *'ley'* cannot be equated with *'a house'* or *'a dwelling'*.
- Can 'Timper' be a form of 'tymp – ærn' (taking the meaning 'stonehouse')? As the name is O.E., it is unlikely, pre-1066, that peasants would live in stonehouses, nor manor houses be built of stone.

On the basis of the facts below, 'tymp' has an affinity with 'stone'.

- Printed evidence from the seventeenth century onwards, associates it with stone.
- Irish/Scandinavian 'tiompan' has the sense *'standing stone'*. (N.B. The author has no proof that 'tymp' derives from this but it is a possibility.)

Careful consideration of all the known facts does justify the conclusion that, on balance, the weight of evidence comes down in favour of the element *'Timper'* equating with 'stone'.

Notes
1. K. Cameron, *English Place Names*, Methuen, 1969.
2. E. Ekwall, *Concise Oxford Dictionary of English Place Names*, 4th edition, 1960.
3. *Introduction to the Survey of English Place Names*, Vol.1.
4. Cumberland Record Office.
5. *Concise Oxford Dictionary of English Place Names*.
6. Mr H. Hulme, pamphlet No.171, Altrincham Reference Library.
7. W.D. Whitney, *Concise Dictionary and Cyclopaedia*, published 1914. See also Murray, *A New English Dictionary*, Clarendon Press, 1933.
8. See manuscript draft of 'History of Timperley' by Lt. Col. C.E. Newton (c.1935). Deposited at C.C.R.O. (Ref. DDX. 137/21).

Abbreviations Used in Chapter 1

A.D.	– Catalogue of Ancient Deeds, P.R.O., London, 1890
An A.S.D.	– *An Anglo Saxon Directory*, T.N. Toller, Oxford University Press, Oxford, 1898
Barraclough	– *The Charters of the Anglo-Norman Earls of Chester, c.1071-1237*, edited by G. Barraclough, Record Society of Lancashire and Cheshire, vol. 126, 1988
B.J.R.L.	– *Bulletin of John Rylands Library*, Manchester, 1950
B.P.R.	– *Register of Edward the Black Prince*, P.R.O., 1930-33
Ch.	– Calendar of Charter Rolls, Cheshire and P.R.O.
Chamb.	– *Accounts of Chamberlains and other Officers of Chester*, Record Society of Lancashire and Cheshire, Vol.59, 1916
Ch. R.R.	– Calendar of Cheshire Recognisance Rolls
Cl.	– Calendar of Close Rolls, P.R.O., London
C.O.D.	– *Concise Oxford Dictionary of English Place Names*, E. Ekwall, eth edition, 1960
Court	– Calendar of County Court; City Court and Eyre Rolls of Chester
Cum. R.O.	– Cumberland Record Office
D.M.	– Domesday Monachorum
D.K.R.	– Reports of Deputy Keeper of Public Records
Earwaker	– *Place Names of Cheshire*, J.P. Earwaker, Vol. 45
E.P.N.S.	– English Place Name Society, *Survey of English Place Names*
Eyre	– Palatinate of Chester: Eyre Rolls of Justice of Chester, in P.R.O.
K.	– Kent
Leycester	– Sir Peter Leycester's *Cheshire Antiquities*
Mx.	– Middlesex
N.E.D.	– *A New Dictionary (Oxford English Dictionary)*, 1953
Not. Cestr	– *Notitis Cestrianis*
N.R.A.	– National Register of Archives
Orm.	– G. Ormerod, *History of Cheshire*, London 1819; also T. Helsby edition, 1892
Pat.	– Calendar of Patent Rolls, P.R.O., London, 1901
Pipe	– *Cheshire in the Pipe Rolls*, Mills and Brown, Record Society of Lancashire and Cheshire, 1938.
Plea	– Deeds, Inquisitions, etc., enrolled on Plea Rolls of City of Chester
Pudsey	– Pudsey deeds, Yorkshire Archaeological Society, Record Series, No.56
R.C.	– *Rotuli Chartorum*, London, 1837
Recog.	– Recognisance Rolls
Tab.	– MSS of Leicester-Warren of Tabley Archive (mostly seventeenth century), CCRO
Tait	– *Domesday Survey of Cheshire*, J. Tait.
T.R.E.	– Tempore Regis Edwardi (i.e. In the time of King Edward)

2

TIMPERLEY: ITS GEOLOGY AND GEOGRAPHY

'Erstwhile a village in the country
Now a suburb of a town.'

Anon.

The couplet above describes, succinctly, the metamorphosis of Timperley township from an agricultural to an suburban area. The process began about 1850 and currently (1988) still continues. If this rate of release – of the limited acres still available for development – is maintained then it is probable that the supply will be exhausted at, or soon after, the year 2000.

Geology

The rock types underlying the Timperley acres,[1] are relatively young in terms of the geological time scale. They belong to two eras and are confined to two geological periods within these eras.

The solid rocks (1 and 2 below) lie in super-position above the much older Coal Measures of the Carboniferous period. The lower bed consists of the New Red Sandstone (1 below) belonging to one of the uppermost beds of the sub-divisions. Above it is the Keuper (Marl) (2 below). Both these beds dip approximately four degrees to the south. When the Timperley quarries were extant, between Shaftesbury Avenue and Stockport Road, the line of the bed could be seen and the marl beds, overlying the sandstone, could be identified at Timperley Brook in the form of thin soft flags jutting out from the banks. In this connection I quote from the text of an interesting lecture, delivered c.1890, on the subject 'The Geology of Altrincham and

ERA	PERIOD	SOLID ROCK TYPE	AGE IN MILLIONS OF YEARS
1. *Mesozoic*	Triassic	@ New Red Sandstone	225-190
2. *Mesozoic*	Triassic	X Keuper (Marl) Sandstone	225-100
DRIFT			
3. *Cainozoic*	Quaternary	Boulder Clay	2.5 *or* less
4. *Cainozoic*	Quaternary	Glacial Sands and Gravel	2.5 *or* less
NB. @ – Consists of four or five subdivisions of sandstone proper. X – A shaly rock.			

District'.[2] The extract deals specifically with Timperley.

'... you will remember the order of super-position of the rock above the Coal series is (1st) Permian Sandstone, a bed lying on the upturned, contorted and eroded surface of the Coal Measures: (2nd) the New Red Sandstone which consists of four or five sub-divisions of Sandstone proper and (3rd) on top of them a shaly rock known as the New Red Sandstone Marl (Keuper); then, omitting succeeding beds (Liassic – Oolite – Tertiary) we come to the period when Boulder Clay was deposited and the subsequent drift of Sand and Gravel. Now we have these beds under us but, you will ask, where can we see them? Let us first go to Timperley and examine the two quarries there...' [When extant they were sited between the present Shaftesbury Avenue and Stockport Road.] '... We shall find that the beds of New Red Sandstone do not lie horizontally but are inclined at angle of about four degrees, dipping toward the south and on examination of this structure of the rock and comparing it with others where the relative position can be more accurately ascertained we find the Timperley sandstone belongs to the uppermost beds of that particular series and we should expect to find the Red Marl very near and above it. Now remembering that the dip is about four degrees to the south and walking southerly we soon reach the Timperley...' [He now relates how he went minnow fishing there as a boy and how he soon learned that the small ones were usually found under 'overhanging ledges jutting out of the bank'.] 'Now these thin flags are what we are looking for; they belong to the Marl beds which overlie the sandstone proper – the sandstone we left at Timperley – and these Marl beds are also at an angle of four degrees to the south...'

Drifts of boulder clay and glacial sands gravel overlay the beds of solid rock.

Boulder Clay

The area of the township with boulder clay drifts is mostly bounded by a line drawn a little to the north of Timperley Brook (on the southern border of the township) running eastward to the Fairywell Brook, then along the line of the Fairywell Brook to a point approximately a quarter of a mile north of Ridgeway Road where its boundary runs away from the brook in a west-north-west direction until it joins Thorley Lane, almost touching the anvil-shaped area mentioned below. It then runs along Thorley Lane to Stockport Road and thence along the line of Stockport Road westwards to the Timperley Brook boundary. It then traverses the golf course to the south of the Old Hall Hotel and then continues to the parish boundary, opposite the junction of White Carr and Clay Lanes.

Glacial Sand and Gravel

This is found in a small anvil-shaped area bounded by Thorley Lane (from its junction with Shaftesbury Avenue to a point a little south of the junction of Thorley and Wood Lanes), then by a line running west (across Warburton's nursery) to Faulkner Drive; thence north-west across Wood Lane, Lorraine Road, to Shaftesbury Avenue, and then east to its junction with Thorley Lane.

Fluvio Glacial Gravel

The remainder of the township to the north of the boulder clay area is overlaid by this drift.

N.B. The boulder clay area has underlying strata with a three degree dip approximately to the south.

Geography

The township is roughly pear-shaped with its narrow end in the north-west, and embraces 1638 acres. Its north-west/south-west axis, Washway Road to Dobbinets Lane, is about two-and-a-half miles long and its north-east/south-west axis is about one-and-a-half miles at its widest point, i.e. the line of Stockport Road from the Fairywell Brook to the Timperley Brook.[3]

It is sited on the southern margin of the wide valley of the River Mersey. In this section of its course the Mersey meanders across its flood plain via Ashton-on-Mersey and Carrington Moss. The northern boundary of Timperley is on the south-eastern edge of Carrington Moss and about two-and-a-half miles from the River Mersey's banks. The Timperley Brook flows through the township on its way to its confluence with the Sinderland Brook at a point north of Washway Road. The Fairywell Brook forms part of the eastern border of the township to its confluence with the Baguley Brook, at a point between the Manchester South Junction and Altrincham Railway Line (MSJ and A Railway), and Woodhouse Lane East, where their combined waters form the Sinderland Brook, which in its turn becomes the border of the township on the east and north. It leaves the township at Washway Road to flow across Carrington Moss and drain into the River Mersey.[4]

Relief

The township is predominantly flat but to the south-east of Stockport Road the land rises to a ridge on its southern border (see section diagram in Appendix 1 at the end of this chapter). The section profile shows that the land surface rises 23 feet (gradient 1:287) between Washway and Stockport Roads over a distance of 1¼ miles. Between Stockport Road and Dobbinets Lane it rises 48 feet (gradient 1:131) over a distance of 1⅓ miles. Along its northern boundary, i.e. the line of Washway Road between Smith's and Siddall's Bridges, the average height above mean sea level is 77½ feet (it only varies between 76 feet and 79 feet between those two features). Between the Timperley and Fairywell Brooks' bridges on Stockport Road the average height is 100 feet above sea level and only varies between 94 feet and 100 feet.[5]

Topographical Features

Woodland

Excluding Fairywell Wood and a small spinney through which the Baguley Brook flows between the canal and Pelican Hotel, and a line of mixed conifer and deciduous trees flanking Brooks Drive, no woodland has survived the intensive residential development of the township.

Rock Outcrops

To the rear of Marston's Joiners' Yard,[6] premises which front onto Stockport Road, the vestiges of sandstone outcrop can be seen. Its was the site of one of the two stone quarries in the township. The other quarry, the Delph Quarry, which has now been built on, was sited nearer to Shaftesbury Avenue. They were actively worked during the seventeenth to nineteenth centuries but have now been defunct for many decades.

Springs

Ground springs occur on the rising land, especially between Ridgeway and Fairview Roads (part of the boulder clay area of the township). One can still be seen flowing through the garden of a house in Fairview Road. (NB. The church cellar often suffered flooding during prolonged periods of wet weather.)

Boundary of the Civil Parish[7]

Starting at the south-east corner of the township (i.e. junction of Fairywell Brook and Dobbinets Lane) it is coincident with the Fairywell Brook and runs in a north-west direction until it joins the Baguley Brook, a little to the west of Beccles Wood (Baguley). En route, it crosses Brooks Drive (about 350 yards south of the Stockport-Warrington Railway), Shaftesbury Avenue, Stockport Road and Beech Playing Fields.

The Baguley Brook, from its confluence with Fairywell Brook, now becomes the boundary. Coursing westward, it traverses the MSJ and A Railway and Bridgewater Canal (about 600 yards north-east of Timperley Station) then skirts the edge of Frieston and Leys Roads to the Washway Road (at Siddall's Bridge,[8] some yards north-east of the Pelican Hotel).

The boundary now leaves the line of the Baguley Brook and runs south-west, coincident with the Washway Road, to the Timperley Brook at Smith's Bridge (about 100 yards east of West Timperley Station Bridge).

It now follows the line of the Timperley Brook, skirting Salisbury Road playing fields (Altrincham), crossing the Cheshire Lines Committee Railway (CLC Railway), Bridgewater Canal and the edge of Skelton Junction, skirts the edge of Navigation Road Playing fields (Altrincham) and crosses the MSJ and A Railway (just north of Navigation Road Station). It now crosses Brook Lane and Wellington Road, before traversing south (along the edge of Woodlands Parkway) to join Stockport Road. It now skirts the edge of the Altrincham Golf Links. At a point about 400 yards south of Stockport Road it departs from the line of Timperley Brook and is coincident with the perimeter of King George's Pool. It rejoins the line of the Timperley Brook at the footbridge (adjacent to King George's Pool).

From this point it courses south-east, crossing the Timperley Brook-Wood Lane footpath (see 5 below), to a point some 100 yards east of it where it again leaves the line of the brook running south-west for 100 yards before turning east. After traversing about 850 yards east (skirting Delahays Road Playing Fields, Hale) it crosses Green Lane and Delahays Road. It then skirts the edge of Old Meadow Lane, Hale and after about 350 yards turns north until it joins the footpath (King George's Pool to Wellfield Lane – see 6 below). It now turns east (along the line of the footpath) and after about 100 yards crosses Wellfield Lane. It now runs south-east and after about 350 yards rejoins the line of Timperley Brook for approximately 100 yards before turning east and, crossing nursery land, rejoins Clay Lane (at its junction with White Carr Lane). It then proceeds north-east along Clay Lane to rejoin Fairywell Brook at its junction with Dobbinets Lane.

Canal

A 1200 yard section of the Bridgewater Canal, running in a north to south direction traverses the northern part of the township.

Railways

Two traverse the township:

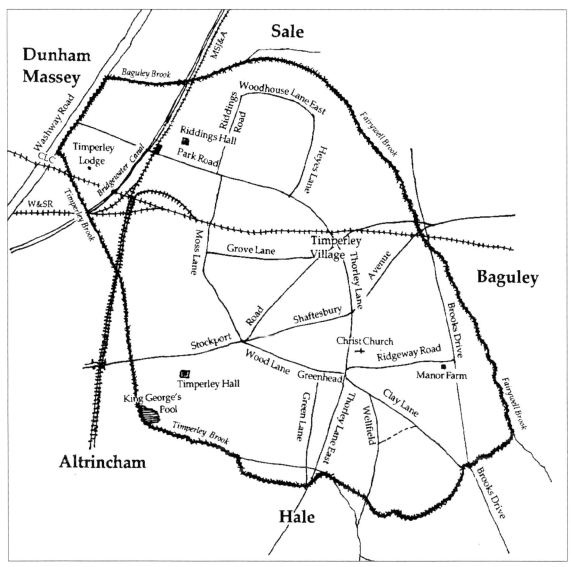

Map 2. Map of Timperley showing the boundary of the civil parish. The boundary is largely defined by the lines of the Timperley, Fairywell and Baguley Brooks.

- The MSJ and A Railway from Manchester to Altrincham, running in a north-east – south-west direction and for the most part parallel and adjacent to the canal.
- The CLC Railway from Stockport to Warrington running east to west across the township from Stockport Road via Skelton Junction to Manchester Road.

Roads
Two A class roads traverse the township:

- A56 – Manchester to Warrington forming the northern boundary of the township.
- A560 – Stockport to Altrincham – runs through the village centre.

Footpaths
A number of ancient paths, most still extant, intersect the township.

1. *Greenhead to Thorley Lane**
From the junction of Wood and Green Lanes to the village centre – runs west of Thorley Lane to join Thorley Lane adjacent to the car park.

2. *Thorley Lane to Hare and Hounds Inn**
Crosses Highfield Road and Green Lane north.

3. *Stockport Road to Thorley Lane**
A western offshoot of 1 above which joins Perry Road to Stockport Road.

4. *Sugar Lane to Clay Lane+*
Skirts the east side of Bowdon Rugby Club's field.

5. *Timperley Brook to Wood Lane*
Joins Timperley to Hale across what is now Altrincham Golf Links.

6. *Stockport Road to Wellfield Lane*
Skirts Timperley Brook, adjacent to King George's Pool and the golf links; crosses 5 above; Green Lane, the bypass extension of Delahays Road and joins Wellfield Lane a few yards south of the Timperley Brook bridge.

7. *Heyes Lane to Baguley Brook**
Crosses Sylvan Avenue and the fields between Sylvan Avenue and the railway line.

8. *Stelfox Avenue to Brooklands Road*
Crosses Beech Playing Fields and Fairywell Brook. Joins Timperley to Sale.

9. *Brookfield Avenue to Brook Lane*
Crosses Skelton Junction by a footbridge and CLC Railway by a tunnel.

10. *Timperley Hall to Stockport Road*
Joins Stockport Road at Timperley Brook road bridge.

11. *Brooks Drive to Baguley*
Traverses the side of Redbrook House[9] and crosses Fairywell Brook.

12. *Brooks Drive to Baguley*
Skirts the south side of Fairywell Wood.

13. *Attenburys Lane to Washway Road**
Runs under the CLC Line and skirts Timperley Lodge; an offshoot connects with Washway Road opposite South Trafford College of Further Education.

14. *Wash Lane to Grove Lane+*
Starts opposite Heyes Lane, crosses the CLC Line and skirts playing fields.

NB
* Parts of these have disappeared following building development.
+ Sugar Lane renamed Ridgeway Road in 1936, Wash Lane renamed Park Road.

Aspects of Boundary Topography
To supplement the bare facts recounted above, listed below are some of the features observed by the author when walking the boundary.

Fairywell Wood
About 250 yards long by about 100 yards wide. Mixed woodland, predominantly oak (mature) but some smaller species, beech (mostly) and holly. There are a number of mature rhododendrons. Not densely wooded. There is thick scrubby undergrowth in places – including honeysuckle – and elsewhere grassy clearings.

Fairywell Wood to Brooks Drive

Fairly steep banks bordered with small willow trees and the occasional oak. On the west bank about 100 yards of open field, east of Brooks Drive. Banks disfigured by haphazard dumping of domestic refuse, evidence of a dearth of concern for the environment by the *nouveau* residents. The field between the brook and Redbrook House is cultivated as a market garden.

Stockport Road to the Manchester South Junction and Altrincham Railway

The brook, now devoid of trees and shrubs, meanders across Beech Playing Fields to its confluence with the Baguley Brook in a field to the north-east of Sylvan Avenue. Along part of its course the gardens of houses to the rear of Sylvan Avenue run down to its southern bank.

Manchester South Junction and Altrincham Railway to the Washway Road

The banks of the Baguley Brook in this section have been landscaped and the brook runs through a spinney of rare black poplar, chestnut, beech and birch trees. Effectively it is a quiet park for the use and enjoyment of the public.

Timperley Brook (Washway Road to Stockport Road)

Its banks are devoid of trees and shrubs. After crossing the canal the brook courses between factory buildings, sited between the canal and railway lines and then traverses the edge of house gardens before crossing the MSJ and A Railway (at a point north of Navigation Road Station) Brook Lane and Wellington Road. More housing development borders its course from here to Stockport Road and the brook runs through a grove of trees.

Stockport Road to Green Lane

Where the boundary skirts King George's Pool it consists partly of a fence with occasional poplar trees and then a fence of iron railings. It rejoins the line of the brook at a sill close to a footbridge adjacent to the pool. From here to the Wood Lane-Golf Road footpath the brook's banks are interspersed with straggly hawthorns. Having left the brook, east of the footpath, it follows the line of a ditch separating the Golf Links from council allotments and crosses the 100 foot contour line. From here it skirts what was originally a brick field and later a fish pond, now drained and developed as playing fields. The level of the land on the Hale side is approximately 10 feet higher than that on the Timperley side and the border is here delineated by a line of tree stumps – approximately 3 feet tall – sited a few yards apart from each other. From here to Green Lane a wire fence, attached to a line of concrete posts, traverses the edge of Delahays School playing fields (in Timperley) and is itself edged by more trees – probably willows – and then the gardens of Kenmore Drive. One of two large trees are prominent and there are signs of a ditch also on the line of the boundary.

Green Lane to Dobbinets Lane

The first 200 yards consists of a wire fence, attached to a line of concrete posts, which borders the council housing estate in Hale. It continues north-north-east following the line of a ditch bordered by a hedge and, at intervals, five small oak trees to the footpath joining Green Lane to Wellfield Lane. Leaving Wellfield Lane by a field gate on its eastern side, it crosses open land, a line of trees and bushes delineating the border. It rejoins the brook about 250 yards south-south-west of Mill Cottage, Clay Lane, but after about 100 yards departs from the brook again and traverses a market garden to rejoin Clay Lane (close to its junction with White Carr Lane). It now follows the line of Clay Lane and Dobbinets Lane until it reaches the Fairywell Brook.

Dobbinets Lane to Fairywell Wood

The boundary is the line of the brook along which willow bushes grown intermittently. It skirts the edge of a house garden and also the field of a market garden, on the east side of Brooks Drive, until its rejoins the starting point at Fairywell Wood.

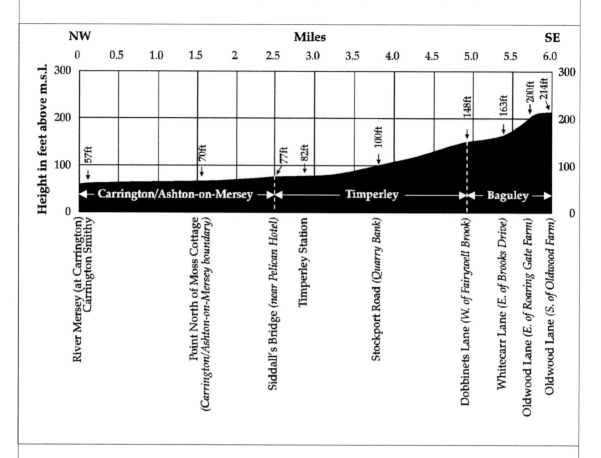

Section on a NW-SE Axis Through Carrington, Ashton-on-Mersey, Timperley and Baguley

NB. This axis divides Timperley into almost equal halves.

The axes of those parts of Stockport Road and Washway Road within the Timperley township boundaries cut the NW-SE axis shown above almost at right angles.

The average height of Stockport Road (within the township) is 100 feet and of Washway Road 78 feet above mean sea level.

Gradients: Siddall's Bridge to Stockport Road 1:287; Stockport Road to Dobbinets Lane 1:131.

Notes

1. Interpolated from O.S. Geological Survey of Great Britain, published 1962, based on 7th Series 1" map sheets 98 Solid and 98 Drift.

2. Delivered to Altrincham Mutual Improvement Society, at Oakfield Road, Altrincham. The manuscript lecture notes are deposited in the Frank Bell Collection under 'Papers of C.E. Newton' at the C.C.R.O. (Reference DDX 131/28). Lt. Col. Newton (Civil Engineer), Overseer of the Parish (1909 to 1936), lived at Watling Gate, Leys Road, Timperley. The house and some land was bequeathed to Altrincham Borough Council in 1937/8.

3. Interpolated from O.S. 6" Sheets 9S.W.-9.S.E.-18N.W.-18N.E. (Cheshire 2nd edition, 1899).

4. In 1992 the MSJ and A was superseded by the Metrolink Light Rapid Transit line from Altrincham to Bury.

5. Interpolated from O.S. 6" Sheets 9S.W.-9.S.E.-18N.W.-18N.E. (Cheshire 2nd edition, 1899).

6. The premises changed hands following the demise of its last proprietor, Mr Norman Hale, in 1984/5. Post 1985 the premises were occupied for some time by Hardy's joinery business.

7. Boundary survey 1982-3.

8. Siddall's Bridge was built in 1795 and refurbished in 1994 (reference article in *Sale and Altrincham Express Advertiser*, 10th January, 1995).

9. Redbrook House has now been demolished.

3

MEDIAEVAL TIMPERLEY – 1060 TO 1500 AD

'...'Tis now become a History little known...' – *Cowper*

When one embarks on a study of the mediaeval history of a small township problems immediately present themselves; the crucial one is the paucity of written evidence pertaining to it – especially for the eleventh and twelfth centuries. Such evidence as is available is principally confined to the legal and financial affairs of the enfeoffed Norman families. Recorded evidence appertaining to the life style of the serf population is, for all practical purposes, non-existent. The principal concern of this chapter is to establish and record the ownership of the Timperley lands during the period 1060-1500. Faced with the inhibiting factors, peculiar to the period in question, one must reluctantly accept that it will be difficult, if not impossible, to establish incontrovertible conclusions; additionally, apparent inconsistencies in the evidence available compound the difficulties. In such circumstances – having weighed the evidence available – one is constrained to advance a theory based on the balance of probability.

Late Anglo-Saxon Period

In Chapter 1 it was stated that Timperley is a place name of Anglo-Saxon origin and form, although no written record of the place name is extant prior to the early thirteenth century.

Although there is no conclusive proof, the Timperley lands probably formed part of a (or even a whole) Saxon manor in the early eleventh century. The theory outlined below supports that conclusion.

The following entry occurs in Domesday Book. Although Timperley is not mentioned by name, it is relevant to the case.

'BAGGILEY'

'... In the Conqueror's time Gilbertus and Ranulfus and Hamo held Sunderland [*sic*] and Baggiley; which at the coming of the Normans were held by Edward and Suga and Udeman and Pat, for four manors, and were gentleman Wasta est Tota...'

Sir Peter Leycester[1] opines re the entry:

'The three first names I take to be Gilbert Venables, Baron of Kinderton: Ranulfus supposed to be the ancestor of the Mainwarings; and Hamon Massey, Baron of Dunham Massey. Sunderland is Locus cognitus[2] within the Town of Dunham Massey... About the reign of King John, Hamon Massey (the then lord of Dunham Massey) gave unto Mathew de Bromhale, Bromhale, Duckenfield and two parts of Baggiley, which the father of the said Mathew held of the said Hamon, as his inheritance in Knight's service, to him and his heirs...'

From the above Domesday Book extract the probable ownership of the Saxon manors is postulated:

- That the four named Saxons must have been the landholders dispossessed by the Normans.
- That it is proven in Domesday Book that the four manors included the lands of Sunderland and Baggiley but their *precise extent* is not delineated.
  It is a reasonable deduction that the said manors embraced all the lands lying between Sunderland and Baguley and *some of those lands comprised what is now the township of Timperley and originally formed one, or part of one, of those manors*, as their geographical location is between 'Sunderland and Baggiley'.
- Sunderland is defined as 'Locus cognitum', i.e. 'in vicinity of' or 'close to' Dunham.
- The four manors were 'Wasta est Tota', i.e. 'Wasteland' or 'Forest'

If the above interpretation is accepted then presumably the four Saxons must have cultivated a portion of their lands for subsistence and part of that cultivation was located in what are now Timperley acres.

Lt. Col. Newton[3] states:

> '... up to 1850 there was evidence of long narrow strips of the open field system carried on in the area west of the footpath connecting the village with Greenhead...'[4]

> '... the local names 'Long Flatts', 'Butty Patch' and 'Long Old Field', in that area, on a map (c.1820) indicates their origin...'

Also

> '... Waste extended from the present village to West Timperley...'

The above extracts suggest that in the eleventh century most of the Timperley acres were wasteland or forest with only a small area cleared for cultivation. The next conundrum may be stated as 'which Saxon manor embraced the Timperley acres?' At the time of the Norman Conquest the township of 'Doneha' (Dunham) bordered, or included, Sunderland and was held by the Saxon 'Aelward' (DB). As spelling forms often varied in contemporary documents it is a strong possibility (similarity of names) that the 'Edward' of the Baguley entry in the Domesday Book could be either an alternative spelling form of 'Aelward' *or* Edward was a close relative of Aelward.[5]

If Newton's opinion is accepted it is a reasonable deduction that Edward held Sunderland, or at least part of it, *or* that Sunderland was a part of the Dunham manor.

The spelling form 'Udeman' suggests an affinity with 'U(n) de (r) man' (i.e. different spelling forms of the same name). Could it be that this 'Udeman' (which prima facie suggests the concept of 'below' or 'under', but in fact means 'part from' or 'separate from') also held land in Sunderland? In point of fact Sunderland is situated adjacent to – and separate from – Dunham. It also happens to be very low lying mossland. If so 'Pat' and 'Suga' would hold manors in what is now the Baguley area which manors comprised lands embracing the contemporary Timperley acres. One of the oldest names in the township is *SUGAR* Lane[6] (renamed Ridgeway Road, 1936). Its affinity with *SUGA*, one of the Saxon manor holders, is glaringly obvious. If the vowels 'u' and 'a' are pronounced as long vowel sounds we get the phonetical pronunciation *SEW* (as in 'pew') *Gar* (as in 'far') which almost shouts at the reader '*SUGA's Lane*'; furthermore the line of the lane connects Baguley with Greenhead which is the area of Timperley associated with the open field system referred to above. Although no conclusive evidence is extant, Suga's manor lands could have then formed part of what is now Timperley and Baguley with the bulk of the lands sited on Timperley acres. The theory outlined above would indicate that the Saxons Pat and Suga held manors comprising the contemporary acres of Baguley and Timperley but which in the eleventh century were designated (DB) 'Baggiley'.

Norman, Angevin, Lancaster and York Periods, c.1070-1485

Following the Norman Conquest Hamon de Mascy was granted by, and held from, the Earl of Chester extensive lands in the Bucklow Hundred and the Wirral. He established his demesne at Dunham Massey – so called to distinguish it from Dunham-on-the-Hill near Chester. In the course of time collateral lines of the Mascy family established themselves in many of the townships in proximity to Dunham (for example, Mascys of Hale, Tatton, Ashley, Sale and Timperley) and also in the Wirral lands (for example, Mascys of Bacford, Puddington and Moreton).

During this period wealth was measured in terms of landholdings and a concomitant of the system, among the enfeoffed families, was the arranged marriage; unions between different branches of the same family were not uncommon. Such inter-family connections are one of the causes of occasional discrepancies and/or omissions in the documents consulted. The Timperley manor is a case in point. Pedigrees compiled by the Royal College of Arms during County Visitations occasionally exhibit such discrepancies, and/or omissions.

For the Timperley manor the principal evidences are the pedigrees of Mascy of Dunham; Mascy of Sale; Mascy of Tatton; Mascy of Bacford and Timperley; Arderne of Timperley; Dutton of Cheadle and Bulkeley of Cheadle families. A chart recording the descent of ownership if the Timperley manor, with explanatory comments is appended at the end of the chapter.

If one accepts the evidence of the pedigrees, then Hamon de Mascy (first Baron),[7] appropriated at least two, possibly more, of the Saxon manors and one was 'Sunderland' (comprising parts of Dunham within it) and the other the manor held by Suga (which contained at least part – if not the whole – of the Timperley lands).

The first clue, re Timperley, occurs in the Dunham pedigree where it is recorded that Cicely (daughter of the third Baron) 'given by her father *Alretunstall* and Sunderland'. This 'Alretunstall' was probably part of the Saxon Suga's manor. Evidence quoted in *Place Names of Cheshire*[8] indicates that it was almost certainly a place in what is now called Timperley. Cicely's status is not recorded; thus it is impossible to say if she was a spinster, or a married woman, or give a date of death. It was usual for daughters to be given land on marriage and her sister Agnes is recorded as 'given a moiety of Bolinton' on her marriage to Sir Geoffrey Dutton of Cheadle. Two other unnamed daughters, sisters of Agnes and Cicely, are recorded as having been given land on marriage but not in the Dunham pedigree. It is most probable that 'Alretunstall' was a moiety of the Timperley manor as when Hamon, the third baron (died c.1216), it is recorded that Agnes had 'Northern Moiety devolve on her as heir to her father'; 'thus it became vested in the Cheadle Dutton family' (see Newton, and the Cheadle Dutton pedigree). This supports the view that Cicely's 'Alretunstall' was in fact the Southern Moiety of Timperley. The Dutton pedigree uses the name 'Timperlegh' (c.1240) to refer to the moiety they held. Henceforward I shall refer to the moieties as the *Northern Moiety* and the *Southern Moiety*.

Northern Moiety

The descent of the Northern Moiety is straightforward and (see chart on p.18) descended via the Dutton of Cheadle family until 1326 when, following the death of Sir Roger de Dutton, his Cheadle estate was divided between his co-heirs, two daughters Clemence, the elder, and Agnes. Agnes' inheritance included the Northern Moiety of Timperley, which went to her husband, Richard de Bulkeley, and henceforward the Northern Moiety formed part of the Cheadle Bulkeley estate. (It descended in the Bulkeley family for almost four centuries.)

Richard de Bulkeley was succeeded by his son William de Bulkeley (d.1379). In their Inquisitions Post Mortem the following is recorded:

> (*Inq. P.M. 1349*) 'Richard de Bulkeley... held a moiety of Timperley of Hugh Le Mascy. (William Bulkeley son and heir) by knight service. Value £12...'

> (*Inq. P.M. 1379*) William de Bulkeley '... held a moiety of Timperley of John Le Mascy by knight service Value £12...'

These Inquisitions Post Mortem support Newton's view that this moiety was held under the overlordship of one of the Mascy families (probably the Dunham branch at this period).

(NB. As will be seen, when the Southern Moiety is discussed on p.19, problems arise in conjunction with the identification of Hugh and John Le Mascy.)

Misfortune struck the family when William's son, Richard, died, aged twenty-one, in 1390. Thus Richard's son and heir was born posthumously: Richard's widow, Margery (née Venables) petitioned the King, Richard II, for 'Livery of Dower' of the estate in April 1391 and later married Randle Mainwaring of Over Peover without the King's Licence. On 14th September, 1391, Randle petitioned the King for 'Livery of his Wife's Dower' which was granted in full in December 1392. In 1395, in consideration of a payment of £230, the King granted custody of the land and tenements to Randle and Margery with 'Wardship and Marriage of Richard Bulkeley son and heir of Richard Bulkeley Deceased'. Richard became of age in 1412 and full livery of all his lands was granted to him on 21st September, 1412. He died in 1454 and his Inquisition Post Mortem states:

> '... Richard de Bulkeley seized in his demesne as of fee of two parts of *half of the Manor* of Cheadle, held of the King as Earl of Chester, by Knight Service together with the reversion of the third part of the said Manor which Margery, his mother, held in Dower at the time of his death. William de Bulkeley s.h. *aet.* 36'

This reversion took place in 1459, in which year Margery died. Margery survived both her first husband and her son, was chatelaine of Over Peover for over fifty-five years and is buried, along with her second husband, in Over Peover Church. Their stone effigies surmount the tomb.

William, her grandson, on payment of a fine of 13s 6d and doing fealty to the Earl of Chester,

THE DESCENT OF THE OWNERSHIP OF THE MANOR OF TIMPERLEY: 1100 TO 1485

Sir Hamon de Mascy
(first known baron)

Sir Hamon de Mascy (2nd baron)

Sir Hamon de Mascy
(3rd baron) s.& h. d.c.1216

John

Robert

Ciceley (?) d.s.p.

NORTHERN MOIETY

AGNES de Mascy m.
Sir Geoffrey Dutton, lord of Cheadle

GEOFFREY de Dutton
(s. & h. d.1294 s.p.)

SIR ROGER de Dutton m. Matilda Mascy
(Brother & Heir of Geoffrey d.1326)

AGNES de Dutton m. Richard de Bulkeley (He d. 1349)
Younger dau. of Roger | younger son of the Eaton Bulkeleys
(d. aet.22 in 1390) |

WILLIAM de Bulkeley (d.1379)

RICHARD de Bulkeley m. Margery Venables (N.b. She survived
| both her husband and son)

MARGERY de Bulkeley m Randle Mainwaring (of Over Peover)
(in dower as Widow of Richard: she d. 1459)

RICHARD de Bulkeley (of full age 1412)
Granted full Livery of all his lands 21st Sept. 1412 (d.1454)
WILLIAM de Bulkeley m. Ellen Griffiths
s. & h. (d.1488)
(Began the Bulkeleys of Beaumaris line: resided in
Beaumaris, Anglesey

SOUTHERN MOIETY

John

(?) Sir John Mascy de Timperley (?)
(Lord of Manor 1270)

Sir William Mascy de Timperley (?)

MATILDA Mascy de Timperley (dau. & H.) m. Sir Hamon de Mascy,
| Lord of Bacford and younger son
| of the Mascys of Sale. (He d.1350
| - Matilda survived him.)

EDWARD de Mascy m. Ellen ?
(2nd son d.1393) |

CECILIA de Mascy m. Richard de Chadderton.
(sole dau. & h. b.1387)* |

MARGARET de Chadderton m. Richard de Radcliffe.
(sole dau. & h. d. 1450) |

Elizabeth
m. Charles Arderne
(elder dau. d.147(?)

Ellen
(d.1477) m. 1. Peter Le Mascy +
| 2. John de Parr

S.W. half of S.M.+   S.E. half of S.M.+
+ Each sister owned a quarter of the whole manor of Timperley.

Notes

1. Hamon (1), Hamon (2) and Hamon (3) were barons of Dunham Massey and Lords of Bacford in the Wirral)

2. The evidence of the pedigrees is imprecise. The JOHN who succeeded Ciceley may have been her brother or her son. As the pedigrees do not indicate if she married, of the two possibilities I take the view that Ciceley's brother John inherited on her death and that Sir John Mascy of Timperley who later inherited was the nephew of Ciceley.

3. Still living in 1443.

18

became possessed of all his Cheadle Bulkeley estates. He did not reside in Cheadle. He married Ellen Griffiths of Caernarvon and lived in Beaumaris, Anglesey where he founded the long line of Bulkeleys of Cheadle and Beaumaris. He died in 1488.

Southern Moiety

The pedigrees of the various branches of the Mascy family, when compared, display, with regard to certain individuals, a vagueness or uncertainty as regards parentage and, occasionally, contradictions and/or omissions during the thirteenth century.

Certainly the Timperley manor was in the sole possession of the Dunham Massey barons until some point during the lifetime of the third baron (died c.1216) when some sub-infeudation took place. The first specific reference to Timperley occurs in the Mascy of Tatton pedigree:

> '... Richard Mascy of Tatton granted free Warren in his Demain lands...' (here follows a list of his lands which includes Timperley).[9]

This proves that the Mascys of Tatton held Timperley in 1294. Establishing ownership of Timperley between c.1216 and 1294 A.D. has proved, to say the least, extremely difficult and one's deductions, from the evidences available, are *not* proven. Certainly a Mascy, or Mascys, held the manor of Timperley under the paramount lordship of the Dunham barons. A Sir John de Timperley held lands in Timperley (c.1270-1580 Visitations of Cheshire – Arderne of Timperley pedigree). Who was he? Certainly he was a Mascy but of which branch of the family?[10]

In the Arderne pedigree he is described as 'Sir John Timperley of Timperley, Bacford and Longdendale'; the Mascys held the manor of Bacford, in Wirral, at this period.

The only John Mascy recorded in the pedigrees in the thirteenth century occurs in the Dunham pedigree. He the son of the third baron and a brother of Cicely and Agnes. Oddly enough, the pedigree records him as having a daughter named 'Cicely'. Did he name her after his sister who held Alretunstall? The thought is intriguing. On the evidence of dates he would be about seventy years of age in 1270.

Two possible theories are advanced:

- He is the brother of Cicely, Agnes and the fourth baron (as listed in the Dunham pedigree).
- He is the son of Cicely and inherited Alretunstall.

The second may be rejected in the absence of any record of Cicely's marriage or date of death.

'Alretunstall' was in all probability the *Southern Moiety* and that on Cicely's death it passed to John her brother. It is most probable that this John Mascy is connected with, or held his moiety from the Mascys of Tatton (see below).

His son Sir William succeeded and in turn Sir William's daughter Matilda (Jane in some pedigrees) inherited on his death. Matilda married Hamon de Mascy, Knight, a younger son of the Mascys of Sale, to whom she brought the Southern Moiety. When he married he was already Lord of Bacford, having inherited as heir to his father, Richard de Mascy of Sale. Richard was left Bacford – as remainderman – by Hamon the sixth baron of Dunham but he predeceased the sixth baron.

Hamon did fealty for his Bacford manor in 1337. He died in 1341. His Inquisition Post Mortem is interesting:

> (Inq. P.M. 1349): '... Hamo de Mascy seized of a moiety of the manor of Timperley of Hugh de Mascy of Tatton.'

This proves that he held under his overlord, the said Hugh, and that the Tatton family had been overlords of the Timperley manor since before 1294, as this Hugh was a close relative of the Richard Mascy of Tatton mentioned above who held Timperley in 1294. Hugh's father was the brother of the aforesaid Richard de Tatton. Richard died without issue and Robert, Hugh's father, succeeded to the Tatton and Timperley lands.

The Bulkeley Inquisition Post Mortem quoted above for the Northern Moiety is added proof that the Tatton Mascys held the whole manor. John Mascy de Tatton, quoted in the 1379 Inquisition Post Mortem, was the second son of Hugh Mascy de Tatton. A later Inquisition Post Mortem, dated 1393, shows that John was still alive then.[11]

1: Small plaque in centre reads (sic): 'This chappell built 35 Henry VI 1456 by Randle Maynwaringe Armiger Regis and Margery his wife whose bodies lie below. Restored 47 Vic. 1884. C.A. Pitt, 3rd. daughter of Sir Henry Mainwaring, Mainwaring of Over Peover.' (Photogragh taken by the author, 1990.)

2: Effigy of Dame Margery. She was the second wife of Randle and widow of Richard Bulkeley. She was chatelaine of the Bulkeley estates when she married Randle. They included the Bulkeleys' Timperley Moiety. (Photograph taken by the author, 1984.)

3: Effigy removed for restoration during late 1980s. It probably dates from c.1460. (Photograph taken by the author, 1990.)

(Inq. P.M. 1393) '... Edward de Mascy de Timperley d. seized of a moiety of Timperley held of John de Mascy of Tatton as of his Manor of Tatton in Socage at a rose rent for all services.'

This Edward de Mascy was the heir of Hamon de Mascy and Matilda (see above). Edward's only daughter and heiress, Cecilia de Mascy, succeeded and on her marriage to Richard de Chadderton she brought to him the Southern Moiety. Their sole daughter and heiress, Margaret de Chadderton married Richard de Radcliffe and again the Southern Moiety passed to daughters. They had two, Elizabeth (the elder) and Ellen, who were co-heiresses. On their father's death the Southern Moiety was split into two halves, each taking a half (i.e. a quarter of the *whole* manor of Timperley).

Elizabeth, who married Charles Arderne, had the south-west quarter of the township, which included Timperley Hall (the manor house) and was about 500 acres in extent. Ellen, who married first Peter le Mascy and second John de Parr, had the south-east quarter of the township. It had no manor house but the principal farm was called Manor Farm. When farming ceased at Manor Farm, situated in Ridgeway Road, the lands and farm building were acquired by Altrincham Borough Council. Following local government re-organisation in 1974, Trafford MBC developed the land and farm building for leisure purposes. For some years it was leased by the Civil Service Social Club: when their lease expired the grounds were unused for some time but in 1994 it was released and is currently used by the Ridgeway Social Club.

Ellen does not appear to have resided in Timperley, but her sister Elizabeth and her husband Charles Arderne appear to have resided at Timperley Hall following their marriage.

Ellen's son and heir, John de Parr, died without issue. Before his death he exchanged his Timperley estate (the south-east quarter of the township) for land belonging to Sir William Booth in Stoke Picton and Chester in 1475.

Thus for over eighty years, due to the lack of male heirs, the moiety passed via the female line from the Mascys, first to the Chaddertons, then to the Radcliffes and then the Arderne family. The sub-division of the Southern Moiety, following the death of Richard Radcliffe (c.1450), marked the beginning of the break-up of the original estate into a number of smaller freeholds.

Notes
1. Sir Peter Leycester, *Historical Antiquities*, written in the late seventeenth century.
2. *Locus cognitus* – in the vicinity (or close to)
3. Lt. Col. C.E. Newton, 'History of Timperley'.
4. Greenhead is the triangle of land bounded by Wood Lane, Thorley Lane and Stockport Road.
5. Newton asserts that if not the same individual... 'Edward was certainly a relative of Aelward who at that time owned Doneha or Dunham...'
6. A lifelong resident – he actually lived in Sugar Lane for many years – with whom I discussed the meaning of the name 'Sugar Lane' suggested it was named after a 'Sugar Plum Tree' which grew near Manor Farm. For various reasons – not least the proven antiquity of the name – the author is unable to accept his version of its origin.
7. The evidence of dates suggests that the *actual* 'first Baron' (c.1086) was the father – or even the grandfather – of the *'first known Baron'* listed in the pedigrees.
8. *Place Names of Cheshire*, Vol.44, Part 1.
9. The actual document, in extremely good condition, is deposited at the C.C.R.O.
10. '... a moiety of the manor of Timperley at a very early age belonged to a family which assumed the local name of 'Timperley' which passed by successive heiresses to Mascys ...' (*Whites Directory of Cheshire*, 1860).
11. John Mascy de Tatton – he died at the Battle of Shrewsbury in 1403 – was a prominent Cestrian figure in the late fourteenth century. Readers are referred to an article which appeared in *Open History*, No.36 (1990), entitled 'A Cheshire Knight in the Hundred Years War: Sir John Massey of Tatton, 1344-1403' by J. Groves.

4

DESCENT OF OWNERSHIP OF TIMPERLEY LANDS –
POST 1500

'Thus our democracy was the most aristocratic, and our aristocracy the most demo-
cratic in the world.'

Macaulay

Northern Moiety

(See chart on p.23.) Following William Bulkeley's decision to reside in Beaumaris, the main line of
the family continued to live there until the end of the nineteenth century. Down the years they occupied prominent positions in the civil and Church establishment in North Wales and also in Ireland. They were Hereditary Constables of Beaumaris Castle; sheriffs of the shire, parsons in Beaumaris and other parishes in North Wales, and ardent Royalists. One was a colonel and another a
captain in the Civil Wars and, post-1660, one was a Master of the Household to Charles II and
James II. In 1643 Thomas Bulkeley was created Viscount Bulkeley of Cashell, Co. Tipperary, Ireland. The title died out, on the death of the seventh viscount, in 1822.

Not until the early seventeenth century did a Bulkeley reside in Cheadle again. Misfortune, in
the form of premature deaths of male heirs, affected the succession.[1] Frances, a spinster, was the
last of the Bulkeleys to reside in Cheadle. Her will, made shortly before her death and dated July
1688, is long and complicated. She inherited the manors of Cheadle, Timperley (moiety) and
Whatcroft near Northwich, and, during her tenure, had continued to honour a number of grants
made to certain estate tenants by her brother Humphrey. Her will reveals that she was apprehens-
ive that her relatives, Robert the second viscount and Richard the third viscount, might renege on
the said grants after the death of her sister-in-law Dorothy, Humphrey's relict. Accordingly she
made a clause to the effect that if the grants were confirmed by them within two years of her death
then her estates, after bequests and expenses, should be conveyed to Richard Bulkeley. If this condition was not met she provided for her manors to go to 'John Bulkeley son of Sir Richard Bulkeley, late of Kingdom of Ireland, Baronet deceased'. In the event Richard the third viscount inherited. Frances's demise was the precursor of the break-up of the Northern Moiety of Timperley.
Both Frances and Lord Robert the second viscount died in the latter half of 1688. In 1702, shortly
before the third viscount's death, his son Richard, fourth viscount, married a daughter of the Earl
of Abingdon and, under the marriage settlement, the manor of Timperley (moiety) was limited in
strict settlement after the death of the fourth viscount[2] upon Richard, son of the fourth viscount,
and his issue male, subject to portions for his younger children.

Richard the fifth viscount was, by 1731, in serious debt. In that year his creditors took legal action to recover what he owed them. He was compelled to enter deeds which limited his estates, in
Wales and Cheshire, to trustees upon trust to sell them and use the proceeds to pay his debts and
retain the balance upon trust for him. In 1733 he held a Court Baron of all his freehold tenants. In
1738 he died without issue having appointed his brother James, sixth viscount, sole executor. Following a suit in Chancery, James was ordered to arrange a further sale of properties (i.e. those
properties in the 1731 deeds remaining unsold) to satisfy creditors of the fifth viscount. James was
allowed to be the best purchaser.

In 1747 James named three trustees to sell and convey his estates in Cheshire. Contracts for the
sale of estates in Timperley moiety were entered into but, before any conveyances were executed,
James died intestate in 1753; In December of that year his wife gave birth to his posthumous son
Thomas James, seventh and last viscount.[3] During his minority his estates were vested in trustees
by Act of Parliament. They completed the conveyance of his estates, as per their contracts, to the
pre-1753 purchasers and dispersed of the remainder in lots.

At this date only seven small farms were left in Timperley. Five of these were situated in The
Heyes, an isolated district forming a little hamlet and originally approached by a road leading off
the common commanded by a gate, known as 'Timperley Gate'.[4] The other two properties were

BULKELEY OF CHEADLE AND BEAUMARIS FAMILY TREE
Northern Moiety: Descent of Ownership Post 1500

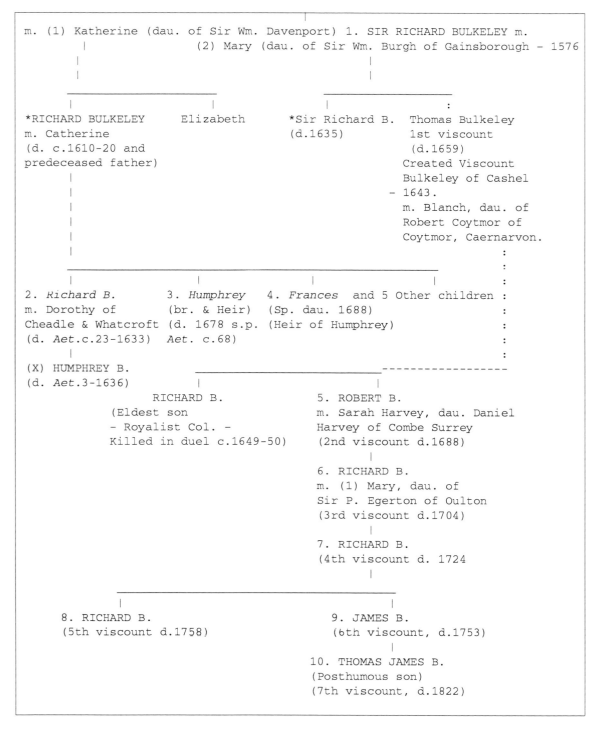

```
m. (1) Katherine (dau. of Sir Wm. Davenport) 1. SIR RICHARD BULKELEY m.
        |                    (2) Mary (dau. of Sir Wm. Burgh of Gainsborough - 1576
        |                                                        |
        |                                                        |
     _____          _____
        |               |                |                    :
*RICHARD BULKELEY    Elizabeth      *Sir Richard B.   Thomas Bulkeley
m. Catherine                        (d.1635)          1st viscount
(d. c.1610-20 and                                        (d.1659)
predeceased father)                                   Created Viscount
        |                                              Bulkeley of Cashel
        |                                                - 1643.
        |                                              m. Blanch, dau. of
        |                                              Robert Coytmor of
        |                                              Coytmor, Caernarvon.
        |                                                          :
     _____            :
        |           |               |               |             :
2. Richard B.    3. Humphrey   4. Frances  and 5 Other children :
m. Dorothy of    (br. & Heir)  (Sp. dau. 1688)                  :
Cheadle & Whatcroft (d. 1678 s.p. (Heir of Humphrey)            :
(d. Aet.c.23-1633) Aet. c.68)                                   :
        |                                                        :
(X) HUMPHREY B.        _____-----------------
(d. Aet.3-1636)            |                       |
              RICHARD B.              5. ROBERT B.
              (Eldest son            m. Sarah Harvey, dau. Daniel
              - Royalist Col. -      Harvey of Combe Surrey
              Killed in duel c.1649-50)  (2nd viscount d.1688)
                                              |
                                     6. RICHARD B.
                                     m. (1) Mary, dau. of
                                     Sir P. Egerton of Oulton
                                     (3rd viscount d.1704)
                                              |
                                     7. RICHARD B.
                                     (4th viscount d. 1724
                                              |
        _____
        |                                   |
   8. RICHARD B.                      9. JAMES B.
   (5th viscount d.1758)              (6th viscount, d.1753)
                                              |
                                     10. THOMAS JAMES B.
                                     (Posthumous son)
                                     (7th viscount, d.1822)
```

NOTES

a. According to the pedigree *Richard and *Sir Richard had the same Christian names, although they were, of course, half-brothers.

b. Richard, 2, was a minor aged eleven years when he inherited in 1621. He died at 'The Peele' (*sic*), Peel Hall on Cheadle lands.

c. It is possible that Humphrey, 3, inherited for a few weeks prior to the birth of posthumous son Humphrey (X): (NB. pedigree says 1640-1). It is not established whether Humphrey (X) inherited. If he did it was only briefly as he died aged three years.

d. Henry, a younger son of Thomas (first viscount) was Master of the Household to both Charles II and James II.

e. An uncle of Richard 1. was Archbishop of Dublin during the first half of the seventeenth century.

f. Note that following Frances' death the Cheadle estates reverted to the descendants of Sir Richard's second wife Mary.

nearer the village. In total they realised less than £2000. The Northern Moiety was now merely a number of freeholds and the divorce from the manorial system was complete.

South-western Half of Southern Moiety

(See chart on p.26.) This portion of the Southern Moiety, embracing approximately one quarter of the whole manor and containing Timperley Hall, came into the Arderne family when Charles Arderne married Elizabeth de Radcliffe. She also inherited part of the Radcliffes' Bacford estate. The main Arderne line is Arderne of Aldford, Alvanley and Harden. The family's Harden estate is in Macclesfield Hundred and located near Stockport, probably in the Bredbury area. The family owned the Riddings estate in the Northern Moiety of Timperley which had passed to them from the Bulkeleys in about 1445 (see Northern Moiety section on p.22).

The ancestry of Charles Arderne is an enigma. He is not listed in any of the Arderne pedigrees. His name suddenly appears, as the first of the Ardernes to own this half of the Southern Moiety, in a pedigree showing his wife's ancestry and, subsequently, their descendants, entitled 'Arderne of Timperley' (1580 Visitation).

Who was he? Careful research of the pedigrees reveals no trace of him. On the basis of the known facts[5] one can deduce that Charles was born c.1400-10; he was the son of 'John Arderne, of Harden, Maxfield (*sic*) Hundred' and his father John was the third son, and heir apparent, of Hugh de Arderne of Alvanley and Harden (*sic*).[6] Whilst it cannot be proved conclusively one is satisfied that the deductions published here fit the known facts. Strangely enough John did not inherit. The inheritance went to his younger brother Ralph. Could it be that Charles was illegitimate and excluded from his father's rightful inheritance? Did John predecease Ralph? The possibilities are intriguing.

The property descended in the main line and to male heirs for four generations and then passed to George Brereton of Ashley when he married Sybilla Arderne, the fifth and last Arderne holder of this part of the Southern Moiety.

Richard, the third Brereton in the male line to hold this estate in Timperley, died without any legitimate issue in 1649[7] and the estate passed first to his brother Thomas who died without issue. He divided the estate into three equal shares and left each of his three sisters a third share. They

4: Built c.1800-10, Timperley Hall replaced an earlier moated hall now demolished. From c.1915 at least it was tenanted by Timperley Golf Club. Following its purchase by Altrincham Council in 1934 it was subsequently opened as a municipally owned hotel called The Golf Hotel. In 1950 it was purchased by Chesters' Brewery Co. and renamed The Old Hall Hotel. Currently it is owned by Whitbread plc and operated as a Beefeater restaurant.

The front and side walls of this Georgian mansion have, as one can see, been 'graced' with various hotel signs. (Photograph taken by the author, January 1981.)

were all married. Frances the eldest, then a widow,[8] had no children and left her third share to her niece Anne (daughter of her sister Anne) as part of her dower on her marriage to Sir Amos Meredith.[9] It included Timperley Hall and, since Lady Anne and Sir Amos were living in Ashley Hall in 1667, it is possible that Anne also inherited her mother's share.[10] The Meredith family held it for four generations when Sir William Meredith sold the estate (c.1770) to George Johnson. His son, the Revd. Croxton Johnson, in turn sold it to James Wood who resided in the Old Hall for some years prior to building the New Hall (c.1800-10).[11] It is still extant and has now been modernised internally and converted to a hotel. The Old Hall was then used as the farmhouse of Timperley Hall Farm and was not demolished until c.1937.

In 1828 the New Hall was tenanted by Mr. Joseph Sutton. In 1857 James Wood, or his successor, sold the estate to Samuel Brooks, the Manchester banker and developer of Brooklands Road. His purchase completed the fragmentation of the south-west half of the Southern Moiety (see also the reference to Brooks below), and from the mid-nineteenth century the theme of Timperley's history is one of decreasing agriculture and increasing suburban development.

South-eastern Half of Southern Moiety

(See chart on p.26.) This portion of the Southern Moiety embraced the lands bounded by Baguley on the east, Hale on the south, the line of Stockport Road on the north and that of Green Lane on the west.

It had no manor house but its principal farm has always borne the name Manor Farm and the original building may have served as the owner's manor house in the fifteenth century. According to Newton, it was sited east of the present building and on the line of what is now Brooks Drive and, when Samuel Brooks cut Brooks Drive from Brooklands' Station to Prospect House, Hale

5: Brooks Drive. The photograph above features part of an unmade, tree lined, carriageway which is named 'Hale Road' on the 1876 25" O.S. Plan. It is, in effect, a continuation of Brooklands Road (which was built by Samuel Brooks) and extends from Stockport Road to Clay Lane at its junction with Roaring Gate Lane. Throughout this century local inhabitants have always referred to it by its colloquial name of 'Brooks' Drive'. It would seem he was responsible for persuading the MSJ and A to build Brooklands Station – named after him. It is said that for a period he lived at Prospect House in Hale Barns and commuted to Brooklands Station via 'Brooks' Drive' in his horse-drawn carriage after 1860. (See Chapter 8.)

Since the development of the Broomwood council estate (post 1952) and subsequently private housing developments on the east side of the drive, the drive has become very dilapidated and overgrown. The photograph shows that in summer the original carriageway is reduced to a footpath.

The photograph features a section of the drive, looking south, at its junction with Ridgeway Road. (Photograph taken by the author, October 1990.)

THE DESCENT OF OWNERSHIP OF THE SOUTH-WEST HALF OF SOUTHERN MOIETY OF TIMPERLEY 1475-1900

1. *Elizabeth de Radcliffe*   m. *Charles Arderne*
   (elder dau. & Co-heiress of
   Richard de Radcliffe)
   (Living 1475)
   |

2. *John Arderne*   m. Ellen, dau. of Thomas Duncalfe
   |

3. *Hamon Arderne*   m. Margaret, dau. of Sir G. Strangwish
   s. & h. Living 1519
   |

4. *William Arderne*   m. Sybilla, dau. of Piers Warburton of Arley
   s. & h., d.1575
   |

5. *Sybilla Arderne*   m. George Brereton (d.1587), s. & h. of
   dau. & heiress, 1st in entail   Richard Brereton of Ashley
   |

6. *William Brereton*   m. Jane (d. 1627), dau. & co-heiress of
   s. & h. d. *aet.* 63-1630   Peter Warburton of Arley
   |

7. *Richard Brereton* – (no legitimate issue), bapt. 1590 – s. & h.
   |

8. *Thomas Brereton*, brother of 7. b.1594, d.1660 s.p.
   |

9. Sisters of 7. and 8.

9a. Frances	9b Katherine	9c Anne
b.1592	b.1596	b.1597
d. s.p.	m. Ralph Ashton	m. Robert Tatton
m. Alexander Barlowe		
		|

   _____

   |

10. **Anne Tatton* (in 1664)   m. *Sir Amos Meredith* of Ireland (d.1669)
          m. 2nd Samuel Daniell of Tabley, d.1708
    |

11. *Sir William Meredith*
    s. & h.
    |

12. *Amos Meredith*
    s. & h.
    |

13. *Sir William Meredith*
    |

14. *George Johnson* of Manchester
    (by purchase from 13.)
    |

15. *Revd. Croxton Johnson*
    (Rector of Wilmslow)
    |

16. *James Wood*
    (by purchase from 15.)
    |

17. *Samuel Brooks*, banker, of Manchester
    (by purchase from 16.)

*Anne was given her third share by her aunt, Frances Barlowe.

THE DESCENT OF OWNERSHIP OF THE SOUTH-EASTERN HALF OF SOUTHERN MOIETY OF TIMPERLEY, 1475 TO 1900

1.	*Ellen de Radcliffe*	m. 1st Peter le Mascy and 2nd John de Parr
	Younger dau. & co-heiress of Richard de Radcliffe (d.1477)	
2.	*John Parr*	m. Alice ?
	s. & h., d. o.s.p. 1494	

By arrangement with Sir William Booth, John exchanged his Timperley estate for lands belonging to Sir William in Stoke Picton and Chester in 1475.

3.	*Sir William Booth*[1]	m. Maude, dau. of John Dutton of Dutton
	(d. 1477)	
13.	*Mary Booth*	m. Harry Grey, 4th Earl of Stamford, d.1768
	Only dau. of h. of George, Earl of Warrington (married 1736)	
14.	*George Harry Grey*	m. Henrietta Cavendish Bentinck, dau. of 2nd
	5th Earl of Stamford, s. & h. Created Baron Delamer of Dunham Massey and Earl of Warrington in 1796 (d.1819)	Duke of Portland
15.	*George Harry Grey*	m. Henrietta Charteris, dau. of Lord Elcho, eldest
	s. & h. 6th Earl, d.1845	son of 5th Earl of Wemyss
16.	*George Harry Grey*	m. 1st Elizabeth, dau. of Mr J. Billage of
	Grandson & heir 7th Earl	Wincanton, d.s.p. 1854 2nd Katherine, dau. of Mr Henry Cocks
17.	*Samuel Brooks*, banker[2]	
	(by purchase in 1857, bought all the Stamford lands in Timperley)	

Notes

1. He was the second in the Booth line to possess the Dunham Massey estate which his father Robert claimed when he married Douce (daughter of William Venables of Bollin – now Wilmslow). Douce was the granddaughter of Sir John Mascy of Tatton and a descendant of the Mascys of Dunham Massey.)

The Timperley lands were held by the Booths for eleven generations and they increased their landholding in the early eighteenth century by purchase of lands in the Northern Moiety (mainly) of the township.

Sir George Booth (d.1684) was created Baron Delamer in 1661. Henry Booth (1652-1694), second Baron Delamer, was imprisoned for treason under James II, but acquitted at his trial. He was created Earl of Warrington on the accession of William III in 1688.

2. Samuel Brooks devised the Timperley lands to trustees for the benefit of his third son Thomas Brooks of Barkby Hall, Leicestershire.

Barns, he demolished it and built the present Manor Farm house some seventy yards west of the line of Brooks Drive (c.1860). The farmhouse together with some of its acres has now been converted to a Civil Service Social Club with extensive playing field facilities on the south and west.

Ellen Radcliffe, the younger of the co-heiresses, inherited this portion of the Southern Moiety together with part of her father's Bacford Estate (in the Wirral). She married twice. Her second husband, John de Parr, owned a small property adjoining hers at Bacford. They do not appear to have resided on their Timperley estate.

Their son, John, inherited and his arrangement with Sir William Booth (see pp.21 and 27) meant that this part of Timperley then descended in the Booth family for eleven generations until 1736 when Mary Booth (sole daughter and heiress of George Booth, Earl of Warrington), married Harry Grey, fourth Earl of Stamford.

During the first half of the eighteenth century the Earl of Warrington increased, considerably, his ownership of Timperley acres by the purchase of farmland – in the Northern Moiety – from the Bulkeley family and so, for many decades, the Grey family, Earls of Stamford and Warrington, were the largest landholders in the township. Five generations of the Grey family held the lands until, in 1857, Samuel Brooks purchased them and also a number of leaseholds and other properties which – at some earlier time – had been alienated from the south-eastern half of the Southern Moiety. At the time of his demise, Brooks held 845 acres, including Timperley Hall which comprised over half the acreage of the entire township. He devised this landholding to trustees for the benefit of his third son, Thomas Brooks of Barkby Hall, Leicestershire.

Notes

1. See chart on p.23.
2. He died in 1724, at Bath, aged forty-one. He was constable of Caernarvon Castle.
3. He died in 1822.
4. Positioned near the contemporary junction of Heyes Lane with Park Road.
5. See Ormerod, Vol.1, p.546.
6. See Arderne of Aldford, Alvanley and Harden Pedigree, Ormerod, Vol.2.
7. Richard had an illegitimate son, William, by his maid servant, Ellen Higginson. See Brereton of Ashley Pedigree in Ormerod, Vol.II.
8. She was the widow of Alexander Barlowe of Barlowe, Lancashire.
9. Anne was the second daughter of Anne (née Brereton of Ashley) and Robert Tatton of Wythenshawe. Her elder sister Mary and her three surviving brothers, William, Robert and Thomas, were all married and settled in life by 1665. In that year Anne married Sir Amos Meredith.
10. Anne Tatton seems to have also given her daughter her share. The 1667 Subsidy Roll shows Sir Amos and Lady Anne Meredith living then at Ashley Hall. Living with them there was Anne's widowed aunt, Frances Barlowe.

In the time of Sir Amos Meredith (died in 1669), Timperley Hall was tenanted. In 1664 Richard Lambe tenanted the hall, according to the Hearth Tax Returns, but the 1667 Subsidy Roll shows that Lambe had returned to Ashley, so the hall was only a short-term tenancy.
11. Sited within the moat and now being excavated by the South Trafford Archaeology Group.

5

RIDDINGS HALL

'An old song... of an old worshipful gentleman who had a great estate.'

Anon.

'Rydding' – A Definition

The word 'Ridding' is a variant form of the O.E. *'Rydding'* meaning a clearing. This suggests that the name, in contemporary English, translates as *'hall in the clearing'*.

It was the reputed manor house of the Northern Moiety of the manor of Timperley and possibly the first Hall to occupy the site had its origins in the late thirteenth, or early fourteenth, century when the moiety was held by the Duttons of Cheadle (see Chapter 3).

Apart from the name, which indicates a M.E. form of 'Rydding', it occupied a moated site which also suggests that it had its origins in the Middle Ages. No concrete evidence is offered in support of this hypothesis.

The last building to occupy the site was latterly used as a farmhouse; it was not demolished until post-1945 when (c.1960) the houses which comprise Riddings Court (off Greenway Road) were built on the site of the Hall and adjoining orchard. Evidences prove that there was certainly a Riddings Hall extant in the latter half of the fifteenth century. Newton opines that the farmhouse was the surviving part of a larger half timbered hall built c.1500. This may well be true, but it is considered such a building would be a Tudor replacement of an earlier building. During the first half of the fourteenth century the Northern Moiety passed by marriage into the Cheadle Bulkeley family. They held the bulk of the Northern Moiety continuously for over four centuries (see Chapter 3).

By 1495 the Riddings Hall estate had passed into the possession of the Arderne family. In that year it is recorded that Sir John Arderne (of Alvanley and Harden)[1] made a settlement of his large estate, which included Riddings Hall.[2] The precise date at which the Arderne family assumed ownership of Riddings Hall is not established but it was probably during the lifetime of Dame Margery Mainwaring, who died in 1459, the widow of Richard de Bulkeley. She remarried following her husband's early demise and also survived their son, Richard de Bulkeley, junior. She held livery of the Bulkeley estate, which included the Northern Moiety, until her son's majority in 1412 and then had one-third of the Bulkeley estate in dower until her death when her grandson had the reversion of her dower.

On the basis of the facts above the probability is that Margery's son, Richard, sold the Riddings Hall estate at some time following his majority in 1412 and his death in 1454; also that the first Arderne to hold the estate was either Sir John or his father Ralph, both of Alvanley and Harden.[3] Three years after making the settlement Sir John, with the agreement of his eldest son, Thomas, sold the estate to Thomas Vawdrey of Bank Hall, Hale, in 1498.

Five generations of the family successively resided in Riddings Hall spanning a period of almost 140 years[4] (see p.31), including Robert, son of the first owner, who lived at Riddings for almost eighty years, spanning the reigns of five Tudor monarchs. His long and detailed will[5] tells us a great deal about him and his children, revealing him as a man of principle who held strong religious convictions. He was also concerned to treat his tenants fairly and ensure their welfare was not neglected. He married twice.[6] Some of his many children pursued a lifestyle which he obviously disparaged as is evidenced by the extracts from his will quoted below.

'... to Margaret[7] at such time as she shall leave her dishonest and uncleane lyvinge for and duryinge all such tyme after as she shall lyve honestlye £5 by years...'

Thomas, the son and heir, was obviously a great trial to his father. His bequest to him is prefaced by a declaration of forgiveness and then recites:

'... of my disobedient son Thomas all those... sums of money which he hath wrongfully received and taken from me and also the sums... which he also is indebted to me... as shall remain unpaid at the time of my decease...'

Robert continues,

'... requiring him to use sobrietie and to leave all evil and drunken company...'

The will then charges Thomas

'... to pray daily on his knees, to have mercy on all creatures and to serve God and live honestly and justly and to cherish his mother and brethren and be kind to his tenants... of the lands which God hath left me and I have left hym...', and abjured him not to exploit his tenants.

Strangely enough, Thomas predeceased his father. Newton[8] conjectures that Robert's cortége must have made an impressive sight as it wended its way from Riddings to Bowdon Church. His wayward son Robert died in 1578 and Thomas probably died some time between 1580 and 1585. Edward, son and heir of the wayward Thomas, grandson of Robert, succeeded. Born in 1571, he lived fifty-one years. During his life he sold the family house of 'Pares' or 'Parrs' Place in Chester. Robert, his son and heir, was connected with the family of Oswald Mosley of the Garratt, Manchester, through his marriage to Oswald's daughter, Margaret. Following a period at Riddings they resided at Ancoats Hall, Manchester.

During the reign of Charles I both he and his cousin Richard refused the offer of a knighthood which would have involved them in costs of about £65 and a journey to London; those who declined incurred a fine of £10.[9] Obviously they considered the fine the lesser of two evils – it saved them at least £50 and the rigours of a journey to the capital.

A distant relative[10] occupied the Hall for a period but when Robert Vawdrey of Ancoats Hall died the estate was sold to Thomas Gerard in 1662. The estate next passed to his daughter and heiress Anne Gerard on her marriage (1650).[11] In turn Anne and her husband had no male heir and the estate passed to their daughter and heiress, Ursula Domville on her marriage in 1675 to William Massey of Sale. The Riddings estate passed in the female line when their eldest daughter, Ann married Henry Taylor in the early eighteenth century.[12]

Riddings now descended through several generations of Taylors until, before 1838, it was owned by Elizabeth Taylor (née Shepley), widow. The Hall was tenanted by farmers continuously from before 1838[13] and probably during the last half of the eighteenth century too.

After 1838 the estate's history exhibits family financial and litigation problems and fragmentation by land sales. Prior to 1838 it comprised lands in Timperley and Sale townships of upwards of 165 acres, of which approximately two-thirds were situated in Timperley – mainly to the south of the MSJ and A railway line and east of Wash Lane. In 1838 the tenant farmer was Mr Samuel Smith.

Elizabeth Taylor had financial problems as by an indenture dated 24th and 25th December, 1838 she mortgaged the estate to Thomas Clayton and Miles Rodgett subject to a proviso for:

'... redemption and reconveyance of the said property to Elizabeth Taylor her heirs and assigns on payment to mortgagers of the capital sum borrowed together with accrued interest...'

Although she defaulted on the conditions, the mortgagers did not foreclose. It is clear from the Abstract of Title that Elizabeth Taylor and her heir, nephew James, both successively raised monies to defray the interest due, from time to time by disposing of parcels of land, in Timperley and Sale, amounting in all to about 35 acres, of which about 16 were situate in Timperley.

18th November, 1840: House with Barn and Outbuildings and Several Fields
           7A. 1R. 22P. to R. Marsland
25th December, 1847: Several pieces of land situate in Sale and Timperley
           4A. 2R. 18P. to MSJ and A Railway Company
(N.B. In December 1840 and December 1842 two plots of land were also sold in Sale.)

Following her demise in October 1850, her nephew James Taylor (formerly James Thomason), son of her sister Esther Thomason (née Shepley) inherited the estate and continued to sell off plots of land.

2nd June, 1852:   Plot of land (part of Moat Field), in all 13453 sq. yds. to Joseph Grave (calico printer).

THE DESCENT OF OWNERSHIP OF THE RIDDINGS ESTATE FROM 1450 ONWARDS

Until c.1450 it formed part of the Northern Moiety of Timperley, which moiety was at that time held by the Cheadle Bulkeley family. It was probably sold by Richard de Bulkeley (d.1453) or his son William de Bulkeley (d.1488). It was purchased by the Arderne family of Alvanley and Harden. The first *Arderne* to hold the Riddings estate was either *Ralph* (d.1446) or his son *Sir John* (living 1506).

1. *Ralph Arderne* or his son *Sir John Arderne* from	c.1450
2. Thomas Vawdrey (of Bowdon, gent.) purchased Riddings estate (m. Anne, dau. of Richard Newton of Pownall)	1498
3. *Robert Vawdrey* (s. & h.) (m. 1. Alice, widow of Ralph Brereton of Wettenhall. 2. Alice, dau. of Ralph Barton.)	d.1578
4. *Edward Vawdrey* (grandson of Robert) (m. Jane, dau. of Robert Hyde of Norbury.) (Buried St. Mary's, Chester.)	b.1571, d.1622
5. *Robert Vawdrey* (s. & h.) (m. Margaret, dau. of Oswald Mosley of Garratt, Manchester) (Buried Bowdon Church)	b.1595, d.1662
6. Thomas Gerard, purchased Riddings estate in 1637 (m. 1. Beatrix, dau. of Robert Hyde of Norbury. NB. Br.-in-l. to Edward Vawdrey.) 2. Catherine, dau. of Richard Brook of Norton	b.1605, 1637
7. *Anne Gerard* (dau. & h.) (m. William Domville of Lymm Hall, 1650.)	1650
8. *Ursula Domville* (dau. & h.) (m. William Massey of Sale Hall, 1675)	1675
9. *Ann Massey* (eldest dau., possessed of Riddings and Lymm Halls) (m. Henry Taylor of Liverpool, early eighteenth century)	1706?
10. Estate descended through several generations of Taylors until	c.1835
11. *Elizabeth Taylor* (widow, née Shepley) (who, pre-1838, mortgaged the estate for £4000 to T. Clayton and Miles Rodgett.)	
12. *James Taylor* (nephew of Elizabeth) (Originally Thomason. Changed surname to Taylor and redeemed mortgage in 1853.)	1850
13. *Mary Hargrave* (widow, sister of James) (née Thomason, formerly Hanlon, widow.) Following civil court action re her will (1919) her grandson inherited.	1904
14. *James Joseph Taylor Hargrave* (grandson of Mary Hargrave)	1919
15. Most of the estate sold for housing development	1924-1935

SOURCES
'Timperley Past and Present', Lt. Col. C.E. Newton's unpublished manuscript.
Ormerod, *History of Cheshire*, Vol.II.

PLAN OF RIDDINGS HALL FARM
from 1838 Tithe Map

Total acreage in Timperley township: 93 acres, 0 roods, 14 perches.
N.B. Over 100 acres if fields 168 and 169, in Sale township, are included.

Scale of Plan (Approximately):
3.3 inches = 1 mile
(NB. Tithe map is drawn to a scale of 26:66 inch to 1 mile.)

Acreages of individual fields are listed in the Tithe Apportionment Schedule.

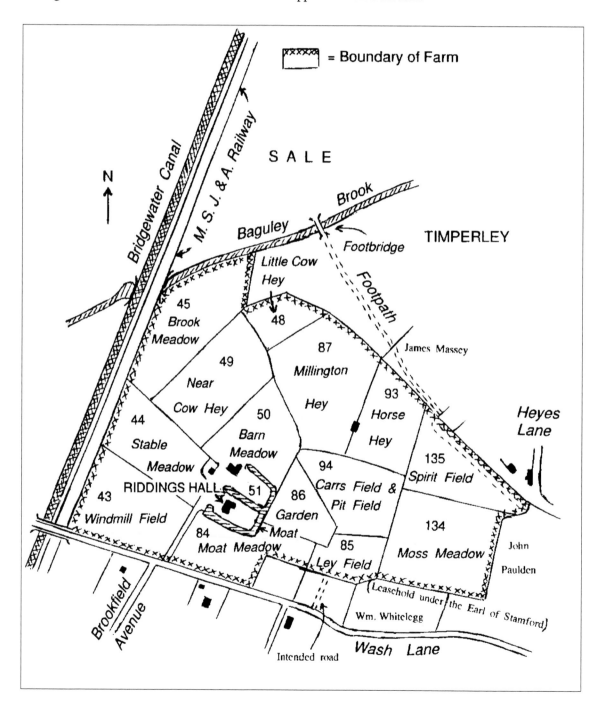

2nd June, 1852:   Plot of land (the other part of Moat Field), in all 7900 sq. yds to Joseph Grave (calico printer).

2nd June, 1852:   Plot of land (part of Carr's Field), in all 8385 sq. yds to William Banks (gentleman).

(N.B. Also in 1852 and 1853 three plots of land in Sale were sold. The dates of the sales suggest interest payable every two years in December.)

James Taylor, having paid all the interest due, repaid his £400 mortgage debt, in 1853, to Miles Rodgett[14] and repossessed the estate, minus the plots sold. James was born James Thomason as his will proves.[15] He resided in Sale, died in 1903, though his will is dated 1859. He appointed two spinsters[16] as his executrixes. They predeceased him and thus the residuary legatee, his sister Mary Hargrave, widow,[17] applied for, and was granted a declaration that the will was valid, in a civil action.[18] Obviously one or more of his brothers (see above) challenged his will.

Mary Hargrave[19] died in 1908 and by her will dated 1905 devised her 'Riddings Hall estate' to her grandson James Joseph Taylor Hargrave and named her son, William George Garibaldi Thomason Hargrave, executor and trustee. Probate was granted in June 1908. Probably J.J.T. Hargrave was a minor in 1908 and did not enter into his inheritance until his twenty-first birthday as the estate was not devised to him until 1915. The executor interpreted the term 'Riddings Hall estate' to embrace only Riddings Hall and its Timperley acres. In December 1917 family litigation was initiated in the Lancashire Chancery Court, Hargrave v. Hargrave, but the action was not heard until late February 1919. The plaintiff was J.J.T. Hargrave and the defendants W.G.G.T. Hargrave, Hilda Hargrave and Bessie Hargrave.[20]

The action turned on the meaning of the expression in the will by which Mary Hargrave devised her 'Riddings Hall estate' to her grandson and '... devised and bequeathed all the residue of her real and personal property to her son W.G.G.T. Hargrave'.

At her death her estate in Sale and Timperley comprised the reputed manor of Timperley and its constituent parts were:

a. Riddings Hall Farm with its attached lands in Timperley.
b. New Farm with its attached lands in Sale.
c. Sale Heys – a freehold house with outbuildings and grounds in Sale.
d. Chief rent on lands in Sale.
e. Chief rent on lands in Timperley.

The plaintiff contended the expression 'Riddings Hall estate construed *ALL* the testatrix's real estate in both Timperley and Sale, whilst the defendants' contention was that whatever may have been the case in the past, *NOW* there is no such thing as a 'Riddings Hall estate' but only the three distinct farm buildings mentioned above and that (b) and (c) are physically severed from (a) by MSJ and A Railway and the Bridgewater Canal. They also submitted that the expression '... devise of the Riddings Hall estate' in the will only included (a) and denied that '... there is any other Riddings Hall estate or that any sums are due to the plaintiff in respect of the said devise by Mary Hargrave...'. The defendants' solicitors[21] wrote to Lt. Col. C.E. Newton of Watling Gate, Timperley, requesting written evidence in support of their case, stating that local tradition has it that the Sale properties are quite separate and no tradition exists that the owner of one property must be the owner of the other. It would appear that Col. Newton's answer supported the plaintiff's case as the court ruled in favour of J.J. Taylor Hargrave, as is proved by the fact that it was he who disposed of the land in the 1930s.

Riddings Hall Farm, in 1917, was let on a yearly tenancy of £245 (about £2.50 per acre in decimal money) and was tenanted continuously from before 1838 to 1945 when the farmhouse and outbuildings were demolished and the land subsequently developed (i.e. Riddings Court estate). The resident tenant farmers were:

Mr Samuel Smith, 1838-1841	Mr John Lancashire, 1881-1901
Mr George Fletcher, 1850-1860	Mrs Maria Chadwick, 1902-1914
Mr Thomas Richardson, 1871-1880[22]	Mr Thomas Garner, 1914-1945[23]

In 1924 J.J. Taylor Hargrave sold two plots of land to developers comprising:

- Part of a field fronting Wash Lane located between what are now Riddings and Greenway Roads.

- Part (or whole?) of a field fronting Wash Lane bounded on the west-north-west by the MSJ and A Railway and on the east-south-east by what is now Greenway Road.

On those plots the developers built, firstly, the row of houses which front Wash Lane between the present Riddings and Greenway Roads and, secondly, those rows of houses which formed the first sections of Greenway Road and Sylvan Avenue. The rows terminated on a line with what is now Cheam Road.

Farming ceased on the remaining lands in the early 1930s. During that period J.J. Taylor Hargrave made further land sales of Riddings acres on which developers built two large housing estates called respectively the Mauldeth and Broadbridge housing estates (see map on p.32).[24] Following the sales only the farmyard, farmhouse and orchard, occupying in all about 3 acres and bounded by the rear boundaries of dwelling houses in Greenway, Cheam and Riddings roads, remained of the ancient Riddings estate, plus some fields adjoining the MSJ and A Railway and extending to the boundary of the township at Baguley Brook. Details of the land sold are listed below.

7th December, 1933   to Herbert Greenhalgh Lonsdale (Architect) 27.4 acres 'Riddings Hall' estate for £19053 2s 6d (about £710 per acre).[25]

1934   to S.V. Broadbridge (Builder) Ltd., 'Sylvan' estate.[26]

Notes

1. Harden is located near Stockport.
2. 'Timperley Past and Present', Lt. Col. C.E. Newton.
3. See Arderne pedigree in Ormerod Vol.III.
4. The Vawdrey family were large landowners in Bowdon parish and Vice Chamberlains in the County's governance until the dissolution of the Palatinate (1540). Besides land and properties in Bowdon parish, they had possessions in other parts of the county, including a house in Chester on Lower Bridge Street (according to Newton).
5. Dated 1567.
6. The pedigree suggests he had four children by his first wife and ten by his second wife.
7. Probably his youngest child.
8. 'Timperley Past and Present', Lt. Col. C.E. Newton.
9. Richard Vawdrey of Bank Hall, son of John Vawdrey of Bank Hall, esquire, and grandson of Robert. Those whom were financially eligible to be a knight but had not so elected and been made knights when Charles I was crowned were fined. It was a ruse to raise revenue. See *Distraint for Knighthood*, Vol.12, Record Society of Lancashire and Cheshire.
10. Robert Vawdrey of Bowdon.
11. Thomas Gerard's father was Rector of Stockport and a member of the Gerard family of Harrow, Middlesex. Through his mother Ursula (née Arderne) he was related to the Ardernes of Harden. (N.B. *Cheshire Directory* dates the purchase as 1660.)
12. The dates of birth, death, etc., of the various owners have been extracted from the pedigrees of Bulkeley, Arderne, Vawdrey and Gerard families, published in Ormerod, Vol.III. See also the Will of William Massey of Sale, esquire, 1706 (C.C.R.O.). William Massey had one son, Robert, and three other daughters, Barbara, Elizabeth and Susannah.
13. See p.33 for their names.
14. T. Clayton had died in 1850.
15. Will states in a bequest '... to his mother Esther Thomason...' and further bequests 'to his brothers Charles T. Thomason, George Thomason and J.H.T. Thomason.'
16. They resided at Rock Ferry, Birkenhead.
17. She was formerly Mary Hanlon, widow.
18. Hargrave v. Thomason, Probate Court, 1904.
19. Mary Hargrave resided at Lostock near Bolton.
20. Hargrave v. Hargrave, Lancashire Chancery Court, Liverpool District, Letter H, No.1819.
21. Simpson, North and Harley of Liverpool.
22. Refer to Kelly's, Pigot's and White's *Cheshire Directories* and the Population Censuses of 1871 and 1881.
23. The Garner family farmed in the district for upwards of sixty years. Prior to tenanting Riddings Hall, Thomas was the tenant of New Farm, Sale, which was also owned by the Taylor family.
24. By 1935/6 most of the Riddings lands were developed.
25. Riddings Hall estate, Mauldeths Ltd (developer). See Chapter 10, Appendix 1.
26. Comprised houses on parts of Sylvan Avenue, Greenway Road and Woodhouse Lane East (up to No.130); also Crofton, Garner and Rosset Avenues.

6

LOCAL GOVERNMENT

'Government is a contrivance of human wisdom to provide for human wants. Men have a right that these wants should be provided for by this wisdom.'

Edmund Burke

The contemporary form of local government that we have today is a comparatively recent phenomenon when considered in a historical time scale. In fact, the forces which have created it were initiated in the middle of the eighteenth century. Its raison d'etre was a necessity to deal with the acute social and economic problems generated by the Industrial Revolution. Prior to the Industrial Revolution the main aim of the King's government was to secure peace, thus facilitating the development of agriculture, craft skills and trade. Its guiding principle was that *good government was a government that governed least.*

To appreciate the workings of local government in a parish today an awareness of the salient factors which have influenced and modified local government down the centuries is essential; also a realisation that the process has been *evolutionary* and not *revolutionary.*

Salient Factors

1. *The Feudal System*
A social order prevailing until the sixteenth century, prescribing rights and duties inextricably bound up with the ownership of land. It provided:
a. A hierarchy of powers from the sovereign down to the humblest inhabitant.
b. A system of county government providing a link between sovereign and parish.
c. A system of parishes providing a network of order.
d. Boroughs: certain small towns with special privileges – they were excluded from county control.
e. Justice – via a dual system of king's courts and local courts.

2. *Thirteenth Century*
The vital innovation of Justices of the Peace. They were a key element in the evolution of local government, being the sovereign's representatives in the counties responsible for keeping the King's Peace. The successful performance of their duties depended on co-operation with the parishes which had a tradition of local self government.

3. *Tudor Period*
During the sixteenth century the J.P.s were brought under the close supervision of the King's Council and much new legislation was enacted, for example:
a. Statute of Bridges, 1530-1531.
b. Highway Acts. (N.B. Parishes made responsible for both these under the supervision of J.P.s)
c. Posts of Surveyor of Highways and Overseer of the Poor added to the traditional parish offices (for example, churchwarden, constable, etc.).
d. Parish officers made responsible for administering Elizabethan Poor Law in 1601.

4. *Stuart Period*
1689 – 'Divine Right of Kings' superseded by an 'Agrarian Aristocracy'.

5. *Georgian Period*
Encompassed the Industrial Revolution which witnessed the metamorphosis of England and Wales from an agrarian to an industrial society with the bulk of the population living in urban communities – generally in unsavoury, crowded and squalid conditions – under a traditional system of local government unable to cope with the social problems engendered by the newly created industrial towns.

6. *Victorian Period*

Occasioned the metamorphosis of the traditional system of local government to its contemporary form, embodying the principle of a central authority (Parliament), controlling and regulating, and a local authority (council) administering the regulations of the central authority.

The unit of local government, the parish, had, down the centuries, developed a tradition of self-help in matters such as crop rotation, maintenance of bridges and footpaths, care of straying animals, poor relief, etc., whilst the J.P.s were responsible for law and order which necessitated co-operation with the parishes. The chain of authority may be shown diagrammatically:

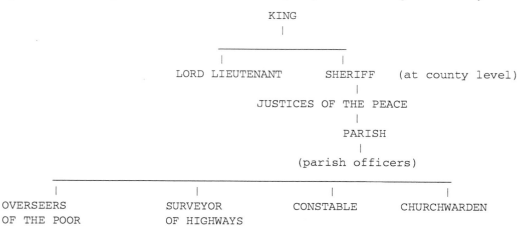

```
                          KING
                           |
            _____
           |                         |
    LORD LIEUTENANT            SHERIFF     (at county level)
           |                         |
              JUSTICES OF THE PEACE
                         |
                       PARISH
                         |
                (parish officers)
   _____
   |                  |               |               |
OVERSEERS          SURVEYOR        CONSTABLE      CHURCHWARDEN
OF THE POOR        OF HIGHWAYS
```

In theory the duties of parish officers were obligatory (unpaid) on all inhabitants, but could be exercised by a deputy. When such duties were customary, limited in extent and unspecialised the traditional system of local government was workable, but the social and economic upheavals of the eighteenth century compelled the parishes to adapt as best they could to the changed conditions. By 1832 this traditional local government system was no longer viable and innovative legislation became imperative, primarily in the new industrial towns. The drive for improvement proved to be intermittent, usually followed extensions of the suffrage, and was designed to alleviate the squalid urban social conditions in the heavily populated new industrial towns. The remedies adopted for these urban communities were often, in modified form, adapted to the needs of the rural parishes, especially in the fields of the Poor Law and public health. These initiatives, out of which our contemporary system has evolved, largely took place during the period 1832-1888, following the Reform Act of 1832. The salient legislation affecting rural parishes (Timperley was one) is listed here.

1. *Reform Act*:	extends suffrage to middle class	– 1832
2. *Poor Law Amendment Act*:	set up unions of parishes, each under the control of a Board of Guardians, responsible for Poor Relief	– 1834
3. *Nuisance Removal Act*:	recognised Board of Guardians as a Rural Sanitary Authority	– 1846
4. *Public Health Act*:	set up local boards to carry out duties re sewerage, drainage, water supply	– 1848
5. *Reform Bill*:	extends suffrage to urban working class	– 1867
6. *Public Health Act*:	reorganised Urban and Rural Sanitary Districts outside the boroughs	– 1875
7. *Local Government Act*:	established elected County Councils; Urban and Rural District councils within county area; most of administrative powers of J.P.s transferred to elected County Council	– 1888
8. *Local Government Act*:	established a. elected Rural District Councils; b. parish councils; c. Parish Meetings	– 1894

Thus by 1894 parish councils occupied the lowest tier in a three-tiered system of rural local government (i.e. county council, rural district council, parish council) which system was itself the result of fifty years of experiment and compromise following the 1832 Reform Bill. It preceded the road transport revolution occasioned by the internal combustion engine; the implementation of the concept of state financed social services (in 1911) and a population explosion (between 1894 and 1921 the population of England and Wales increased from 26 to 38 millions and within this statistic the rural population decreased from 31% to 21% of the total). The system was ill-fitted to cope with the strains and stresses to which it was exposed. Prior to its general revision by the Local Government Act 1929, adjustments to the system were principally expedients to deal with particular problems (for example, road improvements, public health, poor law, housing and town planning). The period also witnessed the gradual development of central control of local government. Post 1928 the following Acts were passed.

Local Government Act 1929
It abolished the Board of Guardians and transferred their powers to County Council and introduced the principle of town and country planning.

Local Government Act 1933
A consolidating Act dealing with services for which local authorities were responsible.

The above factors have, of course, had their influence on the form of Timperley's local government down the years.

In 1832 there were more than 15,000 ecclesiastical parishes in England and Wales which varied extensively in area and population. The original definition of a parish is:

'That circuit of ground in which the souls under the care of one parson or vicar do inhabit.'

Today there are two kinds of parish.

The Ecclesiastical Parish: defined above.
The Civil Parish: which may, or may not, be identical with an ecclesiastical parish in its boundaries. It is simply an area delineated for secular purposes of local government and may contain parts of *one* or *more* ecclesiastical parishes within its boundaries.

Timperley, in 1832, was one of a number of townships in the very large ecclesiastical parish of Bowdon, which parish embraced some 25 to 30 square miles. Such ecclesiastical parishes had a long tradition of local self government. In the case of a small parish it could be administered as one unit for local government. In the case of large rural parishes like Bowdon this was clearly impractical and each township had its own local government organisation for secular affairs. Thus for the secular purposes of local government (for example, Poor Law, highways, bridges, nuisance control, local taxation) Timperley was an individual local government unit.

Legislation enacted during the last decades of Elizabeth I's reign largely determined the form of local government down to the early nineteenth century. In particular it made the parish/township responsible for highways, bridges and the administration of the Elizabethan Poor Law under the general supervision of the J.P.s who were also responsible for law and order.[1] Often a township had no resident J.P.

Having sketched out the salient factors which have occasioned the gradual evolution of local government in England and Wales down to the present time, one can proceed to describe the particular case of local government in Timperley township.

The Feudal Period, Eleventh to Sixteenth Centuries

Following the Norman Conquest, Timperley was one of a number of manors in the fief of the Mascy of Dunham family. During the latter half of the thirteenth century the Timperley manor was split into two moieties (Northern and Southern) and subsequently, in the fifteenth century, the Southern Moiety was itself split into a further two moieties (i.e. each a quarter, approximately, of the whole manor).[2] During this period (eleventh to thirteenth centuries) its inhabitants were subject to the feudal system of government under the Mascys of Dunham. After c.1250 the Timperley manor was split between two lords and later (from the fifteenth century) apportioned between three lords.[3] No documentary evidence is extant to determine how the manor was administered during that period. However, as a small manor with, certainly, no resident lord prior to the late thirteenth century, it is a reasonable conjecture that as regards purely day-to-day matters its inhabitants would hold meetings periodically to regulate their common interests (for example, cultivation of crops, rights of common, etc.) and also take decisions relative to their public duties. In that era the lands would be largely waste and woodland; only a relatively small area would be under cultivation on the open field system, plus some pasture and common. The probability is that the open field was sited in the triangle of land bounded contemporarily by Stockport Road, Wood Lane and Thorley Lane.[4] its population was minuscule, about seventy-five to, at most, a hundred. Evidence from Hearth Tax Returns in the seventeenth century suggests a population of, at most, 200 (c.1670).

The lord of each moiety, being non-resident, would probably administer Timperley through his steward (he would make periodic visits) and the reeve (foreman), normally a villein appointed by fellow villagers, who would supervise the labour of the villagers and keep farm records.

Justice was largely administered by the manor court (halimote or court leet) where the lord of the manor presided to deal with cases, for example, trespass on pastures, bad husbandry, non-performance of duties, brawling, private grievances, etc., and also minor offences against laws governing the King's Peace. Prior to the institution of J.P.s the manor court met, bi-annually, also as a police court dealing with minor legal disputes and law infringements. Residents found guilty of an offence were 'punished' by small 'amercements' (fines). A village failing to perform its public duties could be amerced for all kinds of sins of omission or commission. Any financial impost imposed was assessed on the village as a whole and apportioned 'as the men of the village determined it'. The reeve 'and four better men' represented the village in the shire and hundred courts.

No documentary evidence specifically concerning local government in Timperley during the feudal period is contained in local and county archives. However, in legal records of the period, a number of items appear which concern the township – especially in the Plea and Recognisance Rolls (see Appendices 1 and 2 at the end of this chapter).

Late Sixteenth Century to 1832

From late Tudor times to the close of the Georgian era local government was largely determined by Tudor legislation and was based on two legal factors: the right of all inhabitants to participate in parish business, including the appointment of parish officers; and to perform the duties of parish officers if called upon to do so.

In theory officers were appointed to an 'open' parish vestry – a popular assembly of inhabitants. It had the power to levy a parish rate for financing the township's local government costs. In practice the vestry reflected the economic and social order of the parish or township. Often it became a 'close' or 'select' vestry controlled by an oligarchy[5] dominated by neighbouring J.P.s. It consisted of twelve to twenty-four persons serving for life, vacancies being filled by co-option. The system lent itself to corruption. Some select vestries indubitably exploited their ratepayers but some parishes were governed responsibly and efficiently. To circumvent the disadvantages of unpaid service the select vestry permitted the formal holder of an office to employ a salaried assistant and Surveyors of the Highways were often sanctioned to let out building and repair works to a contractor on a tender basis. Obviously, the system was open to abuse by a parish officer if he chose to utilise the office for his private advantage. By this time (the eighteenth century) there were only some 5,000 J.P.s in the kingdom whose powers had steadily increased down the years. So onerous had their duties become that many eligible persons were disinclined to accept appointment to the bench. During the period 1689-1832 many statutory authorities for special purposes were created to deal with the urgent problems generated by a changing social and economic order, especially in the fields of poor law and roads (making and maintenance).

No documentary evidence is extant on local government in Timperley, prior to 1770, in Altrincham Reference Library. It is, however, probable that in the seventeenth and first half of the eighteenth centuries (in view of the township's tiny population – about 150 in the late seventeenth century[7]) its local government was conducted by Bowdon Parish Vestry, of which parish it was a constituent township at that time. If that, in fact, was the position then local government matters concerning Timperley will be contained in the parish vestry records of Bowdon. The archives available for the period are:

Altrincham Reference Library
The Town's Book, 1770-1833

Cheshire County Record Office
Hearth Tax Returns, 1664 and 1673-4
Land Tax Assessments, 1798-1842
Overseers' Accounts, 1798-1838
Constables' Accounts, 1798-1801

Poor Rate Returns, 1800-1817 and 1821-1834
Plan of Timperley (based on the Tithe Map)
with ownership or occupation annotated for
years 1811 and 1831)[8]

From 1770 onwards at least, Timperley conducted its own local government, administered by officers appointed in 'open vestry'[9] (in practice probably a 'closed vestry'). Each ratepayer in the township was qualified to attend and vote at its meetings. The town's book contains:

Lists of officers appointed annually during the period 1770 to 1833.
Land Tax Assessments for 1784 and 1789 (paid to king).
Tithe Assessments for 1799.
Valuation of Estates for 1799.

A representative selection of officers' names extracted from the lists is below.

Overseers of Poor[10]

1770	Joseph Faulkner (Riddings Hall)	and	William Goulden (Tarvins – *sic*).
1816 to 1820	William Renshaw	and	Samuel Lucas (blacksmith)

Constables of Township[11]

1770	J. Coppock	and	Thomas Warburton
1790	John Coppock	and	John Chorlton
1810	J. Barit (*sic*)	and	James Garner
1832	William Heywood	and	William Davenport

Surveyors of Highways

1770	William Priestnall	and	J. Williamson
1790	Edward Billinge	and	William Whitelegg
1810	William Burgess	and	R. Savage
1832	William Heywood	and	Thomas Carr

Assessors of Poor Rate and Highway Rate

1796	J. Warburton	and	Isaiah Gatley
1810	William Whitehead	and	Samuel Lucas
1820	Samuel Smith	and	James Faulkner
1833	Samuel Lucas	and	William Warren

A careful check of Land Tax Assessments, Tithe Assessments, Valuation of Estates and also the Tithe Redemption Lists (1838), proves that all the officers were substantial residents. Excepting Samuel Lucas (blacksmith), Thomas Carr, William Renshaw and William Davenport (all tenant farmers), they were all landholders, some farming their own lands.

The Land Tax Assessment of 1784 and 1799 assessed the township at £47 16s 0d which was collected from forty-four landholders. In 1784 four landholders (the Earl of Stamford, G. Johnson, Ric-hard Clarke and Mr Taylor) paid collectively £15 4s 6d of the total sum (i.e. one-third of the township's total land tax).

The Tithe Assessment of 1799 shows that forty-three landholders cultivated 558 acres of their lands (about 30% of the total acreage of the township). Those acres were charged to Tithes at 10d (4p) per acre which yielded £22 17s 6d on a 'double ley' basis.

The Valuation of Estates[12] lists twenty estates ranging from one valued at £150 to three valued at £20 each. Typical entries from the lists are below.

NAME	VALUE	CARTS	SHOVELS
James Walker	£150 0s 0d	14½	19
Widow Hulme	£40 0s 0d	5	5
Thomas Warburton	£20 0s 0d	5	5

A lone entry provides an insight into the cost of highway repair and maintenance:

1806 '... Disbursed £71 7s 0d: Recd. by Levy – £34 17s 9d: Recd. by Composition – £4 11s 0d.: = £39 8s 9d: Cash out of Hand – £39 18s 3d.'[13]

E. Billinge (*Overseer*)

Original manuscript records[14] of the work of the vestry officers during the period 1800-1820 and, in some instances, onwards into the 1830s, are discussed below.

Rating Pre-1835

Poor Rate Returns are extant for each of the years 1801-1817 inclusive.[15] The 'Poor Ley' was levied on owners of land and/or property. They were also assessed for land tax (paid to the sovereign), and for constables' and church rates (see below). During the period the returns show that the Poor Ley yield increased from £112 (1801) to £353 (in each of years 1815 to 1817). In 1814 and 1815 the levy yielded £420, suggesting an economic downturn with an associated increased demand for Poor Relief. Unfortunately the rate in the £ levied is not recorded. Assuming an average 'ley' of 2s 6d in the £, it suggests rateable value of about £3000. A breakdown of the figures for a typical year is set out below. Ninety per cent of the asterisked sum was expended on relief.

1817						
Poor Rates	County Gaols and Bridges	Militia	Church and Constables	Salaries	Miscellaneous Expenses	Real Amount Paid to Poor
£353 9s 0½*	£13 7s 4d	NIL	£7 0s 0d	£12 10s 0d	£7 10s 0d	£314 1s 6½d

Constables' Accounts 1799-1801

Each submitted a list of his disbursements which a professional 'writer' compiled into one set of accounts (use of third person 'his' in a specific entry, quoted below, confirms this).

'... Paid the town's writer –... three quarterly payments at 20s, per quarter.'

The constables were obliged to make official journeys to magistrates' courts at Hoo Green[16] and Knutsford.

'To taking an Account of men for Militia 1s-6d and his journey to Knutsford with their names 1s-6d.' [7½p]

'To his journey with the Return of Overseers' of Poor 1s-6d: Paid at the Return of Assessment 2s-6d [12½p] and his journey at the same time 1s-6d.'

'Paid at the Return of the Overseers' of Highways 7s-6d and his journey..., 1s-6d.'

Other items include payment for 'Coal and Gunpowder';[17] 'Postage and Stationery'; 'Sparrows' Heads'; 'Returns of Jurors and Innkeepers'; 'Warrants and Summonses'; 'Coroner's Inquests'; and 'Paid for Liquor at Fire... 5s-0d' [25p] (what a gem of an entry this – doubtless no shortage of volunteer fireman ever occurred).

Vagrants and poor non-residents passing through the township were carefully monitored.

Item: 'Searching for Vagrants – 1s-6d.' [7½p]
Item: 'Payments to sundry passengers...'
(Total relief paid in two years 6s-4d) [32p]

The following item, one of four identical entries, refers to payments of the county rate:

'Paid quarterly payment and his journey at the same time £1-15-5d... and 1s-6d...'

The constables' disbursements averaged £7 5s 0d per annum in each of the two years.

Overseers of Poor Accounts 1817

William Renshaw, the Overseer, farmed Oak Farm.[18] The net amount of the Poor Rate available for Poor Relief purposes after paying various external charges, was £314 1s 6½d (see table above). To this sum must be added a balance of £29, carried forward from 1816, and £63 of bastardy monies collected, making a total of about £406 available for relief, including certain official expenses ancillary to the administration of Poor Relief. Such items are itemised in the Overseer's Return (see Appendices 3, 3b and 3c at the end of this chapter) and are aggregated under particular headings below to the nearest pound.

	£	s	d
Summonses and Warrants	2	0	0
Expenses of Rate Collection	3	0	0
Repairs to School	2	0	0
Bastardy Monies	63	0	0
Official Journeys	9	0	0
Expenses of Town Meeting – Postage and Stationery	1	0	0
Balance Carried Forward (1818)	26	0	0

These ancillary items totalling £106 show that £300 was disbursed entirely on direct Poor Relief, over 70% of the total monies available (i.e. £406 minus £106). Approximately seventy residents were relieved during the year. Unfortunately the entries merely record the recipients' names and the total amount each received. The relief granted was generally for rent, food, clothes or illness. Total *annual* relief to a recipient was generally in the range £2 to £10, usually at a rate of 1s 6d to 2s 6d a week. Only four recipients received more than £10 and only one received a payment for each of the fifty-two weeks. Officers received a fixed sum of 3s expenses for official journeys – usually to Hoo Green or Knutsford (see Appendix 3 at the end of the chapter).

The population of 630 in 1817 suggests that about 9% of the inhabitants received outdoor relief for at least some weeks in the year. Paupers at that time were accommodated at Culcheth in Lancashire.[19]

Between 1821 and 1834 the 'Poor Ley' yielded sums varying from £300 to £400 annually. In any one year the average amount disbursed on Poor Relief averaged £225. In 1826 the Agricultural Levy and the House Levy yielded £259 and £9 respectively.

In 1824[20] and 1832 the Overseers returned completed questionnaires to the Poor Law Commissioners giving factual information about the Poor Rate and rating practice in the township which revealed the following facts:

The township had an open vestry
Was not united with any other parish/township for Poor Law Relief
Had no workhouse
Used Culcheth which had a capacity of fifty persons
Timperley paupers lodged there were paid for at the rate of 2s 1d per week
That unemployed able-bodied men were paid in money only if magistrates so ordered
That the township had four paid officers (i.e. Vestry Clerk, Schoolmaster, Assessment Officer and Overseer of the Poor).

The 1832 Return reveals that for the year ending 31st March, 1832 the township's valuation was £4,097 (assessed on basis of three-quarters the full value of land and houses) and the ley for that year was levied at a rate of 2s 6d in the pound. Answering the questions 'Why was Assessment made on File?' and 'Why is the proportion of rental on lands and houses different?' in both cases the same answer was given, 'Because it is too high'.

We also learn that the township expended nothing and employed no-one on road repairs in 1832; also that four persons from the township were lodged in Culcheth Workhouse. The entries below in the manuscript book, c.1830-35, are interesting.

'Lord Stamford's home quarry occupied by Tom Arnold – assessed at £15 p.a. clear.'[21]

'H. Newberry's home quarry, occupied by J. Mollet – assessed at £5 p.a. clear.'

'Wasteland newly cultivated by W. Royle assessed at 2½ acres at rate of £4 per acre but ¼ to be deducted from outgoings from this valuation.'

'Tolls collected at Timperley Toll Bar rated and assessed at £70 p.a. clear.'

In 1819 an Act of Parliament amended the laws for the relief of the poor. It empowered an 'Open Vestry' to '... select a committee of five (minimum) and twenty (maximum) substantial Householders or Occupiers within a Township...' whose function was '... the management of the Concerns of the Poor...' Its members, nominated and elected annually, constituted the 'Select Vestry'. From amongst its members it elected officers for specific duties.[22] Timperley's first Select Vestry was constituted in 1835 (see below).

1835 to 1894

The written evidence discussed above shows that local government in Timperley from c.1750 to 1834 was conducted in accordance with Elizabethan Poor Law principles. In the 1830s the constantly escalating costs of local government services triggered a demand by ratepayers nationally for central government contributions towards such costs. The principle was conceded and from 1835 central government involvement in local government steadily increased, especially in the fields of finance, law and order, education and highways, via government legislation and grants in aid, for example:

1835	Grants in aid to defray legal charges
1856	Police (Counties and Boroughs Act)
1870	Education Act
1889	Grants in aid towards road maintenance – post abolition of Turnpike Trusts

In 1834 the Poor Law Amendment Act created a central authority, the Poor Law Commissioners, to administer its provisions. It formed groups of parishes into 'Poor Law Unions', each union being governed by an elected Board of Guardians with at least one member from each constituent township.[23] It appointed salaried servants to administer its decisions and levied money calls on township – calculated as a percentage of the rateable value of each – to finance poor relief costs, etc. Timperley was a constituent member of the Altrincham (later Bucklow) Poor Law Union,[24] which embraced Knutsford, Bowdon and Lymm parishes and in all contained forty townships.

The Altrincham Poor Law Union's workhouse was built at Knutsford. Each constituent township administered poor relief through its select vestry and each township's cash payments to the union is carefully listed in the Poor Law Union Minutes[25] (see Appendix 3 for Timperley entries). The creation of the Altrincham Poor Law Union occasioned the formation of Timperley's first select vestry. Ratepayers met at the Hare and Hounds Inn on 6th April, 1835 for this purpose and elected a vestry comprising sixteen members which included its first chairman, Thomas Whitelegg (farmer), the village's blacksmith and joiner and also a number of farmers. The Select Vestry Minute Book[26] shows that it met at approximately monthly intervals and also documents the types of relief applications processed by the Overseers. They were not a *soft touch* (to use the modern idiom). In such a small community they would be cognisant of an applicant's circumstances and thus be able to assess precisely if relief was justified. Relief grants appear to be the minimum commensurate with an applicant's needs (as ratepayers themselves, they had a vested interest in the avoidance of largesse). The evidence of the minutes suggests that they carried out their duties humanely and efficiently. A salaried Assistant Overseer of Poor administered their decisions.[27]

In 1836 the Parochial Assessment Act directed that the poor rate was to be levied on the basis of the nett assessed value of occupied property.[28] In that year the Select Vestry levied a poor rate of 1s 4d in the £ which was increased by 25% in 1837. (Typical items from the Minutes are given in Appendix 4.) Other facets of the work of the select vestry, excluding canal and railway, are now discussed.

During this period the select vestry devoted much time to rating matters, being zealous in its efforts to obtain full value for every penny of public monies expended; the minutes illustrate the scrupulous attention they gave to the township's financial affairs (see Appendix 4). In 1865 Timperley was assessed at a rateable value of £211 4s 10d but only empowered to elect one Guardian of the Poor, whereas Nether Knutsford (rateable value £74 5s 4d) elected two. The Select Vestry protested and requested that the township be granted additional representation. In September 1865 they agreed to support a system for the county rate under which each township paid for its own privileges (for example, the Select Vestry stated '...Timperley has only one policeman... other townships have more...' and deemed it inequitable that '... one township pays for the privileges of another...'[29]

In 1858 the Select Vestry carefully considered the provisions of an Act of Parliament (13-14 Victoria) re small tenements' rating accounts. It finally decided that future assessments for poor and highway rates should be levied on the owners of tenements instead of the occupiers. They decided that any owner prepared to pay the rate whether or not his tenement(s) was/were occupied would be assessed at two-thirds of the amount he would otherwise have been liable for.

Highways

Maintenance and repair of these was the responsibility of two members of the Select Vestry who were elected annually to the office of Surveyor of Highways. Usually they could only devote part of their time to the duties of the office and accordingly appointed a salaried Assistant Surveyor of Highways to administer the highway projects they initiated. This official was responsible for keeping the Surveyor of Highways fully briefed on the progress of work authorised by them; directing and supervising the tasks performed by labourers (for example, infilling pot holes) and monitoring the work carried out by contractors (for example, bridge building). Any major work which the Surveyors of the Highways considered necessary was required to be presented to the full Select Vestry for discussion and approval or rejection. If authorised the necessary expenditure would be sanctioned from the highway rate. Often major works were put out to tender. Subsequently the Select Vestry would select and approve the successful tender. Selected highway minutes illustrate the type of projects dealt with and the vigilance with which the Select Vestry monitored the actions of its Surveyor of Highways. In June 1842 the then Surveyor of Highways, John Dobb,[30] submitted accounts which were disputed by the Select Vestry. They set up a court of inquiry which reported, on 16th June, that Dobb would not settle the matter. Accordingly the Select Vestry felt compelled to place the case in the hands of the magistrates but, at the last moment, Dobb settled by paying the '... sum of £63 6s 2½d to Mr Collier who in turn repaid the cash to the current Surveyors...'. Subsequently, Dobb was billed for £3 1s 3d for committee expenses incurred in the dispute. Obviously no lapse of financial probity was tolerated by members of the Select Vestry. The period occasioned much expense for the building of new, and repair of older, bridges spanning the brooks in the township, as the following minutes illustrate:

23rd November, 1840
Moved: '...£25 out of Rate in 1841 be allocated to defraying expenses of erecting a bridge over brook near Mrs Nancy Hulme's... on condition it is built under direction of Bridgemaster of Bucklow Hundred...'[31]

29th November, 1841
Moved: '... Surveyor of Highways be employed to fill up road leading to bridge over Timperley Brook and to obtain materials at nearest point and on most reasonable terms obtainable...'

20th May, 1857
Moved: '...Meeting to consider estimates laid before Ratepayers of expenses of repairing or rebuilding bridge over brook near Thos. Warburton's and to take opinion of meeting whether new bridge[32] is to be built or the old one repaired...'

N.B. The meeting commissioned the Surveyor of the Highway and two stonemasons to '...inspect and give opinion whether same should be repaired or rebuilt...'. This was done within a week and on 27th May they reported that repair only was needed. The Surveyor was authorised to carry out the necessary repairs.

In 1850 straying cattle were causing concern as the following minute reveals:

4th April
'... Public Notices be given that all horses, cattle, etc. found straying in lanes of township be impounded by Surveyor's servants...'

Public Health

Disease was a major problem in the nineteenth century, especially in the then new industrial towns. Its principal causes were poor and inadequate drainage; primitive, or non-existent, sanitation facilities; polluted water supplies and overcrowded living conditions. The concomitant of these was a high incidence of infectious diseases (cholera, typhoid, smallpox and tuberculosis) which were no respecter of persons; but the poor suffered most. The Poor Law Commissioners, whose aim was to identity and reduce the causes of pauperism were, probably the first to appreciate the scale of the problem; statistics provided by the new Registrar General's Department[33] substantiated their view that, if the condition of the poor was to be improved, action to prevent those basic causes of ill-health must become a prime concern of central government. This burgeoning appreciation of the situation resulted in continuing government initiatives[34] towards the eradication of these health hazards, but progress was relatively slow.

In the rural areas the Nuisance Removal Act of 1846 gave the duty of applying its measures to the Board of Guardians (in each Poor Law Union) who for the first time were recognised as a Rural Sanitary Authority responsible for their Rural Sanitary District (usually this district was identical, or closely related to, the area of a Board's Poor Law Union area). The Board authorised the appointment of Nuisance Removal Committees in the townships comprising the Union. A Nuisance Removal Committee was responsible for identifying health hazards in a township and initiating action to 'abate the nuisance' (as it is euphemistically termed).

The Public Health Act of 1848 created Local Boards with specific duties in connection with sewerage, drainage and supply of water.

Timperley's Nuisance Removal Committee's activities are illustrated by a Nuisance Removal Committee minute book[35] from which typical minutes are quoted below:

2nd July, 1860
'Letter to Mr. Jas. Carter requesting he remove manure lying in a field adjoining Wash Lane.'
'Attention of Surveyor directed to trough adjoining Mr. Kelsall's land.'

18th August, 1860
'A reminder be sent to Mr. Carter re nuisance in his field' (Carried)
(NB. Seems committee were very tardy in monitoring recommended abatements – see item 2nd July above).

3rd September, 1860
'Presentment[36] of Petties in occupation of Sam Whitelegg – on Mr. Dearden's property, having been read it was proposed: "Give notice to Mr. Dearden to remove forthwith."'
'Middens in G. Morgan's yard be inspected and report on state of same to next meeting.'
(NB. Deptn. recommended Morgan remove stagnant water in his yard and in future only vegetable matter be put down.)
'Sur. of Hwys. requested to examine watercourse in Wash Lane and to act as they think fit.'

7th January, 1861
'Presentment by Mr. Suttle of culverts and ditches belonging to Trustees of Duke of Bridgewater be served notice to cleanse same under and parallel to Canal throughout township.' (NB. In March Nuisance Removal Committee reported no reply from Trustees of Duke of Bridgewater – Proposed write them again.)

The Select Vestry formally recorded its opinion that the Nuisance Removal Committee was found to be of great benefit to the township and that the Committee of Ratepayers should be retained (29th April, 1861). On 6th May the committee reported that objections had been raised to the committee retaining its powers – exercised for eighteen months – simply because 'salary paid to Inspector not named in return made by Overseer of the Poor'. Following inquiries he was awarded fixed salary of £5 per annum.

1894 to 1936

The archive material available for the period (both locally and at C.C.R.O.) provides a detailed record of the conduct of local government in the township culminating with its amalgamation with Altrincham in 1936.[37]

1894 was a watershed in the evolution of English local government; the catalyst was the Local Government Act of 1894. It created:

They assumed the powers, duties and liabilities of the Rural Sanitary Authority in each Rural Sanitary District; also the powers of an highway authority in it.

Parish Councils
For townships of 300 plus population, with parish councillors elected by ballot.

Parish Meetings
For townships of less than 300.

Rural District Councillors
Elected by townships to represent a Parish Council on the Rural District Council.

The County Council was the sole general authority over Rural District Councils, Urban District Councils and Parish Councils. In North-east Cheshire the Rural District Councils – of which Timperley was a constituent Parish Council – was called the Bucklow Rural District Council. It embraced parishes around Knutsford, Lymm and Bowdon.

Timperley's period of local government as a parish council with Bucklow Rural District Council was from 1894 to 1936.

The 1894 Local Government Act provided for an annual assembly of parochial electors,[38] election of Parish Councillors (by ballot if necessary), each elector to have one vote in a ballot.

The parochial electors met, on 4th December, 1894, to elect their first parish council. Twenty-seven nominations were received for the thirteen places available. No ballot was called for and, on a show of hands, the top candidate received ninety-four and the thirteenth fifty-eight votes. The members' occupations suggest that they represented a balanced cross-section of the township's residents. The post of Clerk to the Council was a salaried appointment.[39]

Parish Council 1894

Name	Place of Residence	Occupation
Ambler, John T.	Deansgate Lane	Tanner
Ashton, Major Robert	Charlecote, Moss Lane	Private Resident
Bell, James	Woodleigh, Stockport Road	Builder and Joiner
Bell, William	Addison Villas, Wash Lane	Private Resident
Calderbank, Thomas	Moss Lane	Market Gardener
Harrop, Isaac	Moss Lane	Market Gardener
Jackson, Samuel	Sugar Lane	Farmer
Lambert, John	Ribblesdale, Stockport Road	Private Resident
Leech, Sir T. Bosdin	Oakmount, Wood Lane	Gentleman, JP
Muir, Alexander	Quarry Bank, Stockport Road	
Platt, Thomas	Quarry Bank Inn	Beer Retailer and Plumber
Rogerson, William	Deansgate Lane	Market Gardener
Bell, Francis Tait	Ellisland, Stockport Road	Parish Clerk, Assistant Overseer and Collector of taxes
Webb, Edgar	Sans__?	
Jackson, Samuel	Sugar Lane	Farmer

In 1894 Timperley's rateable value is given as £18,911 in Altrincham Poor Law Union records.[40] Cheshire County Council reviewed rateable values periodically and reassessed them as necessary.[41] Any variation was critically examined by the Parish Council and if considered inequitable was challenged. On most occasions reassessments were accepted but it would seem they queried on in 1905, as the following minutes suggests:

11th June, 1905
Letter from Cheshire County Council stating Rate Assessment Committee had revised and altered County Rate basis of Parish of Timperley and fixed same at £24,890. Present Rateable Value is £25,252 (£362 more than proposed basis). Considered satisfactory.' *Resolved*: Be Accepted. (Carried).

The Parish Council levied its own Parish rate – generally at ½d (0.208p) in the pound – which yielded between £40 and £60 as the rateable value increased over the years. With any additional incidental income it was usually more than sufficient to cover the Parish Council expenditure. The Bucklow Rural District Council also precepted the Parish Council for Rural District Council Rates and its Board of Guardians for Poor Law Relief rate. The Poor Relief applications of the poor of the township are contained in the Board of Guardians minutes. The Parish Council minutes reveal that its principal concerns may be categorised under four general headings:

> highways and footpaths (including bridges), lighting, recreation grounds, and nuisance abatement.

Any minutes concerned with the canal, railways and education are dealt with in chapters 8, 9 and 14.

Often liaison with Bucklow Rural District Council was necessary (especially with regard to highway matters) and, as the Parish Council met bi-monthly, 'The wheels of Government turned very slowly.' Often it took months for a project to be approved and completed. Nevertheless, Timperley was governed efficiently and economically. There were three principal reasons which facilitated this high standard of local government:

- The area of the township was small enough to ensure the councillors had an intimate knowledge of every corner of it.

- As ratepayers they had a vested interested in ensuring good value for every penny of public monies spent.

- The office of councillor was elective and unpaid and thus placed a premium on an individual's probity and public spirit.

As the Parish Council's activities are discussed below, the influence of the above factors is seen to be axiomatic.

It held its first business meeting on 13th December, 1894 at Timperley Infants' School, Stockport Road. It elected officers from amongst its members (such as Overseers of the Poor and Surveyors of Highways); appointed Parrs Banking Company, of Altrincham, its bankers and its bank manager (Mr Fairhurst) Council Treasurer and confirmed Mr F.T. Bell as Clerk of the Council. Early in 1895, amongst its first acts, it authorised the purchase of a 'Safe and Stand at a cost of £19...';[42] agreed a hire fee of 3s per meeting for the Infants', School room and appointed F.T. Bell to the office of Assistant Overseer of the Poor at a salary of £125[43] per annum. The Council's actions, as recorded in the minutes, are categorised.

Footpaths

The maintenance and repair of these and their associated bridges – spanning the Timperley and Fairywell Brooks – was a perennial problem for the Council. Certainly, prior to 1920, they were more intensively used, especially for access to adjacent townships. The general procedure adopted was to monitor the condition of the paths and as necessary recinder them; they also instructed owners of land bordering the paths to trim any hedges or trees encroaching on the right of way. Most of the bridges carried the footpaths into adjacent townships and were simple plank bridges with perhaps a handrail. When repair or replacement was necessary they liaised with the adjacent township concerned and the work was done on a shared cost basis. The minutes quoted (see Appendix 5 at the end of this chapter) are self-explanatory.

Highways

During this period the highway authority for Timperley township was Bucklow Rural District Council to which all matters relevant to highways had to be referred for approval. Residents' complaints were often the initiative for action to be taken. The township's principal highway problems may be summarised under four general headings:

Road Maintenance and Widening
Principally poor road surfaces, drainage and constricted road junctions.

Flooding

Often required action to abate, particularly on the lands bordering the course of the Timperley Brook between Brook Lane and the canal. Down the years local newspapers periodically reported the occurrence of flash flooding in that locale, together with the problems and inconveniences suffered by families residing in that area. The residents of Brentwood Avenue were especially vulnerable to flooding. Not until 1984 was the problem finally resolved when a major Flood Abatement Scheme was completed at a site on the Salisbury Road fields.

Sewerage

Periodically the adequacy of the sewerage facilities in the township was considered by the Parish Council, particularly in 1927-8 when housing development in the township generated an urgent need to provide a modern sewerage system.

Special Meeting – 19th April, 1901
Expenditure: Period 1890-1901
About £750 was spent during this period on permanent works (i.e. sewers or extensions for new properties; ventilation shafts; new manholes and covers; workmen's huts and – at the outfall – additional land and new filter beds. (The new filter beds absorbed £200 of expenditure in the year ending 25th March, 1891.) £60 was expended on cleansing the sewers during the period.

A special sanitary rate of 1s 2d (6p) in the pound for 1890 and 1s 6d (7½p) in the pound for 1891 and 1892 was levied.

The lowest rate in the pound was levied (during period 1890-1901) in 1891 and 1892. Councillor Bell's report at the meeting noted: '...Demands of the last few years had prevented maintenance of an even Rate...' and he projected future capital expenditure on sewerage.

Lighting

Occasioned much friction and argument between the Parish Council and Bucklow Rural District Council. When the question of lighting the principal highways in the township was first broached by the Parish Council in 1898, protracted controversy between the two authorities lasted five years and culminated in unilateral action by Bucklow Rural District Council. The Parish Council's reaction is faithfully recorded in the Parish Council Minutes for the period in question.

The Parish Council's actions re the above highway matters are illustrated at the end of this chapter by typical minutes (see Appendix 6).

*

Under the Local Government Act of 1894 the newly created Urban District Councils became the Rural Sanitary Authority and the Nuisance Removal Committees in the townships of Bucklow Rural District Council and continued to function, under the jurisdiction of Bucklow Rural District Council, post 1894. They performed a useful function, though, because of the time lapse between notification of and action to abate, a nuisance could be protracted. Selected minutes of the Nuisance Removal Committee, illustrating typical complaints, are given in Appendix 6.

Timperley's long history as an autonomous unit of local government ended on 1st April, 1936 when its Parish Council was dissolved and the township amalgamated with Altrincham Urban District Council.[44] Henceforth it formed a district of the Borough of Altrincham. The events leading up to this radical change of status are now discussed. The first initiative dates back to January 1912 when Altrincham Urban District Council wrote proposing amalgamation and listed proposals. Following consideration the Parish Council resolved, 'Not to proceed with amalgamation at present.'

Sixteen years elapsed before the subject was broached again. In the interim the Parish Council considered the implications for the township of the Manchester Corporation Bill, 1924. Although no observations on its provisions were offered, the Parish Council would note the city's proposed territorial expansion (Baguley and Wythenshawe) to the eastern boundary of the township and doubtless monitor carefully any actions Manchester initiated which might have implications for the township. Against this background of expansion by Manchester a letter, dated 14th September, 1928, was received from Altrincham Urban District Council inviting the Parish Council to a joint meeting to discuss the question of amalgamation. The Parish Council agreed and informed Bucklow Rural District Council. Following the meeting on 27th September, the Parish Council resolved 'to inform Altrincham Urban District Council that a majority of the Parish Council was in favour, subject to suitable terms and representation being obtained and conditional on a referendum of ratepayers, to be held on 5th October, 1928'. Altrincham Urban District Council replied on 22nd November that they had resolved to engage a firm of accountants to prepare a report on the finances of both districts in order to assess suitable terms. The Parish Council agreed and obtained the permission of Bucklow Rural District Council to this procedure. The report was submitted in May 1929 and delineated the factors affecting various charges (rates, sewage, etc.) in each district in the event of amalgamation. Following consideration, the Parish Council resolved 'To proceed with amalgamation proposals'. Subsequent to a joint meeting on 17th June, 1929, the Parish Council outlined the terms on which it would be willing to amalgamate. Altrincham Urban District Council formally accepted them and both councils resolved 'To amalgamate on agreed terms'. An amalgamation committee was formed which prepared a petition formally requesting Cheshire County Council to take necessary steps to procure amalgamation. This was approved and confirmed by the Parish Council on 24th February, 1930. The projected amalgamation was now subject to a protracted delay by Cheshire County Council. At this time the Cheshire County Council was engaged on a comprehensive review of county districts and was contesting, together with Bucklow Rural District Council, the Manchester Corporation Bill. Until these matters were resolved the Cheshire County Council informed Altrincham Urban District Council they were adjourning consideration of the Amalgamation Petition of the two councils. Despite a joint deputation to Cheshire County Council Parliamentary Committee on 11th June, 1930, for early consideration of the petition, Cheshire County Council declined to action it, As with many bureaucratic processes, further progress towards amalgamation was protracted. On 28th August, 1931, the Parish Council was informed that Cheshire County Council had advised Altrincham Urban District that amalgamation could not take place before 1st April, 1933. Joint amalgamation meetings of the two councils were held on 7th and 25th August and 16th September, 1932 to protest at the delay in any decisions, re amalgamation, being made by Cheshire County Council. On 8th December, 1933 a Special Meeting of the Parish Council discussed a report of Cheshire County Council on 24th November, 1933, under the Local Government Act of 1929, re proposed boundary changes. Cheshire County Council proposed to abolish Timperley Parish Council with effect from 1st April, 1935 and amalgamate almost the whole of the parish with Altrincham Urban District Council except for about 24 acres in the vicinity of Dobbinets Lane which it was proposed to transfer to Ringway (Ringway was subsequently to form part of Hale Urban District Council). Also it was proposed to incorporate Dunham Massey in Altrincham.

These proposals formed part of the North Cheshire Regional Town Planning Scheme upon which Cheshire County Council had been engaged for some considerable time. It adopted the suggestions contained in the joint petition, submitted by Altrincham Urban District Council and Timperley Parish Councils (including proposals to divide the township into three wards, each electing three councillors to sit on Altrincham Urban District Council). The resolution of the differential rating problem was left to the Ministry of Health following full consultation with Altrincham Urban District Council and Timperley Parish Council. The Cheshire County Council formally resolved 'That that portion of Timperley proposed to be added to Altrincham should be taken out of the North Cheshire Regional Town Planning Scheme and that Altrincham should be the burial authority for the extended district'. The Ministry of Health inquiry into the North Cheshire Regional Town Planning Scheme was held on 16th October, 1934 and subsequently the Minister informed Cheshire County Council that 'It was not possible to activate any part of Cheshire County Council's proposals made under the Local Government Act 1929': This meant yet another postponement of amalgamation. At this juncture Altrincham, with Timperley Parish Council's approval, made an application to be incorporated as a borough which was granted by the Privy Council. Ultimately, on 18th June, 1935, the Ministry of Health approved the proposed amalgamation – subject to minor boundary adjustments with Sale, at Siddall's Bridge.[45] An order giving effect to amalgamation with effect from 1st April, 1936, was received on 28th February, 1936. On 30th March Timperley Parish Council held its final meeting when it formally dissolved itself; and its representatives on Bucklow Rural District Council retired from the council with effect from 1st April, 1936.

In its final year the Parish Council's income was £1158 15s 5d, expenditure £870 19s 5d. A cheque for the balance of £287 16s 0d was forwarded to Altrincham Urban District. The Clerk, Mr Frank Bell, was thanked for his service, of over twenty-five years, as Parish Clerk.[46]

Post 1936

Amalgamation terminated an era of, at least, 250 years during which the township was a separate and largely autonomous unit of local government. Henceforward Timperley's local government was centred on and administered by Altrincham Borough Council. Following the 1914-18 war the township experienced an accelerating transition from a rural to a suburban lifestyle. The first steps towards this radical change were taken in the 1850s[47] but prior to 1900 their impact was marginal and largely confined to villa type development catering for professional and commercial families who, thanks to the railway, were able to reside in more congenial surroundings than the Manchester industrial conurbation could offer and commute to their offices and warehouses in the city. The pace of development quickened post 1920 and especially during the 1930s. The war years, 1939-45, temporarily halted the trend but development intensified and continued apace post 1950. Today, except for public leisure spaces and a few small market gardens,[48] the township lands are almost completely developed. This process will continue and it is justifiable to forecast that the few acres still undeveloped, if released by Trafford Council, will have been built on before the dawn of the twenty-first century. Already it is a thriving and heavily populated dormitory suburb whose working population consists largely of commuters. Prior to 1945 they commuted to the Manchester conurbation by rail. The post-war years have witnessed a trend towards industrial and commercial decentralisation, coupled with a revolution in communication and information technology, and a private car owning population. These factors will accelerate the rapid pace of change which the twentieth century has witnessed in the township. Following amalgamation with Altrincham in 1936, the hub of local government moved from the village centre to Altrincham. Less than forty years later, in 1974, it experienced another radical change when a regional local government re-organisation turned the borough of Altrincham into a unit of the newly created Metropolitan Borough of Trafford. This had the effect of once again moving the centre of gravity of Timperley's local government to Stretford and tended to reduce still further the village identity of the parish. One can only trust that, despite the pressures for change in society, Timperley's village heritage will continue to survive and flourish in the years to come.

Parliamentary Elections: Enfranchisement

Pre-1832 in rural townships like Timperley enfranchisement for Parliamentary suffrage was restricted to freeholders[49] possessed of land worth 40s a year or more. Such electors voted in Parliamentary elections to choose MPs to represent the county at Westminster.

During the period 1730-1830 it is probable that only twenty-five freeholders[50] in Timperley were so qualified. The Reform Act of 1832 extended the franchise to £20 copyholders; £10 long leaseholders and £50 short leaseholders, and increased the total national electorate by 50%. On the assumption that Timperley's qualified voters increased by the national average, the number of electors in the township would have increased to forty or forty-five[51] out of a total population of 752, of whom about 200 were adult males aged twenty-one plus. The 1867 Reform Act enfranchised all £12 householders for Parliamentary elections for county seats. The 1871 List of Timperley Electors contains 100 names. This figure included thirty-two qualified by virtue of ownership of property (i.e. as per the 1832 Act) and sixty-eight qualifying as £12 householders (i.e. as per the 1867 Act).[52]

The 1884 Reform Act introduced household suffrage in both county and town elections. Excluding town constituencies, the country was divided up into single member constituencies and henceforward Timperley electors voted to choose an MP for their local constituency. In 1884 there were about 600 adult males in the township but the precise number of householders would only be about 300 as enfranchisement was restricted to men over twenty-one years of age, excluding those employed in domestic service.

The extension of enfranchisement to women over thirty in 1918, women over twenty-one in 1928, also the great increase in the township's population during the decades post-1920 and the enfranchisement of citizens aged eighteen plus has vastly increased the electorate in the township. Today the village electorate numbers 18,672 out of a total population of 24,343 (1971 Population Census).

Notes

1. In 1832 there were only 5,000 J.P.s – patently an inadequate number to administer efficiently their many duties.

2. See Chapter 3.

3. Ibid.

4. 'Timperley Past and Present', Newton.

5. For example, tenants of the local squire, employers of pauper labour, etc.

6. Responsible for liquor licensing laws, recognisances, rates and drainage.

7. Extrapolating from Hearth Tax Returns 1673/4.

8. The Overseers' Accounts, the Constables Accounts and the Poor Rate Returns are all included in a manuscript book deposited at the C.C.R.O., reference PC52.

9. Answer to a questionnaire returned by Overseer of the Poor in Appendix 3c at the end of this chapter.

10. Overseers' of Poor List terminates in 1820.

11. See Constables' Accounts for year ending 1801, Appendix 3b at the end of this chapter.

12. List probably incomplete.

13. Suggests the highway rate was underspent in 1805.

14. See C.C.R.O. Archive list.

15. See Appendix 3 at the end of this chapter. The years ran from Easter to Easter.

16. Hoo Green is situated on the Warrington – Knutsford Road between Mere Corner and High Legh.

17. The term 'Gunpowder' probably denotes a particular type of tea.

18. Oak Farm (now demolished) occupied a site at the junction of Thorley and Wood Lanes. Farm labourers' cottages, still extant, stand on the south side of the junction.

19. Culcheth is situated in Lancashire, nine miles north-west of Timperley. The township did not use the Altrincham Workhouse, in Broadheath, which was built in 1756.

20. See transcript of the 1824 Return in Appendix 3c at the end of this chapter.

21. Lord Stamford's quarry was sited between Stockport Road and what is now Shaftesbury Avenue, immediately behind Marston's premises (now Hardy's) on Stockport Road. Newberry's quarry was to the south of it, close to Shaftesbury Avenue. W. Royle's land bordered the canal west of Timperley Station. (Reference: 1838 Tithe Map.)

22. Overseers of the Poor, Poor Rates Assessors, Constables, Surveyors of Highways, etc.

23. In 1865 Timperley asserted it was entitled to more than one representative.

24. It met in Altrincham.

25. Altrincham Poor Law Union Minutes 1844-48 (C.C.R.O.).

26. Timperley Select Vestry Minute Book (Altrincham Reference Library).

27. Assistant Overseer's Salary increased from £7 7s 0d p.a. in 1832 to £45 in 1867.

28. A facsimile of Timperley Select Vestry Return for 1835 is shown in Appendix 4.

29. Another example of the zeal with which the Select Vestry supervised the financial interests of the township.

30. J. Dobb resided at Delahays House in Green Lane and was a farmer.

31. Most probably the bridge over Timperley Brook in Deansgate Lane.

32. The bridge in Green Lane. Many generations of the Warburton family have farmed the surrounding lands. A Warburton still cultivates the land as a market garden (1988) and resides in the farmhouse.

33. Created in 1837.

34. Including 1875 Public Health Act.

35. Covers period 1860-61.

36. A formal complaint of an offence.

37. Parish Council Minutes, 1895 to 1936 and Parish Council Accounts, 1895 to 1910; declarations and acceptance of office by councillors (1899 to 1934); Parish Council Allotments – Cash Book, 1914 to 1936; and Parish Council Postage Book, 1926 to 1936 (Altrincham Reference Library). Altrincham Poor Law Union Minutes and Accounts 1844 to 1928; Local Government Board Assistance Committee Minutes 1904 to 1929; Altrincham and District Out Relief Order Books 1928 to 1934; and Records of Removals to Workhouse 1915 to 1929; Workhouse masters 1898 onwards; Records of Non Poor Law Duties, 1862 onwards; Bucklow Rural District Council Minutes, 1896 to 1915 (C.C.R.O.).

38. Held within seven days of 25th March annually, at Timperley Infant School on Stockport Road.

39. Francis T. Bell. He and subsequently his son filled the office from 1894 to 1936.

40. See list in *History of Altrincham and Bowdon* by Alfred Ingham.

41. See Account sheet for 1897 in Appendix 4 at the end of this chapter.

42. Parish Council Minute dated 8th March, 1894.

43. Parish Council Minute dated 19th April, 1895.

44. By Ministry Health Draft Order, Section 46, Local Government Act 1929.

45. Adjacent to the Pelican Hotel.

46. The duties of the Parish Council Clerk were performed by one family from the Parish Council's inception in 1894 to its dissolution in 1936. Francis Tait Bell (father of Frank Bell) served as Clerk from 1894 to 1910.

47. For example, Woodlands Park.

48. Mostly in the south-east corner of the township.

49. The 1838 Tithe Awards list about fifty freeholders. Not all of these would own land worth 40s plus.

50. The average population during the last half of the eighteenth century was about 500, which included about 175 adult males (Electoral Roll of October 1778).

51. In 1831 the township population was 752 and included about 200 adult males.

52. The 1871 Population Census shows a total population of 2,112 and included about 600 adult males.

CENTRAL GOVERNMENT RECORDS FOR THE MANOR OF TIMPERLEY IN THE FEUDAL PERIOD, 1100-1500

(A number, in manuscript, are extant and principally concerned with legal and financial affairs. A selection of them, with comments, are appended.)

Cheshire County Record Office

1294 – Grant

(Original inspected personally.)

'A Grant of Free Warren in all his demesne lands, providing the lands are not within the boundaries of the Royal Forest' by Edward I to Richard Mascy Kt. dated 4th December, 1294 '... No one to enter lands to hunt or take anything that belongs to them... without Richard Mascy's leave on pain of forfeiting £10.'

Witnesses

Anthony Beck, Bishop of Durham; William of Louth, Bishop of Ely; William of March, Bishop of Bath and Wells; William de Valery; Henry de Lacey, Earl of Lincoln; Reginald de Gray; Walter de Beauchamp (de Belle Campo); Richard of the Wood (de Bessa). *Under the Great Seal*, dated 4th December, in the twenty-second year of Edward I.

Comment

The lands described included Timperley. The original grant is in Cheshire County Record Office (Ref: DDX 464/Acc. 2364). It is in excellent condition. Richard Mascy resided at Tatton. He was Sheriff of Cheshire in the 1290s.

1295 – Plea Roll

'Margaret (wife of Sir Geoffrey Dutton, of Cheadle) sued Hamon de Dutton for Dower of a moiety of Timperley.'

Comment

Hamon, lord of Ashley, was the younger brother of Sir Geoffrey. On Geoffrey's demise, Geoffrey (son and heir) of Sir Geoffrey succeeded but predeceased his mother. Thus Hamon (uncle of Geoffrey) succeeded and obviously did not provide for Margaret (his sister-in-law). Hence her plea.

1300 – Plea Roll

'Roger de Dutton, of Cheadle, and Hamo de Dutton. A Fine of the Manor of Timperley in favour of Roger.'

Comment

When Geoffrey above died aged twenty-eight his younger brother, Roger, was the rightful heir. Thus Roger had to sue his uncle Hamon for his manor of Timperley and he was successful. Doubtless, Hamon was rather unpopular with Margaret and her family.

1336 – Plea Roll

'Richard de Honford and his wife Ellen, late wife of Hamon de Ashley, against Richard, son of Robert de Bulkeley (senior) and Agnes his wife, Dower of 200 Acres of Land, 50 of Wood and 160 Acres of Pasture in Timperley and Hale. Richard and Agnes vouch for the Warranty of Robert de Bulkeley...'

Comment

Agnes, daughter of Sir Roger de Dutton of Cheadle and wife of Richard de Bulkeley, brought the Timperley moiety to Richard on marriage. Ellen and her second husband continued to harass the Bulkeleys as her first husband had harassed Agnes' father. The result of the plea is not recorded but it seems certain that judgement would be in favour of Richard and Agnes.

1397 – Recognisance Roll

'Edward de Mascy of Timperley, John de Mascy (parson of Stockport), Sir Richard Mascy and Tomas [*sic*] de Mascy. Recognisance for £50 to the Earl of Chester.'

Comment

Henry Mascy (son and heir) of his father died aged ten and the manor was taken into the wardship of the Earl. Edward, the younger brother of Henry and his heir, eventually inherited. The recognisance was to ensure he was recompensed for all issues and profits received to the use of the Earl, of the lands which were inherited by Henry Mascy for the whole time it should be found that Edward had been of full age till the making of the above fine.

1397 – Recognisance Roll

'John de Timperlegh grantee of the Livery of the Crown (Sagittarius de Corona) with 6d per day for life.'

Comment

At least one Timperley bowman was a member of Richard II's company of archers.

1399-1413 – Dunham Massey Rental

(Reprinted in Ormerod, Vol.I, p.546)

'In the rentall of Dunham Massey: 3 Henry IV, Ranulphus Mainwaring tenet de uxoris suae medicatem villae de Timperley cum clausura in eadem vocato Chesnall, in soccagio: et reddit per annum termina Johannis Baptistae duodecem denarios Et de Stuth, alia dictum Sheriffe Tooth, 2d ob...'

Comment

In 1401 Randle Mainwaring held, by right of his wife, half of Timperley at a rent of twelve pennies per annum on the feast of John the Baptist or 24th June.

1402 – Recognisance Rolls

'Nicholas de Mascy of Timperley commissioned with others to arrest Robert del Fere for Arson and Ravishment.'

Comment

The criminal came from the township of Millington near Dunham Massey.

1413-1422

(Reprinted in *Cheshire Sheaf*, Vol.6, 1906)

'Names of Timperley archers recruited from the Bucklow Hundred during the reign of Henry V (1413 to 1422) viz.:

John'nes de Forest de Tymperley; Thomas Massey de Tymperleigh; Thomas Aleyn de Tymperley.

Comment

They probably served at Agincourt.

1475

(Information in Newton and Ormerod, Vol.II)

'In this year the three owners of the Timperley Lands viz: William Bulkeley (Northern Moiety); John Arderne (south-western half of Southern Moiety) and Sir William Booth (south-eastern half of Southern Moiety) agreed to enclose Timperley Moss and Common. A straight ditch was cut (over a quarter of a mile long) down the middle of the common, from east to west. William de Bulkeley took land to the north of the ditch and some of the moss land at the west end. John Arderne and Sir William Booth divided the southern half between them. At that time no roads existed in the central area of the township, only tracks across the common which later developed into the first roads, or lanes in the township.'

Comment

Newton opines that the line of the ditch could still be seen in 1936. He suggests that the moss and common, at that time, consisted of land between the present village centre and what is now Broadheath.

Notes

Plea Rolls

Date from 1194 and are the first legal documents written by clerks recording the cases pleaded in the king's courts.

Recognisance Rolls

These are records of bonds entered into by which a person engages before a court, or magistrate, to observe some condition. If broken it incurred a fine of the amount stated.

EARLY MODERN RECORDS OF THE MANOR OF TIMPERLEY FROM 1495 ONWARDS

(As for the pre-1500 period, a number are extant in manuscript and, similarly, are principally concerned with legal and financial affairs. A selection is appended with comments.)

1495 – Plea Rolls

'Robert Vawdrey exempted from Jury Service.'

1502 – Plea Rolls

'John Arderne of Timperley grants to Elizabeth Barlowe (widow) all his lands in Timperley in tenure of Laurence Hunt and Edward Legh. Also to William Tatton, Robert Tatton (rector of Warton) and James Barlowe, for life of Elizabeth who was the wife of Henry Barlowe, the fields called Wheatfield, Kedelwood Field and other lands and the Milnefield, Marled Croft, Kylnefield and Alton Field all in Tymperlegh.'

Comment

The Arderne family owned the Riddings estate in the Northern Moiety from c.1445 until at least 1498.

1504 – Plea Rolls

'John Arderne of Timperley exempted from Jury Service.'

1510 – Plea Rolls

'Thomas Vawdrey v. John Arderne of Tymperleigh and Hamo Ardern his son and heir. Recovery of 2 Messuages, 52 Acres of Land, 10 Acres of Turf and 20 acres of Pasture in Tymperlegh.'

Comment

'Recovery' is a legal process for gaining possession of some property by the verdict or judgement of the court. Often it concerned disputes about entailed properties.

1511 – Plea Rolls

'Geoffrey Barlow v. John Arderne of Tymperlegh. Recovery of one Messuage, One Cottage, 17 acres of Land, one of mead, five of pasture, eight of heath and four of turf in Tymperleigh.'

Comment

It would seem the two families had to resort to the courts frequently to resolve their differences re lands in Timperley.

1531 – Plea Rolls

'Hamnett Ardern of Timperley. Deed leading the uses of a recovery suffered by the said Hamnett to John Legh of Baguley, James Massey of Sale, John, son of William Brereton Kt., and Richard Legh of Stockport, of the manor of Timperley, 10 Messuages, 80 acres of land, 20 of meadow, 50 of pasture, 4 of Wood and a 100 of turf therein. Habend. to use of Hamnett for life. remainder as to one third to Margery, his wife, for life; a messuage to use of Robert, his second son, for life remainder as to all the premises and reversions to use of William, son and heir of Hamnett in tail. remainder to Robert in tail, remainder to Hamnett's heirs.'

1535 Plea Rolls

'Roland Bulkeley and Hamo Arden of Timperley and Margery ux. dj. Fine of a Messuage, 12 Acres of Land, 2 of mead[ow] 6 of Pasture and 25 of Moss and Turf in Timperley.'

Comment

Ux. = *uxoris* - wife;   dj. = *de jure* - by right of.

c.1537 – Plea Rolls

William Arderne (son of Hamon and grandson of John) was involved in a dispute over ownership. He claimed that his father's estate in the manor of Timperley consisted of ten messuages, 80 acres of land, 20 acres of meadow, 50 acres of pasture, four acres of woods and 100 acres of turbary and that his father Hamon had given him (the supplicant) this estate on 8th February, 1535/7. Anne Arderne (an infant niece of William's and daughter of his deceased brother John) claimed it (or part of it) through her guardian Elizabeth Booth (of Dunham) described as 'aged 60 or more' and Richard Legh of Baguley described as 'Siclye and aged' who, with their servants and others, took possession of certain premises, consisting of three messuages and one close called 'New Field parcel' with swords, bucklers and daggers, staves and other weapons' and took the rents but refused to produce their evidence of ownership which, it was suggested, were in a locked bag. They denied that they carried anything but 'such weapons' as they daily used.

Comment
The result of the action is not recorded.

c.1538 – Plea Rolls

William Arderne was concerned in another lawsuit. He accused ten people, who, by order of George Booth and Elizabeth Booth (widow), had taken William's turves and frightened William's servants away. He blamed George Booth and said his father, Hamon Arderne, had been forced to flee to London.

Comment
William seems to have had a propensity for creating problems with his neighbours. Seems to make highly coloured complaints and they do not ring true. The result of the lawsuit is not recorded.

1541 Plea Rolls

'George Booth, William Allen, George Booth, William Booth and Margaret his wife. Two Recoveries and a fine of a Messuage, 20 acres of land, 6 of mead[ow], 40 of Pasture and ten of Heath in Timperley.'

1544 Plea Rolls

'Thomas Vawdrey and another v. Robert Vawdrey. Recovery of Messuage and Lands.'

1567

(See also transcript of will in Newton – copy in Altrincham Library.)
The Vawdrey family purchased the Riddings Hall estate (1498) and held it until 1637 when it was sold to Thomas Gerard. Robert Vawdrey, the second of the Vawdreys to own the estate, lived almost eighty years at Riddings Hall during five reigns of Tudor monarchs. His will (dated 1567) has been reprinted in *Wills and Inventories*, Chetham Society, Part II, Vol.51. It is a long and most interesting document and well worth reading.

1631 Newton

Robert Vawdrey, the fourth Vawdrey to own the estate (b.1595 – d.1662), married Margaret, a daughter of Oswald Mosley, and left Riddings to live in Ancoats Hall, Manchester. He, along with his cousin, refused a knighthood in 1631 which would have cost him £60 or £70 and a journey to London. Those who declined were fined £10.

Comment
He was obviously a person who thought things through before committing himself to expenditure.

1666 Leycester 'Cheshire Antiquities'

(See also Pedigree of Vawdrey of Riddings and Bank – Ormerod, Vol.II.)

Charterers now in Timperley

'Thomas Gerard of Riddings in Timperley (gent.). These Freehold lands belonged to Vawdrey of Riddings and were not long since purchased by said Thomas Gerard. These lands were originally granted away by John Arderne of Timperley and Thomas, his son and heir, unto Thomas Vawdrey and his heirs rendering yearly £1 13s 4d. Dated 10 August, 13 Henry VII – 1498. Original in possession of Thomas Gerard aforesaid.'

'William Steele, of Nether Knutsford, hath three cottages in Timperley. These formerly belonged to the Riddings.'

'George Ward of London[1] one cottage formerly belonging to Riddings.'

'Robert Hield, of Etchells,[2] one cottage in Timperley.'

'Peter Parker, of Altrincham,[3] hath about an acre in Timperley formerly belonging to the Riddings.'

Comment

The Gerards of Timperley stemmed from the Gerard family of Harrow, Middlesex. They were related by marriage to the Arderne family. The second son, Richard Gerard, of the Harrow family, was Rector of Stockport (d.1614) and he married Ursula (daughter of Ralph Ardern of Harden) a member of the Arderne family which previously owned Riddings. The rector's son Thomas purchased Riddings in 1637. He was brother-in-law to Edward Vawdrey (son of Robert above).

Notes

1. The Wards were a Timperley family. An eighteenth century descendant of George Ward, Benjamin Ward, was one of the wealthiest men in Timperley.
2. Robert Hield or Heald had about 60 acres in Etchells, so he probably leased this cottage and land in Timperley.
3. Peter Parker died in 1664 (will and inventory in CCRO). According to the 1667 Subsidy Roll, his widow Mary succeeded him.

APPENDIX 3
TRANSCRIPTION OF
POOR RATE RETURN
FOR THE TOWNSHIP OF
TIMPERLEY,
1800 TO 1817

(Note: Accounting year runs from 1st April to 31st March.)

For what year to Easther [sic]	Poor Rates	Law expences	County Goals & Bridges	Militia	Church & Con'bles rates	Salaries	Other expences	Neat [Net] amount p.[d] to y[e] poor
1801	£102.0.0					£1.10.6	£0.12.0	£99.17.6
1802	£126.19.0	£1.2.0					£2.8.0	£123.9.0
1803	£160.2.5				£4.6.6		£2.10.6	£155.5.5
1804[1]	£160.2.5				£5.0.6	£0.12.0	£2.10.0	£155.19.11
1805	£209.4.0		£18.9.7	£38.9.3	£3.0.0		£3.2.0	£146.3.2
1806	£174.7.6		£2.10.4	£24.6.6	£4.6.2			£143.4.6
1807	£209.5.3	£5.1.8		£15.16.4	£19.4.0		£0.14.2	£168.9.1
1808	£209.0.0				£10.7.10		£3.3.0	£185.9.2.
1809	£246.10.10			£40.0.0	£7.16.10		£2.2.0	£196.12.0
1810	£280.8.0½		£18.8.0		£6.7.6			£255.11.6
1811	£244.18.3		£17.8.3		£7.0.0		£7.2.0	£213.8.0
1812	£353.9.0½		£38.5.0		£4.18.0		£2.2.0	£308.4.0½
1813	£419.0.8	£15.0.0	£36.0.8		£9.0.0		£8.4.0	£350.15.0
1814	£419.0.8	£2.0.0	£49.0.2		£6.7.0	£10.0.0	£1.12.7	£350.11.0
1815	£353.9.0½		£36.15.0	£3.10.0.	£8.9.1	£10.0.0	£4.6.6	£293.18.5½
1816	£353.9.0½		£14.10.1.	£2.17.6.	£5.9.2	£12.10.0	£8.0.1	£310.2.2½
1817	£353.9.0½		£13.7.4		£7.0.0	£12.10.0	£7.10.0	£314.1.6½

Note

1. Some of the totals may be incorrect, with possible errors in the totalling of items of expenditure in the years 1803, 1804, 1809, 1813, 1814 and 1815. For example, for 1804 the total should be £164 2s 5d.

APPENDIX 3B

TRANSCRIPT

OF

CONSTABLES' ACCOUNTS

(In facsimile form)

The Accounts of Richard Savage Constable of Timperley from Oct. 29 1799 to Nov. 3rd 1801

	£	s	d
Paid when sworn in 1/2^d & for a Lead of Coal 1s 0d & for 1^{lb} of Gunpowder 2/8^d	0	4	10
Paid for Liquor at the Fire	0	5	0
Paid the 1st Quarterley pay £1-18-4 & his Journey at the same time 1/6	1	19	10
To taking an acct. of men for Militia 1/6, & his Journey to Knutsford with their Names 1/6	0	3	0
Paid the Expences of Warrant for Jno Brundret 7/6^d & at the Returning of Overseers of the Poor 2/-	0	9	6
His Journey with the return of Overseers of the poor 1/6^d. Paid at the return of assess 2/6 and his Journey at the same time 1/6	0	5	6
Paid a Quarterley pay £1 13^s 11^d and his Journey with the same 1/6	1	15	5
Paid for 12 score sparrow-heads at ½^d p[er] Head and 6 score at ¼^d p[er] Head	0	12	6
Paid to sundry Passengers	0	5	0
Paid at returning Jurors 6^d and his Journey with the return of the same 1/6^d	0	2	0
His Journey returning Inn-holders	0	1	6
Paid a Quarterley Pay £1 13^s 11^d & his Journey with the same 1/6^d	1	15	5
Paid at the return of Overseers of the Highways 7/6 & his Journey with ye same 1/6	0	9	0
Searching for Vagrants	0	1	6
Paid to Jno Renshaw for making 2 schedules in order to number the people	0	3	0

The Accts. of Josiah Faulkner Constable of Timperley from Oct. 29th 1799 to Nov. 3rd 1801

	£	s	d
Paid when swore in	0	1	2
Paid to Sundry passengers	0	1	0
Paid for sparrows' Heads	0	1	4
Paid a Quarterley pay £1 13^s 11^d & his Journey with the same 1/6	1	15	5
Paid to Sundry Passengers	0	1	4
Paid on Acct. of the Coroner's Inquest on a man – kill'd at Altrincham warehouse	0	5	0
Paid the Towns writer, as agreed by a Meeting held for the Purpose, 3 Quarterley pays at 20^s p[er] Quarter	3	0	0
Josiah Faulkner's total D[isbursement]	5	5	3
Richd Savage's D[isbursement]	9	1	6
Total of both	£14	6	9
rec.^{d} of their antecedents	0	2	3
Do. by Levey	14	6	4½
Total rec.^{d}	14	8	7¼
Ballance in Hand	£0	1	10¼

TRANSCRIPT OF THE ACCOUNTS OF WILLIAM RENSHAW, OVERSEER OF THE POOR OF THE TOWNSHIP OF TIMPERLEY FOR THE YEAR ENDING 31ST MARCH, 1817

	£	s	d
Paid Ann Adshead	7	2	0
To Thomas Ackerley	0	6	0
To Martha Aldcroft	6	10	0
To Eliz[a]b[e]th Ackerley	6	10	0
To Mary Aldcroft	2	15	0
To John Ackerley	8	15	6
To Samuel Ackerley	0	5	0
To Hannah Bailey	2	12	0
To Eliz[abe]th Bailey	1	5	0
To Jane Billinge	3	5	0
To Peter Bate	2	9	0
To John Brooks	0	5	0
To Alice Brundrett	6	10	0
To ? Banks	5	19	0
To Mary Brundrett	5	4	0
To Jane Bailey	2	17	6
To George Broom	9	2	0
To Mary Derbyshire	5	4	0
To John Dunster	2	11	2
To Ann Davenport	5	4	0
To George Cotterhill [Cotterill?]	2	17	0
To John Compton's Bill	4	7	6
To Will[ia]m Dickinson	4	11	0
To Thomas Epplestone	0	2	0
To Ann Epplestone	3	8	7
To Mary Dunster	18	12	4
To Alice Garner	4	8	0
To Henry Gibson	1	6	0
To Sarah Goodier	5	9	6
To Alice Garner's [?]	3	5	0
Carried over	131	7	7

Brought Over	£	s	d
	131	7	7
To John Garner	18	14	?
To Gropnall at sundry times	15	15	?
To Sarah Hankinson	5	4	?
To Eliz[abeth] Greenhalgh	4	1	?
To Martha Hankinson	0	10	?
To Mary Greenwood	5	4	?
To Mary Goodwin	0	6	11
To Timothy Harrop	0	15	?
To Thomas Hewitt	0	10	?
To Mary Hulme	5	4	?
To James Hulme	0	9	?
To Maria Harrop	3	0	?
To Richard Holt	4	18	?
To Eliz[abeth] Holt's Rent	5	0	?

	£	s	d
To Thomas Harrop	6	1	6
To John Hankinson	0	18	?
To James Hankinson	4	17	6
To Theophilus Hewitt	21	2	?
To Will[ia]m Holt	0	17	?
To Eliz[a]b[e]th Hewitt	7	15	?
To Robert Artless	0	10	?
To Eliz[a]b[e]th Holt	5	4	?
To Lounds Hannah	5	11	9
To Do	1	5	?
To Mary Moss	5	4	?
To George Massey	0	9	?
To Thomas Pine	0	5	?
To John Mollett	0	2	?
To Tho[ma]s Pearson's Rent	5	0	?
To Will[ia]m Renshaw	11	5	?
To Eliz[a]b[e]th Ridgeway	5	15	?
To Anne Royle	2	15	?
	291	9	3½

	£	s	d
Brought up	291	9	3½
To Joseph Smyth	9	0	0
To Joseph Smyth	6	16	10
To Archer Smyth	0	8	6
To British Smyth	1	12	6
To Charles Smyth	10	14	11½
To Martha Sarndell 52 Weeks @2/-	5	4	0
To Eliz[a]b[e]th Smyth	2	18	0
To Thomas Torkington	9	13	1
To Richard Warrington	5	8	5
To Ellen Warburton	7	16	0
To Mary Ward	3	7	6
To Isaac Worthington	0	2	10
To One Warrant for Andrew Sympock	0	3	0
To Charles Smyth @	0	3	0
To Tho[ma]s Greenhalgh @	0	3	0
To A Journey with @	0	3	0
To Signing and publishing of a Book[1]	0	3	0
To a Warrant for Ja[me]s Garner	0	3	0
To summonses	0	2	0
To expenses of Geo[rge] Garner	0	3	6
To papers for Assess[in]g	0	5	0
To 4 Quarterly Paym[e]nts County Rates	13	7	4
To John Hulme Const[a]ble	5	17	3
To Geo[rge] Davenport @	1	4	6

	£	s	d
To taking John Garner and Ja[me]s Greenhalgh	1	6	6
To Sundry Expenses Hannah Lounds	4	4	6½
To Expenses of Town's Meeting	0	5	6
To Collecting	2	10	0
To Journey to Hoo Green	0	3	0
To 4 Summonses and 3 W[a]rr[an]ts	0	19	0
To j[ou]rn[e]y to Newton L[a]ne	0	3	0
To George Stelfox	1	17	6
To Salary for serving as Overseer	12	10	0
To 9 J[ou]rn[e]ys to s[u]ndry places	1	10	0
To Warr[an]t for J[oh]n Bailey	0	3	0
	403	1	9
Brought over	403	1	9
To J[ou]rn[e]y to Cheadle	0	3	0
To S[i]gn[in]g and Pub[lishing] a Book	0	3	0
To J[ou]rn[e]y to Newton Lane	0	3	0
To a Journey to Distley Rink	0	3	0
To a Journey to Moberley	0	3	0
To a Journey to Hoo Green	0	3	0
To a Journey to The New Bailey	0	3	0

	£	s	d
To W[a]rr[a]nt for W[illia]m Redford	0	4	0
To a Journey to Manchester	0	3	0
To a Journey to Cheadle	0	3	0
To a Journey to Hoo Green	0	3	0
To a Journey to Withinshaw [sic]	0	3	0
To a Journey to Stockport	0	3	0
To a Journey to Manchester	0	3	0
To a Journey to Knutsford	0	3	0
To 15 Journeys to sundry Places			
To 7 Ditto	1	1	?
To a Macclesfield 'Note' [sic]			
To the Post, For 4 Letters	0	2	?
To Paper and Books	0	2	?
To John Dunster	0	4	?
To Dr Pearson's Bill to R. Warrington	0	5	?
To Will[ia]m Worthington for making 3 suits of Clooths	0	15	?
To the Schoolmaster for Writing	1	11	?
To Repairing the School	2	0	?
	414	16	?[2]

Notes

1. This was the signing and publishing of accounts before a meeting or before a magistrate.

Sums disbursed in official expenses amounted to about £77. Deducting this sum from the total leaves a sum of £337. Deduct balance of £23 carried over to 1818 leaves £314 spent wholly on Poor Relief to successful applicants. Thus almost 76% disbursed in relief.

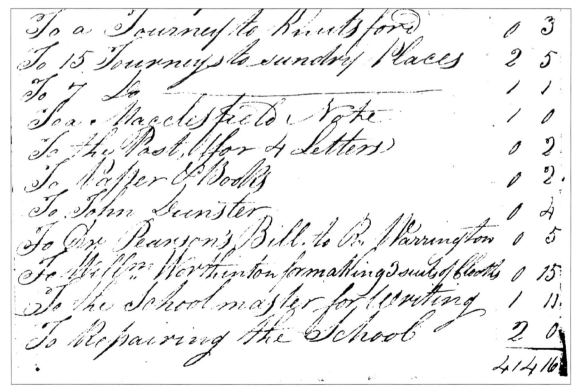

Extract from William Renshawe's Overseers Accounts for 1817. Note: the pence column in this part of the Accounts is unreadable. (Records in Cheshire Record Office are reproduced here by permission of Cheshire County Council and the owner/depositor to whom copyright is reserved.)

QUESTIONNAIRE FROM POOR LAW COMMISSIONERS, 1824

Responding to the poor Law Commissioners' circularised twelve point Questionnaire requesting details of Poor Law Relief, granted during the year of 1824 to 'Lady Day'.[1] The Overseer of the Poor in Timperley township returned the following answers to the questions posed.[2]

	Question	**Answer**
1.	Have you any local Act for Management of Poor?	No
2.	Is Parish united with Others for Management of Poor?	No
3.	Has it a Board of Guardians or Elected Vestry?	No
4.	Has it a Workhouse? (We use the workhouse at Culcheth)	No
5.	How many persons will the Workhouse accommodate? at present time – Including 2 Timperley Persons.	50
6.	Have you any rules for management of Workhouse?	Yes
7.	State if Indoor farmed by contract (or how otherwise supplied)?	Yes
8.	State weekly cost per head per head of Paupers in Workhouse for year of 1824?	2s 1d
9.	Do you pay Able Bodied Poor in Money without employment? (Nb. Occasionally if ordered by Magistrate or if they have been in work.)	Yes
10.	Have you any paid Officers employed in management of Poor? (i.e. Vestry Clerk, Assessment Officer and Overseer of Poor)	Yes
11.	State number of persons relieved during year of 1824 to Lady Day.	

Males

Able-bodied	–	4
Totally Disabled	–	5
Partially Disabled	–	4

Females

Able-bodied	–	13
Totally Disabled	–	9
Partially Disabled	–	2

Children under 9

Total	–	34
Able to Work	–	1
Unable to Work	–	1

1. 25th March
2. Copy of their Return to the Poor Law Commissioners contained in the book of Accounts covering period 1798 to 1847 (C.C.R.O., Ref. PC52).

Altrincham Poor Law Union

Quarterly calls for Poor Relief monies levied on the township of Timperley by
the Board of Guardians

Year: 1844 Assessed Value: (each quarter) £2 0s 2d											
Call %	13th May 30%				19th August 35%				11th November 40%		
	£	s	d		£	s	d		£	s	d
	60	12	0		70	14	0		80	16	0
	12	14	11		11	17	5		12	16	10
Add/Deduct Bal. Last quarter	73	6	11		82	11	5		57	19	2
Call paid (to nearest £)	73	0	0		83	0	0		58	0	0

Year: 1848 Assessed Value: (each quarter) £2 1s 8d			
Call %	3rd February 40%		
	£	s	d
	76	6	0
	13	14	7
Deduct Bal. last quarter	62	11	5
Call paid (to nearest £)	63	0	0

Bucklow Union

General Ledgers: extract showing Timperley township entry for year ending Lady Day 1897

* At passing of Union Assessment Act
+ Assessment Value under Agricultural Rate Act

Note
Ledgers are at C.C.R.O., ref. LRB 38/2.

According to Valuation Lists of Union Assessment Committee						
Area	Population	Population	Rateable Value	Rateable Value	Rateable Value	Rateable Value
1628 acres	2241 (1881)	2441 (1891)	£8926 (1862)*	£19399 (1896) September	£19286 (1897) March	£17622 (1897)+

Diagram of Poor Law Organisation in the Nineteenth Century After the Poor Law Amendment Act 1834

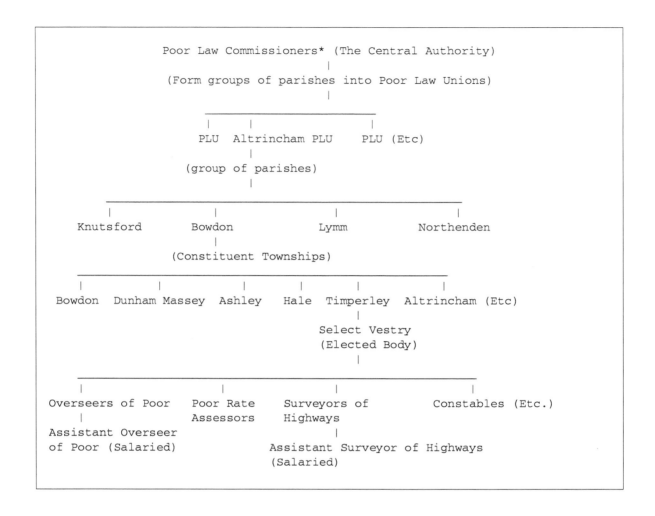

Note

In 1847 the Poor Law Commissioners' powers were transferred to the new Poor Law Board with a Minister (President of the Poor Law Board) responsible for its actions to Parliament.

In 1871 the Poor Law Board was amalgamated with the Public Health Board and was designated the Local Government Board and the Poor Law Union became the Rural Sanitary Area with the Board of Guardians becoming the Rural Sanitary Authority. As well as Poor Relief, the Board of Guardians now had responsibility for public health in the area.

In 1894 the Local Government Act established Rural District Councils which inherited the power, duties and liabilities of the Rural Sanitary Authority and also the powers of any highway authority in the area. The Altrincham Poor Law Union was now renamed as Bucklow Rural District Council. The 1894 Act also established parish councils and Timperley became at this time designated a parish council, being a rural parish. It elected Rural District Councillors to represent it on the Rural District Council and such representatives also represented the parish on the Board of Guardians.

TIMPERLEY SELECT VESTRY MINUTES, 1835 TO 1894
Selected Extracts

1835

5th October

'Ordered Richard Warrington be received into workhouse at Culcheth: Overseer to provide him with suitable clothing.'

'Ordered application of J. Wyatt's wife for allowance for Surgeons charges for attending husband... to be left in Overseer's hands till next meeting.'

November

'Application of Agar Gardner on behalf of Maria Goulden, who had fractured leg, for increase of weekly pay. Ordered that Overseers ascertain if she be recovered and allow her a further sum of 1s 6d per week until next meeting.'

1836

4th January

'Application of Sarah Walker to be allowed sum of £1 5s 0d towards sister's funeral expenses. Order Application dismissed.'

March

'Ordered Overseer allow Mary Jones of Chester, whose husband has left her, the weekly sum of 1s 6d.'

4th April

'On application of John Garner for relief of work ordered Surveyor be requested to find him employment, when requisite, for roads until next meeting.'

2nd May

'On application of Nancy Aldcroft, whose husband was killed last week, ordered Overseer to allow her 3s 0d per week for next month.'

June

'Ordered payment to Nancy Aldcroft be advanced to 3s 6d per week for next month.'

The collection of 'Bastard Money' (*sic*) due caused difficulties for Overseers. Payment arrears frequently occurred, causing a drain on Poor Rate as the minutes below reveal.

1835

4th January

'Upon application of J. Wyatt for payment of arrears of 'Bastardy Money' due to his daughter, Jane, from Noel Gatley. Ordered that Overseers refrain from paying any further sum until same collected from father.'

1836

4th January

'Ordered that Overseer make best arrangements he can with Noel Massey and Sam Boardman for Bastardy Money due to Township.'

Rating Matters

1842

3rd November

'Services of J. Bradford (Petty Constable) dispensed with as unnecessary as Ratepayers had nominated 6 Constables to officiate...'

1844

'J. Aimson's [village wheelwright] Bill challenged. Had been paid £10 on account and balance refused until Ratepayers satisfied with correctness of Bill.'

1849

26th April

'*Moved*: Summonses be issued to Hoo Green for parties owing rates unless they pay before next meeting.'

1851

7th August

'List of uncollected rates from 11 Ratepayers with reasons for default recorded viz:

'Five had run away – one Hannah Warburton to America.'

'Two had died and two houses empty for six months.'

'Railway Rates reduced at a meeting on 16th Jan resulting in a loss of £4 15s 0d on original Assessment'

'*Total Uncollected*: £8 15s 0½d'

Miscellaneous

1855

27th August

'Mr Dearden stated Demand made on him for £1 19s 11d by Mr Greenwood (Bailiff) under Court Baron of Dunham Massey alleged to be amercement [fine] upon Surveyor which had not been paid. Neither he nor his colleagues had rec[eive]d notice of "Officeing" day.'

'*Moved*: Dearden and two other members to wait on Mr F. Smith and Mr. Heron to confer... re liability of inhabitants to repair road in question and Surveyors be empowered to take legal advice if necessary in opposing notice of such amercement from Court Baron of Dunham Massey.'

1860

2nd April

'*Proposed:* Rate of Payment for Team Work be 6s 0d for one Horse and cart; 9s 0d for 2 horses, man and cart. as far as possible, work to be by Contract. All Bills... to be submitted weekly to Surveyors.'

1861

24th January

'*Meeting:* To Consider... making a Sewer down Wash Lane to Canal Bridge.'

1863

5th January

'*Proposed and Carried*: Deptn. wait on owners of Property in Wash Lane and other parts of Township for Support and Subscription towards making sewer along Back Lane... and lost fall brought up from junction with Mr Skelton's land and sewers enlarged... negotiations to be at once entered into with Railway Company for larger culvert under line and same to be properly constructed.

Moved and Carried: Surveyors requested to repave, repair and reinstate as well as possible... that is cartway and footpath from Four Lane Ends to Railway Station.

25th January

'*Moved:* Surveyors attention called to Back Lane, Wood Lane and Deansgate Lane as waywardens... threatened by J. Platt[*] that if not reported within fourteen days he will bring magistrates over roads.

Moved: Waywarden required to get competent man (from Timperley if possible) who can keep accounts and time on road. (Carried)

[*] Platt was a farmer who lived at 'The Grove' a house in Back (now Grove) Lane.

The Select Minute book for period 1868-1894 merely records the Vestry's Annual Meeting in March. The bulk of the business they transacted consisted of the appointment of the parish officers for the forthcoming year. The reports and accounts of the parish officers are not contained in it. Only rarely did they need to hold a Special Meeting.

1868
16th March
The average attendance at most of their meetings was less than twenty.
Committee appointed for obtaining all necessary information re working of the Local Government Act and to call a General Public Meeting of Inhabitants of Township.
'*Moved*: Tho[ma]s Holt be excused paym[en]t of 10s 9d owing for Poor Rate unpaid by him. *Carried*.'
1870
2nd June
'For purpose of considering property of governing Trustees of Samuel Brook permission to open Township sewer in Wash Lane near Four Lane Ends, for purpose of widening and deepening same. Meeting adjourned to 7 June.

7th June
'Permission granted subject to Select Vestry having power over said drain.'

1872
February
'To consider propricty of repair of road by canal side – Deansgate Lane to Station.'
'*Moved*: Committee appointed to ascertain to whom road belongs.'
'*Moved*: Heyes Lane as far as J. Whitelegg's be repaired by Township and resolution be sent to Highways Board requesting they do repair.'

21st March
'*Proposed*: 7s per day be given for man, horse and cart working on Timperley roads and that hours be from 7am – 12am and 2pm to 6 pm each day.'

1874
19th February
'*Purpose*: Appointing Parochial Sanitary Committee – Plans and Statements relative to drainage of Timperley laid before meeting.'

1875
No Date
'Moved: Salary of Assistant Overseer fixed at £75 p.a.' – (carried)

1876
26th March
'Committee appointed to consult with J. Platt, Waywarden re construction of new bridge near to Kemps.'[1]
'*Proposed:* Highway Board be requested compel Property Owners on each side of Heyes Lane to repair said lane with a view to putting on Townships Books.'

1877
16th March
'Proposed: Guardians be requested oppose... introduction of Union Fever Receiving House in Township and if legally necessary to establish local receiving house for infectious complaints; that Guardians be urged to procure site for same at a distance from the High Road and all Dwelling Houses.'

1879
17th March
'Proposed: J. Cookson Assistant Overseer be paid additional remainder of £15 p.a. for additional duties re preparing Accounts of Sanitary Rate for Special Drainage purposes – paid half yearly out of said rate. *Approved*.
'*Resolved*: All roads in Townships be taken on books of Highways Board for purpose of repairing them – especially Heyes Lane and Road from Deansgate Lane to Station.' – (Carried)

1880

22nd March

'To decide Remuneration of Salaried Officers for keeping Sanitary Rate Accounts for year ending 25 March 1880 and future years. *Resolved*: £15 p.a. for Current and Future years.'

1882

'*Resolved:* Waywarden to instruct owner of Manor Farm to restore old footpath to Public use which had been ploughed up by Tenant, J.C. Rogerson – in case of non compliance question be taken before Highways Board for them to deal with.'

'*Resolved*: That Meeting having heard that recommendation made by Ministry of Health to erect Hospital for Infectious Diseases in Township protests most strongly against such a step – copy of protest sent to Sanitary Authority.'

1885

5th March

'To consider proportionate basis for County Rates as submitted to Overseers by a Committee appointed for that purpose.'

'*Resolved:* Meeting strongly objects to sum of £20379 as basis upon which to charge County Rates against this Township because s[ai]d sum already reduced by appeals before Assessment Committee also objets to being charged on £1836 a sum in dispute with Cheshire Lines Committee and which they are now appealing against in a London court because should the Railway Assessment be reduced by that sum we should be paying County Rates on nearly £2000 more than our actual Rateable Value.'

16th August

'*Resolved:* Assistant Overseer's Salary made up to £100 p.a. in consideration of his executing Overseer duties and making out and collecting Special Rates of Township.'

28th September

'Clerk to the Sanitary Authority recommends calling of meeting of Ratepayers to discuss propriety of Sewering Moss and Wood Lanes. Estimate of cost submitted.

Resolved: Question of sewering be NOT entertained. (*Carried* unanimously.)

1890

17th July

'A number of candidates proposed for post of Assistant Overseer. Poll Held. 24th July, 1890. Mr Bell elected.'

'*Moved:* Salary of Assistant Overseer be £100 p.a. as before' Mr Brown moved amendment that Salary be £80 p.a. Amendment lost. (Original motion carried.)

This occasioned the nomination of a number of candidates and a Poll became necessary.

1892

24th March

'Meeting accepted Resignation of Assistant Overseer followed by discussion of amount to be paid to Assistant Overseer. General feeling was an increase was necessary because of extra work load due to erection of new property.'

1894

12th April

'Special Meeting re Circular Letter from Cheshire County Council as to whether Township be Divided into Wards. Following discussion general feeling against as it was likely to cause unnecessary trouble and expense of electing Councillors.

Resolved: Township should not be divided into Wards but remain entire Township.

14th November

'Resolved: Representative Committee to be appointed to select 13 suitable candidates representing various interest in Township to report to adjourned meeting on 28th November, 1894. [Final entry in Minute Book].'

Note

1. Kemps was in Wellfield Lane, so the 'new' bridge was over the Timperley Brook where it crosses the said lane.

APPENDIX 4B

TIMPERLEY SELECT VESTRY

A Transcript of the Return of the Nett Annual Value of Property in the Township upon which the Poor Rate was calculated.

(The levy in 1835 was 1s 4d in the pound)

A Return made for the purpose of equalizing County Rates, May 4, 1835

1	2	3	4	5
The total amount of the full and fair Annual value of such of the several Estates and Property in this Township as consists of the following Particulars viz	The full and fair annual productive value of such Property as is rated without regard to the amount in the rate	The full annual amount of such Property as is rated as per last Rate allowed and published	The full and fair annual productive value of such Property as is not rated	The total fair and just annual value being equal to the sum of columns 1 and 3
1. Lands Farm Buildings and Tithes	£2782 0s 3d	£2090 19s 10½d		£2782 0s 3d
2. Dwelling houses Buildings without Lands; Factories; Mills; Print and Bleach Works	£382 6s 1d	£268 12s 0d		£352 6s 1d
3. Railroads; Canals; Navigations; River; Market and other Tolls and Dues; Ferries; Waterworks; Gas Works; Collieries; Quarries; Brickworks and other rateable property	£272 11s 6¾d	£204 8s 8d		£272 11s 6¾d
Total	£3406 17s 10¾d	£2561 0s 6½d		£3406 17s 10¾d

State when was the Valuation made upon which the present year's rate is laid?   Ans: in 1831 since which period any requisite alterations have been made

APPENDIX 5

EXTRACTS OF PARISH COUNCIL MINUTES RELATING TO FOOTPATHS AND FOOTPATH BRIDGES

1895

4th October

'Letter read from Sale Urban District Council re dangerous condition of plank bridge over Baguley Brook and requesting co-operation in providing new planks and a handrail'. Committee appointed to deal with same.

1897

5th March

'Letter from Baguley Parish Council re new plank bridge and handrail over Fairywell Brook.' *Resolved*: Baguley to do work Timperley pay half cost.

1899

22nd September

'*Proposed*: Path behind Lyme Grove be recindered.' *Carried*. 'Clerk instructed to have swing gates and railings repaired on path leading from Lyme Grove to Wash Lane.'

1901

22nd March

'Attention drawn to untidy state of hedges along footpath behind cottages in Deansgate Lane.' 'Clerk instructed to write to property owners adjoining path requiring them to have hedges trimmed.'

1903

27th March

'Condition of paths in parish discussed. Committee appointed to inspect and report back.'

17th April

'Report on paths considered.' *Resolved*: 'Fifty tons of cinders be obtained from G. Bonson of Ashton-on-Mersey at 3s 3d per ton delivered to canal side: same to be put on paths where necessary.'

15th May

'Letter from T.A. Fitton re path adjoining his property, in West Timperley: his attention having been drawn to alleged encroachment. As his reply considered unsatisfactory resolved Bucklow Rural District Council be requested to take steps to remove same.'

3rd July

'Path encroachment West Timperley: Clerk instructed to write to Bucklow Rural District Council requesting what steps taken by them.'

1905

24th March

'Attention drawn to unsatisfactory state of plank bridge over ditch on path leading through Riddings Hall Farm from Heyes Lane to Canal side.'
Resolved: 'Two sound sleepers to be obtained and fixed there; considered this would meet the case.'

8th December

'Attention drawn to unsatisfactory state of plank bridge over Timperley Brook on path from Wood Lane to Hale Moss.'
Resolved: 'Approach Hale Urban District Council to see if they would bear half cost of plank bridge with handrail.'

1906

February

'Letter from Hale Urban District Council [about bridge mentioned above]
Resolved: 'Parish Council agrees to pay half cost (not exceeding cost of £5 5s 0d) if Hale agree work to be carried out. Further resolved: One Tender to be obtained by Hale and one by Timperley... work to be given to lowest Tender.'

12th October

'Brookfield Avenue encroachment: Paths Committee to investigate and take action as necessary; also to examine condition of several paths reported in bad state of repair and take necessary action to improve them.'

14th December

'Report of Paths Committee: Decided to recinder path behind Deane Avenue leading from Deansgate Lane to Black Bridge; also one at the bottom end of Brookfield Avenue; also path between Lyme Grove and railway bridge and path leading from Green Lane towards Altrincham.'

1907

22nd February

'Re plank bridge over brook on path from Heyes Lane to Brooklands – Urgent: Clerk has written to agents of the owner adjoining land requesting they have embankment made good to secure the bridge. Letter received from agent agreeing to comply.'

19th April

'Attention drawn to state of path from cricket field to Hale Moss.' 'Clerk requested to write to Secretary of Timperley Golf Club asking him to improve condition of path.'

1910

11th February

'Letter from Timperley Golf Club claiming £5 for trespass and damage to links in carting cinders on to paths crossing the Links: *Resolved*: Golf Club be referred to tenant farmer, Mr. H. Bradbury, who had given permission to Parish Council.'

14th March

'Clerk having mislaid copy of letter to Golf Club re damage claim.' *Resolved*: 'All important letters be copied in a letter books and produced at next meeting.'

1911

8th September

'Reported Plank Bridge on Heyes Lane to Brooklands path destroyed by fire.' 'Clerk instructed to replace.'

1914

13th November

'Mr. J. Clarke... accorded Parish Council permission to divert public path from Hawthorn Terrace to Wash Lane across his land and to substitute new road from Wash Lane to Hawthorn Terrace. Mr. Clarke to defray all expenses in this matter.'

1923

20th April

'Footpath Baguley to Hale Road (i.e. Brooks Drive) application by J.H. Brown to divert it and provide new path in lieu; Plan submitted – fenced and 6 feet wide. Brown stated recently bought field between his house and brook and allowed a Wireless Society to use plot. Path close to their mast and Crossed by wire carrying high voltage occasionally. Path census showed only 4 people used it in one week. Agreed path would be slightly longer for users going to and from Parish Church from Baguley.' *Resolved*: Council Permission refused.'

10th August

'J.H. Brown submitted amended plan. Request Parish Council's observations.' *Resolved*: 'Paths Committee to inspect and report back.'

14th September
'Following Paths Committee report re Path.' *Resolved:* No objection to diversion on lines suggested by Brown's Solicitors.'
'Clerk Reported that subject to proposed straightening of Timperley Brook. Mr Thompson would allow path through his land from Brentwood Avenue to brook. Agreement entered into and acknowledgement of 5s 0d paid and Path to be Closed 1 day per week.'

2nd November
'Letter from G.A. Shawcross stating he had fenced path through his field leading to Thorley Lane and requested Parish Council to cinder same.' *Resolved:* Path to be recindered also Clerk to draw attention of Clibrans and W. Austin to condition of paths through their fields.'

1928

9th March
'Two boats loads of cinders obtained: used for recindering paths: 1. Across Golf Links: 2. Oak Farm: 3. At Lark Hill.'

24th August
'Letter from Bucklow Rural District Council agreeing to pay half cost of painting footbridge over Timperley Brook on path across Golf Links.'

1929

18th January
'Clerk reported trial wagon of cinders obtained from LMS and used on St. Andrews path and found suitable. Three more wagons of cinders ordered @ 7s 0d per wagon load to complete path and recinder Lyme Grove path. Action confirmed and path to rear of Timperley Lodge ordered to be recindered.'

25th October
Resolved: 'Paths Committee should meet at Deansgate Lane to consider erection of Posts on path in order to prevent cyclists using same.'

1930

'Complaints re Cyclists using enclosed field footpaths near St. Andrews Avenue and behind Heyes Leigh.' *Resolved:* 'Requested Bucklow Rural District Council have notices placed at each end of paths prohibiting cycling.'

1934

'Special Meeting Letter from Bucklow Rural District Council.' 'At a Meeting of Bucklow Rural District Council, 7 March request of S. Broadbridge and S.V. Broadbridge to Council. Consent to stopping up Public Path from Riddings Road and running north-west for 315 yards and ending in footpath over Fairywell Brook... subject to public use of diverted path and Bucklow Rural District Council being indemnified against all charges.' *Resolved:* 'Timperley Parish Council agrees to proposal.'

1935

26th July
'Special Meeting: Footpaths Committee: reported on meeting with Sparke and Stephens, 12 July re proposed path diversion, Hare and Hounds – Timperley Church – in connection with proposal for building 396 houses and arrangements of various new streets.' *Resolved:* 'Expedient public path leading from Hare and Hounds in a south-east direction for 636 yards be diverted, turned and in part stopped up in following manner: Path should leave Stockport Road at point 60 yards north-east from present entrance and pass in south-east direction for 60 yards along proposed Seymour Grove then for 525 yards in south-east direction along proposed Clover Road until it reaches existing path proposed to be called Green Lane North.' *Resolved:* 'Consent given.'

A SELECTION OF PARISH COUNCIL MINUTES
RELATING TO HIGHWAYS IN THE TOWNSHIP

Road Maintenance

1895

6th December

'Clay Lane: Width considered: Proposed Parish Council would be satisfied with a road 30 feet wide. Clerk instructed to advise Earle.' (NB Agent of Samuel Brooks.)

1896

7th February

'Clay Lane: Letter from Earle suggesting a 24 foot carriageway. Deputation to call on Earle to discuss.'

30th March

'Earle consents to 30 feet wide road in line with plans from estate office.'

1897

15th January

'Clerk reported Manchester Carriage and Tramway on 27th November deposited plans for proposed extension of tramway along Manchester Road to Peel Causeway and requested Parish Council's support. *Resolved*: No action at present.'

1900

16th March

'Proposed Bucklow Rural District Council be requested to have names of principal roads and lanes fixed on suitable and prominent positions in district.'

1903

15th May

'Question of watering Stockport Road in Timperley discussed. *Moved*: Parish Council to write to Cheshire County Council to check if cost of providing water cart and also of watering said road devolves on Parish Council or Cheshire County Council and if on Parish the estimated cost.'

1904

10th June

'Watering of main roads in summer months discussed again.' *Resolved*: Bucklow Rural District Council be requested to proceed with arrangements for road watering and if water cart cannot be hired one to be purchased for township.'

1907

19th April

'Attention drawn to unsatisfactory state of road at Navigation crossing end of Woodlands Park; also dangerous corner in Brook Lane at that point. Clerk instructed to write to Altrincham Urban District Council asking them to remedy.'

14th June

'*Brook Lane Corner*: Clerk reported meeting with Altrincham Urban District Council: suggested road needed widening: Committee constituted to liaise with Altrincham Urban District Council. Committee as to possible action.

9th August

'*Brook Lane*: reported Altrincham Urban District Council surveyor had promised to submit plan showing proposed alteration and as bridge over brook considered too narrow thought matter might have to be referred to Bucklow Rural District Council who might be disposed to pay half cost of widening and Altrincham Urban District Council the other half.'

11th October

'Letter from J. Jackson re narrow and dangerous condition of Quarry Bank corner of Bloomsbury Lane. Requested steps be taken to have lane widened at this point. Committee appointed to inspect and report back.'

13th December

'Committee reported on Quarry Bank corner. Recommended road should be widened to at least 18 feet in addition to footpaths on each side. *Resolved:* Bucklow Rural District Council be asked to do this – at present narrow and dangerous.'

1908

14th February

'*Quarry Bank Corner:* Committee reported action taken. *Resolved:* Parish Council recommends Bucklow Rural District Council to proceed with widening of lane and to make best terms possible with Cross and Bell in purchasing a plot of land at junction.'

1910

'Many complaints re condition of Stockport Road resulted in consideration of Tar spraying of all the length of this road within parish boundaries. County surveyor estimates cost at approximately £140 of which Parish contribution would be about £50. *Resolved:* Bucklow Rural District Council consult Cheshire County Council requesting them to proceed.'

1915

10th September

'Following request of Parish Council to Bucklow Rural District Council reported 'Dangerous Cross Road' signs had been placed by Cheshire County Council on Stockport Road near Four Lane Ends.'

1920

10th September

'Letter from Cross and Bell suggesting road improvement at junction of Moss Lane and Stockport Road and Wood Lane with plan outlining proposals. *Resolved:* Bucklow Rural District Council be approached with view to widening these roadways and doing away with existing greensward.'

1921

8th July

'Discussion re position of 'Dangerous Cross Road' sign on Altrincham side of Hare and Hounds corner. Decided Clerk to consider if overhanging branches of trees could be cleared to prevent sign being obstructed.'

11th November

'Parish Council considered triangular plots in Clay Lane should be removed. Considered dangerous. *Resolved:* inform Bucklow Rural District Council Parish Council will not be satisfied until this done; necessary to facilitate traffic on this road.'

1922

'Letter from Bucklow Rural District Council stating Wellfield Lane inspected. Decided that breaking up of old grit setts would be considered in next estimates – also widening of lane provided necessary land could be secured.'

1923

20th April

'Sanction obtained for repairs to roadway over two railway bridges in Wash Lane.'

9th November

'Letter from Bucklow Rural District Council: Worst holes in Wood Lane patched – road should now stand over until next financial year. *Resolved:* Bucklow Rural District Council asked to inspect and make safe and passable for Winter.'

1924

14th March

'Report of meeting with Bucklow Rural District Council on 19th February re Holly trees Wash Lane. Bucklow Rural District Council stated not prepared to remove trees but would not object if adjacent owner, Mr Bannister, did.' 'Re Beech tree corner of Wash Lane – Bucklow Rural District Council considered it dangerous and nullified widening and rounding off of corner which was carried out 3½ years ago: Bucklow Rural District Council would consider if they were legally responsible for any damage caused by accident arising if tree left in situ; if so would propose tree be removed.' Parish Council equally divided on question – matter to be discussed at later date.'

7th October
'Bucklow Rural District Council be asked to rescind resolution of few months ago to remove big tree at Wash Lane corner until Bucklow Rural District Council decide to widen road when public opinion would not be against its removal.' (Nb. Motion passed on casting vote of chairman.)

12th December
'Letter from Bucklow Rural District Council stating engineer instructed to prepare plan of proposed road improvement at Wash Lane corner, in order to take maximum advantage of land purchased. Plan showed work consisted of felling tree and setting back kerb thus widening carriageway about 4 foot. *Resolved:* Parish Council approve, by a majority decision, proposed plan.'

1925

13th February
'Letter from Bucklow Rural District Council stated Engineer to report and estimate cost of improving Wellfield Lane, also that it had been decided to remove rubbish from side of Clay Lane and to erect notice warning against depositing rubbish.'

11th September
'Bucklow Rural District Council acknowledge receipt of letter re Buses. *Resolved:* Bus companies be asked if they can adopt 1d stages in Timperley.'

13th November
'Letter from Altrincham Motor Services stating fares from Hare and Hounds to Altrincham reduced to 1d;[1] from Deansgate Lane to Moss Lane corner 1d; Kingsway, Altrincham[2] to Deansgate Lane 1d and Moss Lane corner to village 1d; Also reported North Western Road Car Company had also reduced fares from hare and Hounds to Altrincham on their Stockport route.

1926

'Complaint by Councillor Rook of danger to public by large motor buses on narrow roads in Timperley. *Moved:* Bucklow Rural District Council to be asked to prohibit use of large motor vehicles and service be maintained by smaller buses: Carried.'

1927

16th December
'Letter from Bucklow Rural District Council stating necessary steps taken to change name of Wash Lane by placing a name plate on road and by a public notice in paper.'
'Discussion on Timperley highways maintenance by Bucklow Rural District Council. *Resolved:* Letter be sent expressing strong dissatisfaction with state of roads and warning if matters not improved legal action to be considered.'

1928

6th July
'Letter from Bucklow Rural District Council stating circumstances had prevented Brook Lane widening scheme being implemented. Current position would be considered by Bucklow Rural District Council.'
'Parish Council considered condition of Timperley highways. *Resolved:* Committee be appointed to inspect and report back with view to complaint to Cheshire County Council. if necessary under Section 16 of the Local Government Act 1894.'

1929

10th May
'Highways complaint by Parish Council. Cheshire County Council investigation committee reported that since last inspection Bucklow Rural District Council had spent £2016 more this year than last on maintenance of roads thus must have been just cause for complaint. Bucklow Rural District Council referred to road surface damage caused by intensive building development in parish and their heavy commitment to Highway work in other parishes. Cheshire County Council expressed hope that Bucklow Rural District Council and Timperley Parish Council would work in harmony in future.'

6th September
'Re complaint to Cheshire County Council Highways report received from Cheshire County Council dated 1st August, 1929. report states Timperley Parish Council complaint justified (in their evidence Bucklow Rural District Council stated 637 houses built in Timperley since 1921 and a further 350 planned).'

1930

19th April
'Clerk reported proposed widening of Stockport Road would not affect trees at corner of Woodlands Park but building line would allow building on a third of the plantation... decided letter be sent to owner of plantation suggesting arrangements be made to preserve the trees as considered an asset to neighbourhood.'

1931

28th August
'Completion of Tarmacadaming of Wellfield Lane not covered by current year's estimates: Bridge scheduled for reconstruction during Summer and when completed remainder of road can be tarmacadamed to parish boundary when funds available.'

1932

8th July
'Petition from Wellfield Lane residents complaining of neglected condition of this portion of lane. *Resolved*: Petition by sent to Bucklow Rural District Council with recommendation road should be resurfaced.'

23rd September
'Letter from Bucklow Rural District Council re Petition: Would receive attention – asphalt had been placed at entrances to petitioners' houses.'

1933

3rd March
'Enquiries re possibility of robot signals to control traffic at Four Lane Ends being installed.'

24th March
'Letter from Highway Surveyor Cheshire County Council advising installation not possible until Ministry of Transport consent received also Park Road widening scheme in abeyance due to economic situation.'

1934

'Thorley Lane: complaint by Mr Timpson of Hale re dangerous part of lane – too narrow at Granville Road junction. Letter sent to Bucklow Rural District Council who replied stating work would be costly for various reasons. Clerk requested to ascertain from District Surveyor if any alteration had been made in Town Planning Scheme which showed Thorley Lane to be widened to 50 feet and also the present position with regard to this road.

1936

'Reported Direction post in Thorley Lane repaired and name plates – which had disappeared – had been replaced at Grove and Wellfield Lanes.'

Flooding
1920

26th March
'Letter from Bucklow Rural District Council re Grove Lane. Reported no further flooding opposite Mr Jackson's farm but road under water at Pickering Lodge corner. *Resolved*: Bucklow Rural District Council Highways Surveyor have his attention drawn to the flooding at the corner.'

1922

10th March
'Complaints re flooding of road and houses in Brentwood Avenue – allegedly caused by recent diversion of brook course by Cone Tube Co.: *Resolved* Bucklow Rural District Council to be notified and report back.'

21st April

'Flooding – Brentwood Avenue: Report submitted by Bucklow Rural District Council that banks of diverted section have given way in places due to frost and heavy rainfall – debris had thus accumulated. Cone Tube Co. interviewed – had promised to clear obstruction and improve slope of banks and raise level of bank in one place.'

1930

14th November

'Complaints re flooding in Thorley Lane due to ditch overflow in Mr J. Lanceley's garden. Highway surveyor requested to investigate pointing out possible causes (e.g. piping of open ditch near 'The Hollies' or silting up of open watercourse through grounds of 'Lark Hill').

1931

3rd March

'Letter from Highways Surveyor re flooding Thorley Lane. Stated receiving attention but as regards 'Lark Hill' may be delay before private owner could give it necessary attention.'

28th August

'Complaint re flooding due to ditch overflow at Lyme Grove adjacent to public path also: Question left in abeyance.'
'Thorley Lane flooding: Bucklow Rural District Council had inspected in conditions of heavy rain – decided to recommend new road drain to remedy.'

Sewerage
1896

7th February

'Condition of public sewers discussed as several complaints made of smells from manhole grids: Clerk instructed to liaise with Stretford and Urmston re their methods of ventilation.'

1899

13th October

'Special meeting to consider treatment of Sewerage. *Resolved*: Parish Council not prepared to join Altrincham Urban District Council in sewerage scheme. *Proposed*: Assuming existing outfall and sewage works at Dark Lane cannot be modified Council oppose joint sewerage scheme with Dunham Massey.'

1900

8th December

'Letter from Bucklow Rural District Council re proposal to take up and relay 450 yards of Timperley outfall: *Resolved*: be left to discretion of Bucklow Rural District Council Councillors and our two representative on Bucklow Rural District Council are of course aware of the Parish Council's feelings on matter.'

1915

4th June

'Letter from Bucklow Rural District Council advising decision to make extensions at Timperley sewage works costing about £400 which would put matters right for at least five years. Necessity for work explained by Lt. Col. Newton. *Resolved*: No objection.'

1926

16th April

'Reported cost of several extensions to sewers now in progress would necessitate heavy increase in current year's rates: Loan suggested over a period of years. Would necessitate Ministry of Health inquiry. Recently Altrincham Urban District Council had offered to deal with Timperley sewage at their outfall works. Would consider Altrincham Urban District Council terms.'

17th December

'Reported Bucklow Rural District Council and Altrincham Urban District Council had considered report of Altrincham Urban District Council re sewerage works necessary to enable Timperley sewage to be dealt with by Altrincham Urban District Council Sewage Farm. *Resolved*: Bucklow Rural District Council to prepare scheme for Timperley new outfall works to compare costs. Altrincham Urban District Council scheme cost £1789 meaning a rate increase of 1s 3d in the pound for a minimum of 15 years.'

1928

12th April

'Special Meeting of Parish Council with Bucklow Rural District Council re new sewerage outfall works. Bucklow Rural District Council stated new works necessary. Plans approved by Bucklow Rural District Council and forwarded to Ministry of Health. Timperley sewerage troublesome for some years and extensive building development make new outfall works essential. Various schemes considered but rejected: proposed scheme recommended by Bucklow Rural District Council. Serious pollution in Sinderland Brook at Dark Lane works. Extensive polluted effluent at sewage works and works out of action in flood conditions and polluted storm water overflow near Woodcote Farm. New scheme must be a pumping scheme. Site not practicable for a gravity scheme. Present works two miles from Timperley boundary. Proposed purchase of 13 acres on opposite side of brook to Bucklow Rural District Council sewage farm and to construct works on it to treat sewage by bacterial putrefaction method which would cut out last mile of Timperley sewerage. Lane is about same level as incoming sewage and electric motor pumping necessary. Present pop. 6900. Projected population – figure required by Ministry of Health when new works planned – 8600. Layout provided for future extensions – Cottage to be built for man in charge. Estimated cost £22,606 including Special rate of 1s 2d in £; interest on loan 5%. Special expenses of Parish increased by £1817 (including £380 for additional maintenance).

5th October

'Letter from the Ministry of Health stating Public Inquiry in Parish on 10th October re Bucklow Rural District Council application to borrow £22,606 for sewage works. Legal representative engaged to oppose scheme and support Gravitation scheme costing £13,600. *Resolved*: Parish Council joins with opposition to Bucklow Rural District Council scheme and to question if possibility of amalgamation with Altrincham Urban District Council can be raised at inquiry as Parish Council considers it undesirable to incur Capital expenditure on sewage works in view of uncertainty re future of local government proposals.'

22nd November

'Clerk reported on Ministry of Health inquiry (10th October) re new sewage works. *Inter alia* Cheshire Lines Railway Company objected to increased use of level crossing – only means of access to land on proposed site. Ministry of Health decision awaited.'

1930

'Report presented to joint meeting – 22nd January – between various local authorities re Bill promoted by Cheshire County Council for formation of a North Cheshire Sewerage Board for an area including Timperley. Estimated cost £868,000; anticipated Government grant of 75% for 15 years and then 37½% for further 15 years. Cheshire County Council would also apply a ½d rate over whole county when loan charges exceeded a 3d rate in areas concerned. Pointed out one of main trunk sewers would pass through undeveloped part of Timperley: also that all Timperley sewage would be picked up at Park Road/Manchester Road junction and new outfall works built for whole area. Would replace Bucklow Rural District Council's £22,606 scheme for Timperley alone which entailed a 1s 2d rate in £. *Resolved*: Parish Council in favour of North Cheshire Sewerage scheme and approved generally of North Cheshire Sewerage Board Bill.'

Lighting
1898

11th March

'Special Meeting. Councillor Bell explained estimated cost spread over 5/6 years. Report approved – copy affixed to minute book. Electricity rejected; Gas only practical alternative. Hale and Dunham canvassed as to cost of plan and maintenance.'

1901

10th May

'Suggested Bucklow Rural District Council asked to provide lighting for main roads. Considered Parish Council should undertake. *Resolved:* Ratepayers be consulted.'

14th June

'Lighting Committee reported. Recommended Parish Council support (at Ratepayers' meeting) 1898 scheme for lighting as terms available from Altrincham Gas similar to 1898 terms with small addition for extra cost of lamp pillars.'

'Local Government Board advise Timperley that the Parish is not competent to adopt Lighting and Watching Act of 1833. Possible for Bucklow Rural District Council to delegate such powers to Parish Council.' *Resolved*: Letter to Local Government Board asking them to rescind order as far as it relates to Timperley.'

8th October
'Letter from Local Government Board stating they agreed to rescind (with reference to Timperley) their order of 31st May 1900 conditional on Timperley adopting Lighting and Watching Act 1833.' *Resolved*: Parish Meeting convened to consider adopting 1833 Act (as far as it concerns lighting and that 1898 Gas scheme be recommended to Parish meeting.'

20th December
'Bucklow Rural District Council request Parish Council to formulate Lighting scheme and submit for consideration. Bucklow Rural District Council will consider if they will delegate such powers to Parish Council. *Resolved:* Inform Bucklow Rural District Council they decline to take further steps re lighting at present.'

1902

1st April
'*Resolved:* Oppose Bucklow Rural District Council's activation of Timperley Lighting scheme until ratepayers' views ascertained.'

18th April
'Local Government Board advise that on suggestion of Bucklow Rural District Council they had rescinded provisional order giving Timperley ratepayers power of adopting Lighting and Watching Act 1833.'

8th August
'Copy of letter received by Bucklow Rural District Council from Local Government Board giving them sanction to apply for loan of £400 for purpose of lighting Timperley township. *Moved*: Letter to Bucklow Rural District Council complaining of manner business had been transacted throughout and Special Meeting of Parish Council be convened to consider draft of such letter.'

15th August
'Letter drafted expresses surprise at Bucklow Rural District Council application being sanctioned by Local Government Board for Loan of £450 without previous Parish inquiry... Reminds Local Government Board Parish Council in favour of adopting Lighting and Watching Act of 1833 but favourable poll not obtained... must be realised those voting in favour understood work would be carried out by Parish... considers Bucklow Rural District Council act unreasonably... by-passing Parish Council. Parish Council intend to raise matter at later date according to law. Would have been willing to abide by and carry out decision of ratepayers... Parish Council enters protest at precipitate action of Bucklow Rural District Council... considers against spirit of Local Government Act 1894.'

1903

11th December
'Suggested Bill of Cheshire Electric Power and Gas Co. considered. *Resolved*: Parish Council considers bill should be opposed and request Cheshire County Council and Bucklow Rural District Council takes such action.'

1904

7th October
'Bucklow Rural District Council requests Parish Council's opinion re additional lamps in Grove Lane. *Moved*: For public Lighting. Altrincham Gas Co. should carry mains in Grove Lane from Grove House to Moss Lane within twelve months and Parish Council will support Bucklow Rural District Council to that end.'

1909

12th February
'*Resolved*: Suggested lamps be fixed half way down Orchard Place and Baker Street and that surveyor should do this before next winter.'

1914

13th November

'Attention drawn to unsatisfactory lighting on Railway Bridge over Cheshire Lines Company Railway in Wash Lane. *Resolved*: Bucklow Rural District Council required to improve by having existing lamp on village side moved 12 yards nearer to the village and additional lamp paced on the other side of bridge.'

1919

21st November

'Clerk to write to Bucklow Rural District Council requiring installation of incandescent burners on certain lamps at junction of Moss Lane and Brook Lane and corner of Moss Lane at Hall's cottages and entrance to Lyme Grove. Bucklow Rural District Council advised request being complied with.'

1920

10th September

'Bucklow Rural District Council proposes to install clockwork controlled lamps at selected points to provide night and morning lighting at those dangerous points during Winter (i.e. cross roads at Hare and Hounds, Thorley Lane and Clay Lane and Four Lane Ends). *Resolved*: Approved subject to proviso one lamp to be fixed at Wash Lane/Manchester Road Junction instead of Clay Lane corner.'

1921

9th September

'*Resolved*: Recommend Bucklow Rural District Council order that lamps should be lighted throughout season and do away with break of three or four nights at each full moon.'

1925

13th February

'Letter from Bucklow Rural District Council stating Engineer instructed to prepare plan for improved future lighting arrangement in Timperley.'

1926

17th December

'Letter from Bucklow Rural District Council stating lighting Grove and Wellfield Lanes would be considered. Reported additional lamps placed in Grove Lane.'

1929

18th January

'Letter from Bucklow Rural District Council stating they had advanced time for lamp lighting in certain circumstances; also extensions of gas main in Green Lane would allow for erection of three lamps – now authorised; also offered to have suitably protected lamp fixed to subway of Skelton Junction bridge if Parish Council considered necessary. Clerk instructed to inform Bucklow Rural District Council complaints still being received re late lighting of lamps Wood Lane and required earlier lighting of same; also Parish Council considered Skelton Junction offer and decided lighting was necessary provided lamp could be suitably protected.'

1930

14th November

'Letter from Bucklow Rural District Council stating decided to erect lamp in Deansgate Lane and hoped to arrange renewed lighting of lamp at Skelton Junction.'

1931

17th April

'Complaints re certain street lamps unserviceable for long periods and dirty state of some lamps; also necessity for improved lighting for Grove Lane-Stockport Road. *Resolved*: Clerk interview Bucklow Rural District Council re problem.'

12th June

'Lighting complaints: All Timperley lamps inspected at night by Bucklow Rural District Council: 1. Skelton Junction lamp inoperative due to wilful damage to supply pipe – now fully protected and clock timed to activate at a late hour...: Grove Lane/Stockport Road junction: agreed improvements should be considered and Bucklow Rural District Council required to provide additional lamp at this corner; Timperley representatives given power to act – decided to give additional lamp at this corner and to move next lamp to a new site opposite Mayfield Road.'

1932

'Clerk reported meeting of Bucklow Rural District Council Lighting Committee on 1st April: new lamps recommended Beech Avenue: boundary Stockport Road and Manchester; Brookfield Avenue and footbridge over Cheshire Lines Committee Railway line; two new lamps at dangerous corner of Brook Lane and altering position of existing lamps. Question of further lamps at Four Lane Ends deferred.'

4th March

'Letter read from Highway Surveyor re telephone kiosk Brook Lane. Difficulties with supply authorities re connections to box – would pressure authorities concerned.'

24th March

'Lyme Grove residents require lighting of Grove and would be prepared to pay installation costs. *Resolved*: Bucklow Rural District Council required to draw up scheme for submission.

21st April

'Letter from Bucklow Rural District Council re Lyme Grove. Offered to erect two lamps at cost of 11s 0d per house. Council to undertake future lighting and maintenance of such lamps.'

1935

30th March

Final meeting of Parish Council when it formally dissolved itself and withdraw its representatives from Bucklow Rural District Council by resignation.

Nuisance Removal

1896

7th February

'Complaint: offensive matter turned into Timperley Brook from drainage connected with Brook Steam Laundry. Clerk instructed to write to Nuisance Inspector requesting early attention.'

3rd July

'Bucklow Rural District Council's attention again drawn to unsatisfactory condition of effluent from Steam Laundry into Timperley Brook – requests steps to abate nuisance.'

1900

12th October

'Nuisance by smoke emission from chimney of Stannard and Co., Deansgate Lane. Clerk to request they abate same.'

1901

19th April

'Complaints still being received re obnoxious fumes from Tannery Chimney, Deansgate Lane. Clerk to write to Bucklow Rural District Council asking them to abate it.'

1906

15th June

'Complaints re dusty condition of main roads. *Moved*: Surveyor's attention be drawn to matter – that he sees roads are well watered regularly in dry months.'

1907

19th April

'Clerk write Bucklow Rural District Council re arrangements for watering trials and request they send watering cart oftener and earlier in day.'

1911

10th February

'Complaint by two residents requesting Parish Council to ask appropriate authority to prevent children playing in village street whilst suffering from scarlet fever. *Reported*: discussion with Bucklow Rural District Council Sanitary Inspector but no grounds for prosecution.'

1915

10th September

'Complaints re pollution nuisance of open ditch – rear of Haddon Grove – allegedly from sewage entering ditch from houses in Posy Row. *Resolved*: Bucklow Rural District Council's attention called to complaints.'

1916

21st January

'Letter from Bucklow Rural District Council stating Statutory Notices served on owner of houses in Posy Row, to remedy defects and abate nuisance.'

9th June

'Letter from Mr. S. Chadderton re recent drowning of Grandson in pit off Brook Lane requesting if steps could be taken to prevent further accidents. Pit is in private grounds. Letter sent to property agent drawing attention to problem and requesting fences be put in good order to prevent access by children.'

1919

16th March

'Complaint from Mrs Wallwork re condition of Cow Lane. *Resolved*: letter to Brooks's estate office requesting road be improved.'

1920

13th February

'Complaints re waste paper litter, etc., from Cone Tube Co.'s works, Deansgate Lane, also smoke emission. Nuisance Inspector alerted.'

16th April

'Letter read from Cone Tube Co., Brookside Works, asking Parish Council's assistance to obtain permission to straighten course of Timperley Brook adjoining works and to divert brook into underground culvert. *Resolved*: Refer to Bucklow Rural District Council.'

10th September

'Letter from Bucklow Rural District Council stating Cone Tube Co. informed Bucklow Rural District Council has no objection to proposal for straightening course of brook as shown on plan – provided permanent boundary marks fixed to centre line of present course of brook which forms the boundary between Timperley and Altrincham – also disused portion of brook to be filled up to level of adjoining land.'

1921

22nd April

'Resolved inform Bucklow Rural District Council of complaints re paper blowing from tip in Heyes Lane. Bucklow Rural District Council asked to instruct men to collect and burn all paper refuse on tip.'

8th July

'Letter from Bucklow Rural District Council promising action re Heyes Lane tip following a residents' petition complaining of offensive smells and tip stated to be on fire. *Resolved*: Parish Council consider complaint serious. Request Bucklow Rural District Council remedy within seven days.'

11th November

'*Resolved*: letter to Ministry of Health re complaints of insanitary condition of houses in Olive Grove and Bloomsbury Lane. *Resolved*: Bucklow Rural District Council to be notified if complaints upheld.'

1922

January

'*Reported*: notice served on owner of Olive Grove houses by Bucklow Rural District Council to carry out necessary repairs. Due to financial problems decided to allow payment by owner to be spread over seven years – subject to proper agreement signed.'

21st April

'Further complaints re condition Olive Grove cottages – especially long delay in repair work. *Resolved*: letter to Bucklow Rural District Council requiring immediate action to repair roofs.'

30th June

'Letter from Bucklow Rural District Council stating contract entered into for repairing Olive Grove. Work to commence that day.'

1923

20th April

'Attention drawn to stagnant pool in 'Larkhill', Thorley Lane; health hazard. *Moved*: Nuisance Inspector's attention drawn to the pond – to remedy.'

1927

4th March

'Complaints re method of emptying ashpits, Orchard Place. Clerk to report to and liaise with Sanitary Inspector to remedy.'

16th December

'Gem Laundry Nuisance:– Inspector to be advised Parish Council would be pleased to have his report on nuisance complaints made by residents.'

1929

8th March

'Reported Gem Laundry nuisance not abated. *Resolved*: Bucklow Rural District Council requested take action.'

19th April

'Gem Laundry: Bucklow Rural District Council stated Sanitary Inspector instructed take series of time tests.'

10th May

'Attention drawn to Timperley Brook. Pollution at weekends by foul discharge from Brookside Paper Works. *Resolved*: Sanitary Inspector be notified.'

19th July

'Pollution Brookside Works: Sanitary Inspector stated reported to Mersey and Irwell Joint Committee.'

25th October

'Bucklow Rural District Council reported Statutory notice served on Brookside Paper Co. re smoke nuisance. Mersey and Irwell Joint Committee informed of Timperley Brook pollution by this works – alleged nuisance – offensive odour – should be investigated.'

1930

15th April

'Reported Sanitary Inspector taking observations of smoke emission Brookside Paper Co. following residents' complaints. Clerk requested to draw attention of Inspector to offensive odour from works especially on Monday mornings.'
'Question of footpath pollution by dogs: as this problem experienced by Hale Urban District Council. Agreed Parish Council should ascertain Hale's solution to this problem.'

26th September

'Fouling by Dogs: reported Hale had failed to get Cheshire County Council to pass Bye-Law – but had published notices warning residents unless nuisance minimised council would seek statutory powers to deal with owners concerned.'

14th November

'Following Clerk's inspection of Nuisance problem Brookside Paper Co. and liaison with Altrincham Nuisance Inspector he reported Mersey and Irwell Joint Committee had taken up the matter; also further samples revealed offensive and polluted effluent. Mersey and Irwell Joint Committee resolved. 'Notice be served on Company inviting them to appear before committee to show cause why legal proceedings should not be taken against them under Mersey and Irwell Joint Committee Act Part 3, Section 5, 1892.'

1932

20th March

'Brookside Paper Co.: no reply from Sanitary Inspector re pollution. Ascertained question of taking effluent into Altrincham Urban District Council or Timperley sewers being considered. Mersey and Irwell Joint Committee monitoring problem.

1933

29th September

'Letter from Sanitary Inspector stating observation being made with view to checking black smoke emission from Brookside Works also effluent problem being investigated.'
(Nb. since date of the letter above works destroyed by fire. Cottages close to works saved from destruction by Fire Brigade.)

1934

4th May

'Letter from Mr G.A. Faulkner, Southwood, Stockport Road complaining of erection of large advertising hoarding on Railway Bridge near his house. Considered injurious to amenities of neighbourhood. *Resolved*: Cheshire County Council be informed.'

13th July

'Complaint from Mr. T.R. Pool, Woodlea, Park Road, re litter nuisance of used bus tickets at stage near his house...' Bucklow Rural District Council asked to provide suitable receptacle for litter.'

14th December

'Hoardings Stockport Road Railway Bridge: letter from Cheshire County Council opined proceedings against Railway Company would not succeed. Railway Company had offered to remove Co-op board on understanding no objection to the other two hoardings: Railway Co. also offered to remove some of signs at Timperley Station. Parish Council decided to ask Cheshire County Council to try to negotiate removal of hoarding objected to by Mr. Faulkner in lieu of the one offered to be removed by Railway Co.'

1935

4th October

'Following further complaint re the hoarding at Hare and Hounds Clerk interviewed Director of the Railway Co. and the hoarding had now been removed.'

Note

1. 1d was equal to 0.4p approximately.
2. Kingsway, Altrincham was the site of the old bus station, nearly opposite the present bus and train terminus.

7

THE BRIDGEWATER CANAL,
TIMPERLEY SECTION

'Never be entirely idle but either be reading... or endeavouring something for the public good.'

Thomas a Kempis (1380-1471)

By an Act of Parliament[1] the Duke of Bridgewater was empowered to construct a canal from Worsley to Manchester with a spur to Longford Bridge, Stretford. This spur was completed by the end of 1761.

A second Act of Parliament[2] empowered the Duke to extend his canal from Longford Bridge to the Mersey estuary, near Runcorn. It is this length of his canal which traverses the north-west corner of the Northern Moiety of Timperley over a distance of about 1200 yards.

Clause 2 of the Act appointed a number of commissioners to:

'... settle all differences between the Duke of Bridgewater and persons interested in any lands that may sustain damage by powers granted under the Act...'[3]

Clause 18 empowered landowners near the canal to '... make wharfs or quays or landing places on their own lands...'

The Timperley section of the canal enters the township when it crosses the Baguley Brook and leaves it when it crosses the Timperley Brook. Both brooks, which mark the boundaries of the township, had to be culverted under the canal.

Research suggests that the Duke purchased lands for his canal from two principal Timperley landowners: the Taylor family in respect of lands forming part of their fields between the Baguley

6. Close up of Canal Basin with ramp which provides vehicular and passenger access to canal bank from Wash Lane. Used extensively, especially in the pre-railway era, for the on and off loading of passengers and freight. (Photograph taken by author, October 1990.)

Brook and Wash Lane;[4] and the Earl of Stamford (Harry Grey, fourth Earl) in respect of lands forming part of his fields between Wash Lane and Timperley Brook.[5]

This Timperley section was excavated during the period 1764-6. One can easily imagine the radical change it would occasion in the lifestyle of the rural community in this section of the township; scores of navigators (navvies) descending on the township, carts constantly coming and going transporting the excavated earth, builders bridging over the line of the canal where it crossed Wash Lane and eventually a permanent and unique change to the topography of the township. It was the beginning of the transformation of a wholly rural community and precursor of the changes that were to follow in the next century with the coming of the Railway Age (see Chapter 8).

By 6th June, 1766 the canal was in operation as far as Broadheath when

'On 6 June 1766 the first tolls were taken on the new line to Altrincham, in October the canal was cutting through to Dunham, in September 1767 the Bollin had been crossed and at Altrincham coal prices had already been reduced by about half. By 1769 the canal had reached Lymm.'[6]

Passenger carrying began in 'October 1767 between Broadheath (Altrincham) and Manchester, in early 1769 was extended to Lymm, and later to Stockton, using converted barges'.[7]

'On 1st September 1774 the Duke was reported just to have built two packet-boats for the same run, one carrying 120 passengers and the other 80-. Each had a "Coffee-room at the Head, from whence Wines &c are sold out by the Captain's Wife. Next to this is the first Cabbin, which is 2s 6d, the second Cabbin [sic] 1s 6d, and the third Cabbin 1s for the Passage."'[8]

In 1788 two boats were working a service through to Runcorn.

	Timetable[9] (Monday to Friday)	
	Down Boat	Upboat
Manchester	0800	c.1600 to 1700
Altrincham	1000	c.1430 to 1530
Lymm	1130	c.1300 to 1400
Stockton Quay	1300	c.1130 to 1230
Preston Brook	1600	c.0800 to 0900

Chester passengers travelled to or from Preston Brook by connecting coach, whilst Liverpool passengers travelled to or from Stockton Quay by connecting coach.

7. Canal Basin and associated ramp providing access to the canal bank from a point on Wash Lane (Park Road) opposite to Timperley Station entrance. This particular ramp was most probably built c.1850 when the railway line was constructed. (Photograph taken by author, 1990.)

Coal was the principal freight carried and during the period 1773-1790 267,536 tons were transported between Worsley, Manchester and Liverpool. Some of this would doubtless be unloaded at Timperley for the village's solid fuel supplies. Tolls, freight, warehousing and porterage generated a revenue of £61,143 in 1791.[10]

It is most probable that the wharf or basin, beneath the Wash Lane bridge, and a sloping ramp connecting it with Wash Lane, were constructed at this time to facilitate the on and off loading of goods at Timperley.[11] The then owner of the land would have utilised Clause 18 to his pecuniary advantage.

By 1794 the Duke's packet boats, in addition to carrying passengers on business or pleasure, functioned as a goods delivery service, conveying parcels, cloth, groceries, etc., to country stores sited at places on or close to the canal.[12] The Timperley wharf would certainly be utilised by the village community for this purpose.[13]

In 1794 the fare from Manchester to Altrincham in the first class or front room was 1s (5p) and 9d (3.75p) in the second class or back room.[14]

In the following century it is probable that the Runcorn sandstone, used in the construction of the parish church, was transported from Runcorn by canal to the Wash Lane wharf. Despite competition by the burgeoning railway systems in the North-west, the canal packet boats were still plying between Manchester and Runcorn at least up to the middle of the nineteenth century. They included a new type of packet boat which had a narrower beam and was lighter in weight than the standard packer boat design. It was drawn by:

'... two horses at a gallop, the horses being changed several times on the run.'[15]

Doubtless the sight of these boats plying the canal would be a constant source of interest to the villagers, especially the boys, in the township.

It would appear that by the fourth decade of the nineteenth century the canal was heavily polluted, if a note from a contemporary publication is accurate:

'... and within a dozen miles of Manchester the water of the canal is as black as the Styx and absolutely pestiferous from the gas and refuse of the manufactures...'[16]

In August 1865 the canal was again polluted, so Timperley's Select Vestry sent a deputation to meet the Trustees of the Duke of Bridgewater, along with deputations from other canalside townships, to see what could be done about the same. (See Appendix 1 at the end of this chapter.)

In 1828 the canal company was contributing to the township's rate, income being assessed at a rateable value of £400[17] on a length of 1167 yards of its canal. Assuming an average rate of 1s in the pound it would pay about £20 a year.

The Bridgewater Canal, 1830 to 1995

As publications treating of the canal's history in depth are readily available, it is only necessary here to sketch the salient events germane to the waterway's evolution during the nineteenth cen-

8. Bridge carrying line connecting Skelton Junction, via West Timperley Station, with Cheshire Lines Railway at Glazebrook (see Chapter 8 for more information). (Photograph taken by the author, October 1990.)

tury and beyond. In this connection it should be appreciated that, in addition to the waterway, the canal company's assets included land, collieries, warehouse and office properties.

On 8th March, 1803, Francis Egerton, 3rd Duke of Bridgewater died. Under the terms of his Will[18] his industrial estates in Lancashire and Cheshire were to be placed in trust for the benefit of George Granville Leveson-Gower, Marquess of Stafford, during his lifetime: following his demise the benefits of the trust were to devolve on his second son Francis Leveson-Gower, subject to the proviso that he changed his surname to Egerton. The trust was administered by three trustees and lasted one hundred years.

During the first quarter of the nineteenth century the estates prospered with profits averaging £66,000 between 1803 and 1820 – mostly provided from canal revenues.

Liverpool merchants were actively considering, during the decade 1820-30, the construction of a rail link with Manchester. Their proposals encountered stiff opposition from the Bridgewater Trustees, who foresaw a formidable threat to their near monopoly of freight and passenger carrying between the two towns. The problem was resolved when the Marquess of Stafford invested £100,000 in the railway project and was authorised to nominate two directors to the board of the railway company. The Parliamentary Bill authorising the Liverpool and Manchester Railway was enacted in 1826 and the line opened for traffic in 1830. It marked the beginning of the 'Railway Age' and heralded the slow decline of the canal as a commercial waterway.

In 1833 the Marquess of Stafford[19] died and his second son Francis Leveson-Gower duly changed his surname to Egerton and received the benefits of the trust. Already the 'new' railway had overtaken the canal in terms of passengers and freight carried. Throughout the 1830s the waterway's proportion of the carrying trade declined relative to the railway and its concomitant was rapidly falling profits. Henceforward, the canal's fortunes fluctuated but the overall trend was one of a continuing slow decline in profitability. Initially, new investment and modernisation – it included the buy-out of its competitor the Mersey and Irwell Navigation Company – brought a revival in its fortunes during the period 1837-45.[20] This improvement was shortlived as, post 1845, the country experienced the age of 'Railway Mania' when schemes promoting railways proliferated – not least in Lancashire and Cheshire with ominous implications for the Bridgewater Canal's future prosperity. From thence the story is one of severe price competition, squeezed margins and declining profitability. One of the canal's initial setbacks was the passenger service between Timperley and Manchester following the opening (1849) of the MSJ and A Railway. In c.1851 the trustees agreed to terminate the passenger boat services ex-Runcorn at Timperley in return for a large tranche of shares in the said railway. It resulted in passengers between Timperley and Manchester having to disembark or embark at Timperley and travel by rail between Timperley and Manchester.

Following the amalgamation of a number of small railway companies into the London and North Western Railway Company, during the 1860s, the trustees lost their boardroom influence on the Liverpool and Manchester Railway. At that juncture the trustees resolved to sell their waterway interests. A sale was achieved in 1872 when the Bridgewater Navigation Company Ltd,[21] purchased both canal undertakings from the trustees for a consideration of £1,120,000.

In 1885 the Manchester Ship Canal Company, under the Manchester Ship Canal Act, paid the Bridgewater Navigation Company Ltd, £1,710,000 for the whole of their properties subject to the proviso:

'... that the Bridgewater canal be well maintained and freely open to those who wish to use it...'

In 1923 a new company was formed to acquire the estates (owned by the Ellesmere family in Worsley and other parts) and was incorporated as 'The Bridgewater Estates Ltd'.

During the 1920s the Bridgewater Collieries were sold to Manchester Collieries Ltd and this latter company was nationalised in 1948.

The canal's commercial activities continued post-1918 but its traffic volume continued to decline. Its function as a commercial waterway ceased in 1974 and the canal is now administered and controlled by the Manchester Ship Canal Company and has metamorphosed into a purely leisure waterway.

Notes

1. 33 Geo. II (March 1760).

2. 2 Geo. III (1762)

3. They met bi-annually in March and September alternately at one of two venues, one of which was '... the home of Widow Newhall by the sign of the Unicorn, Altrincham...'

4. The family had owned the Riddings Hall estate since the early eighteenth century when a female descendant of the Domville family (previous owners) married Henry Taylor (Mayor of Liverpool).

5. He owned a large part of the Northern Moiety following his marriage to Mary Booth, sole heiress of the Earl of Warrington, in 1716.

6. Charles Hadfield and Gordon Biddle, *The Canals of North West England. Volume 1*, p.31.

7. Ibid, p.35.

8. *Derby Mercury*, 9th September, 1774, quoted in *The Canals of North West England. Volume 1*, p.35.

9. Deduced from figures in Lewis's *Directory for Manchester and Salford, 1788* and also reproduced in *The Canals of North West England. Volume 1*, p.35. As only the Up-Boat Departure Time ex-Runcorn is quoted in the source consulted arrival times at staging points en route to Manchester have been interpolated from the Down Boat schedule listed herein. The takings for the years 1776 to 1790 rose from £1,303 to £2,905.

10. Ibid, p.36.

11. Its importance increased post-1847. See Chapter 8.

12. *The Manchester and Salford Directory* for 1802 contains the following '... the sail from Manchester to Runcorn is very amusing... at Lymm boat stops a quarter of an hour, and passengers have opportunity of getting refreshments at a neat and clean Public House...' (Quoted in *The Canals of North West England. Volume 1*, p.94.)

13. Comparison of the carriage prices per ton of goods, etc., clearly illustrates the competitive position of the Bridgewater Canal vis à vis river and land navigation: by river 12s; by land 40s; by Bridgewater Canal 6s. Lime, manure and building materials were also carried by canal. Figures from *The Canals of North West England. Volume 1*.

14. *The Canals of North West England. Volume 1*, p.94.

15. Ibid, p.118.

16. *A Home Tour Through the Manufacturing Districts of England in the Summer of 1831* by Sir George Head.

17. Timperley Overseers of the Poor Account book (C.C.R.O., ref. PC.52).

18. One of the lengthiest in legal history.

19. He became 1st Duke of Sutherland a few months before his death.

20. A profit of some £76,000 was declared in 1844.

21. Many railway shareholders invested in it.

BRIDGEWATER CANAL

Minutes appertaining to the Bridgewater Canal contained in the Select Vestry and Parish Council Records

Select Vestry Minutes

1864

24th January

Moved: 'Immediate attention of Trustees of late Duke of Bridgewater called to road by canal side from Deansgate Lane as it is impossible for foot passengers to get along road'. (Carried.)

1865

1st August

Meeting: 'To consider effects of recent decision in Queens Bench re introduction of foul water into canals whereby same are polluted and rendered public nuisances.'

Meeting: 'Opinion of meeting that state of canal from Manchester onwards for considerable distance is most objectionable and an intolerable nuisance prejudicial to health, comfort and property and requests early abatement.'

Moved: 'Deputation be appointed to co-operate with deputations from other townships along line of canal to concur in suitable measures deemed best to effect object in view.'

Nuisance Committee Minutes

1861

7th January

'Presentment by Mr Suttle of culverts and ditches belonging to Trustees of Duke of Bridgewater brought before meeting.'

Proposed: 'Trustees of Duke of Bridgewater be served notice to cleanse same under and parallel to canal through township.'

4th March

'Trustees of Duke of Bridgewater having disregarded letter sent proposed to be written to again.'

Parish Council Minutes

1899

20th January

'Clerk instructed to write to Secretary of Bridgewater Canal Company re dangerous state of road alongside canal near Timperley Station and ask them to fence it off.'

24th March

'Clerk reported letter from Manchester Ship Canal Company stating fencing would be done.'

1924

7th October

'Surveyors attention drawn to state of path in Brook Lane and fact that lamps on canal bank... had not been lit this winter.'

1927

4th March

'Messrs. Meldrums complained of very poor state of roadway adjacent to works [i.e. on canal side]. Had written to Highways Surveyor in January but no reply received. currently refused to pay rates. Clerk reported surveyor had agreed to apprise Parish Council, on which promise firm paid rates. *Resolved:* Meldrums' letter be sent to Bucklow Rural District Council.'

8

RAILWAYS IN TIMPERLEY

'Travel... is a part of Education... a part of experience.'

Bacon

The term 'Railway Mania' encapsulates the nationwide proliferation of schemes to construct railways during the middle decades of the nineteenth century. During that time Timperley acres were acquired to accommodate one of the then new railway lines. In the course of time this 'new' transport phenomenon was to prove the catalyst which transformed the township from an agricultural to a densely populated dormitory suburb. Railway entrepreneurs were attracted, especially, to the burgeoning industrial region of North-west England which embraced the industrial areas centred on the towns of Manchester, Sheffield, Leeds and Liverpool.

By the early 1840s a number of railway companies had built lines with termini at Manchester. These enterprises had been constructed in isolation and their respective termini were sited on the perimeter of Manchester and thus separate from each other, in some cases by over a mile. Clearly, this was an inefficient arrangement, especially for freight routed via Manchester, as it entailed transhipment there from one railhead to another. In the case of three of these lines Liverpool and Manchester Railway which used the Liverpool Road Terminus, Manchester and Birmingham Railway which used the London Road Terminus, which it shared with the Sheffield, Ashton-under-Lyne and Manchester Railway it was patently obviously that a junction connecting them would be highly desirable as it would obviate the need to tranship goods between railheads, cut freight costs, expedite delivery times and, most importantly, improve profit margins. Such considerations were the raison d'etre behind a scheme to construct a junction connecting the railheads to be called the Manchester South Junction Railway.

9. MSJ and A Railway, Timperley Railway Station, entrance and booking hall. Sited on the east side of the bridge carrying Park Road (originally Wash Lane) over the railway line. (Photograph taken by author, 1989.)

Shortly after this photograph was taken work commenced on the conversion of the Altrincham – Manchester Line to the Metrolink Light Rapid Transit System. Timperley is now provided with two lifts affording access to the platform below the level of Park Road. The new rail system opened on this section of the Metrolink in c.May-June 1992.

The Manchester South Junction and Altrincham Railway

Prior to work commencing the scheme was modified to include a branch line to Altrincham from the projected MSJ Railway. Obviously such a line would affect the commercial interest of the Bridgewater Canal Company which, between Stretford and Timperley, ran parallel to the projected Altrincham branch. Accordingly, the support of Lord Francis Egerton[1] was sought and obtained. He agreed to guide the Bill through Parliament, provide some of the land required, including a three and a quarter mile stretch between Stretford and Timperley, and to obviate competition by terminating the passenger 'flyboat' service at Timperley, thus compelling 'flyboat' passengers to use the rail service between Timperley and Manchester. In return the Bridgewater Trustees received £50,000 of shares[2] in the railway company. Following agreement the name of the company was modified to the Manchester South Junction and Altrincham Railway Company and the Act of Incorporation received the royal assent on 21st July, 1845. Work on the Altrincham branch was completed and the line opened for traffic on 20th July, 1849.

Having outlined the background of this first railway to cross Timperley, this study is now only concerned with that part of the line which came within in the township's boundaries.

The Timperley section of the line is about 1300 yards long and enters the township at its north-north-east corner where the boundary is the line of the Baguley Brook. It then runs parallel with the canal until it reaches Timperley Station where it turns away from the canal in a southerly direction.

The MSJ and A Railway Company purchased a strip of land about 20 yards wide and 1300 yards long from the then owners of the land in 1847. Approximately 600 yards of this land was then part of the Riddings Hall estate (from the parish boundary at Baguley Brook to the station bridge at Park Road) and was taken out of three fields (the Little Brook Meadow, the Stable Meadow and the Windmill Field) all situated in the parish. The Riddings Hall estate then owned land in Sale and the owners also sold land in their Nearer Six Acre field, situated in Sale, to the railway. The following extract from the indenture between the MSJ and A Railway Company and the vendors is apposite:

> '... and receipting by Indenture of Release, dated 4 August, 1847 the said T. Clayton and M. Rodgett of the 1st part; Esther Shepley (Widow) since deceased of the 2nd Part; said E. Taylor of the 3rd Part and Manchester South Junction and Altrincham Railway Company of 4th Part, several pieces or parcels of land comprised in the said Indenture of Mortgage of 25 December 1838 situated in Sale and Timperley aforesaid required by the said company for the purpose of their railway and works authorised to be constructed by the Manchester South Junction Railway Company, Act, 1845 containing the whole by admeasurement 4 Acres 2 Roods and 14 Perches Statute measure or thereabouts and being part and parcel of the said fields or close of land called The Nearer Six Acre; The Little Brook Meadow; The Stable Meadow and The Windmill Field were granted and released to the said company their successors and Assigns freed and discharged from the said Mortgage debt...'[3]

The remaining strip of land (about 600 yards) from the Station Bridge to the parish boundary at Timperley Brook was held by a number of tenants on leasehold from the Earl of Stamford in 1840 (see Tithe Awards for Timperley dated June 1840) and thus it is reasonable to assume that the MSJ and A Railway purchased the railway land in this section of Timperley from the Earl of Stamford. The land purchased traversed ten fields. The table below lists these fields beginning with land nearest to Timperley Bridge and moving south-south-west.

Tithe Award No.	Description	Type of Tenure
53	Enclosed Lands	Leasehold from the Earl of Stamford
54	Lane and Cottage	Ditto
55	Canal Field	Ditto
56	Field	Ditto
57	Field	Ditto
59	Corner Field	Ditto
60	Canal Field	Ditto
61	House Field	Ditto
62	Canal Field	Samuel Starkey, Freeholder
63	Old Lane Field	Anne Hulme, Freeholder

10. Signal box and railway crossing, Deansgate Lane. Note Wyvern Cottage, the original railway house, which was built in 1848. It was probably for the crossing keeper/signalman. (Photograph taken by author, 1990.)

To obviate competition, the canal trustees terminated their passenger boat service to Manchester at Timperley[4] and boat passengers were obliged to use the railway between those two stations. The ramp road, still extant, provided access to both rail and canal for horse-drawn goods vehicles.

According to the 1876 O.S. 25 inch plan the platform was then situated adjacent to the canal basin. The 1899 O.S. 6 inch map sited the station platform in its contemporary position, which suggests the platform was relocated on its present site between 1876 and 1897.

The signal box controlling the Timperley section of line was sited adjacent to the Deansgate Lane level crossing on the canal side of the line. The signalman/level crossing keeper was accommodated in a purpose built dwelling close to it.[5] The original signal box has long since been replaced by the present box sited on the east side of the line at Deansgate Lane.

11. Railway house and bridge carrying Brooks Drive over the Stockport, Timperley and Altrincham Railway at Baguley (view looking east towards Southmoor Road). (Photograph taken by the author, 1990.)

Stationmasters of Timperley Station	
Charles Latham[6]	1849 to 1862 (?)
Robert Farrow	1863 (?) to 1889
James Warburton	1889 to 1891
Clement Latham	1892 to 1905
Thomas Broady	1906 to 1915
W. Pardoe	1916 to 1922
James Berry	1923 to 1937 (?)
William Battersby	1938 to 1942 (?)
(?) Available records inadequate to establish these dates precisely	

The Warrington and Timperley Railway

During the period 1840-60 a number of railways were constructed in the South Lancashire-North Cheshire region and especially between Manchester and Liverpool. Warrington, due to its geographical position,[7] was at the hub of most of them. Intense inter-company rivalry for traffic was the norm and the competition thus engendered had important repercussions for Timperley.

The first project to impinge on the township was the Warrington and Altrincham Junction Railway, which was constituted by an Act of Parliament dated 3rd July, 1851. It authorised a line connecting Arpley near Warrington with Timperley. On 4th August, 1853 a further Act was obtained authorising an extension of the line to Stockport and changing the name of the company to the Warrington and Stockport Railway Company. The line was opened as far as Broadheath but, due to engineering delays in bridging the canal, it was not until 1st May, 1854 that the connection to the MSJ and A line at Timperley (via a railway viaduct over the canal and an embankment sloping to the MSJ and A line) was completed. This line was closed down in 1962 and the embanked line, connecting it with the MSJ and A at Timperley, demolished.

By 1860 a mosaic of railway lines encircled Manchester. The MSJ and A Railway enabled the Manchester, Sheffield and Lincolnshire Railway (MS and L Railway) and the Great Northern Railway (GN Railway) to operate services from Manchester to Liverpool via Timperley and engendered acute rivalry with the London North Western Railway Company (LNW Railway) which regarded the rail services around Liverpool as its private preserve. The MS and L Railway Company had, by January 1863, connected its Marple line with Stockport and now successfully floated a scheme to link it with the former Warrington and Stockport line at Broadheath thus securing a direct line from Stockport to Liverpool. This line, called the Stockport, Timperley and Altrincham Railway Company, was authorised by an Act dated 22nd July 1861 and the line was opened for traffic to Deansgate Junction[8] on 1st December, 1865. It was connected with the former Warring-

12. *Bridge carrying the Warrington and Stockport Railway line, connecting Skelton Junction with Broadheath, over Deansgate Lane. (Photograph taken by the author.)*

13. *Skelton Junction (view from Moss Lane Bridge). Note the double track curve connecting with the MSJ and A Railway, the single track bridging canal (unseen) and connecting with West Timperley Station and Warrington and Stockport Railway.*

The junction of the single line with the line to Lymm (track now lifted and line closed) can be seen in centre of photograph as a white patch. (Photograph taken by the author, February 1993.)

ton and Stockport Railway Company's line at Broadheath, via Deansgate Junction, on 1st February, 1866. The railway company purchased the necessary land for the junction from Mr John Skelton (gentleman), a prominent Timperley landowner, so the junction is called Skelton Junction. His residence was Pickering Lodge.[9]

A further line connecting the Stockport, Timperley and Altrincham Railway Company line to what became the Cheshire Lines Committee Railway line, from Manchester to Liverpool, at Glazebrook was sanctioned by an Act dated 5th July, 1865. The line opened for traffic in 1873. Thus by 1875 Skelton Junction was a complete entity and formed the hub of a railway system connecting Stockport with Timperley, Altrincham, Manchester, Warrington and Liverpool and, later, Knutsford, Northwich and Chester. It also linked these places directly, by rail, with the North, Midlands and Yorkshire.

For a brief period the MS and L Railway Company operated a circular service between London Road (later Piccadilly Railway Station) and Central Station (now GMEX Centre) stations in Manchester via Stockport, using a short curve linking the ST and A Junction with the MSJ and A Railway line at Skelton Junction. It only attracted minimal traffic and was terminated in March 1880.[10]

14. *Railway houses on Moss Lane at Skelton Junction. (Photograph taken by the author, October 1990.)*

15. South side of the bridge approach. (Photograph taken by the author, 1990.)

Subsequently, in 1903, the short curve was removed.

The Stockport to Liverpool line via Glazebrook was closed to passenger traffic under the Beeching Reorganisation in 1962, and has only been open for freight traffic since then. Today the wheel has turned full circle as British Rail opened in May 1989 a passenger service between Altrincham and Stockport via Skelton Junction.

It is intriguing to learn that if the views of the township's Select Vestry members had prevailed, Timperley would never have had railway lines traversing the township as the extract from the Select Vestry minutes on p.96 shows:

30th December, 1844
Meeting at Schoolroom Moved: 'That this Township... opposes the MSJ and A and Stockport, Birkenhead and Cheshire Junction Railway Bills and all railways of any kind that shall pass through the township.'

The Select Vestry minutes and those of its successor, the Parish Council, covering the period 1847-1936, illustrate the close liaison that later developed and was maintained between the railway companies and the township.[11]

Locally, post 1970, a vast increase in traffic flow along Park Road occasioned acute traffic congestion, during business hours, in the vicinity of the bridge carrying the road over the Stockport, Altrincham and Warrington Railway. To relieve the problem a road modification scheme was begun in 1985 on that section of the road between the Triangle and Dudley Road. It involved widening the bridge, on its western side, and realigning the road to eliminate the acute bends on the approaches to it.

16. Cast iron mile post, Brooks Drive. (Photograph taken by the author, August 1982.)

94

17. A cast iron panel, which is self-explanatory, on the railway bridge carrying Brooks Drive over the Stockport and Warrington Railway line. The bridge is sited in Baguley township where it borders Timperley. Sadly the panel has been defaced by graffiti. (Photograph taken by the author, March 1987.)

Mile Post and Panel

A cast iron mile post (still extant in 1990), but largely obscured by undergrowth, is sited on the west side of Brooks Drive[12] to the south of Davenport Green Farm. The Timperley section of the Drive is now very dilapidated. The unmetalled carriageway is largely overgrown and traversed by new roads, consequent on the post-1950 housing development on its borders. The Drive connects Brooklands with Hale Barns, and is tree-lined. A similar post, now disappeared, stood on the west side of the Drive, about 100 yards north of Ridgeway Road.[13]

Notes
1. Chief Trustee of the Bridgewater Canal Company. He became the Earl of Ellesmere in 1846.
2. Returning 8½% per annum.
3. A copy of this abstract is quoted in the title deeds of a house built on the Riddings Hall estate by Mauldeth and Co. (Builders) in 1933. The house, 13 Cheam Road, was owned by my father from 1933 to 1987.
4. They embarked and disembarked at the canal basin, still extant, sited beneath Park Road bridge to join trains at the adjacent rail platform.
5. It is called Wyvern Cottage, and is still extant and lived in. A wall plaque dates it precisely as 1848.
6. Charles Latham is listed in the 1851 Census. His address was 16a Deansgate Lane, Timperley and he was born at Bunbury, Cheshire c.1810. His son, Clement, was ten years of age (according to the census) in 1851. He took over his father's old post in 1892. The Cheshire directories were consulted for most of the other tenures of office, also the Altrincham directories
7. The first point upstream where the River Mersey could be bridged.
8. The original name for Skelton Junction.
9. An 1850 Cheshire Directory contains the following description of Pickering Lodge:

   '... A handsome stuccoed residence pleasantly situated and beautified with extensive Pleasure Grounds...'

   It was originally a small tenement farm on land enclosed from Timperley Moss. John Skelton purchased it c.1845. The farmhouse was utilised as the nucleus of the residence. The house and grounds, post 1936, came into the ownership of Altrincham Borough Council who developed the grounds as a public park and recreation ground. Sadly the house, structurally unsound by then, had to be demolished. The lodgekeeper's house is still extant and occupied. (See Chapter 10.)
10. It only operated for four months.
11. See Appendix 1 for a selection of minutes appertaining to the railways.
12. Originally called Hale Road. Colloquially known as Brooks Drive after Samuel Brooks, the man who built it to connect his Brooklands estate with his house in Hale Barns.
13. Originally called Sugar Lane; O.S. 25 inch to the mile plan, 1876 edition.

APPENDIX 1
A SELECTION OF MINUTES APPERTAINING TO RAILWAYS IN TIMPERLEY PARISH

(Extracted from the Minute Books of the township's Select Vestry (1847-1867) and its successor, the Parish Council (1894-1936). The period 1868-1894 has not been researched but is available at Trafford Local Studies Centre.)

Select Vestry
1844
30th December, 1844
Meeting at Schoolroom Moved: 'That this Township... opposes the MSJ and A and Stockport, Birkenhead and Cheshire Junction Railway Bills and all railways of any kind that shall pass through the township.'

1847
30th December
Meeting considered notices from the MSJ and A Railway re alterations to be made at Timperley Bridge and its approaches.
Moved: 'Approaches to Parliament for extension of Act for alteration of bridge at Timperley over the canal be opposed until approaches thereto made more easy.'
Small committee appointed to liaise with MSJ and A and solicitors to ascertain precise plans and report back.

1848
4th September
'Committee appointed to inspect Timperley Bridge and act to best of their judgement for benefit of township.'

1851
16th January
Meeting considered: 'Subject of rates and rating of Railway.'
Agreed unanimously: 'That Overseers to instruct Mr Simpson (Select Vestry's solicitor) of intention to withdraw opposition to Railway Company with regard to assessment of line.'
Small Committee appointed: '... to wait on Railway Company and make best arrangement possible with them.'

8th March
Meeting Discussed: 'Desirability of assenting or dissenting from Level Crossing at Deansgate Lane by intended line of Warrington and Altrincham Junction Railway.'
Moved: 'Meeting does not sanction Level Crossing and a petition be presented to Parliament.'

1864
25th January
Meeting Considered: '... steps to be taken re Railway bridges to be built.' *Resolved*: 'Deposition to wait on Engineer of Stockport, Timperley and Altrincham Railway re bridges and call his attention to culvert over Fairywell Brook. Meeting wishes it to be made equal to the culvert under the MSJ and A line.'

10th February
Meeting to Consider: 'Bridge about to be built in Wash Lane as now there is possibility of Railway Company and Township coming into an arrangement.' *Proposed*: 'Committee to negotiate with Railway Company re bridge in Wash Lane.'

24th March
Moved: 'Attention of J. Kirkman (Secretary of MSJ and Altrincham) be called to dangerous state of Level Crossing near Timperley Station and hope he will see propriety of placing man at gates.' Meeting pleased to observe provision already made to appoint a gateman.

Minute Book ends.

Parish Council
1895

1st February

'Deputation to Railway Company appointed to confer with representative of Cheshire Lines Committee re footpath at Level Crossing connecting Grove and Wash Lanes.'

8th March

Deputation (above) reported back re meeting with CLC on 1st March '... Considered proposed deviation of path between Grove and Wash Lane would be a public improvement and subject to agreement being signed offered £20 towards expenses. Chairman and Clerk appointed 'to meet Sir W. Brooks' agent Mr Earle to discuss proposed deviation and enlist his support.'

1st April

Proposed: 'Meeting approves diversion of footpath between Wash Lane and Lyme Grove to do away with level crossing over Cheshire Lines Railway.'[1] Motion carried.

14th June

'Following meeting with Mr Earle, Clerk instructed to write Mr Burgess to forward estimate of cost of path.' *Proposed:* 'Following receipt of plan of proposed alteration of path from Mr Earle deputation instructed to continue business re path.' *Proposed:* 'Letter to Secretary MSJ and A Railway advising Level Crossing gates near Timperley Station are locked during the night and being a public road requests it must be made available to public for traffic at all times.'

10th July

'Question of diversion of path Lyme Grove-Wash Lane be brought to attention of Knutsford Rural District Council and sanction obtained for same if possible.'

2nd August

Resolved: 'Would be a public improvement to divert existing path between Lyme Grove-Wash Lane to adjoining occupation road and over railway bridge. Steps to be taken to carry out same.' Carried. Letter from Secretary MSJ and A re level crossing: 'Clerk instructed to write to Cheshire Lines Committee insisting on access to road along canal at all times.'

4th October

Letter from MSJ and A read: 'Clerk to write insisting on public access at all time to road alongside of canal and requiring copy of plans of proposed alteration of roadway for approval before work commenced.' *Resolved:* Confirm 2nd August decision (Lyme Grove-Wash Lane path). 'Clerk to consult Altrincham magistrates re steps necessary for completion.'

6th December

Letter from Secretary MSJ and A advising arrangements made to put extra man in signal box at Level Crossing so that road alongside of canal open day and night.

NB. The original path connected Grove Lane (before Lyme Grove was built) with Wash Lane. The new railway line traversed it and pedestrians had then to walk across the railway line when using the path. The path was thus diverted in a westerly direction from Lyme Grove and thence over the rail bridge of accommodation road to join Wash Lane opposite Heyes Lane.

1896

7th February

Agreement with MSJ and A (Wash Lane-Lyme Grove path) received from Nichols Lindsell and Harris Solicitors – duly signed and returned by Council.

21st April

Committee appointed to superintend construction of path Wash Lane-Lyme Grove and complete as soon as possible.

1923

20th April

Reported: Path over railway bridge (Lyme Grove) needs repair – Paths Committee to inspect and report back. Sanction obtained for repairs to roadway over two railway bridges in Wash Lane.

(Nb. The bridge over the railway, adjacent recreation ground, was extensively widened and the road approaches straightened out in 1985.)

1924

11th January

'Clerk reported steps and handrail leading from railway bridge on Moss Lane had given way: railway company notified.

Letter from railway company... stated considered part of public footpath and Parish Council responsible from repairs.

Resolved: railway company to be informed path is on railway company land and had always been maintained by railway company. Council does not hold itself responsible for maintenance of steps or path.'

1927

4th March

'Complaints made that new train service on MSJ and A inconvenient for Timperley residents between 7-30 and 8-30 am. Clerk instructed to write to MSJ and A advising them of complaints.'

22nd April

'Letter from MSJ and A stating train laid on departing Altrincham 7-46 am; Timperley arrive 7-49 am; Stretford arrive 8 am.'

1933

7th July

'Letter read from railway company re gap in fence on rail embankment at Timperley Station suggesting Parish Council consider erection of flight of steps up the slope. Special meeting convened to consider suggestion.'

21st July

'Special meeting held at Timperley Station. Following inspection of bridge and discussion of provision of footpaths on both sides of it. *Resolved:* Cheshire County Council's attention be drawn to "death trap" (*sic*) and Parish Council suggests bridge be widened on shops' side to enable proper footpaths to be provided on both sides of roadway.'

9
TIMPERLEY IN 1838

'O, call back yesterday, bid time return.'

Shakespeare

During the second quarter of the nineteenth century, by virtue of an Act of Parliament, Tithe Commissioners for England and Wales were appointed and empowered to commute tithes (hitherto paid in kind to the Church of England) into a rent charge levied on all landholders. The Act was administered at ecclesiastical parish level, each township in a parish being assessed separately.

To effect this assessment it was necessary to

- produce an accurate plan of each township delineating every field, building, lane, etc., and number each unit for reference;

- draw up detailed schedules listing each and every unit of territory owned by a landowner, its area and the rent charge assessed; also, where applicable, the name(s) of the occupier(s) of land rented from a landholder.

From this wealth of documented information can be derived an accurate and detailed description of the economy, land use and demography of a particular township at a precise point in time.

In the case of Timperley township the plan and schedule were completed in the space of ten months and provisionally agreed on 21st November, 1838 by the Tithe Commissioners.[1] The assessors for Timperley were James Cawley and Thomas Smith.

Area of township		1637.8 acres[2]
Population	1834	732
	1838	890
	1841	947[3]
(By interpolation)		

The general picture, created by the Tithe Schedules, is of a compact, largely self-sufficient, agricultural township traversed on its western boundary by the Manchester-Chester Road and the Bridgewater Canal and by the Stockport-Warrington turnpike road traversing the central north-east/south-west axis of the township.[4]

The hub of the village clustered around the Church Inn[5] which stood on the south side of the central turnpike.[6] A few meagre lanes and paths connected the village centre to the outlying parts of the township. The village was, as yet, not connected to the burgeoning railway systems.

1555 acres, 95% of total, were cultivated.

Arable	876 acres
Meadow/Pasture	622 acres
Common	4 acres
Market Gardens	26 acres
Cottages with gardens	55 acres
Bridgewater Canal	8 acres
Private Residences and Grounds	8 acres
Roads, Lanes, Woodlands and Waste	about 40 acres
Tradesmen's premises	about 2 acres

Number	Landowner	Farmer (Occupier)	Area to Nearest Whole Acre
1	Elizabeth Taylor	Samuel Smith	93
2	James Wood	Thomas Carr	146
3	Devisees of the late James Massey	John Marsland	57 (D)
4	Joseph Hodgkinson	James Barton	48
5	Henry Newbury	Charles Leigh	42
6	Samuel Starkey and William Pass	Samuel Starkey	4
7	William Stelfox	John and Amos Rogerson	60
8	Mary Worthington	Samuel Hulme	(L) 44 (D)
9	Mary Worthington and William Coppock	Thomas Rogerson	(L) 35 (D)
10	William Marsland	Joseph Cookson	45
11	Thomas Barton	Samuel Rowbotham	part (L) 34
12	William D. Cooper and wife	John Dobb	65
13	Goostrey Church (part) and John Tetlow	James Hulme	44(D)
14	John Barratt	James Barlow	48
15	John Barratt	William Davenport	53
16	Elizabeth Berry	Herself	52
17	Joseph Atherton	William Kinsey	24 (L)
18	Martha Bridgewood	Sarah Frank (Pelican)	20
19	William Cluley	John Howarth	25 (L)
20	Devisees of P. Fletcher	William Renshaw	20
21	William Goulden	John Chorlton (Hare and Hounds)	26
22	William Kemp	Himself	52 (L)
23	John Hankinson	William Leigh	19 (L)
24	Anne Hulme	Herself	20
25	James Holland	William Brown	5
26	William D. Cooper	Thomas Roberts	15
27	John Paulden	John Sherlock	43
28	John Paulden	James Thomason	12 (L)

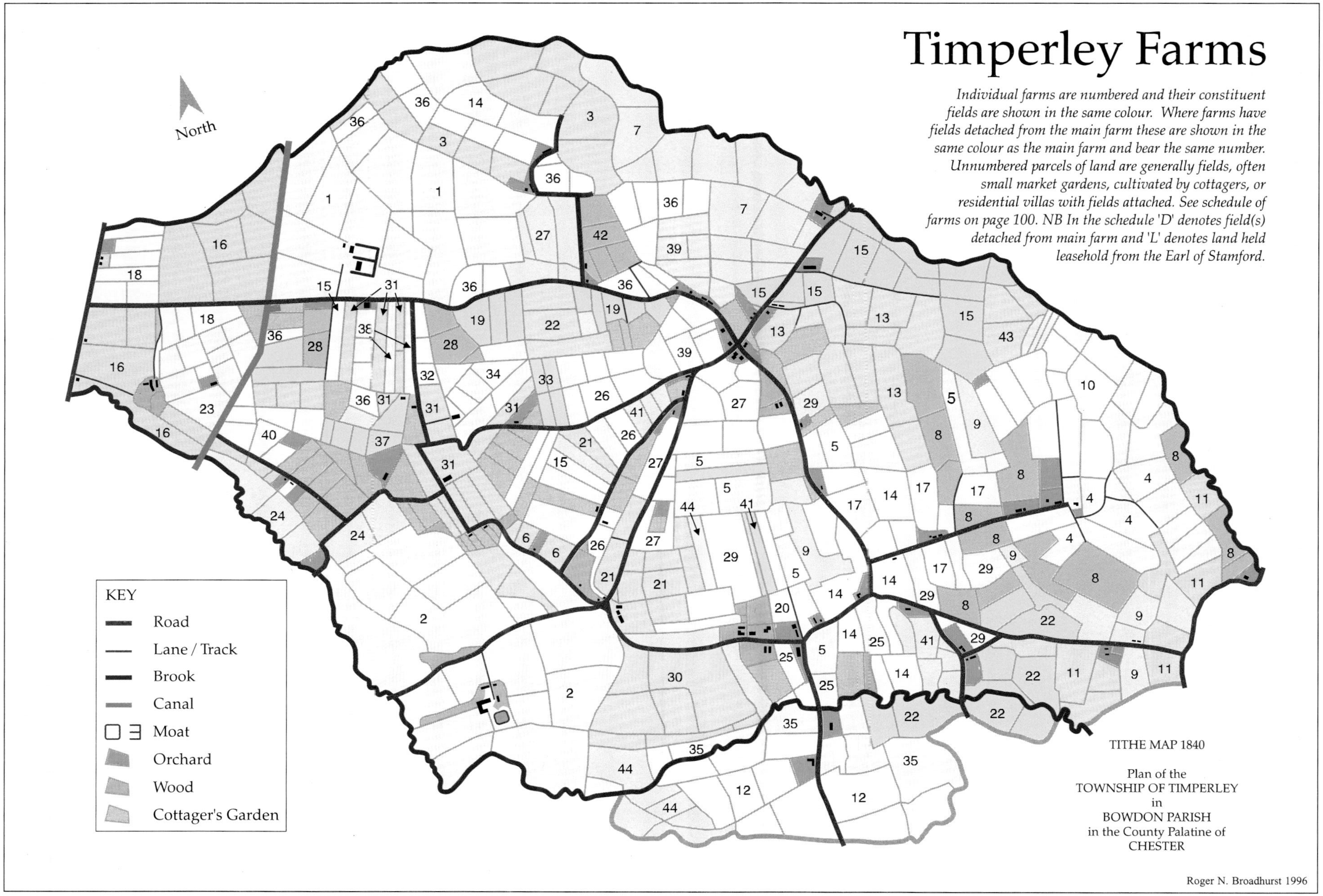

Timperley Farms

Individual farms are numbered and their constituent fields are shown in the same colour. Where farms have fields detached from the main farm these are shown in the same colour as the main farm and bear the same number. Unnumbered parcels of land are generally fields, often small market gardens, cultivated by cottagers, or residential villas with fields attached. See schedule of farms on page 100. NB In the schedule 'D' denotes field(s) detached from main farm and 'L' denotes land held leasehold from the Earl of Stamford.

North

TITHE MAP 1840

Plan of the
TOWNSHIP OF TIMPERLEY
in
BOWDON PARISH
in the County Palatine of
CHESTER

Roger N. Broadhurst 1996

KEY

Road	
Lane / Track	
Brook	
Canal	
Moat	
Orchard	
Wood	
Cottager's Garden	

Map 4. Timperley Farms, based on the Timperley Tithe Map 1840 in the Cheshire Record Office, ref. EDT 397/2.

29	William Pass	James Garner	24
30	William Pass	John Kaye	36
31	William Pass, Robert Woodall and John Ridg	Thomas Hulme	(D) 30 part (L)
32	Mary Pearson	William Lamb	4
33	James Pitts	Himself	5
34	James Taylor	Joseph Morgan	14
35	John Warburton	Himself	27 (L)
36	William Whitelegg and Ringway Chapel	Himself	46 part (L)
37	Elizabeth Taylor	Esther Aldcroft	8
38	George Baxter	Mary Burgess	11
39	John Barratt	Anne Renshaw	11
40	Jeremiah Brundrett	Himself	11 (L)
41	George Burgess	James Garner	4
42	John Marsland and Devisees of J. Massey	John Marsland	57
43	Robert Marsland	Himself	9
44	William Pass	Himself	24
			Total 1472

Note: Lord Stamford had 290 acres of his Timperley lands let on leasehold terms as follows: to farmers 276 acres; to cottagers, etc., 14 acres.

Of the forty-two farms listed, nine exceeded 50 acres and two of these, Riddings Hall and Timperley Hall, each had about 100 acres or more. Thirteen were between 25 and 50 acres and fourteen between 10 and 25 acres. Analysis of the two largest farms, cultivating about 230 acres between them, reveals they held thirty-four fields in total. In 1838 they were farmed as follows:

Meadow/Pasture	12 fields =	98 acres
Arable	22 fields =	130 acres
Vegetable Gardens		about 2 acres

The land use revealed by the 15% sample above (see map and schedule on pp.100-103) suggests that the smaller farms pursued a similar pattern of cultivation and it is therefore reasonable to state that the township was mixed dairy and arable. The main crops were wheat, barley and oats but they also grew root vegetables and had vegetable gardens and orchards for their domestic needs.

On the fringe of the township, and principally on the moss land in the Deansgate and Brook Lanes area, there were a number of small market gardens producing cash crops for local markets,[7] catering especially for the burgeoning urban populations of Manchester, Altrincham and Stockport.[8] Two of the farmers were also publicans.[9]

The demographic statistics below illustrate accurately the various occupations followed by the population in 1838.[10]

Population			
Males	450	Females	440
No. of Families	170	No. of Persons in Families	760
Others	130		

(From the Tithe Schedules and 1841 Census.)

Occupations			
Farmers/Market Gardeners	55	Servants (male and female)[11]	55
Blacksmiths	2	Shoemakers (including apprentices)	8
Tailors	2	Schoolteachers	2
Housewives/Widows	140	Stonemasons	2
Agricultural Labourers (15+)	100	Children (under 15)[12]	400
Wheelwrights	4	Joiners/Sawyers	3
Brickmakers	3	Butchers/Grocers	2
Independent and/or Unclassified	80	Other Tradesmen and/or Apprentices	32

Most of the tradesmen occupied business premises (often their home too) in the vicinity of the village centre. The blacksmiths and wheelwrights had premises on what is now Aimson Road (Vantage Garages car lot today is the approximate site of their workshops). The shoemakers mostly occupied cottages on Wash Lane[13] and Thorley Lane. Often the same families (for example, father/son/brothers) are shown, by the records, as following the same trade.

In 1838 the schoolhouse was sited on the library side of Stockport Road.[14] The only listed place of worship in the township was a Methodist chapel sited at the corner of Heyes Lane and Wash Lane.[15]

Only nine large houses, standing in their own grounds, are listed; for the most part they would be inhabited by families of independent means. Apart from one, in the vicinity of the Chester Road, named Timperley Lodge,[16] all the rest were sited near to the turnpike road.[17] Some of them could justly be described as mansions (see Appendix 1).

Apart from the farmhouses, market gardeners' house and private houses, the great majority of the population were accommodated in 109 cottages[18] each of which would probably have an average occupancy rate of five or six. Most of these cottages were situated in the Deansgate lane area or in the vicinity of the village centre. Apart from the two major roads traversing the township there were few thoroughfares and none of them could be classified as roads. They consisted of Wash, Heyes, Thorley, Wood, Clay, Green, Sugar, Moss, Brook, Deansgate, Bloomsbury and Grove Lanes. Only Thorley, Wood and Deansgate Lanes are actually named on the Tithe Map. It is probable that in 1838 the others were little more than paths giving access to farmers' fields from the turnpike road.

The large number of inhabitants (about 37% of the total population) residing in the Deansgate/Brook Lanes area of the township were living in the most unhealthy part of the township as it was largely reclaimed moss land and thus low lying. Doubtless dampness in the houses would be a problem and in periods of prolonged wet weather flooding of houses near Timperley Brook would be a further hazard.[19] One of the residents, listed as occupying a house close to Timperley Lodge, was a Dr J. Webster. If he was a doctor of medicine he would have many patients from this area needing treatment for a variety of complaints occasioned by poor housing in an unhealthy location. However, whether or not they could afford his fees is another matter.

Flooding was a periodic hazard for householders in this part of the township until the early 1980s, their hardships being graphically reported in the *Altrincham and Bowdon Guardian*. In the 1980s a comprehensive flood abatement scheme was completed adjacent to Salisbury Road, West Timperley, which eradicated the problem permanently.

It is interesting to note the gross rent charge levied on the township by the Tithe Commissioners:

To Vicar of Bowdon	£49 0s 0d
To Lord Bishop of Chester	£225 17s 0d
Total	£274 17s 0d

This value was expressed in terms of what the land would have to produce to realise the rent charge:

Cereal	Price per Bushel	Bushels
		(to 5 decimal places)
		(bushel 8 gallons
		dry goods or 36.4 litres)
Wheat	7s 0d	260.98516
Barley	3s 11½d	462.90527
Oats	2s 9d	666.30303

Old Farm Buildings

18. Manor Farm, Ridgeway Road

Sited at the eastern end of Ridgeway Road (formerly Sugar Lane), it was built c.1860-1865. This was one of the three largest farms in the township. Its lands extended on each side of Brooks Drive. It replaced an earlier building possibly dating back to the sixteenth century. (Photograph taken by the author, 1990.) It was leased by the Civil Service Sports' Club. When their lease expired it was empty for some time. Now it is leased by the Ridgeway Sports' and Social Club (1995).

19. The Barn of Sugar Lane Farm

Sited on the north side of Ridgeway Road at its eastern end, the barn was probably built in the late eighteenth century. It is now utilised as a garage called Ridgeway Motors. It was converted to its present use c.1970. (Photograph taken by the author, 1990.)

20. Delahays Farm Barn, Green Lane

Sited on the west side of Green Lane and built pre-1876, possibly in the first half of the nineteenth century, post 1950 the barn was converted to residential use, possibly flats. Note the addition of windows. Brick infilling (see centre frontage of photograph) suggests access to the barn was afforded originally through large threshing barn doors. (Photograph taken by the author, October 1990.)

21. Warburton's Farm, Green Lane

This is situated on the eastern side of Green Lane and on the southern side of Timperley Brook. The house, now extensively modernised, is close to, but on the other side of the road, to Delahays Farm. Branches of the family are still resident in the township including one branch who run a flourishing garden centre on part of the farm lands. (Photograph taken by the author, 1990.)

Notes

1. A supplementary agreement on arrangements for the first payment of rent charges was signed on 28th November, 1838.

2. O.S. map dated 1872-6. The Tithe Commissioners assessed acreage at '1628 Acres 2 Roads 26 Perches'.

3. Pigot's *Directory for Cheshire* 1834 and 1841 Census.

4. The Toll House stood at the corner of Moss Lane approximately on the site of the present Ringway Motors Petrol Station.

5. One of the three inns then extant, see Chapter 11.

6. Site now occupied by Roger Dean, Estate Agents.

7. Especially rhubarb and strawberries.

8. Transport would be by horse and cart.

9. The Pelican and the Hare and Hounds (see Chapter 11 for more information on these inns).

10. By 1841 over 37% (about 350) of the population were resident in the Deansgate/Brook Lanes area.

11. Often the term meant farm workers.

12. Those aged ten plus probably employed.

13. Vicinity of what is now Dudley Road.

14. Approximately opposite the site of Vantage Garage showroom, on the corner of what is now Baker Street.

15. The old Methodist chapel on Stockport Road was built in 1846/47 (see Chapter 11).

16. Timperley Lodge is still extant on Attenburys Lane. A complete history of the house is contained in a 'History of Timperley' (up to c.1935) by Lt. Col. Newton (Trafford Local Studies Centre) unpublished.

17. See Appendix 1 for details.

18. At least some of these cottages still stand, for example, Pott's Cottage, Grove Lane (c.1834) and a block of four cottages in Sugar Lane, Numbers 12, 14, 16 and 18.

19. Culverting the brook beneath the canal did not help.

20. See the article by Robert Warburton, published in the *Timperley Independent Free Newspaper*, dated 25th June, 1993.

PRIVATE HOUSES LISTED IN
THE 1838 TITHE SCHEDULE

Note: the Tithe Schedules, with the possible exceptions of the two halls, do not list the names of the house. The names annotated are those that the houses are called on the 1876 O.S. 25 inch to the mile plan.

Name of House	Location	Owner	Occupier	Size: A	R	P
Timperley Hall[1]	Stockport Rd: Sited some 100 yds from road frontage	Mr J. Wood	T. Carr	1	0	2
Riddings Hall[2]	Wash Lane: (Park Rd) Sited some 40 yds from north side of rd, frontage & approx. opposite St. Hugh's R.C. School	Mrs E. Taylor	S. Smith	3	0	32
Oakmount[3] (Parkfield) (O.S. 1876)	Wood Lane: south side – 100 yds west of Green Lane	Mr J. Holland	William Brown	2	0	15
Oaklands (O.S. 1876)	Wood Lane, north side about 200 yds west of Green Lane	Mr J. Kaye	Himself	1	1	33
Rose Cottage (O.S. 1876)	Wood Lane: north side about 70 yds west of Green Lane North	Mr J. Bruckshaw	James Reynolds	0	2	06
Larkhill	Thorley Lane: west side about 165 yds south of Thorley Lane junction.	Mr W. Chambers	Himself	2	1	07
Timperley Lodge[4]	Chester Rd: south side. Sited some 100 yds from road frontage, opposite South Trafford College	Mrs E. Berry	Dr J. Webster	1	3	38
House	Sited in grounds of Timperley Lodge	Mrs E. Berry	Herself	0	0	39
The Hollins[5]	Stockport Rd. Sited at side of present Stelfox Av. and some way from road frontage	Mr W. Stelfox	? Whitelegg	0	2	25
House (O.S. 1876)	Stockport Rd. Sited on west corner of its junction with Park Rd (Wash Lane)	Mr J. Chorlton	Mary Withington	0	2	25
Brook House	Brook Lane: sited on north side, about 100 yds west of Deansgate Lane	Mr J. Taylor	P. Dumville	0	0	37

Notes

1. The present Hall replaced a mediaeval moated hall c.1800-10. It is now a hotel.

2. The Hall was used as a farmhouse prior to demolition c.1960. The site has now been redeveloped.

3. The building was renamed Parkfield, probably post-1900. For many years, probably post-1930, it housed a boys' remand home until 1991/2. The house was then demolished and redeveloped with an estate of c.20 detached houses (1994/5). The access road from Wood Lane is named Oldbrook Fold.

4. There is a detailed history of this house and estate from its origins in the eighteenth century up till 1935 in 'Timperley Past and Present' (unpublished manuscript) by Lt. Col. Newton.

5. The listing description for the Hollins, the next house and Brook House is not precise and it is possible they were merely smallholdings.

10

TIMPERLEY: ITS METAMORPHOSIS, POST 1838

'Change is inevitable. In a progressive country change is constant.'

Benjamin Disraeli

1850-1900 Period

The previous chapter portrayed the wholly agricultural profile and lifestyle of the village at a precise point in time. If the cutting of the Bridgewater Canal section across its northern fringe and the construction of about four private mansions during the first decades of the nineteenth century is excluded, the township in 1838 presented much the same appearance as it had in 1700. The decade 1840-50 marked its apogee as an archetypal English village. Circa 1850 an era of radical change was inaugurated, which, in the course of less than a century, transformed the township from a small agricultural area to a densely populated dormitory suburb with some industrial development in its north-west sector. 'The Locust Years' is perhaps the apposite phrase to describe the rate at which agricultural land was devoured by developers. Most of the township's 1638 acres have been developed and the revolution is now almost complete. The few remaining untouched acres will doubtless fall victim to the bulldozer before the dawn of the twenty-first century.

The factors which occasioned this economic and social metamorphosis were principally geographical (i.e. proximity to a large urban conurbation; an ideal topography for ease of development; excellent road and rail communications).[1] The comparative statistics below illustrate vividly the radical changes made during the 'Locust Years'.

ITEMS	1838	1987
Total Acreage of Village	1638	c.125 to 150 (undeveloped)[2]
Acreage farmed	1555	c.50 to 75
Roads	15	270 plus
Houses	c.180	8200 plus[3]
Agricultural employees (including wives and children over 10)	c.550	50 to 100
Population	c.900	24,950 (1983)

The pace and scale of housing development has been spasmodic rather than gradual, periods of relatively little interspersed with periods of intensive building construction.

During the four decades 1811-51 the housing stock only increased from 121 to 201 and included a number of private mansions located principally in the Wood Lane/Thorley Lane area. A few cottages were also built.[4]

Following the village's connection to the railway system in 1847, its rural environment became attractive as a domicile for professional people, as commuting to their places of work was now a practical proposition. Thus a demand for residential development burgeoned and the period 1851-1901 witnessed the first phase of housing construction in the township, the metamorphosis had begun. It was mainly concentrated on, or adjacent to, the section of Park Road between its junction with Moss Lane and Manchester Road, Stockport Road between its junction with Moss Lane and Park Road and what is now the Woodlands Parkway area.[5] Some rows of terraced houses were also built and created new roads during the latter half of the period (1875-1900).[6]

1900-1925 Period

This period witnessed a gradual, albeit slow, increase of population, averaging about fifty per annum. Thus housing development was minimal and largely restricted to terraced properties located principally in the Deansgate Lane and Park Road north areas. In the process, some ten to fifteen new roads were created.

The Parish Council, however, was cognizant of a future demand for housing in the township as the Parish Council minutes, quoted below, reveal. They were the precursors of developments which transformed the face of the township during the inter-war years.

1920

12 November

'Parish Council Deputation attended Bucklow Rural District Council, 21st September to discuss land acquisition at Skelton Junction... to purchase 16 acres plus farmhouse and five cottages... Housing Inspector stated scheme too large for Timperley and suggested census of housing needs to be taken. Cost of site averaged £250 per acre and Parish Council considered price should not exceed £200 per acre.'

1921

14th January

'Parish Council Deputation attended Bucklow Rural District Council, 11th January to consider report re Census of Housing Requirements. Report stated... Houses required by people working but not residing in Timperley – 51; Written applications received for 26 houses; People in Lodgings required – 30 houses; Others – 3; Total required 110; Plus normal requirements of Timperley in next three years estimated – 150 giving overall total of 260.'

'Reported Tenders considered that day for 25 Houses of "B" type on Heyes Lane Estate. Estimated cost per house on lowest tender £1130. Considered exorbitant. Committee resolved not to proceed. Deputation expressed opinion it was unnecessary to acquire further land in Timperley for housing until Heyes Lane site fully utilised. Bucklow Rural District Council informed of decision.'

1926

21st May

'Reported Bucklow Rural District Council to proceed with Housing Scheme for thirty houses of Non Parlour type at Heyes Lane (63 applicants had applied for them of whom 26 were Timperley residents – good demand also for Parlour type houses). Bucklow Rural District Council decided all houses should be of Non Parlour type.'

'Parish council resolved that in its opinion houses to be built under Housing Acts in Heyes Lane should include a fair proportion of Parlour type houses having regard to character of existing houses in locality and the demands for this type of housing.'

10th September

'Letter from Bucklow Rural District Council, re Heyes Lane Housing Scheme: Bucklow Rural District Council had resolved not to depart from decision made: also letter from Ministry of Health saying following consideration of Parish Council's representations of May 22nd he would not withhold sanction to Bucklow Rural District Council proposals for 30 Non Parlour type Houses.' Parish Council formally resolved that it regretted the decision as it considered it ignored the needs of applicants for Parlous type of house.'

It would appear that these houses were the first council houses to be built in the township.

1925-1939 Period

A succinct Parish Council minute, dated 10th May, 1929, sets the scene for this period. It quotes a report, received from a committee of Cheshire County Council, in response to a complaint by Timperley Parish Council, re the standard of highway maintenance in the township by Bucklow Rural District Council, the local highway authority. It refers to:

'... the amount of building development in the township over the past five years with consequent heavy traffic due to the haulage of materials to sites causing damage to road surfaces...'

and

'... the breaking up of road surfaces for the necessary Power, Water and Sewerage connections to houses...'

During this period Timperley experienced one of the two most intensive phases of housing construction in its history and in the process hundreds of acres of agricultural land were converted to residential use.

Between 1925 and 1929 development was limited to a number of relatively small areas. Based on the evidence of contemporary street directories and voters' lists, they included:

A NEW HOUSE SENSATION

YOU CAN NOW BUY A SUPERIOR
MAULDETH MODERN HOME
FOR THE STARTLING PRICE OF

£325

DEPOSIT ONLY £22·12·0

Balance on Mortgage to approved purchasers £302 8s. 0d.

TOTAL WEEKLY INCLUSIVE ESTIMATED COST **13'1** **CLEAR**
Everything in · General Rates, Water Rate. Mortgage and Interest & Chief 13/1 Weekly ALL IN.

No Stamp Duty • No Legal Charges • No Mortgage Charges • No Other Fees and No Extras

These 3 BEDROOMED MAULDETH HOUSES

have a Square Hall, Large Living Room, 19 ft. in length, Separate Bath and W.C. Scullery with Bay Window, Separate Larder, Coal house, Bay Windows at front and Good Gardens. Only finest quality materials used in construction. Choice locality - not merely a builder's plot - really charmingly residential.

At such a small outlay and including cost of travelling to town, it is definitely cheaper to own your own Mauldeth Home at Timperley than to rent a house in Manchester.

- **NUMBER TO BE**
- **BUILT STRICTLY**
- **LIMITED** •

All terms are exactly as advertised here - no second Mortgages and no Extras whatever. Now you know all the facts.

SEE THE SPECIMEN HOUSE NOW READY FOR YOUR INSPECTION
MAULDETHS·LTD
Riddings Hall Estate, Park Road, Timperley.
Immediately outside Timperley Station.

1933 leaflet for Mauldeth homes. (Original document in author's possession.)

RIDDINGS HALL ESTATE,

Riddings Road, Park Road, Timperley.

Park Road Bus Stop (Manchester to Altrincham Buses).
Second Road on left past Timperley Station. Electric Railway from Oxford Road).

Financial Particulars, "1934" Type Houses.

PRICE - - £325.

	£	s.	d.
Deposit - - -	22	12	0
Building Society Mortgage,	302	8	0
(To Approved Purchasers)			
	£325	0	0

Estimated Total Annual Cost.

	£	s	d
Mortgage repayable at the rate of £1 16s. per lunar month, inclusive of Interest	23	8	0
Estimated Nett Assessment for Rates, £12—present Rates being 8/5 in the £	5	1	0
Annual Water Rate, based on the estimated nett rateable assessment at 1/6 in the £	0	18	0
Annual Chief Rent, say	5	0	0
The Estimated Annual Cost is therefore	£34	7	0

Being an Estimated Weekly Outlay of only 13s. 2d.
No Stamp Duty, Legal or Mortgage Charges.

Builders = = Mauldeth's Ltd.,

Estate Office, Park Road, Timperley.

Phone —SALe 2606.

1933 leaflet advertising new houses. (Original document in author's possession.)

No. 2534

BUCKLOW RURAL DISTRICT COUNCIL.

WATER CERTIFICATE.

Local Government Act, 1894.   56 & 57 Vict., c. 73.
PUBLIC HEALTH (WATER) ACT, 1878.   41 & 42 Vict., c. 25, s. 6.

Township of *Timperley*,

Plan No. *2118*

Date of approval of Plan *29th June 1933*

Owner *Messrs Meredith's Ltd.*

To *Messrs Meredith's Ltd.*
of *Estate Office Park Road, Timperley*

Whereas the Dwelling-house *Situate in Chear Road Timperley as No. 13*

in the Rural District of Bucklow, in the County of Chester, has been erected, or pulled down to (or below) the ground floor, and rebuilt, after the date of the commencement of the Public Health (Water) Act, 1878, namely, on or about the *11th* day of *Dec.* 19*33*, and is provided with such supply of Water as is hereinafter mentioned: *from the mains of the Manchester Corporation*

The Rural District Council of Bucklow, **hereby Certify** in pursuance of the said Act, that there is provided within a reasonable distance of the said Dwelling-house such an available supply of wholesome Water as appears to them, on the report of their Sanitary Inspector, to be sufficient for the consumption and use for domestic purposes for the inmates of such Dwelling-house.

Given by the said District Council, this *13th* day of *December*, 19*33*.

Renshaw
Sanitary Inspector.

NOTE.—All Communications with regard to Water Certificates to be made in writing and addressed to—
The Sanitary Inspector, 27, Station Buildings, Altrincham.

Water certificate for a house on the Riddings Hall estate. (Original document in author's possession.)

Claremont Drive	The Crescent	Dalveen Drive
Foxhall Road	Mossgrove Road	Thorley Drive
The Triangle	Greenway Road (Part of)	Sylvan Avenue (Part of)
Grange Road	Park Road*	
*Some houses, mostly between Riddings and Greenway Roads.		

The necessary authorisation for housing development in the area (of which Timperley was a constituent unit) was provided by a Ministry of Health order approving proposals for development in connection with the North Cheshire Regional Planning Scheme. It authorised the local authority concerned[7] to grant permission for the development of estates and building schemes '... to proceed in conformity with proposals in the approved statement for the purpose of protecting development and building from the risk of removal or alteration...'

Prospective developers now had 'the green light' and they took full advantage of their opportunities. Between 1930 and 1939 a number of large housing estates were developed in the township by various development companies. The principal areas they developed are lands bounded by:

> Wellington Road, Stockport Road and Woodlands Parkway;
> Deansgate Lane, Moss Lane and the Cheshire Lines Railway;
> Thorley Lane, Wood Lane and Shaftesbury Avenue;
> Stockport Road, Aimson Road, Shaftesbury Avenue and Thorley Lane;
> Lands adjacent to Brook Lane;
> Lands adjacent to the east and west sides of Park Road.[8]

A feature of these developments was what can only be described as the 'bargain basement' cost of housing in the 1930s. Semi-detached properties were bought for £325 and good detached houses could be obtained for £550.[9] During the brief but enormous house price boom of the late 1980s these houses sold at between 100 and 150 times their initial cost.

1945-1985 Period

The second intensive phase of housing development in Timperley occurred during the period 1945-1960 and was a direct consequence of the amalgamation of the village with Altrincham in 1937. In common with many other local authorities the borough was faced with an acute housing shortage in the immediate post-war years. Its principal causes were three-fold:

- A virtual cessation of construction during the period 1938-1945.

- A slum clearance requirement in the old Victorian terraced housing areas in Altrincham.

- A population boom in the borough fuelling the demand for housing.

Radical action was required if the problem was to be surmounted within a reasonable time. In its wisdom the borough council resolved to utilise land in Timperley for the main part of its public housing programme.

Its first major development was the Grange council estate, adjacent to Heyes Lane, which was built c.1945-8.[10] This was followed by the largest housing estate in the borough when the Broomwood council estate, west of Brooks Drive, was constructed during the period 1952-1959. Many Altrincham families were moved into the estate when their old terraced properties were demolished, many young married couples were also housed on the estate.[11]

Post-1960 development has been largely confined to the private sector. The principal developments have been on land east of Brooks Drive on the Baguley boundary, and include the Maunders estate and further council housing centred on Redbrook Road. There have been a number of small private developments, mostly restricted to schemes of about twenty-five to seventy-five units and usually limited to one road or drive. They have infilled the numerous small plots available for development, usually on the perimeters of pre-war housing estates.[12]

If the golf links, cricket ground, public parks and recreation grounds, and playing fields of private clubs[13] are excluded plus land scheduled in the Green Belt, then one can state that the few acres still remaining will most probably have been developed before the end of the twentieth century and metamorphosis will be complete.

The housing stock is varied and contains examples of the different styles built since the beginning of the nineteenth century. Many examples of early Victorian detached and terraced properties are still extant.[14] Late Victorian terraced properties are quite numerous.[15] Between the wars detached and semi detached houses on large housing estates were the vogue. Post-1960 development, whilst continuing the provision of detached and semi-detached types of houses, has witnessed a trend towards bungalows, blocks of flats, housing association units and, latterly, small blocks of two storeyed apartments designed for retired couples.[16]

Houses built in the Nineteenth Century

22.Parkfield House

This mansion stood in its own grounds with a frontage to Wood Lane, between what are now Laurel Drive and Faulkner Drive. It was built in the 1830s and for over a century was named 'Oakmount'. In 1838 it was owned by Mr J. Holland and occupied by Mr William Brown (see 1841 census and 1876 O.S. 25 inch plan). In 1948 the house was purchased by the Church of England Temperance Society and the premises used as a Boys' Probation Hostel. The new owner renamed the house 'Parkfield'. In December 1992 the house and site were sold and the hostel closed down. In 1994 the site was re-developed with c.20 large detached houses. The developer has named this new estate 'Oldbrook Manor' and the access road Oldbrook Fold. The photographs feature the western façade of the house which stood at right angles to Wood Lane. (Photograph taken by the author, October 1990.)

23. Parkfield just prior to demolition. (Photograph taken by the author, November 1992.)

24. Athol Villa

Sited on the north side of Bloomsbury Lane near its junction with Moss Lane, Athol Villa was built before 1876. (Photograph taken by the author, 1990.)

25. Yew Tree Farm

Formerly the premises of 'Freshnest', a greengrocer's shop, was located behind this house. Parts of this farmhouse dated from the eighteenth century, when it was owned by the Chorlton family, but most of it dated from the nineteenth century. It was demolished, along with 'Freshnest', in February 1996 to make way for sheltered housing. (Photograph taken by the author, February 1993.)

26. Vale Cottage, Stockport Road

Vale Cottage, Stockport Road, was built before 1840 and is possibly eighteenth century. In the 1841 Census it was occupied by Samuel Hill, dancing master, his wife, his six children and two other children.(Photograph taken by the author, 1990.)

27. Farm Cottages, Ridgeway Road

These cottages, 12 to 18 Ridgeway Road, date from before 1840. For many years water could be obtained from a well sited in the garden on the left of the block. Ridgeway Road was originally called Sugar Lane. New residents, in houses built c.1935, successfully petitioned the council to have it renamed. (Photograph taken by the author, 1990.)

28. Wyvern Cottage, Deansgate Lane

This was built in 1848 by the MSJ and A Railway Company, probably to house a crossing keeper/signalman. It was bought from British Rail in 1983. Since then the owner has renovated and extended the cottage. (Photograph taken by the author, 1990.)

29. Potts Cottage, Grove Lane

Built 1834, it was probably the home, in the Victorian era, of a prominent Methodist family of that name. (Photograph taken by the author, 1990.)

30. Cottages in Moss Lane

These cottages, which were built prior to 1876, are sited near the junction of Moss Lane with Mossgrove Road. They were modernised and renovated between 1975 and 1985.(Photograph taken by the author, 1990.)

31. Terrace of cottages, Clay Lane

This terrace of cottages in Clay Lane was built before 1876. It has been extensively modernised with a car park for residents created at the western end of the site. (Photograph taken by the author, 1990.)

32. Cottages, off Ridgeway Road

This pair of cottages was certainly built before 1840 and are probably late eighteenth century. In 1985 these cottages were converted into one house, re-roofed, extensively redesigned and modified internally when the land to the rear was redeveloped for housing. An access road was built from Ridgeway Road to the houses. (Photograph taken by the author, 1990.)

33. Holly Tree Cottage, Clay Lane

Sited on the north-eastern corner of Clay Lane near the boundary of the township, Holly Tree Cottage was built prior to 1876. The cottage was renovated and modernised internally during the early 1980s. (Photograph taken by the author, 1990.)

34. Beech House, Clay Lane

Beech House was probably built prior to 1876. It is sited within a few yards of the Hale border on Clay Lane, opposite the junction with White Carr Lane. It probably replaced a tiny cottage next to it now used for storage. (Photograph taken by the author, 1990.)

35. Agricultural Workers' Cottages, Bloomsbury Lane

The two blocks, of five and four respectively, were built c.1865 and are sited on the west side of Bloomsbury Lane. A large detached called Bloomsbury House stood adjacent to them before it was demolished. At least three similar blocks were sited on the other side of the lane nearer to its junction with Stockport Road. One of them is still extant. (Photograph taken by the author, 1990.)

36. Agricultural Workers' Cottages, Bloomsbury Lane

The front façade of this block of four cottages is located on the left of photograph No.35. Modern doors have replaced the originals and the two houses in the centre of the terrace have had porches added. (Photograph taken by the author, 1990.)

37. Quarry Bank, Stockport Road

Built before 1876, Quarry Bank is a terrace of four houses sited on Stockport Road close to its junction with Bloomsbury Lane. Named after the stone quarry which was sited on land opposite. The village joiner and undertaker's premises occupied the quarry site until the early 1980s. (Photograph taken by the author, 1990.)

38. Newfoundwell, Wellfield Lane

Newfoundwell is a house with outbuildings and was originally a small farm with almost 4 acres of land situated in Wellfield Lane, on the southern edge of the township. A dwelling plus outbuilding were here in 1831 (see map in C.C.R.O. ref. DXXI/31). During the post-war years it was modernised extensively. It has changed hands a number of times post-1930. It last changed hands in 1985. (Photograph taken by the author, 1990.)

39. Cambridge House, Wellfield Lane

Cambridge House is a cottage in Wellfield Lane with some agricultural land attached. Probably the owner/occupier was a small market gardener. Apart from windows being replaced and possibly the addition of the porch, its façade has not changed. (Photograph taken by the author, 1990.)

40. Oak Cottages, Wood Lane

This pair of cottages, built after 1876, probably housed agricultural workers employed at Oak Farm which, prior to demolition, stood opposite them. They are sited on the south side of Wood Lane at its junction with Thorley Lane. They have been extensively modernised post-1970. Note the absence of chimney stacks, new windows, addition of porches and cement facing. (Photograph taken by the author, 1990.)

41. Agricultural Workers' Cottages, Wellfield Lane

These are sited on the west side of Wellfield Lane . They were modernised after 1970. Note the absence of chimney pots, addition of porches and modification of paths to provide parking for cars. At least one pair was built before 1876.[18] (Photograph taken by the author, 1990.)

42. Willowbank, Moss Lane

This is a block of three houses, built before 1876, sited on Moss Lane, opposite Wellington Road High School. The houses are cellared and may possibly date back to 1850. (Photograph taken by the author, 1990.)

43. Ellisland

Built between 1895 and 1900, this pair of semi-detached houses on the north side of Stockport Road, mid-way between Moss and Bloomsbury Lanes, was the home of the Bell family. Francis Tait Bell and his son Frank Bell between them occupied, consecutively, the post of Parish Clerk from the inception of the Parish Council in 1894 until the civil parish was amalgamated with Altrincham in 1936.
(Photograph taken by the author, 1990.)

44. Brookbank, Brook Lane

This terrace block of houses called Brookbank was built before 1876. It is sited on the north side of Brook Lane, close to Navigation Road Station, on the western edge of the township. (Photograph taken by the author, 1990.)

45. Gatehouse of Pickering Lodge, Moss Lane

Built in about 1850, Pickering Lodge was small estate. It was owned from c.1850 to 1865 by Mr John Skelton, originally of Pickering, Yorkshire, for whom the house was built, and subsequently by Mr George Hardy, who owned Hardy's Crown Brewery. The gatehouse is all that now remains of the large house and estate. (Photograph taken by the author, 1990.)

46. Branksome, Clay Lane/Wellfield Lane

A mansion was built pre-1876 at the junction of Clay Lane and Wellfield Lane. Named 'Laurel House' on the 1876 25 inch O.S. plan, the premises are currently owned by the Altrincham Lodge of Freemasons who, in 1985, built an almost identical building – partly seen on the right. The front garden accommodated the original fountain which initially graced the Trafford Park mansion of Lord de Trafford. The owners have renamed the premises 'Ashcroft House'. (Photograph taken by the author, 1990.)

47. Addison Villas, Park Road/Acresfield Road

Built in 1852, Addison Villas is sited at the junction of Park Road and Acresfield Road. Originally it was a pair of large semi-detached houses, but between 1975 and 1980 it was converted into a nursing home and renamed 'Beech House'. (Photograph taken by the author, 1990.)

48. Watling Gate, Leys Road

The house was designed and built in 1904 (it replaced an earlier building) by Lt. Col. C.E. Newton in the grounds of his landed estate called Timperley Park. When he died c.1936/37 his family had resided on the lands for upwards of sixty years. In 1840 the land was owned Mrs E. Berry of Timperley Lodge and subsequently sold by her. Details of the estate's history are recounted in Chapter 15. (Photograph taken by the author, 1990.)

Industry and Commerce in the Township

Before 1900 only two commercial concerns with addresses in Timperley are listed in the street directories[21] the Brookside Tannery, off Deansgate Lane[22] and the Brook Steam Laundry, at the rear of the south side of Wood Lane.[23] Both appear to have closed down before, or during, the First World War. During the period 1900-1914 only one additional listing appears: the British Mat Company, Deansgate Lane.[24] This suggests it only traded briefly in the township.

Prior to 1910 the principal effect of the railway connection had been to stimulate some private residential development, mainly for the families of businessmen who commuted to Manchester, Altrincham, etc. The village economy remained predominantly agricultural; this changed radically during the inter-war years.

During the last decade of the nineteenth century the advantages of the Altrincham area for industrial development were quickly appreciated, i.e. excellent rail, road and canal communications with a main port (at first Liverpool, then, after the opening of the Manchester Ship Canal, Manchester), and the industrial areas of Lancashire, Yorkshire and Staffordshire; proximity to coal supplies for necessary steam power; availability of a suitable work force.

Accordingly, industrialists established between 1895 and 1910 a number of engineering factories at Broadheath, adjacent to the Bridgewater Canal, which flourished and the area soon became a thriving industrial estate. Between 1918 and 1935 industrial development came to Timperley with the arrival of a number of engineering firms, adjacent to Broadheath, in the north-west corner of the township and on each side of the canal between Deansgate Lane and the railway station on Park Road.[25] They employed some hundreds of personnel who incidentally increased the demand for houses in the township. The only other commercial venture listed is the Gem Laundry in Cow Lane (now Aimson Road) which traded until the early 1930s.

These industrial firms flourished for many years. However, the post-1945 trend to the rationalisation of heavy industry and towards high tech and service industries has taken its toll. Most of those inter-war concerns have now been closed down. In many cases, their buildings and sites have been redeveloped and/or modified to cater for the new trends in industry, for example:

John Sherratt and Sons Ltd
Closed and the building utilised by Forest City Signs (Plant Hire) Ltd, producing road signs, bollards, etc.

W.A. Copley and Son (W.P.M. Ltd)
Closed and the site redeveloped by Peerglow Park Estate into seventeen small industrial units leased to small businesses.[26]

Meldrums Destructors Ltd
Business closed down. The factory is unoccupied but the office premises are now leased for administrative offices for technical and service businesses.

Baldwin and Francis
Manufacturers of mining equipment, etc. Timperley premises closed down c.1968/9 and business transferred to new premises in Broadheath.

A number of small manufacturing and service orientated enterprises, established post-1945, now flourish in premises adjacent to the canal and Deansgate Lane. They include: Rotalac Plastics (plastic extrusion products); Crown Corrugated Ltd (paper and cardboard packaging products, etc.), G. Taylor (gear cutting and general engineer).

Service industries in the township include many which are automobile orientated, for example, garages offering car sales, rentals, servicing and petrol facilities. They are sited, almost exclusively, on the Manchester and Stockport Roads, and at least two of the garages were founded in the township in the early 1920s.[27]

The decades post-1960 have witnessed an influx of professional services businesses, mostly with premises located in the village centre on Stockport Road, catering for various personal needs of the large population.[28]

Before 1925, with the exception of one or two corner shops of the off-licence/general store variety in the Deansgate, Heyes and Clay Lane locales, all the shops were located in the village centre on Stockport Road. Catering principally for the basic needs of the inhabitants, they included a baker, butcher, newsagent, sweet shop, ironmonger, draper, greengrocer, post office, off-licence and a bank.

Between 1930 and 1939 the shopping facilities were extended in the village centre when purpose-built blocks of shops were built[29] and also a large Co-operative wholesale store .

Most of the new housing estates also incorporated blocks of shops to serve the basic needs of the estate residents. Clothes, furniture, carpets and capital goods, etc., were then only generally available at local town centres, for example, Altrincham or Sale. The post-war years, especially post-1965, have witnessed a great expansion of shopping facilities which have significantly increased the variety of shops and goods available in the village centre. The shop accommodation requirements have been met by a mixture of purpose-built blocks, with shop units on the ground and office units on the first floor levels,[30] the conversion of dwelling houses on the fringe of the village centre, and large purpose-built stores.[31] One or two businesses, founded in Victorian times, have redesigned and extended internally to meet modern requirements (for example, Percy Rook, ironmonger). Currently about seventy retail shops are trading in the village centre. In addition to the essential post office/newsagent/stationery shop, chemist and food retailing shops, they include businesses allied to the leisure industry (for example, travel, betting, video tape, 'do it yourself', car accessory and cycle shops). There are also an optician's, laundrette, jeweller, ladies' and gentlemen's hairdressers and ladies' and children's clothes shops.

Notes

1. See Chapter 8.

2. Includes acres still farmed.

3. Includes flats and apartments.

4. For example, Potts Cottage, Grove Lane (built in 1834) and a block of four cottages on Ridgeway Road (built in c.1835), which have already been mentioned in the previous chapter.

5. For example, Egerton Terrace on the corner of Brookfield Avenue and Park Road, Ellesmere Villas on Brookfield Avenue (both still extant and occupied), Quarry Bank on Stockport Road, Willow House on Moss Lane (all still extant and occupied).

6. For example, Brookfield and Westwood Avenues, Baker Street and Orchard Place and Lyme Grove.

7. Cheshire County Council and its local agent Bucklow Rural District Council.

8. See Appendix 1 for detailed description of the developments and see Appendix 3 for the list of roads.

9. At that time the price was exclusive of road charges. When the roads were made up householders were charged according to the frontage as a proportion of the road length. The average charge came to c.£30 so the total charge for a £325 house inclusive of road charge was between £350 and £360.

10. See the detailed description of the developments in Appendix 2 and also see the list of roads in Appendix 3.

11. Ibid.

12. Ibid.

13. British Airways, Bowdon Rugby Club (Clay Lane) and the Civil Service Club (Ridgeway Road) until c.1992, but now (1995) Ridgeway Social Club.

14. For example, Ellesmere House (Brookfield Avenue), Egerton Villas (Park Road), Quarry Bank Terrace (Stockport Road), Willow House (Moss Lane).

15. For example, roads in Deansgate Lane area; large semi-detached (Stockport Road, west of Bloomsbury Lane) and Lyme Grove (off Grove Lane).

16. For example, bungalows (Shaftesbury Avenue, Whitegates Close, Thornycroft Road), Housing Association (Peter's Court off Ridgeway Road), apartment blocks (Wood Lane and Redbrook Road area).

17. For more information see *Story of Timperley Methodism 1833-1933* by E.H. Wright.

18. 1876 25 inch O.S. plan.

19. Hazel Pryor, *Looking Back at Timperley*.

20. See Chapter 15 and Appendix 3 for the house plans.

21. Various street directories for the Altrincham District, such as Kelly's and Slater's.

22. Brentwood Special School has now been built on the site.

23. Old Laundry Nursery now occupies the site.

24. Various street directories for the Altrincham District.

25. Meldrums (canal side), John Sherratt and Sons Ltd and W.A. Copley and Son (wallpaper machinery manufacturers).

26. Copley's factory was modified to accommodate some of the units.

27. Jackson and Edwards (Manchester Road) and Jacksons (Stockport Road).

28. For example, four estate agents, five solicitors' and accountants' businesses, three dental surgeons' and a number of general practitioners' practices and a health centre, this latter in Grove Lane.

29. Adjacent to Mayfield Road.

30. For example, Charles Court (a redeveloped site) on Stockport Road/Thorley Lane corner.

31. For example, Lennons' Supermarket and Shoppers' Paradise Supermarket.

SCHEDULE OF PRINCIPAL HOUSING DEVELOPMENTS IN TIMPERLEY, 1930-1939

Estate or Building Scheme Developer or Builder	When Built	Approximate No. Houses	Approximate No. Shops	Names of Principal Roads
Realty Development Company	1930-1	100	6	Greenwalk; Green Drive; Hardy Drive
?	1930-2	95	NIL	Banbury; Malpas; Marbury; Ridley & Rochester Drives & Cholmondeley Avenue
Mauldeth Ltd	1931-3	*225	*10	Downs; Bollin & Upton Drives
?	1931-3	165	NIL	Balmoral & Windsor Drives; Buckingham; Kensington; St. James' & Windsor Groves; Hampton Grove
W. Burton Day	1932-4	100	NIL	(part of) Brook Lane & Brook Avenue
Mauldeth Ltd	1933-5	*310	*16	Riddings; Olive; Cheam; Heath & Arderne Roads; Eaton & Hodgson Drives & Tabley Grove
Tyrrell & Westlake	1933-5		NIL	Ash Grove; Dale & Bridge Groves; Marley; Mosley Closes
Broadbridge	1934-6	525	7	**Sylvan Avenue & Greenway Road; Burton; Crofton; Garner & Rossett Avenues; (part of) Woodhouse Lane East
Frank Whiteley	1934-6	145	NIL	Brookfield; Park & South Drives; South Meade; Oakleigh Avenue; Meadowbank
Gough & Gurney	1934-7	235	NIL	North Vale; West Vale & Thorsby Roads; Beeston Avenue; South Vale Crescent; Bexhill Close & St. Leonards Drive
Sparke & Stevens & Other builders	1935-6	395	*10	Attwood; Clover; Lorraine & Thornycroft Roads; Stanley & Wingate Drives; Laurel Drive; Seymour Grove; Deane Avenue; Crowley; Mosley & Perry Roads; Merton Grove; Thornycroft Close
?	1938	45	NIL	Cloverley Drive; Henson Grove & Drayton Grove
?	1938	145	NIL	Kelsall; Bedford; Marsden & Conway Drives; Greenhill Road & Cawdor Place
Total No. units				2485

* On two sites.
** Parts of

SCHEDULE OF PRINCIPAL HOUSING DEVELOPMENTS IN TIMPERLEY, 1945-1985

Estate or Building Scheme Developer or Builder	When Built	Approximate No. Houses	Approximate No. Shops	Names of Principal Roads
Borough Council (Grange Estate)	1944-9	275	NIL	Fairywell Road; Grange & Ladybrook Avenues; Whitley Place & Whitley Gardens
Borough Council (Broomwood Estate)	1952-9	685	15	Broomwood; Briarfield; Eldercroft; Grasmere; Hempcroft; Merefield; Mossfield; Nethercroft; Marshfield & Keswick Roads; Mainwood Road; Carrfield; Greystoke; Hollinscroft & Longfield Avenues
Borough Council (east side of Brooks Drive)	1960-70	315	NIL	Capesthorne & Redbrook Roads; Adlington & Ryefield Closes; Bamford & Hartford Gardens; Ambleside & Dee Avenues; Redesmere Close
Various Developers (?)	1965-75	145	NIL	Shaftesbury Avenue
Various Small Private Developments	1969-70	40	NIL	Riddings Court (off Greenway Road)
Each of these roads developed separately	1960-70	65	NIL	(Heyes Lane area) Denson Road; Fairlie & Halton Drives; Heyes Avenue
	1960-70	60	NIL	(Wood Lane area) Faulkner & Haydock Drives
	1960-70	95	NIL	(Grove/Bloomsbury Lanes area) Holly & Pickering Closes; Fairbourne Drive; Wentworth Avenue
	1960-70	45	NIL	(Park Road south area) Lindsgate Drive; Kelvindale Drive; The Green
	1960-70	60	NIL	(Park Road north area) Berisford & Whalley Closes
	1960-70	80	NIL	(Moss Lane area) Hardy; Henley Drive; Forest and Tulip Drives; Thorndale Grove
	1970+	90	NIL	Langdale & Kendal Closes (Stockport Road); Whitegate Close (Wood Lane); Goodwood Crescent (Hargreaves Road); St. Hughes Close (Park Rd north); Westmead Drive (Heyes Lane); Larkhill Close (off Thorley Lane)

Maunders Housing Association	1975-8 1972-5	220	NIL	Bowness Road; Derwent & Rotherdale Avenues; Colindale & Patterdale Walks Greenwood Close; Norwood Drive; Troutbeck Road
Each of these roads developed separately	1981-3	40	NIL	Downham Chase (near Perry Road)
	1982-4	10	NIL	Spring Gardens (off Fairview Road)
	1984-5	26	NIL	Buckingham Way (off Grove Lane)
	1983-5	?	NIL	Vale House site (off Stockport Road)
	1984-6	68	NIL	Threshfield Drive (off Fairywell Road)
Total		2319	15	

LIST OF ROADS IN TIMPERLEY WITH APPROXIMATE LOCATIONS AND YEAR OF OPENING WHERE ASCERTAINABLE, OTHERWISE AN APPROXIMATE OPENING DATE

Key

Letter symbols against each entry denote the nearest highway to a particular residential road, avenue, drive or close, etc

			Pn.	=	Park Road (north)	
Bl.	=	Bloomsbury Lane	Pc.	=	Park Road (centre)	
Br.	=	Brook Lane	Ps.	=	Park Road (south)	
Bd.	=	Broomwood Estate	Ri.	=	Riddings Road	
Ch.	=	Chester Road	Su.	=	Sugar Lane	
De.	=	Deansgate Lane	St.	=	Stockport Road	
Gr.	=	Grove Lane	Th.	=	Thorley Lane	
Gn.	=	Green Lane	Wo.	=	Wood Lane	
He.	=	Heyes Lane	(Pre)	=	Pre 1838	
Mo.	=	Moss Lane				

Entries in italics are cul-de-sacs.

Name of Road	Location	Date	Name of Road	Location	Date
Abbotsford Grove	Pn.	1909	Bollin Drive	Pn.	1931/3
Acresfield Road	Pc.	1930/5	Bowness Road	Su.	1976
Adlington Close	Bd.	1970	*Bradley Close*	Bl.	1965
Aimson Road[1]	St.	1933	Bramhall Close	Bd.	1970
(formerly Cow Lane)			*Branson Walk*	Bd.	1954/8
Alexander Drive	Gr.	1934/7	Brentwood Avenue	De.	1870/5
Ambleside Avenue	Bd.	1969	Briarfield Road	Bd.	1953/6
Appleby Avenue	Bd.	1954/6	Brackenfield Walk	Bd.	1955/7
Arderne Road	Ri.	1934	Bridge Grove	Mo.	1934/5
Ash Grove	Mo.	1934/5	Brook Avenue	Br.	1910
Ashlands Road	Ri.	1945/6	Brook Close[2]	(Pre)	1838
Attenburys Lane	Pn.	1934/7	Brook Lane	(Pre)	1838
Attwood Road	Wo.	1936/9	Brooks Drive[3]	St.	1860/5
Ashleigh Road	He.	1934/7	(formerly Hale Road)		
			Brookfield Avenue	Pc.	1900
Baker Street	St.	1876	*Brookfield Drive*	Ps.	1934/8
Balmoral Drive	Pn.	1931/3	Brookway	Mo.	1965/9
Bamford Gardens	Bd.	1970	Broomwood Road	Su.	1952/4
Banbury Drive	Pn.	1930/2	Broomwood Gardens	Ri.	1954/8
Barnfield Walk	Bd.	1954/8	*Buckingham Grove*	Pn.	1932/4
Bedford Drive	St.	1938	*Buckingham Way*	Gr.	1984/5
Beech Avenue	He.	1928/31	Burton Avenue	Ri.	1934/5
Beeston Avenue	St.	1934/7			
Berisford Close	Pn.	1960/5	Canal Road	Pn.	1850+
Bexhill Close	St.	1934/7	Capesthorne Road	Bd.	1964/7
Birley Close	Mo.	1934/5	Carlin Gate	Bl.	1932/4
Bloomsbury Grove	Bl.	1962/4	*Carrfield Avenue*	Bd.	1955/7
Bloomsbury Lane	(Pre)	1838	Cartmel Drive	Bd.	1970/5

Cawdor Place	St.	1938		*Glen Rise*	St.	1936/8
Chatsworth Close	Su.	1986/7		*Goodwood Crescent*	Th.	1976
Cheam Road	Ri.	1933		*Granby Road*	Ri.	1934/6
Cholmondeley Avenue	Pn.	1930/2		Grange Avenue	Pc.	1943/7
Claremont Avenue	Ch.	1926/9		Grange Road	Pc.	1933/8
Claremont Drive	Ch.	1920/2		Granville Road	Th.	1933/5
Clay Lane	(Pre)	1838		Grasmere Road	Bd.	1956/8
Clifford Avenue	Gr.	1938		Green, The	Ps.	1962/4
Clover Road	Wo.	1935/6		Green Drive	Mo.	1928/31
Cloverley Drive	Wo.	1938		Green Lane	(Pre)	1838
Colebrook Road	Gr.	1935/8		Green Lane North	Wo.	1965
Colville Grove	Bl.	1933/5		Green Walk	Mo.	1928/31
Colwick Avenue	Bl.	1948/50		Greenfield Close	Bd.	1956/8
Coniston Walk	Bd.	1979		Greenhill Road	Th.	1939
Conway Drive	St.	1938		Greenway Road	Pc.	1930/2
Crescent, The	Mo.	1925/9		*Greenwood Close*	Su.	1972/5
Crofton Avenue	Ri.	1934/5		Greystoke Avenue	Bd.	1956/9
Cross Grove	Ri.	1934/5		Grove Lane[4]	(Pre)	1838
Crowley Road	St.	1936/8		(formerly Back Lane)		
Curzon Drive	St.	1945/6				
				Haddon Grove	Br.	1904
Dale Grove	Mo.	1933/6		Hall Avenue	De.	1934/5
Dalveen Drive	Mo.	1924/8		Halton Drive	He.	1966/8
Deane Avenue	Wo.	1936/8		Hampton Grove	Pn.	1931/3
Dee Avenue	Bd.	1969		Hardy Drive	Mo.	1965/8
Denson Road	He.	1962/4		Hartford Gardens	Bd.	1969
Denver Drive	St.	1936/8		*Hargreaves Road*	Th.	1938
Derwent Avenue	Bd.	1970		Hawthorn Avenue	Pn.	1915
Drayton Grove	Wo.	1938		*Haydock Drive*	Wo.	1963/5
Downham Chase	St.	1981/2		*Hayfield Walk*	Bd.	1955/8
Downs Drive	Pn.	1931/3		*Heath Road*	Ri.	1934
Dudley Road	Ps.	1946/8		Hempcroft Road	Bd.	1954/6
Durley Avenue	He.	1930/2		Henley Drive	Mo.	1965/7
				Henson Grove	Wo.	1938
Eaton Drive	Ri.	1934/5		*Heyes Avenue*	He.	1962/4
Edenhurst Drive	Th.	1973		*Heyes Drive*	He.	1933/5
Eldercroft Road	Bd.	1954/6		Heyes Lane	(Pre)	1838
Ennerdale Road	Pc.	1936/8		*Highfield Road*	Wo.	1935/8
Eskdale Drive	St.	1972/3		*Holly Close*	Bl.	1964/5
				Hodgson Drive	Ri.	1936/8
Fairbourne Drive	Bl.	1966/8		Hollincroft Avenue	Bd.	1954/6
Fairfax Avenue	Bl.	1945/6		*Houldsworth Avenue*	De.	1936/45
Fairfield Road	Su.	1945/6				
Fairlie Drive	He.	1966/8		Kelsall Drive	St.	1938
Fairview Road	Th.	1930/4		*Kelvindale Drive*	St.	1969
Fairywell Road	Pc.	1946/7		*Kendal Close*	St.	1978
Farndon Drive	Bl.	1937/9		*Kenmore Drive*	Gn.	1944/6
Faulkner Drive	Wo.	1962/4		Kensington Grove	Pn.	1930/2
Forest Drive	Mo.	1966/8		Kersal Drive	Bd.	1978
Fox Close	Br.	1933/5		Keswick Road	Bd.	1956/9
Foxhall Road	Br.	1927/32		*Kingsley Road*	Ps.	1945/6
Frieston Road	Pn.	1916/20				
				Ladybrook Avenue	He.	1943/7
Garner Avenue	Ri.	1935/6		*Langdale Close*	St.	1971/3
Garth Avenue	St.	1935/8		Langham Grove	He.	1931/4
Gawsworth Close	Bd.	1970		*Laurel Drive*	Wo.	1934/8
Gerrard Avenue	Ri.	1934/5		*Lawn Drive*	De.	1936/8

Name		Date	Name		Date
Lawson Drive	Bl.	1933/5	*Rainford Avenue*	St.	1946/8
Leicester Avenue	Ri.	1933/5	*Raven Road*	Ri.	1938
Leslie Grove	Bl.	1935/8	Redbrook Road	Bd.	1969
Leys Road	Pn.	1915	*Redesmere Close*	Bd.	1970
Lime Grove	Gr.	1894/8	*Riddings Court*	Ri.	1969/70
Lincoln Avenue	Wo.	1933/5	Riddings Road	Ri.	1934
Lindsgate Drive	Ps.	1962/4	Ridgeway Road[6]	(Pre)	1838
Longfield Avenue	Bd.	1954/7	(formerly Sugar Lane)		
Lorraine Road	Wo.	1935/6	Ridley Drive	Pn.	1934/7
Lowther Avenue	Bl.	1936/8	Rochester Drive	Pn.	1934/7
Lynton Grove	St.	1936/8	Rosset Avenue	Ri.	1934/6
			Rosslyn Grove	Bl.	1930/2
Mainwood Road	Bd.	1952/4	Rotherdale Avenue	Bd.	1976/8
Malpas Drive	Pn.	1930/2	Ryefield Close	Bd.	1962/4
Marbury Drive	Pn.	1930/2			
Marley Close	Mo.	1934/5	St. Andrew's Avenue	De.	1906
Marsden Drive	He.	1938	St. George's Avenue	Pc.	1930/2
Marshfield Road	Bd.	1954/6	St. George's Crescent	Pc.	1930/2
Marsland Road	Gr.	1938	St. Hugh's Close	Pn.	1984/5
Mayfield Close	St.	1946/8	*St. James's Grove*	Pn.	1934/5
Mayfield Road	St.	1915	St. Leonard's Drive	St.	1934/8
Meadowbank	Pc.	1934/8	Seymour Grove	St.	1935/6
Merefield Road	Bd.	1952/4	Shaftesbury Avenue	St.	1937/8
Merton Grove	St.	1935/8	Shap Avenue	Bd.	1962/4
Millom Crescent	Bd.	1971/3	*South Drive*	Pc.	1934/8
Milton Drive	Ri.	1935/6	Southfields Drive	Pc.	1935/8
Mosley Close	Mo.	1945/6	*South Meade*	Pc.	1934/8
Mosley Road	St.	1935/8	South Vale Crescent	St.	1934/8
Moss Lane	(Pre)	1838	Spring Gardens	Th.	1983/4
Mossfield Road	Bd.	1956/8	Stanley Drive	Wo.	1933/5
Mossgrove Road	Mo.	1926/30	Stelfox Avenue	St.	1935/8
Mottram Drive	St.	1933/5	Swan Road	Ri.	1934/6
Mullion Drive	De.	1933/5	Skelton Road	De.	1955/65
			Sylvan Avenue, part of	Ri	1930/2
Nethercroft Road	Bd.	1954/6	Sylvan Avenue, part of	Ri	1934/5
Newstead Terrace	Mo.	1900/05			
North Vale Road	St.	1934/8	Tabley Grove	Ri.	1934/6
Norwood Drive	Su.	1972/5	*Thorley Drive*	Th.	1926/9
			Thorley Lane	(Pre)	1838
Oakdene Road	He.	1930/2	*Thorndale Grove*	Mo.	1962/4
Oakleigh Avenue	Pc.	1934/8	*Thornycroft Close*	Wo.	1962/4
Oldfield Drive	Mo.	1935/8	Thornycroft Road	Wo.	1935/7
Old Heyes Road	He.	1936/8	Thorsby Road	St.	1934/8
Olive Road	Ri.	1935	Threshfield Drive	Ps.	1984/6
Orchard Place	St.	1870/1	Trafford Drive	He.	1935/8
			Triangle, The	Ps.	1925/7
Park Avenue	Pn.	1902	Troutbeck Road	Su.	1969/72
Park Close	Pn.	1936/8	Tulip Drive	Mo.	1968/72
Park Drive	Pc.	1934/8			
Park Road[5]	(Pre)	1838	Upton Drive	Pn.	1931/3
(formerly Wash Lane)					
Patterdale Walk	Bd.	1978	Vale Road	St.	1935/8
Perry Road	St.	1936/8	Vaudrey Drive	Ri.	1934/5
Pickering Close	Gr.	1962/4	*Victoria Avenue*	De.	1908
			Victoria Road	Gr.	1944/6
Radlet Drive	Ri.	1934/5	Victoria Close	Gr	1963/5
Raglan Drive	Pn.	1934/7			

Westwood Avenue	Pc.	1895/8	Windsor Drive	Pn.	1931/3
Wellfield Lane	(Pre)	1838	Windsor Gardens	Bd.	1969
Wellington Road	St.	1930/1	*Wingate Drive*	Wo.	1936/8
Wentworth Avenue	Gr.	1966/8	Woodhouse Lane East	Ri.	1935/6
West Vale Road	St.	1934/8	*Woodlands Lane*	St.	1933/5
Westmead Drive	He.	1982	Woodlands Parkway[7]	St.	1902
Whalley Close	Pn.	1966/8	(formerly Albert Road)		
Whitegates Close	Wo.	1971/3	Wood Lane	Wo.	1838
Whitley Gardens	Ps.	1943/7	*Wood Mount*	Wo.	1962/4
Whitley Place	Ps.	1943/7	Wood Road	Ri.	1938[8]

Notes

1.. Aimson Road was designated Cow Lane at least to 1933.

2. Originally part of Brook Lane. When Woodlands Parkway was extended to Brook Lane that part of Brook Lane which was cut off was renamed Brook Close.

3. Brooks Drive was designated Hale Road on nineteenth century maps and plans.

4. Grove Lane was designated Back Lane at least up to 1876.

5. Park Road originally joined the railway station to the Chester Road. A section from Riddings Hall to the village was called Wash Lane (see *Slater's Directory*, 1906). Wash Lane was renamed Park Road in 1927.

6. Sugar Lane was renamed Ridgeway Road in 1936.

7. Woodlands Parkway was originally called Albert Road.

8. Dates have been ascertained from O.S. maps, street directories and voters' lists.

Nb: Roads built post-1988/9 are not included in this list.

11

LICENSED PREMISES IN THE TOWNSHIP

'There is nothing which has yet been contrived by man by which so much happiness is produced as by a good tavern.'

Samuel Johnson

Not everyone would endorse wholeheartedly the sentiments expressed above but indubitably the village hostelry has always played, still plays and will continue to play its essential role in the social life of a community.

The term Public House embraces 'The Inn' (a name which conveys the sense of a place providing overnight accommodation, liquid refreshment and food for travellers and, prior to the automobile era, their horses also) and the 'Alehouse', 'Beerhouse' or 'Tavern'. These latter names, especially the first two, denoted domestic premises licensed to sell ale or beer brewed on the premises.[1]

Prior to the mid-nineteenth century the basic design of a purpose-built inn changed little down the ages. The plan of an eighteenth century coaching inn resembled its Roman counterpart, i.e. a four-sided building constructed around a courtyard with an opening on its road frontage providing access to the courtyard. It origins trace back to the first century A.D., when the Romans established inns and alehouses on the roads they constructed. After them followed the monastery hospitals of the seventh to sixteenth centuries which provided free food and accommodation for travellers (especially pilgrims). With the number of travellers in the Middle Ages increasing and overtaxing the available hospital provision, the monks built lodging houses called 'inns' outside the confines of the monastery. A few secular inns were also built. During the sixteenth century the Dissolution of the Monasteries cut off the hospital facilities and this resulted in the building of many more secular inns in towns and villages located on main roads. During the eighteenth century they were followed by the coaching inns specifically designed to cater for the burgeoning era of coach travel. In turn these were superseded and entered a period of decline with the arrival of the Railway Age. The railways generated a demand for a new type of hostelry, the railway inn or hotel[2] sited in close proximity to the new railway stations. 'The twentieth century has witnessed the advent of the 'Automobile Era' and, post 1950, a phenomenal increase in private car ownership. Its concomitant, convenience of door to door transport, has revived the fortunes of the country inn and additionally brought about the innovation of the 'Motel', the modern counterpart of the coaching inn. It has also proved the catalyst for the conversion of old country mansions into 'up-market' hotels and/or restaurants catering for the leisure needs of the ubiquitous private car owners.

The next few pages will show that Timperley can boast examples of each of the above categories of hostelry and that the origins of its licensed houses can be traced back for at least 350 years.[3]

Prior to 1753 alehouse keepers were required to enter into recognisances and provide sureties before magistrates at the Quarter Sessions or the more frequent Petty Sessions. The details were enrolled in Quarter Sessions files. One such file, covering the period 1629-1650 survives for Cheshire.[4] The following entries for Timperley in Bucklow Hundred are recorded for the year 1640:

Alehouse Keeper	Sureties
Hamnett Simpson of Timperley	Thomas Jenkinson
Nicholas Bentley	Randal Barton of Altrincham and Thomas Jenkinson

No inn signs are listed but the entries prove, indubitably, that the two alehouses are the oldest in the township. Subsequent registers show that they are now identified by the signs of the Old Pelican and the Hare and Hounds.

Both contemporary hostelries are the linear descendants of those two seventeenth century alehouses. The omission of inn signs makes it impossible to state with certainty which of the above licensees occupied a particular hostelry. The 1664 Hearth Tax Returns for Cheshire lists forty-four hearths in the township.[5] Extrapolating, on the basis of about four people to each hearth, this would suggest the population of the township in the mid-seventeenth was about 200. On that estimate the probable clientele for the hostelries would be about 100/125 adults plus travellers traversing the roads through the township. It also suggests that the landlords were not exclusively publicans. The evidence of contemporary documents[6] proves that they were also farmers, at least until the latter part of the nineteenth century. An Act of Parliament (26 Geo. 2) required Clerks of the Peace to keep registers of alehouse licenses. The aleseller was required to enter an annual recognizance to be of good behaviour and provide two sureties.[7] Generally, no inn signs are recorded, the only exception being 1828. However, by backtracking from 1828 through the recorded names of licensees it is proven that the two alehouses recorded in the 1640 Quarter Sessions files are, in fact, the Old Pelican and the Hare and Hounds respectively which we know today. These two houses are the only two Timperley hostelries recorded in the Cheshire directories prior to 1834. All the other licensed premises in the township have nineteenth or twentieth century origins.

Particular Licensed Houses

The Old Pelican

During its long history it has metamorphosed from an alehouse to a coaching inn, thence to an hotel and recently to its current status of a motel.

Sited on the premier highway traversing the township, and almost on its eastern boundary, its status as the premier hostelry in Timperley was assured. It originally formed part of a farm of about 15 acres enclosed from common land. For many years the licensees combined the occupations of farmer and alehouse keeper. Prior to 1690 it formed part of the Bulkeley moiety lands in Timperley, which family had held their lands in the township since c.1330 (reference Dutton pedigree 'Visitation of Cheshire, 1580'). This property, together with other farms in the moiety, were sold c.1689 by the Bulkeley family. Its origins trace back at least to the early seventeenth century.[8] The ownership changed hands a number of times during the eighteenth century, though always between relatives. Between 1688 and c.1727 the owner was John Higginson. In 1727 he willed it first to his son-in-law, Edward Aldcroft of Timperley, and then to his grandson John Aldcroft,

49. *The Old Pelican, Manchester Road in 1905, in the time of Walter Bruton (see Appendix 1). (Photograph reproduced here by courtesy of Trafford Local Studies Centre, Sale Library.)*

50. The Pelican as it is today. The building here was erected in the 1930s behind the old inn, which was then pulled down, leaving a forecourt. (Photograph taken by the author, 1990.)

later of Carrington.[9] In 1740 John Aldcroft sold it to his aunt, Elizabeth Holt the elder of Altrincham (see Appendix 1). By 1766 it was owned by Ann Holt,[10] who could have been one of Elizabeth Holt's daughters, and in the same year she transferred a half share in the property to Jonathan Worthington and Thomas Smith of Manchester.[11] It appears that subsequently the whole half share became vested in the said Thomas Smith as it is recorded he later mortgaged it to a Henry Ridgeway of Mobberley. Subsequently Thomas Smith was made bankrupt and apparently, after 1766, Henry Ridgeway purchased the other half share[12] as the deeds[13] record that in 1799 the property was conveyed '... by Henry Ridgeway and the Assignees of Thomas Smith' to '... Thomas Warburton of Altrincham'. Thus it is probable that Ridgeway foreclosed on Smith.

From 1681 to 1687, or possibly before, the alehouse was called 'Hardie's Tenement'. From 1688 to 1740 the alehouse was 'called and known by the name of "Higginsons of the brook"'. By 1766 the deeds record '... formerly known by the name of "the Coach and Horses" but now as "The Lamb and Punchbowl"'.[14]

By 1799, it had adopted its present sign of the Old Pelican. Seemingly the original building was replaced (c.1820-1837) by a purpose-built inn. The known facts are that:

- In 1838 the licensee, Sarah Frank, is described (Tithe Awards) as '... Renting a Public House, Orchard and Yard also nine fields in all over 20 acres...'.

- In 1841 she is listed as licensee and also three agricultural labourers are recorded as living on the premises (1841 census).

- On census night two adults, hawkers by trade, are recorded as resident on the premises (1841 census).

- It is described as an inn '... having two beds for travellers and accommodation for supplying refreshments for forty persons...' (Return of Licensed Houses, 1891).

The present building replaced the old 'Hostelry building' c.1930. During rebuilding certain artefacts were found in the foundations, i.e. glass pieces of c.1600 plus numerous clay pipes and bone ivory bobbins (these latter used for lace making), all eighteenth century vintage.

Additions were made to the building in 1934, 1938 and 1935 (Altrincham Council Minutes) which included a large lounge and extensions to the restaurant. In 1982 major alterations were made including a motel development around a courtyard.

It was a coaching inn and even in 1891 boasted

'... Three Stables and thirteen Stalls'
(Return of Licensed Houses, 1891).

Coaches plying certain routes to and from Manchester passed the house and those listed below called, some being rehorsed by the proprietor (reference Cheshire directories 1821, 1822, 1824).

Stage Coach Timings		
Destination	**Coach Name**	**Departs Manchester**
London (Royal Mail)	'London Flying Machine'	8 pm
Chester	'The Dart'	6 am (Daily except Saturday)
Chester	'The Pilot'	9.30 am (Daily except Sunday)
Knutsford	'The Bang Up'	7 am (Daily)
Nantwich	'Royal William'	3 pm Mon, Wed, Fri, Sat
Northwich	'The Nettle'	4.30pm (Daily)
Northwich	'Sir Oliver'	6 pm (Daily)
Northwich	'Velocipede'	5 pm (Daily)

The Hare and Hounds

This house also was originally an alehouse. Its site, opposite a toll bar, on the Stockport-Warrington Road and close to the township's western boundary ensured it, in addition to its local clientele, a passing trade from travellers, both on foot and the local stage coach services, that passed it. Originally a farm of more than 26 acres, the licensee combined the occupations of publican and farmer. It continued as a farm until the second half of the nineteenth century. The present house, which replaced an earlier building, dates from c.1810. The first Register entry,[15] which proves conclusively that it eventually took the name Hare and Hounds, is in 1774 when William Goulden was the owner/licensee. It would seem that William died in 1800 as the Registers record that Elizabeth his wife took over the licence in 1801 and remained the licensee up to and including 1808. In 1809 John Chorlton replaced her as the licensee and held it for ten years until 1818. He was a Timperley resident who had owned and farmed land which included the present recreation ground adjacent to Park Road. When he became a publican he rented out his village centre farm and he himself rented the Goulden property (i.e. the public house – probably part of the farm-

51. The Hare and Hounds in the early 1900s. It then had a Dutch barn to the left-hand side of the photograph, on the present site of Le Bon Viveur restaurant, in which the Timperley Prize Band used to practice. (Photograph reproduced by courtesy of Trafford Local Studies Centre.)

142

52. The Hare and Hounds in 1990 showing the changes in progress. (Photograph taken by the author, 1990.)

house – orchard and thirteen fields) from Elizabeth Goulden. He held the licence for twenty years.

By 1873 it was a tied house, the lessees being the Altrincham brewers Siddeley and Kent. A Mr Edward Stelfox of Comberbach, Cheshire, was at this period the owner of the house and land.[16] Between 1892 and 1902 the lease was transferred to George Henry Podmore.[17] In 1891 it is listed[18] as having

> '... One Stable with three Stalls... and two beds for Travellers and accommodation for supplying refreshments to twenty four persons...'

The remarks column states:

> '... Old House, good accommodation, refreshments other than drink frequently supplied...'

Obviously by this time, probably before, its status had changed to that of an inn. Its site was still comparatively rural up to the early 1930s as the anecdote which follows, for which I can vouch, confirms. It occurred c. 1934 on a vintage summer's day. My paternal grandfather was enjoying a lunchtime reviver on this day. All the inn doors were open. Suddenly a rabbit sped through the

53. The redesigned bowling green and pavilion. (Photograph taken by the author, 31st August, 1992.)

143

54. *The renovated Hare and Hounds and the redesigned road junction. (Photograph taken by the author, 31st August, 1992.)*

rear door, hotly pursued by a dog. It ran through the lounge and out through the front entrance. My grandfather opined that he considered the inn's sign an inspired choice.

The building was extended at its eastern end and the bowling green reduced in size for the ubiquitous car park in the early 1970s and later a new restaurant block extension was added behind, and attached to, the main structure.

Changes to the Hare and Hounds in 1990-1

The building and its site, together with the adjacent road junction and the cricket ground site each underwent extensive alterations and refurbishment during 1990-1. These works completely changed the appearance of the locale and it seems fitting to describe the various developments here.

The Hare and Hounds was extensively renovated and extended at the rear of the premises. In addition, the access and egress to the car park was completely redesigned. This was achieved by building an access road from Wood Lane and opening an egress to Shaftesbury Avenue. The bowling green was attractively fenced in and a pavilion provided. The front entrance had a porch added and a stone wall with railings was built on the frontage to Shaftesbury Avenue (see photograph)

The thoroughfares of Wood Lane, Moss Lane and Shaftesbury Avenue join the Stockport Road adjacent to the Hare and Hounds, the whole forming a complex road junction. During the 1980s traffic flow problems at the junction had become acute. Shortly after the works described above, Trafford MBC commenced a major redesign of the junction. It involved a widening of Wood Lane and Stockport Road on their frontage to the cricket ground. Approximately thirty yards of the low sandstone wall on each road was taken down and re-erected a few yards back. Also an intricate system of traffic lights and pedestrian crossings was installed. The scheme was completed c.1991.

Ringway Motors Petrol Station, occupying a site at the corner of Stockport Road/Moss Lane, was in the first half of 1992 demolished and a new state-of-the-art petrol station erected in its place.

These combined works have completely altered the appearance of the locale and vastly improved the traffic flow at the junction.

The Timperley Cricket Ground, an old established ground, has, especially post 1945, greatly extended its facilities, notably in the provision of floodlighting on its tennis courts. Its latest innovation in 1991-2 was the provision of an all-weather surface for hockey and football. Surrounded by a high metal fence and floodlit, it also had access from Wood Lane to a car park. The site borders the golf links. The path across the links had to be diverted for approximately 50 yards to the east of its original line to provide space for the access road for cars.[19]

A feature of the four oldest hostelries still extant was that each boasted a bowling green. Sadly, only one is still extant,[20] the others have fallen victim to the requirements of the public houses for car parks and beer gardens/children's play areas. The Hare and Hounds is easily the most attractive of the township's hostelries with its early nineteenth century façade and open aspect across the village cricket ground.

The two inns above remained the sole licensed houses in the village until 1828.[21] Between then and 1834 they were supplemented by two retailers of beer, John Arnold and William Yearsley.[22]

The Church Inn

John Arnold's premises, rented from the owner Mary Barlow and described as a 'Beerhouse and Orchard' in 1840, occupied a site on the south-east corner of the junction of Thorley Lane and Stockport Road.[23] An old photograph suggests the building was originally a pair of cottages. In 1841, the house is listed as the Church Inn and the new licensee as George Brundrett.[24] It would seem the choice of name was fortuitous as it preceded the building of both the Methodist Chapel in 1847 and Parish Church in 1849. By 1891 it had become a tied house of Hardy's Crown Brewery Co., Manchester and is listed as:

'... Beerhouse... with... Two beds for Travellers and Refreshment accommodation for six persons...' and classified as a '...Moderate House...'[25]

By 1903 its ownership had changed to the Openshaw Brewery Co. Ltd, and the licensee was one Abraham Goodwin. The brewery relinquished the licence in 1913 as the following entry in the Cheshire Register of Licences records.[26]

'Sign of House: 'Church Inn'   Holder of Licence: Rose Hazlehurst
Regd. Owner: 'Openshaw Brewery Co. Ltd, Brook Street, West Gorton, Manchester.
Remuneration Paid: 'To Owner – £1217, To Licensee: £300, Total £1517."

Following the licence relinquishment it would appear the establishment changed to a 'Beer Retailing Shop' as it is so listed in post-1914 directories. The premises were subsequently demolished c.1918-25 and the site redeveloped with retail shops.

A Beerhouse, Heyes Lane

A William Yearsley owned a pair of cottages at the junction of Heyes and Wash Lanes, one at least of which the beerhouse occupied.[27] At some date between 1841 and 1850 the beerhouse was closed as it is not listed in either the 1851 census or Cheshire directories. The reason for the closure becomes apparent in the next section.

55. The Stonemasons Arms in Timperley Village. (Photograph taken by the author, 1990.)

Stonemason's Arms Inn

56. Stonemasons Arms inn sign, Timperley Village. (Photograph taken by the author in 1981 at Watling Gate, Leys Road, Timperley.)

In 1840 its site was part of a field owned by William Stelfox. By 1841 the building was completed and had opened with John Arnold, stonemason as its first licensee. It was the first purpose-built hostelry to be erected in the township. John Arnold, with entrepreneurial initiative, had moved from the Church Inn to his new appointment. 'Translated from the Church' as it were. He combined the twin occupations of stonemason and publican, hence the apposite house sign. He advertised his trade by having sculptured, in sandstone, the figure of a nude male child flanked by the tools of his trade, tri square and pestle, the whole surmounted by an urn in the Greek style. It was incorporated in the fascia of the inn and gave rise to the colloquial name of the hostelry, 'The Naked Child'.[28] When the building was demolished in 1926 to make way for the contemporary building it was removed and ultimately found its way into the Watling Gate Museum. Unusually the sign, incorporated in the wall, followed the Roman tradition in contrast with the contemporary vogue for a 'Gibbet' type sign. John Arnold's eldest son William took over the inn when his father died in the 1840s. The Stonemasons Arms was renown for its good stabling which it advertised, along with its bowling green, as an attraction in 1896.

The original building was sited nearer the road and was flanked by a cobbled forecourt. Internally the present building was refurbished in 1985 and the windows, externally, canopied with wine coloured awnings. At this juncture it retained its locally renowned bowling green, but latterly it has been converted into a beer garden and children's area. At the same time the high brick wall, screening it from its frontage with Park Road, was demolished.

Other Public Houses

During the period 1842-64 three beerhouses were licensed to sell 'Beer and Cider' on the Premises' and at various dates between 1874 and 1890 they adopted the signs listed below:

Sign (post 1874)	Location	Licensee	
Gardeners' Arms	Deansgate Lane	Samuel Marshall	(grocer)
Quarry Bank Inn	Bloomsbury Lane	Thomas Perrin	(shoemaker)
*Railway Inn	Stockport Road	James Renshaw	(wheelwright)

*Following the opening of the Stockport-Warrington Railway this house was replaced by a purpose-built inn, hence its adoption of this sign. The building was demolished c.1955/8 and the licence transferred to another new purpose-built house on Mainwood Road, which assumed the sign of The Broomwood Hotel. From 1988 onwards the empty site was utilised as a car lot by Vantage Garages Ltd.

After 1864 but before 1871 another beerhouse, licensed to sell 'Beer and Porter on the Premises' and named 'The Blue Pig', opened in a terraced house on Clay Lane. Subsequently, c.1890 it became an off-licence and general store before eventually closing down c.1970/5.

During, or preceding, 1864 two off-licences opened: one at Four Lane Ends run by Mrs Lucas, wife of the village blacksmith;[29] and the other at Quarry Bank run by James Renshaw, wheelwright.

Between 1873 and 1890 a grocer's shop, located at the corner of Brook and Deansgate Lanes obtained an off-licence for the premises. Thus at the end of 1891 there were eleven licensed outlets for alcohol in the village.[30]

The Licensing Act of 1902 required all clubs to be registered. Timperley had two licensed clubs: Timperley Golf Club, which had 294 members and whose licensing hours were 8 am to 10 pm, and Timperley and Baguley Conservative Club, which had thirty-five members and whose licensing hours were Saturdays to 11 pm.

Refreshment house keepers also had to register. One entry for Timperley reads:

'*House*: Manchester Road, *Owner*: Mr Attenbury; *Licensee*: J Clarke (Resident) Wine Licence only.'[31]

A concomitant of the post-1920 intensive residential development is the building of a number of Licensed houses and the conversion of existing buildings into hotels catering for the vast population increase in the township (see below).

Sign	Year Opened	Sign	Year Opened
Sylvan Inn	1938	Woodlands Hotel[*32]	1961
Broomwood Hotel	1957	Old Hall Hotel[33]	1955
Moss Trooper Hotel	1958		
NB. *Private hotel pre-1961.			

The following clubs also have licences to sell alcohol to members:

Timperley Conservative, Liberal and Labour Clubs.
Bowdon Rugby and Kersal Rugby Clubs.
Timperley Sports and Social Club, Ridgeway Social Club and British Airways Sports Club.[34]

An interesting statistical comparison is provided by the ratio of licensed houses to population in the years 1891 and 1983 respectively:

1891 – 11 outlets	Ratio of Licensed Houses to Population 1 : 223
1983 – 36 outlets	Ratio of Licensed Houses to Population 1 : 676[35]

Notes

1. See *Open History* Offprint No.3, 'The Move from Ale to Beer in Sixteenth and Seventeenth Century North-west England' by Jill Groves.

2. The name 'hotel' comes originally from the French 'hôtel' meaning large town house. It arrived in England in the nineteenth century and denoted a more exclusive type of inn. Its twentieth century derivative 'motel' denotes hotels with purpose-designed facilities for motorists, or as we might say, their 'mechanical horses'.

3. Alehouses have a tradition tracing back many centuries. As the suffix 'house' indicates, they were not purpose-built but rather domestic premises, i.e. farmhouses or cottages, in which a family (in practice the wife) brewed ale or beer for its own consumption and also for retail sale. Usually it was secondary to the principal occupation of the husband or head of the household. For many years the Hare and Hounds was a classical example of the genre. Readers who wish to study the topic in greater detail are referred to sources listed in the bibliography.

4. The Quarter Session records are deposited at Cheshire Record Office, and are now on microfiche. (Ref. C.C.R.O., QDL 2/1 and 2/2.)

5. The Hearth Tax Returns deposited at Cheshire Record Office. (Ref. P.R.O. 1644, E179\86\145 and 1673/4, E179/86/155.)

6. Local directories, Tithe Awards 1838, Census Enumerators' Returns.

7. Only two registers survive for Cheshire covering the period 1743-1828. However, there are gaps. The records for the following years are missing: 1758 to 1773; 1788 to 1798; and 1822 to 1827 inclusive.

8. See Appendix 1.

9. The will of John Higginson of the Brook, Timperley, yeoman, dated 1727 (CCRO). The brook was the nearby Baguley Brook.

10. See Appendix 1.

11. Respectively calico printer, and dealer and chapman.

12. Presumably Ann Holt's half share.

13. Original deeds held by Greenall Whitley plc during the 1980s, when this chapter was written. They trace back to at least 1680.

14. It is possible that the term 'Lamb' has religious connotations, the term 'Punchbowl' probably had political overtones. Punch was the fashionable drink of the Whigs in the late seventeenth century. It may have indicated a hostelry with Whig sympathies. In later years when 'Whiggery' was in decline the then landlord may have deemed it wise, for commercial reasons, not to give the impression the house was partisan.

The name 'Lamb and Punchbowl' could also refer to 'lambswool', a popular drink of the seventeenth and eighteenth centuries, made with hot, spiced ale and the pulp of roasted apples. It was served in a punch bowl. Hence the inn's name could promise a hot, comforting drink. (See Peter Brears (1993) 'Celebrations in Hot Ale', in C. Anne Wilson, editor, *Liquid Nourishment*, Edinburgh University Press Food in Society Series, pp.108-9, 124-5, 134.)

15. Alehouses and Alesellers' Register.

16. Ibid.

17. Ibid.

18. Return of Licensed Houses (CCRO).

19. See p.178.

20. The Hare and Hounds. Since this chapter was written the bowling green of the Stonemason's Arms has been converted to a garden with tables on the lawn.

21. Ref. local directories.

22. Ref. local directories.

23. Tithe Awards, 1840

24. 1841 Census.

25. Return of Licensed Houses.

26. CCRO Ref. QAL/5, Licensing Act 1904.

27. 1841 Census.

28. The author photographed it in 1981 at Watling Gate. It can be clearly seen in the wall of the inn on old photographs.

29. Probably occupied site of the present Rook's ironmongers shop.

30. East side of the junction of Bloomsbury Lane and Stockport Road.

31. Altrincham District Licensed Houses Return.

32. Conversion of two large houses.

33. Internal conversion of Timperley Hall.

34. These clubs occupy premises and playing fields in the township.

35. No significant difference in the population figure is anticipated when the 1991 census returns become available. Accordingly this 1971 ratio will probably show little, if any, change when compared with the forthcoming 1991 population returns.

APPENDIX 1
NAMES OF LICENSEES

Pelican		Hare and Hounds	
1640	Hamnett Simpson	1640	Nicholas Bentley[1]

Registers Missing 1650 to 1742

Pelican		Hare and Hounds	
1746-1748	George Warburton		
1749	No Entry		
1750	Thomas Warburton		
1751	No Entry		
1752	Thomas Ashley		
1753-6	No Entry		
1757	George Warburton		
1758-1773	Entries Missing		
1774-1782	Richard Rowlinson	1774-1800	William Goulden
1783-1787	John Williamson Jnr.	1801-1808	Elizabeth Goulden
1788-1798	Entries Missing	1809-1818	John Chorlton
1799-1801	Robert Worsencroft	1819	Hannah Chorlton
1802	George Hardy	1820-1849	John Chorlton
1803	Hannah Hardy	1850-1863	John Ashley
1804-1810	Joseph Warburton	1864	James Platt
1811	John Becket	1865-187?	John Ashley
1812-1814	Richard Hargreaves	187?-1872	Charles Whittaker
1815	Henry Slater	1873	Hannah Whittaker
1816-1821	Thomas Barton	1874-1888	Mrs Ann Whittaker
1822-1827	Entries Missing	1889-1890	Amelia M. Whittaker
1828-183?	William Gregory	1891-1903	Joseph Gatley
183?-1837	William Frank	1904	William Plant
1838-1846	Sarah Frank	1905	Eliza Plant
1847-1852	John Savage	1906-1937	Albert Hoole
1853	Isaac Warburton	1938-1949	Robert H. Peake
1854	James Houghton	1960-1965	Herbert Horsley
1855-1856	Samuel Taylor	1966-1975	Geoffrey Gibson
1857-1861	William Houghton	1976-1985	James B.W. Cunningham
1862-1873	John Knowles	1986-1989	Nicola Gough
1874-1877	Mrs John Knowles	1990	Leonard Winstanley
1878-1881	Mrs Elizabeth Knowles		
1882-1890	James Seddon		
1891-1897	Charles Higginbotham		
1898-1901	George Walton[2]		
1902-1905	Arthur Manchester		
1906-1915	Walter Bruton		
1916-192?	Thomas W. Horton		
192?-1947	Arthur H. Hodgkiss		
1948-1949	Bridget F. Dowling		
1950-1961	William H. Mintern		
1962	Ralph G. Walsh		
1963-1967	Clifford Barber		
1968-1975	Daniel J. Campbell		
1976-1984	Harold F. Foulger		
1985-19	Andrew C. Spink		

(NB. Only two registers survive for Cheshire which cover the period 1743-1828. However, there are gaps in them viz: 1753 to 1773 inclusive, 1788 to 1798 inclusive and 1822 to 1827 inclusive.)

Notes

1. The only Alehouse Keepers' Register to survive for Cheshire covers the period 1629-1650. No inn signs were given. Thus it is impossible to state categorically whether Hamnett Simpson was at the Pelican and Nicholas Bentley at the Hare and Hounds. It could be vice versa.

2. It is possible that Mrs M.A. Walton held the licence in 1901.

12

TIMPERLEY PARISH CHURCH: ITS HISTORY

*'"Let us now praise famous men" – men of little showing –
For their work continueth, And their work continueth,
Broad and deep continueth, Greater than their knowing.'*

Rudyard Kipling

Introduction

Second only to a village's place name, its church is, generally speaking, its oldest surviving link with its past and architecturally its finest building. Furthermore, it embodies and manifests in its fabric much of the religious history of the parish and preserves, in the parish chest, the written records of that history and also the written records of the principal events in the lives of many of the parishioners it has served down the years. Especially in those rural communities which have escaped the traumas of industrialisation and/or urbanisation, it is still the hub around which much of the social life of the village revolves.

Christ Church: Its Raison d'Etre

Christ Church, which celebrates its 150th anniversary in 1999, is a mere infant in the annals of church building. What were the factors which influenced its conception? One must first appreciate that for many centuries Timperley was one of at least ten townships within the vast ecclesiastical parish of Bowdon. Consequent on the creation of the new parish of Ashton-on-Mersey in the early fourteenth century out of Bowdon territory its size was slightly reduced. Accordingly by the end of the eighteenth century only eight of the original townships remained within Bowdon Parish.[1] Imagine also that an observer standing on the ramparts of Bowdon church surveys, from that vantage point, the full extent of the parish territory. He/she would note Bowdon church occupies a magnificent ridge site dominating the surrounding countryside but, as his/her eyes traversed the parish boundary, would be compelled to admit that its position is geographically inconvenient for many of its parishioners as it is sited barely a mile from the southern boundary of the parish.

- The Birkin Brook to its confluence with the River Bollin
- The River Bollin to the point where it is crossed by The Bridgewater Canal
- Thence the western boundary of Partington to the Manchester Ship Canal
- Thence the line of the Red Brook and Sinderland Brook
- Thence the Sinderland Brook and along line of the Baguley Brook to its junction with Sale Hedge
- Thence Baguley Brook to the Fairywell Brook
- Thence the eastern boundary of Hale and Ringway
- Thence the boundary of Ashley to Mobberley Brook and then the line of that brook to its junction with the Birkin Brook at the southern end of Tatton Park

At that time Bowdon Parish embraced eight townships and parts of three others:

Altrincham	Partington
Ashley	Timperley
Bowdon	Part of Agden
Carrington	Part of Ashton-on-Mersey
Dunham Massey	Part of Baguley
Hale (including Ringway)	

Parishioners residing on the eastern and northern fringes on the parish were distanced from the church, some of them facing a return journey of seven miles to worship at Bowdon (for example, some Timperley and Baguley residents), a daunting prospect, especially during the winter months. The predominantly agricultural economy of the townships meant that the bulk of the male, and some of the female, population laboured long hours in the fields. Such a regime is not one calculated to inspire enthusiasm for a journey of over five miles return, on one's sole day of leisure, in order to worship at the parish church.

In 1841 the combined population of Timperley and Baguley was 1447. Between 1825 and 1840 a small influx of families of independent means had occurred, mostly business and professional people. They built their villas and took up residence. A directory of 1850 contains the following description 'Timperley contains many genteel houses which are principally owned by manufacturers and merchants of Manchester'. Among the gentry it names approximately fifteen families residing in the township. Included amongst these 'nouveau' families were members of the Church of England who, together with long established residents, quickly appreciated the urgent need for an Anglican place of worship in the immediate vicinity, especially now that Timperley was about to be linked by railway with Manchester. In addition, these new residents had the professional expertise essential for the planning, financing and building of a church. They lost no time in initiating action to that end.

In accordance with an Act of Parliament (1/2 and 7/8 William IV), and in May 1847, the then Vicar of Bowdon, the Revd. W.G. Mann, Mr E. Joynson of Bowdon and Mr B. Bagnall of Timperley met and resolved to inaugurate a scheme to erect a church and vicarage in Timperley and to raise the necessary funds. Once initiated the rate of progress was phenomenal. The Bishop of Chester gave practical expression to his full support by donating £500 to the endowment fund and £50 to the building fund.

A building committee was formed whose members were the Vicar of Bowdon; James Barratt, attorney of Manchester; Edward Joynson, cotton merchant of Bowdon; Benjamin Bagnall, manufacturer of Timperley; and John Skelton, gentleman of Timperley. Mr John Mort, linen draper of Altrincham, served as honorary secretary.

An active campaign for subscriptions prospered so well that the committee commissioned, and subsequently adopted, plans for a church drawn up by James Bayley, architect of Sandiway, Altrincham.

The two cardinal priorities were a site for the church and a site for the new vicarage.

The acquisition of the church site was resolved by Mr John Barratt[2] who donated a plot of land, containing 4885 square yards, being part of a field known as the Nearer Carr, arguably the finest site in the township for the purpose. It had frontages of 72 yards with Thorley Lane, 66 yards with Sugar Lane and an eastern boundary of 76 yards.[3] A conveyance, dated 1st February, 1851, transferred the land into the names of the trustees (see below).

The vicarage site was acquired when two of the trustees, on 24th June, 1850, entered into an agreement with John Paulden, leaseholder, to purchase from him a plot of land 2654 square yards in extent, on the west side of Thorley Lane, for a cash sum of £10 and a rent of £2 p.a. Subsequently, on 19th December, 1850, the Earl of Stamford executed a grant of the said plot to the church trustees.[4] The new vicarage, together with its outbuildings were soon built and the vicar was able to take up his residence there in May 1851. On 24th June, 1852, the devisees of John Paulden, deceased, executed an agreement with the trustees confirming the 1850 agreement (i.e. rent of £2 p.a.) for a period of ninety-nine years commencing on the day of the 1852 agreement.[5]

Prior to the completion of the new church a meeting of subscribers appointed the first trustees of the patronage, viz:

Revd. W.G. Mann	Vicar of Bowdon;
Thomas W. Tatton	esquire of Wythenshawe Hall;
Mr B. Bagnall	manufacturer of Timperley;
John Skelton	gentleman of Timperley;
James Barratt[6]	attorney of Manchester.

Less than eighteen months after the project was first mooted the foundation stone was laid and the building work completed less than eleven months later. The first service in the new church was held in late September 1849 (see below for details). One can only admire the expedition and efficiency with which these Victorian worthies converted a concept into a reality. The modern appellation 'whiz-kid', strictly in its speed connotation, seems apposite.

Excluding the bishop's initial donations, the whole cost of the venture was defrayed by public subscription, the parishioners having responded magnificently to the financial challenge presented by the project.

The guiding principle of the diocesan authorities, 'Only incur the minimum cost of any Scheme we authorise', is patently obvious.

Following completion, the architect issued four certificates, each dated 22nd August, 1850, certifying the inadequacy of accommodation for all parishioners in existing churches in the parish; the seating capacity of the new church; its fitness for use; and the cost of building it.

1. 'I the undersigned being the Architect under whose superintendence the new Church called Christ Church at Timperley in the Parish of Bowdon has been erected and fitted up in a good sound and substantial manner in every respect and that the same is now fit for use and consecration as witness my hand this twenty second day of August 1850.'

James Bayley

2. 'I the undersigned... do hereby certify that the existing Churches and Chapels in the Parish of Bowdon do not afford sufficient accommodation for more than one third of the inhabitants thereof, by actual admeasurement thereof. As as witness... 1850.'

James Bayley

3. 'I James Bayley do hereby certify that Christ Church... will accommodate four hundred and ninety seven persons independent of the Minister and Churchwardens' pews as witness... 1850.'

James Bayley

4. 'I James Bayley of Altrincham... architect and surveyor do hereby certify that the cost of erecting and fitting up of the new church... amounted to the sum of two thousand and thirty eight pounds one shilling and no more. As witness my hand... 1850.'

James Bayley
Architect and Surveyor

Schedules attached to the Sentence of Consecration

'Pew No. 14 reserved for the Minister... and his family and pews nos. 63 and 64 for the use of Churchwardens... for the time being and no rent or assessment shall be made or charged on either of them.'

'... one third at least of the Sittings... shall be and continue for ever as free sittings or charged at such low rents as the Bishop shall... decide'

'That the Pews... as aforesaid, shall be let by Churchwardens... according to the scale of Pew Rents set forth on the said Plan... herein to the amount of £156... said Churchwardens shall pay or apply rents to the Minister... and for the performance of Divine Service and Offices therein subject to reservations... set forth hereafter:–
    '£6 p.a. (or as may be altered from time to time) together with a sum of £4 17s 6d secured by Indenture dated 3rd March, 1851 for repairs...
    '£10 p.a. for salary for Clerk, Beadle, Pew Openers and all other officers including salaries of Singers, charges for books, coals, candles and lights, Bread and Wine... cleaning of pews etc... Residue to Minister for his absolute use... by way of stipend in addition to annual Rent Charges of £71 2s 0d.'

'Right of nominating Vicar vested in the Trustees.'

'Right of nominating Organist, Singers, Clerk, Vergers and all officers vested in the Vicar.'

'Incumbent is to pay the Bishop at the Feast of Easter five shillings for Synodials and three shillings for procuration at every Episcopal Visitation...'

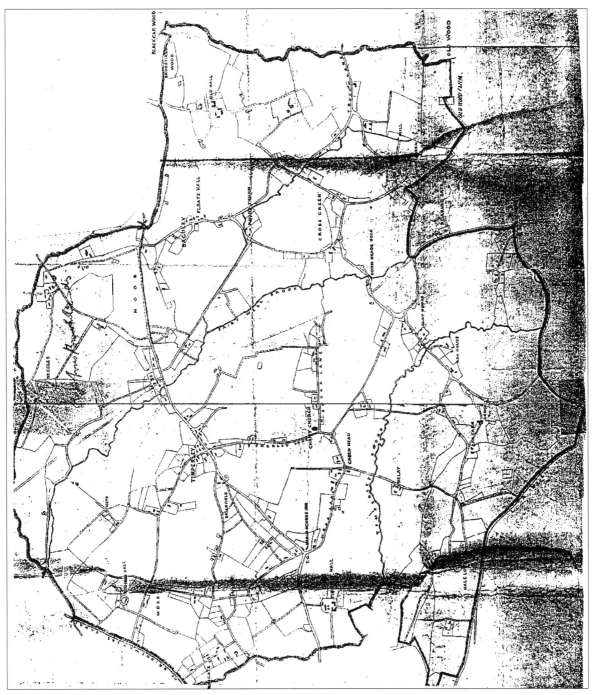

Map 5. The map of Timperley parish carved out of Bowdon Parish in 1852. The deed delineating the parish boundaries is dated 7th May, 1852. A few years later most of Baguley was taken out of the Timperley parish and became St. John's parish of Baguley, although some of that township was retained in Christ Church parish. This map is a copy of the official map deposited with the deed in the parish chest. Parts of Hale are still within Timperley ecclesiastical parish. (Reproduced here by courtesy of

The inaugural service in the new church was held on 20th September, 1849 when the preacher was the Revd. H.W. McGrath of St. Ann's Church, Manchester. The first Sunday Services were held on 24th September, 1849; the vicar preached at the morning service and the Revd. H. Stowell, Vicar of Christ Church, Salford, at the evening service. The total offerings for the three services amounted to £261 14s 0d.

The consecration of the church was much delayed. The original licence to perform divine service is dated 15th September, 1849 and was granted for '... one year or until the church is consecrated whichever is the sooner...' Two extensions were granted, dated respectively 14th September, 1850 and 13th September, 1851. Not until 23rd October, 1851 did consecration take place. The 'Sentence of Consecration' ran

> '... and we consecrate this church by the name of Christ Church... and the yard and cemetery attached... to remain from this time an Holy Place and Holy Ground by virtue of this our Sentence...'

It was read and 'promulged' (sic) in the presence of the Bishop of Chester's Secretary, C.I.W. Parry (notary public), Revd. I. Hordern (rector of Rostherne) and Revd. Edward Woolnough M.A. (rector of Northenden). It listed a number of schedules, principally concerned with the application of pew rents and other charges.

The inordinate delay, almost two years, was caused by the demise of the donor of the church site prior to the signing of the conveyance vesting the land in the names of the trustees. The formal conveyance, dated 1st February, 1851, states that the land belonged to James Barratt and Samuel Barratt, trustees under the will of the late John Barratt.[7]

On 23rd October, 1851, in the presence of a large gathering of clergy from both Manchester and Chester dioceses, parishioners and friends, Mr Parry read the 'Petition to the Bishop' for consecration and the 'Sentence of Consecration' was read by the Revd. J. Kingsley (curate of Bowdon).[8] The Bishop of Chester preached the sermon on a text from Romans XV (i.e. 'How beautiful are the feet of them that preach the Gospel of Peace and bring tidings of good things').

Doubtless local residents in the congregation would reflect that the reference to 'feet' was singularly apposite; no longer would attendance at church entail an extended walk to Bowdon and back, ensuring that they returned home 'footsore and weary' from their Sunday devotions. From that time and henceforward they had a church, literally 'on their doorstep'.

Initially it was a 'chapel-of-ease' but Christ Church became a parish in its own right when, on 7th May, 1852; a district was taken out of the mother parish of Bowdon which comprised most of the township of Timperley, together with parts of Baguley and Hale townships, to form the new ecclesiastical parish of Christ Church, Timperley. In 1868 Christ Church parish itself was reduced in size when a district was taken out of it to form the new parish of St. John of Baguley.

Boundary of Christ Church, Timperley, Ecclesiastical Parish

This is precisely delineated in the instrument creating it, dated 7th May, 1852 (see Appendix 1).[9] Commencing at a point on the boundary of Altrincham and Hale, where it crosses Hale Road.[10] It follows the line of Hale Road, to its junction with Shay Lane. It then traverses the line of Shay Lane to Davenport Green Farm from whence it follows the line of Roaring Gate Lane to its junction with White Carr Lane and thence along White Carr Lane to Newall Green Hall Farm. Here it turns right and continues to Oldwood Farm and then 'along the line of a fence until it joins the Baguley Brook'. The boundary is now co-incident with the Baguley Brook, only leaving it briefly to skirt Black Carr Wood, until the brook passes under the Bridgewater Canal (between Timperley and Brooklands). It now takes the line of the Bridgewater Canal until it reaches a point where the Timperley Brook passes under it. It now leaves the canal and is co-incident with the Timperley Brook until it reaches the footpath across what is now the Municipal Golf Links. It now traverses the line of the footpath, towards Golf Road, for a short distance before veering right across the (then) fields (now North West Gas premises) until it reaches and crosses Moss Lane (at its junction with Mayors Road) and continues across Stamford Park (then Hale Moss) to emerge at the junction of Stamford Park and Charter Roads. It follows the line of Stamford Park Road until it turns along the line of Ashfield Road, for about 65 yards, before turning east and crossing the line of Finchley Road to a point midway between Finchley and Hawthorn Roads. It now turns south crossing the line of Elm Road to reach its starting point on Hale Road.

That part of Timperley township on the Chester Road side of the Bridgewater Canal is not included in the ecclesiastical parish but of course forms part of the civil parish. The part of Hale township within Christ Church ecclesiastical parish is bounded by the lines of Hale Road, Shay Lane, White Carr Lane to its junction with Clay Lane and its boundary with Timperley and Altrincham townships back to Hale Road. The part of Baguley township within Christ Church parish is bounded by the line of White Carr Lane to Oldwood Farm and the line of the Baguley Brook to its junction with the Bridgewater Canal. The parish of Christ Church only existed in its entirety for sixteen years. In 1868 some lands were taken out of it to form part of a new parish, St. John of Baguley on Brooklands Road. Those lands, part of Baguley township, were bounded by a line commencing at the canal and crossing fields to join the Fairywell Brook, thence the line of the brook to Stockport Road and the line of Stockport Road to the boundary between Baguley and Northenden townships thence the line of Baguley Brook back to the Bridgewater Canal.

Church Endowment – Financial Provisions

In this connection the trustees were required to comply with certain Acts of Parliament regulating the '... promoting and building of additional churches in populous parishes...' Those Acts state that '... an endowment of £40 p.a. arising out of Houses, Land, Titles, Rent Charges or other Hereditaments... shall be considered equal to a sum of £1000 which shall be secured before the Bishop may grant the perpetual right of nominating a Minister under the above Act.' Also 'A fund is to be provided for repairs to the said church equal in amount to £5 for every £100 of the original cost of erecting and fitting out such church... secured on lands or money...' and '... a further sum be reserved out of the pew rents at the rate of £5 per £100...'

The trustees, after paying for the building of the church and vicarage, invested most of the balance of the fund in the purchase of chief rents, secured on lands and houses in Manchester and Salford, which secured a perpetual income of £71 12s 0d p.a. as part of the vicar's stipend and £4 17s 6d p.a. for the Repair Fund.

		Monies Invested to Endow Benefice[11]			
Date	No.	Rent Charge on Land Sited at	Area Sq. yds	Amount Secured P.A.	Capital Cost
19th March, 1851	1	East side of MONTON STREET, Chorlton-on-Medlock.[12] (Nb. Parallel and about 150 yards west of Lloyd Street)	3167	£71 2s 0d	£1493 2s 0d
19th March, 1851	2	CLARENDON STREET, Hulme (with two houses on the site) (Nb. Between Great Jackson Street & City Road.)	195	£4 17s 6d	£110 0s 0d
8th August, 1860	3	JACKSONS ROW,* on South side (Off Cross St., with an inn,) the Green Man, built on it	?	£12 0s 0d	£276 0s 0d
5th July, 1861	4	PARK STREET,* Salford, Lancashire (nr. Windsor Bridge).	428	£10 0s 0d	£225 0s 0d

Note: items marked * were the gift of Mrs E. Bridge, widow, of Oakmount, Wood Lane, Timperley.[13]
Nos. 1, 2 and 3 are all in Manchester

The disbursement of the Building and Endowment Fund is listed below:

Erection of Church and laying out of churchyard	£2038 1s 0d
Erection of Vicarage (see p??)	£800 0s 0d
Purchase of Chief Rents (Vicar's Stipend)	£1493 2s 0d
Purchase of Chief Rents (Church Repair Fund)	£110 0s 0d
Witnesses' Fees	£1 0s 0d
Balance in hand	£369 2s 1d
	£4811 5s 1d

57. Christ Church, Thorley Lane, built in 1849. Major building works were undertaken in 1864 when the north and south transepts, a new chancel and an organ chamber were added. (Photograph taken by author, c.1986-8.)

The vicar's income was augmented by pew rents. The Sentence of Consecration empowered the churchwardens to let the pews subject to qualifications 'laid down in the schedules thereto' (see p.152). If all the pews were let the vicar would receive, nett, £140 p.a., making a total of £201 2s 0d when the income from the chief rents was added. In 1850 the endowment was supplemented by Mrs E. Bridge, a parishioner, who purchased two additional chief rents, securing sums of £12 and £10 p.a. respectively.

Church Architecture – External

Apart from the slated roof,[14] the exterior material used is Freestone, a good quality red sandstone from Runcorn, with a brick lining. Perhaps the local Timperley sandstone was not of a suitable quality. One can only guess at the reaction of local masons to this fact. Unless, of course, it was brought in rough hewn for them to dress into suitably sized blocks. There is no trace so far of any documentation describing the method of transportation but it was probably brought by canal to Broadheath or Timperley berths and thence by cart to the site. The tranquil and pastoral location, little changed for centuries, must have undergone a major upheaval and doubtless the multifarious building activities would have formed a major topic of conversation in home, shop and inn.

The original building comprised a chancel, nave and gallery, tower and spire.[15] In contrast to church tradition, it is built on a north-south axis with the chancel located at the northern end. There seems no valid reason why the architect chose not to build on the conventional east-west axis with the chancel at the eastern end.

It is built in the Norman style, with all the main windows stone-framed and of rectangular form with semi-circular heads. Each side of each frame embraces a slim, circular, engaged pillar terminating in a small urn shaped capital. The semi-circular heads are bordered by a string course.

The Nave

Its original dimensions were 59 feet by 33 feet and comprised five bays, each pierced by a window on the east wall, whilst the west wall has only four bays pierced by windows with its southernmost bay embracing an engaged stone porch serving as the main entrance to the nave. This porch has a small window in each of its north and south walls. Each nave wall is supported by buttresses terminating in mitred heads. The buttresses at the south-west, south-east, and north-east corners are clasped. The mitred heads terminate just below a course of blind arcading which is patterned with a stone circle over each buttress head. This arcading is located just below the line of the eaves.

The south wall is pierced by two large windows, each approximately 9 feet high, which flank each side of the tower.

The Chancel

This was originally approximately 12 feet square in plan with a single window piercing its north wall (see section below headed 'Subsequent Building Modifications').

The Vestry

This was contained in, and filled the angle between, the west side of the north wall of the nave and the west wall of the chancel. Structurally speaking, it was an extension of the nave on its west side. It had a small window and/or door in its west wall and access to the nave via a door in the south side (i.e. an internal door).[16]

The Tower and Spire

The lower storey of the tower, square in plan, is engaged with the south wall of the nave, the whole consisting of three tiers and the spire. Each tier is slightly smaller in plan section than the one beneath it.

First Tier

This is approximately 15 feet high with clasped buttresses, mitred at the top, at its south-west and south-east corners and also buttresses, mitred at the top, close to its engagement with the nave wall. It has a semi-circular arched doorway on the south wall the stone frame of which contains engaged circular stone pillars on each side terminating in a capital . The design matches the window frames of the nave bays. A small metal lantern is attached to the wall above the door. The east and west walls are pierced by single windows, each approximately 6 feet by 8 feet.

Second Tier

A course of blind arcading below a slightly overhanging stone cornice separates it from the first tier. Part of this second tier is above the nave eaves level and thus all its corners are encased by clasped buttresses. It is approximately 12 feet high with windows, approximately 6 feet by 1 foot, piercing its east and west walls and of the same shape as the nave windows but without pillars on each side of their frames. A string course borders the semi-circular tops of the windows. A circular hole (now blocked up) pierces its south wall. Originally, it may have been a window or an opening for a clock face.

Third Tier

This tier is separated from the second tier by a string course. It has slender circular engaged pillars at each corner but no buttresses. All its walls are pierced by stone framed double louvres each with a double semi-circular head. Matching the tower windows they are bordered by a stone string course supported at each end by small semi-circular corbels. The top of this tier appears to be bridged with slightly projecting stone beams, of square section, laid on an east-west axis ad whose function is probably to support, in conjunction with the tower walls, the weight of the spire.

The Spire

This is octagonal in section and approximately two-thirds the width of the third tier at its base. It is broached to the top of the tower by courses of sloping stone tiles. The bottom course of the tiles slightly overhang the walls of the third tier and rest on the projecting beams (see above). The apex is surmounted by a wind vane whose swivelling pointer represents a cock bird. The spire was renovated in the early 1930s.

The whole building is well-designed and constructed and a credit to both its architect and builder, especially the pleasing proportions of the tower and spire when viewed from a distance.

Subsequent Building Modifications

During the period 1850 to 1865 the pace of development in the parish quickened. Three principal factors occasioned it:

- the new railway line connecting Altrincham and Manchester;
- the eminent suitability of the local terrain for housing development;
- the purchase of over half the land area of Timperley by the banker and developer Samuel Brooks.

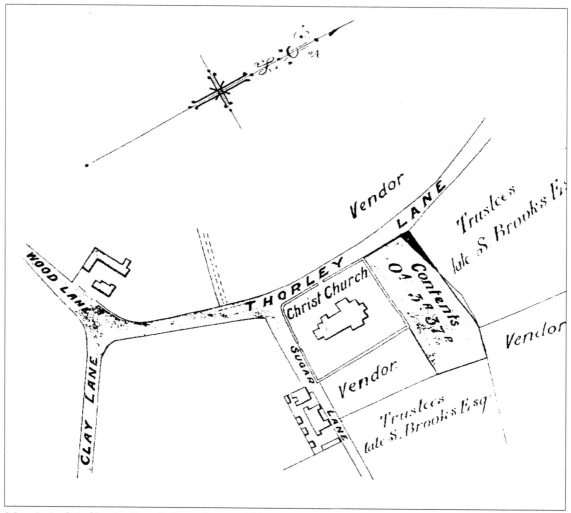

Map 6. A plot of land – 3 roods 7 perches – sold by John Arnold (auctioneer) to Ecclesiastical Commissioners for £275 by a conveyance dated 22nd August, 1905. The land was used as an extension to the churchyard. A consecration certificate for the plot, dated 15th June, 1907, is held in the Parish Chest. (Reproduced here by courtesy of Christ Church parish.)

These factors were largely responsible for a 50% increase, to 2250, in Timperley's population during the decade 1851-1861: most of the new residents were business or professional people.

During the early 1860s the vicar and certain prominent residents considered that the pew sittings were inadequate on the basis of the total number of parishioners resident in the townships within the parish. Accordingly, on 27th February, 1864, they convened a meeting of parishioners at which it was resolved to enlarge the church in accordance with a plan submitted to the meeting:

1. 'Taking down of the (then) Chancel and Vestry in order to add North and South Transepts[17] with a Chancel, Organ Chamber and Vestry.

2. To remove Font from its (then) position in "West Gallery" (*sic*) ... to a room or chamber on South corresponding to the vestry on the North Side.

3. To add seats in the space gained by the removal of the Organ from "West Gallery"... the choir benches being placed in the Chancel... and to remove the Pulpit and Reading Desk from their present positions to new positions denoted in the Plans, deposited in Probate Registry at Chester, giving 330 extra places of which 110 are free.'

The faculty for these major works, according to plans by Mr J. Lowe, architect, of Manchester, was applied for and granted by the Bishop on 2nd June, 1864. The church was closed while the building work, which included the church wall, was in progress. The enlargement was completed and the church reopened on Easter day, 16th April, 1865, a period of ten months. One can only marvel at the dynamism and the efficiency of the Victorians! The organ, which previously had been sited in the gallery, was removed and installed in the new organ chamber. The total cost of the work was £1973 5s 11d and was defrayed by public subscription.

Post-1850 Samuel Brooks, banker, became, by purchase, the owner of over half the land area of Timperley and also lands in Baguley township. Circa 1860 he developed Brooklands Road with large mansion type houses and subsequently founded and endowed the church of St. John the Divine. On 18th July, 1868 the church was allocated portions of Christ Church, Timperley and St. Anne of Sale parish lands and such lands formed the new parish of St. John of Baguley (see p.153).

Between 1885 and the present time Christ Church has been granted a number of faculties authorising various alterations, improvements and renovations to the building which works have subsequently been carried out. In all cases, the costs have been defrayed by public subscriptions (see above for details). The principal works are described below:

1887

A scheme for opening out an arch into the organ chamber, stripping off plaster (in bad repair) from internal walls of nave and replacing with terra-cotta.[18]

1899

A scheme to enlarge the vestry; install a new and larger organ; raise roof of the vestry to accommodate the new organ; to partly offset cost by agreement with suppliers (Wadsworth Bros.) to accept the old organ in part payment.

1905

The churchyard was enlarged (see plan on p.158). A plot of land, of area 3 roods 7 perches, forming part of the field known as the Nearer Carr (from which original land for the church was taken) was conveyed on 22nd August, 1905 by John Arnold and others to the Ecclesiastical Commissioners. It was consecrated on 15th June, 1907.

58. This window was inserted in 1882 and replaced a three-light window inserted in 1865. It has ogee tracery above the lights. The stained glass rectangular lights portrays Our Lord flanked by disciples and followers with cherubin and seraphim in the upper halves of the four panels flanking the centre panel.

It is one of the most impressive features of the church. Unfortunately, at a later date, a fine rear altar panel was placed in front of the window, which obscures one's view of the lower third of the window when viewed from the nave, thus inhibiting a full appreciation of its beauty. (Photograph taken by the author.)

1908

The holy table and reredos were removed and installed in St. Andrews Mission School. In its place a new holy table, of oak, inscribed with the Lord's Prayer, and the ten commandants, together with a new panelled reredos, were installed.

The reredos was a memorial to the Revd. C. Wilkinson.

1923

The organ chamber was extended eastward and a new arch constructed in the north wall of the east transept. Also the existing organ was taken down and rebuilt and installed in the enlarged chamber with mechanical pumping apparatus and radiator.

1933

The then existing communion rails were removed from the chancel and new communion rails, of oak, bearing a memorial inscription to William Bell installed.

1960

The electrical wiring, shades and fittings were renewed.

1968

The choir stall, pulpit and lectern were resited; some nave and transept pews were removed and a free standing holy table with three-sided communion rail introduced. These alterations reduced the seating capacity of the church.

Church Architecture – Internal

When this description was written in the 1980s, the interior appearance of the building exhibited only minor changes from its aspect following the major structural alterations of 1865. For convenience the description below is divided into sections. The numbers in brackets refer to the position of an item on the plan on p.164.

Chancel

Its walls are tiled almost to the roof level. originally plastered, they were tiled post-1865. The first ten courses, from ground level, are of red terra-cotta; the medial ten courses are cream coloured with each alternate tile having a leaf motif which gives a draughtboard pattern effect (9) to the til-

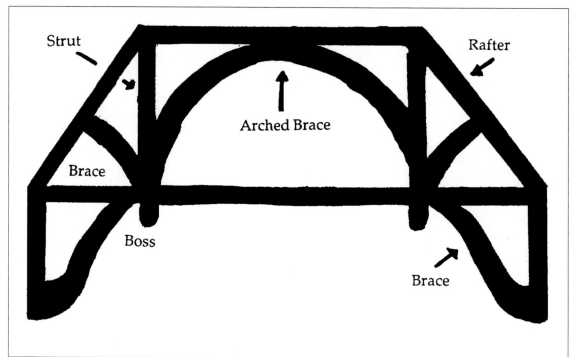

Drawing 1. Chancel. Roof truss rests on corbels, and forms part of the new enlarged chancel added to the church in 1865. (NB. Roof trusses in both transepts are identical with this.) (Drawing by author.)

Drawing 2. Chancel: a window in the north-east corner of the east wall. The present chancel, added to the nave in 1865, replaced a smaller chancel which formed part of the original church. (Drawing by author.)

ing; the upper four courses are separated from the medial courses by a string course and each of the tiles has a lozenge shape split into quarters and each quarter being heavily patterned with a fleur-de-lys motif, also the spandrels. A line of blind arcading, about 30 inches in height, borders the tiling and completes the wall covering. Each arcade bears a red shield motif on a blue field. The whole effect is both neat and most attractive. The north wall was pierced by a three-light window in 1865 but subsequently in 1882 it was replaced by a new five-light stained glass window. Of the lancet design, the centre, tallest, window portrays Jesus in its upper half and the smaller flanking windows portray angels in their upper halves and the disciples in their lower halves. The lower half of the centre window portrays Mary and a disciple. The lancets are surmounted by stained glass ogee-shaped lights.

The holy table is backed by a fine carved oak reredos,[19] approximately 12 feet wide by 10 feet high. It is bordered by a gold

and silver coloured leaf motif. The face of the reredos has three fine carved panels. The two rectangular side panels are also edged by a gold and silver coloured motif and the larger, square, centre panel has a large circular motif carved in it, as also have the corners outside the circle. Whilst it is an exceptionally fine reredos, unfortunately its height obscures the lower halves of the three inner lights of the five-light window thus marring its beauty. Three stone steps, spanning the north end of the chancel, give access to the holy table which stands on a patterned tile floor. The fine oak communion rail (3) stands on the first of the steps. The east wall is pierced in its north-east corner by a window; (7) by a door leading to the organ chamber and an arched opening which accommodates the organ manual. A doorway, giving access to the vestry, pierces the west wall. Two rows of choir stalls, in pine, flank each side of the chancel aisle.

Drawing 3. Nave, chancel and transept walls: tiles, design as above, are laid alternatively with plain tiles on the upper courses of the walls. The patterned tiles have a coloured motif. (Drawing by author.)

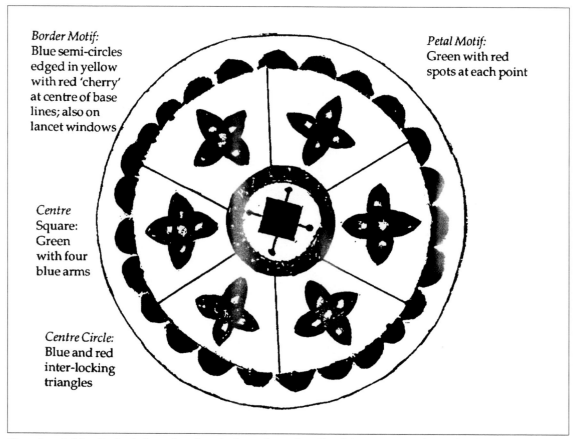

Border Motif:
Blue semi-circles edged in yellow with red 'cherry' at centre of base lines; also on lancet windows

Petal Motif:
Green with red spots at each point

Centre Square: Green with four blue arms

Centre Circle: Blue and red inter-locking triangles

Drawing 4. Identical windows (as above) pierce the end walls of the transepts. (Drawing by author.)

The Transepts

The walls of both are tiled and arcaded identically with the chancel and nave. The west transept has an outer entrance door and a finely carved double inner door which is encased within a very fine carved wooden door frame (c.1870). The lower halves of the double door are intricately carved and the upper halves are of clear glass. This doorway is surmounted by a fine circular stained glass window identical with one in the east wall of the east transept. (4) Each of the north walls of the transepts are pierced by single windows and each of the south walls are pierced by two windows. The east wall of the east transept is pierced by two windows flanking each side of the circular stained glass window. A small altar, flanked by communion rails, sits against this east wall of the east transept.

The north wall of the east transept is pierced by an open arch which accommodates the organ pipes and an open rectangular light, arched at its top, screened by metalwork tracery.

The Vestry

It was built initially in 1865 but was enlarged in 1899. Its north wall is pierced by a two light lancet window (8) and two identical two-light lancet windows pierce its west wall, flanking each side of the open-sided entrance porch of the vestry. This porch gives access, via a flight of stairs, to the vestry entrance door. Basic toilet facilities are accommodated in a cellar beneath the vestry, access to which is by a flight of stairs beneath the porch.

The accommodation is divided into the vicar's vestry and the choir vestry, this latter providing access to the chancel by a door piercing the east wall of the vestry.

The Organ Chamber[20]

This was added in 1865 but has since undergone a number of modifications.

1899
Roof of the chamber raised and a new organ installed.

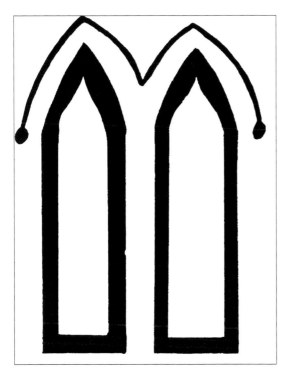

Drawing 5. The window in the east transept is flanked by two identical lancet windows (see left). The transepts were added to the nave in 1865. The stained glass is by Edmonson and Son of Manchester. (Drawing by author.)

1923

Chamber extended eastward and an arch pierced in its south wall, to accommodate a rebuilt organ with mechanical blowing equipment.

19??

Bay window added to north wall. (8)

The Nave

This has two aisles providing access to a main centre block and two side blocks, all of box pews of typical traditional design and installed when church was built. A transverse aisle gives access from the sole entrance door, at its south-west corner, to the main aisles and also additional box pews sited beneath the nave gallery. The white stone font is now positioned on this transverse aisle, immediately behind the centre block of pews. When originally installed, before 1865,[21] it was sited at the chancel end of the nave. The semi-circular headed rectangular nave windows, one in each bay, are mainly stained glass memorials. (5) Of the nine nave windows three only are of clear glass. Each window is fitted into a chamfered stone surround, flanked on each side by stone pilasters (6) of cylindrical section. Each pilaster is decorated with a spiral string course in which a leaf motif is carved. The nave walls tiling is identical with that of the chancel and transepts.

The Nave Gallery

Spans the south end of the nave and is supported in the centre by two iron pillars of circular section. The front face of its parapet consists of blind arcading. Each individual arch of the arcading is decorated with either a rose or fleur-de-lys motif. It accommodates rows of bench pews. The only

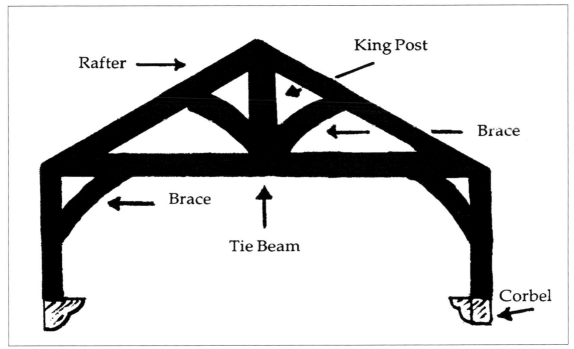

Drawing 6. Nave: six roof trusses support the nave roof, design as above. They were constructed in 1849. (Drawing by author.)

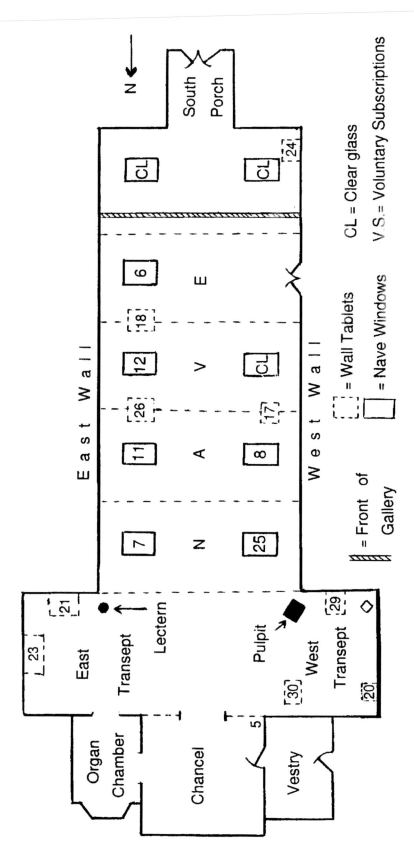

Plan of Christ Church Following Its Enlargement in 1865

Notes

1. This fine brass eagle lectern, a memorial to George Faulkner of Oaklands, Timperley, was given to Christ Church by his widow and family.

2. As it is built on a north-south axis its chancel, unconventionally, is situated at the north end of the building. The numbers marked in the 'boxes' refer to the reference number of the appropriate faculty listed in the pages following.

3. Dotted lines delineate the four bays of the nave.

4. The plan of the church shows the locale of items which are the subject of faculties (for example, wall tablets, etc.). Each location is numbered on the plan: the reference number indicates the number of the faculty in the lists of the faculties in the following pages.

access to the gallery is by a door opening into it from the first floor storey of the tower. The pews were installed in 1865 following the removal of the organ from the gallery.

The Tower and Spire

Contains a three-tiered flight of balustraded stairs leading to the nave gallery and belfry. The belfry houses a single bell and bellrope, now no longer used. After 1960 recording equipment has been used to broadcast recordings of a appropriate peals and chimes from the belfry. It would perhaps be preferable, if practicable, to revert to hand ringing, the sound quality would be much better than that offered by a recording.

Faculties Granted to Christ Church by the Bishop of Chester[22]

Notes for Guidance

Unconventionally Christ Church is built on a north-south axis with the Chancel at its north end. In the Bishop's Registers the church walls are listed, erroneously, on the basis that the building lies on an east-west axis. Thus in the Faculties the east and west nave walls are listed as 'south' and 'north' walls respectively; similarly the east and west transepts are listed, erroneously, 'south' and 'north' transepts respectively.

The plan of Christ Church is orientated correctly. Where an orientation is incorrectly recorded in the Bishop's Registers it is set in italics (for example, *west*) in the brief Faculty descriptions.

The plan of the church shows the location of items which are the subject of Faculties (for example, stained glass windows, wall tablet, etc). Each location in numbered on the plan: the reference number indicates the number of the Faculty in the lists of the Faculties in the following pages.

Key to Abbreviations used in the list
V.S. = Voluntary Subscription;　　　　　　B.R. = Bishop's Registers
The numbers relate to numbers on the plan on p.164.

No.	Cost Defrayed by	Brief Description of Faculty	Year	B.R.
1	V.S.	Enlargement of Church including the removal of original chancel and vestry: adding north and south transepts with new chancel, vestry and organ chamber: also new stained glass windows. (J. Lowe, architect, Mr. Terras, builder, both of Manchester.)	1864	22
2	Church	To remove painted glass in *east* window and place it in windows at *west* end of nave. To modify *east* window and place stained glass in modified window. (By Heaton, Butler and Bayne of London.)	1882	30
3	V.S.	To open out arch in organ chamber. To strip poor plaster from walls and reline walls with terra-cotta tiles	1887	30
4	V.S.	To enlarge vestry; raise roof of organ chamber and install new organ. (Mr. T. Bushel, architect, of Manchester.)	1899	30
5	V.S.	To erect new holy table and reredos in oak and open window in *south* side of chancel in plain glass. Reredos a memorial to Revd. C. Wilkinson. (Mr Edgar Wood, architect.)	1908	30
6	V.S.	Stained glass window representation figure of 'Faith' with inscription – memorial to Hattie Bell	1908	30
7	Sister and V.S	Stained glass window representative female figure 'Patience' with inscription – memorial to Mary Wood.	1911	30

8	Members of Family	Stained glass window representative 'Diligence' with inscription – memorial to Sir Thomas Bosdin Leech, Kt.[23] and Edith his wife, of Oakmount, Timperley	1913	31
9	V.S.	For erection of St. David's Church, Hale	1914	31
10		Recites: '...Sequestration issued to ... Churchwardens enabling them to receive revenues of church and pay a competent curate for officiating during vacancy	1917	31
11	Father	Stained glass window representative St. George representing 'Courage'. Memorial to Captain K.C.G. Wray (killed in action France, 1916)	1917	31
12	Father	Stained glass window representing St. Louis of France as a 'Crusader' with inscription. Memorial to 2nd Lt. John Swift (killed in action Mesopotamia, 1917)	1918	31
13	G. Sichell	Brass tablet mounted in oak with inscription on south wall of vestry. Memorial to Theodore Sichell deceased, married in this church 1866. Died November 1917	1918	31
14	V.S.	Tablet of alabaster and marble with inscription. Memorial to Revd. J.A. Dibben, vicar, 1880-1890 (ref. west wall of Chancel)	1919	32
15		In Churchyard: cross of stone; in Church: tablet of oak each with inscriptions. Memorial to men of parish killed in action	1920	32
16	V.S.	For extending organ chamber *eastward* and (north east wall of transept) constructing new arch in *east* wall of *south* transept. To take down and rebuild organ in enlarged chamber with mechanical blowing apparatus and radiator	1923	32
17	V.S.	Tablet of vitreous tiles framed in oak with inscription. Memorial to James H. Fisher deceased, sometime warden.	1925	32
18	V.S.	Tablet of vitreous tiles framed in oak. Memorial to Charles Fitton.	1926	32
19	V.S.	To remove existing communion rails and insert new ones in oak. Memorial to William Bell.	1933	33
20	Family	Circular plaque: Deborah, wife of Wilfred Lyon of Moatfield House, Wash Lane, Timperley. (North side of west wall of west transept.)	1866	?
21	Family	Stone tablet south wall of east transept: to Betsy, wife of Charles Moore, M.D. of Hollybank, Timperley (died October 1867)	1868	?
22	Family	Lozenge shaped plaque: Benjamin Bagnall (died 1874) south side of west wall of west transept	1875	?

23	Husband	To enlarge tablet, already erected to memory of Fanny and Thomas Southam, by placing beneath it further tablet of marble with inscription 'Memorial to Marion Southam deceased, wife of T.F. Southam M.D. of Southport'.	1934	33
24	T.F. Tattersall	Tablet of repousse (rose bronze) mounted in oak with inscription recording recent reconstruction of spire. Memorial to F.A. Tomlinson	1935	34
25	Daughter	Stained glass window: figure of St. Gabriel inscription 'Memorial to Anthony F. Obegin and Jessie Adeline his wife.'	1938	34
26	Church	Roll of Honour – Parishioners who gave their lives in 1914-1918 War.	?	?
27	Church	Renewing of electrical wiring with new shades and fittings.	1960	3?
28	Church	For alteration and improvements to *eastern* end of Church, including resiting of choir stalls, pulpit and lectern, removal of some pews in nave and transepts and introduction of free standing communion table with three-sided communion rail. (Alterations reduce seating capacity.)	1968	3?
29	Family	Tablet: William Hobday, died 1848, and his daughter Ann Milward, died 1860. South side, west wall of W.T.	1860	?
30	Church	Tablet: to Revd. Edward Dowling M.A., first vicar of Christ Church, Timperley. North wall of west transept.	1880	?
?	V.S.	Major repairs to Church involving: complete reroofing of the nave (January to June); complete reroofing of chancel, transepts and vestries (September to January)	1988 / 1988/9	

List of the Vicars of Christ Church

1849-1880	Revd. Edward Dowling MA
1880-1890	Revd. John A. Dibben MA
1890-1905	Revd. Samuelus Wilkinson MA
1906-1917	Revd. G.D. Wray MA
1917-1926	Revd. George C. Briggs MA
1926-1934	Revd. Albert William Tomlinson MA
1934-1946	Revd. Walter St. John Lindars MA, DD
1946-1956	Revd. Leonard Morley
1956-1964	Revd. Roy Duffield BA
1964-1971	Revd. Arthur L. Manning BA
1972-1992	Revd. Desmond Probets RD*
1992-1995	Revd. P.W.G. Burwell

(NB. Portrait photographs of the incumbents are hung in the vestry of the parish church.)

*The Revd. D. Probets, vicar for twenty years, retired in March 1992.[26] His successor, the Revd. P.W.G. Burwell, was inducted into the benefice on 4th November, 1992, at a service conducted by the Bishop of Stockport.

The Old Vicarage

No documents (i.e. building plans, bills, etc.) dealing with the building of the vicarage are deposited in the parish chest. The *Golden Jubilee Souvenir Booklet* of 1899 (page 5) quotes: '... does not appear to be any record of commencement of Vicarage...' This suggests that if any such documents were produced they have either been lost or deposited elsewhere.

From terriers early in the twentieth century (i.e. c.1905) it is recorded that the vicarage 'is built of white brick and comprises, Dining Room, Drawing Room, Study, Kitchen (2 Pantries and Sculleries) all cellared, seven bedrooms and Dressing Room, Bathroom and W.C. with outbuilding and a garden of about half an acre...'.

In 1901 the building was badly in need or repair (evidence of settlement in parts of building and also resiting of drains necessary). The vicar borrowed, on mortgage, a sum of £141 from the Governors of Queen Annes Bounty (a charity for maintenance of clergy) to cover the cost of repairs. The money also covered the cost of painting the building (including the front gates and lamp) with two coats of paint; the end of the house was given two coats of colour wash by the painter J.C. Davenport, of Stockport Road at a cost of £12; certain joinery works by C. Marston and Son (builders), Stockport Road. (NB. he listed his joiner as being paid at a rate of 11d per hour, labourers at 8d per hour and apprentices at 6d her hour.) The resiting of drains and structural repairs were also completed. The building was demolished (c.1963) and the present vicarage erected on the site.

The New Vicarage

On 1st September 1963 a mortgage was taken out with the Church Commissioners for £5,899 repayable in twenty-five years at 5% interest on the reducing balance 'Chargeable on all glebe, rents and other profits arising from said Benefice'... 'Towards cost of erecting house and offices.'

Modern Repairs to the Church and Churchyard

Churchyard Works

During the latter half of 1980, 1981 and part of 1982 the Manpower Service Commission provided a working party of youths who undertook various works in the churchyard which included taking down numerous headstones and laying them horizontal. Surplus earth was piled as a bank adjacent to the access path[24] to a market garden site east of the churchyard.

During the latter half of 1985 a number of overgrown rhododendron bushes were removed from the east wall of the nave. They obscured the nave wall to a height of at least six feet and were a source of damp to the wall. Their removal was well justified.

59. The New Vicarage, Thorley Lane. It was built in 1963 on the site of the original vicarage (built 1850), about 200 yards south of the village centre. (Photograph taken by the author, 1990.)

Church Fabric Renovations

A survey revealed extensive repairs to the fabric of the building were imperative. Following a public appeal to raise £100,000, parishioners raised £25,000 by the end of 1987. This enabled the most important of the repairs, reroofing of the nave, to be started in January 1988 and the work was completed in June 1988. The following September the second phase was begun, reroofing of the transepts, chancel and vestry. Following the Harvest Festival Service on 25th September, 1988, the church was closed for three months while the second phase of the repairs was undertaken.

The Church Spire

A survey revealed that it had developed a list – for a number of years this 'lean from the vertical' could be seen by the naked eye – and urgent action was necessary. During January 1992 work to take down the spire began. By the end of January the scaffolding work and necessary access ladders were in place and on 30th January the weather cock and vane were removed.[25] Then the stonework was carefully taken down, the pieces numbered and cached in the churchyard under tarpaulins. The stump was covered in lead. The work was completed by the middle of February 1992. It is understood that when funding is available it is intended to rebuild the spire. The spire had stood for over 140 years and was a notable landmark in the parish and beyond.

Church Buildings Ancillary to Christ Church

The population of the ecclesiastical parish has increased continuously since its formation in 1852. A concomitant of this trend was a burgeoning need for chapels, ancillary to the mother church, sited so as to provide convenient facilities for worship for those parishioners who happened to reside on the periphery of the parish. To cater for this need a mission school and three chapels-of-ease have been built, at various dates, within the parish.

St. Andrew's Day School and Mission House

This project was the first initiative undertaken by the church trustees. During the first half of the nineteenth century the most densely populated area of the parish was located in its north-west corner and centred on Deansgate Lane.[27] In 1873 the trustees purchased a plot of land, fronting on Deansgate Lane, with the aim of building a day school on it. Financial problems prevented imme-

60. *Christ Church spire before...* (*Photograph taken by the author, January 1992.*)

61. *Christ Church spire after...* (*Photograph taken by the author, February 1992.*)

diate development.[28] Ten years elapsed before a meeting, convened on 20th May, 1882 met to:

'...consider a scheme for building a day school and mission school on the Deansgate Lane site...'

A committee was formed and subscriptions solicited and obtained. Subsequently a building, to the designs of Mr E.J. Thompson (architect), was erected at a total inclusive cost, for the site, building and furnishing, of £937 3s 10d. It opened on 8th October, 1888. In addition to its principal function, a day school, it also functioned as a mission room where church services were conducted. Following extensive alterations to the chancel of Christ Church, in 1908, the original holy table and reredos were removed and installed in the mission room. It catered for worshippers residing in the Deansgate Lane area of the parish for almost forty-five years (see below).[29]

St. Andrew's Church

The mission room was superseded by a purpose-built chapel-of-ease in 1932, which was named St. Andrew's. The service of dedication was held on 30th November, 1932 and conducted by the Bishop of Chester. It continues to serve the needs of parishioners residing in the Brook and Deansgate Lanes area of the parish. It occupied a site on Brook Lane at a point where the lane curves towards its junction with Moss Lane and stands opposite to the building known as Fox Farm. After 1960 a short new road was constructed connecting Brook Lane, from the site of St. Andrew's, to the junction of Moss and Grove Lanes. St. Andrew's now occupies the angle between Brook Lane and its junction with Brookway, the new road.

St. David's Church

On 6th August, 1914, Christ Church was granted a faculty to erect a new church. What were the factors which persuaded a committee of local church incumbents to make the application for a faculty and the Diocesan authority to grant the faculty? A pamphlet[30] published by a committee of local incumbents and laity provides the answer to that question.

It outlines the fact that Christ Church ecclesiastical parish embraces part of the township of Hale within its confines consisting of the lands bounded by:

62. St. Andrew's, Brook Lane. It was built in 1932. (Photograph taken by author, 1989.)

63. St. David's, Grove Lane, Hale. It was built c.1915. (Photograph by author, 1989.)

'... on the north by the Civil Boundary between the townships of Timperley and Hale; on the south by Hale Road, from Queen's Road to Hale Barns then along Shay Lane to a point where it joins Rolling (sic) Lane.[31] On the east by Rolling Gate Lane to White Carr Lane; on the west by Queen's Road...'

The area was centred on a house called The Hermitage[32] which lends its name to this district of Hale. The area was then being redeveloped for residential purposes and in view of the consequent rapid increase in population – already it contained 380 houses and 1650 residents – the church worthies formed a considered opinion that new church accommodation in this section of the parish to cater for the needs of the parishioners was urgently needed. The result of their deliberations was:

a. They should erect a *Temporary* church (author's italics) as soon as possible.
b. A clergyman should be placed in sole charge of the new church district.
c. That it was their aim that the new church district should become a parish in its own right in the future.
d. That the curate in charge 'shall be guaranteed' a stipend of not less than £150 p.a. which it is hoped will be supplemented by the congregation so as to 'raise the stipend to at least £200'.
e. An appeal for subscriptions should be launched to build a '... temporary Church of an artistic design, not an iron building...'

Plans on these premises were considered and it was found that a suitable building to accommodate 250 persons could be built for £600. No costs were involved as regards the site as a suitable plot of land:

'... has been generously offered by Mr. Macnamara... of c. One Acre... having a frontage on Grove Lane of about 80 yards...'

This site was almost equidistant, about one mile, from both Christ Church and St. Peters; and about one and a quarter miles from Hale Barns' Mission Church; and about one and a quarter miles from St. John's Church.[33]

These plans were soon put in hand and what was in effect a chapel-of-ease for Timperley parishioners was built and opened for worship.

The committee's resolutions have proved to be far sighted as residential development has continued in the district, especially post-1945.[34]

In one respect the committee's hopes have not been realised as the church is still part of Christ Church parish. Possibly its hopes will be realised in the future.

St. Catherine's Church

Occupies a site which was originally part of Riddings Hall Farm. In 1852 a Mr J. Grave (calico

64. Brookfield House, Park Road. It was built in 1905. Now renamed St. Catherine's House, it is the residence of the curate in charge of St. Catherine's Church. (Photograph taken by the author, 1989.)

printer) purchased a plot of land of c.1¾ acres (about 135 yards by 65 yards), which comprised parts of the Moatfield and Carrsfield. It had a frontage to Wash Lane of c.135 yards. On it he built a large mansion, with associated outbuildings and gardens, and enclosed the whole site, on its western, northern and eastern boundaries, by a high brick wall (c.7 feet high).[35] The house and outbuildings were demolished in 1904 and the site re-developed. The initial re-development was a large detached house and grounds, called Brookfield House (1905) with a frontage of 40 yards to Wash Lane, which occupies that part of the Moatfield House site taken out of Carrsfield. Its western boundary, now the western side of Acresfield Road, is delineated by the original western wall of Moatfield House. The Moatfield part of the Moatfield House site was redeveloped with three pairs of semi-detached houses. All seven properties are still extant and occupied (1989). From, at least, 1938 to 1957 Brookfield House was the home of a Mr and Mrs G. Beedle. A 1942 directory contains the following entry:

'Brookfield House Junior School: Head: Mrs E.G. Beedle, 97 Park Road.'[36]

At some date subsequent to 1958 the house and grounds were acquired by the diocesan auth-

65. St. Catherine's, Park Road. It was built in 1969. (Photograph taken by the author, 1989.)

66. The Parish Hall, Thorley Lane. It was built in 1968/75. It occupies the site of the old National School (built in 1856 and demolished in c.1962-5). It is sited at the junction with Mainwood Road. (Photograph taken by the author, 1990.)

orities and planning permission obtained to build a church on part of its site. St. Catherine's Church was eventually built, c.1968/9, on the undeveloped western side of the plot. It opened for worship in March 1969. Brookfield House was then renamed St. Catherine's House and is the residence of the curate in charge of this daughter church of Christ Church.

It caters for parishioners who reside, principally, in the north-east sector of the parish which embraces, approximately, that part of the parish bounded by the Bridgewater Canal, the Cheshire Lines Railway Line between Stockport Road and Moss Lane and the line of the Fairywell Brook between Stockport Road, and the canal. Strictly speaking it is, like St. Andrews and St Davids, a chapel-of-ease for a peripheral sector of the parish.

Notes

1. At that time Bowdon parish embraced eight townships: Altrincham, Ashley, Bowdon, Carrington, Dunham Massey, Hale (including Ringway), Partington and Timperley and also parts of Agden and Ashton-on-Mersey. A few fields of Baguley township were in Northenden parish.

2. John Barratt was a grocer, maltster and wine merchant of Altrincham and a landowner in Timperley.

3. The original legal documents are all deposited in the Parish Chest.

4. Ibid.

5. Messrs Bagnall and Joynson negotiated with John Paulden. He was tenant of the field on which the vicarage was built. It formed part of Fir Tree Farm and was called Hope Ridding field. At that time Fir Tree Farm was farmed by James Thomason. Presumably he rented it from the leaseholder John Paulden.

6. The son of John Barratt.

7. See document entitled 'Case of John Barratt's will', deposited in the parish chest.

8. The vicar of Bowdon was absent due to illness.

9. A copy is deposited in the parish chest.

10. A point approximately midway between Ashfield and Hawthorn Roads.

11. The indentures covering these rents were vested in the trustees who were required to apply the income to the vicar's stipend and the Repair Fund as delineated thus '... on Trust by consent of Bishop of Chester...'.

12. Rents Nos. 1-3 and 4 to vicar's stipend; No.2 to Repair Fund.

13. This mansion was, many years later, renamed 'Parkfield' and for many years housed a Boys' Remand Home. In 1992 it was demolished and the site redeveloped.

14. For some lengthy period prior to 1988 the nave roof had been giving cause for concern. In 1986 a Roof Restoration Fund, aiming to raise £100,000 was launched. Work commenced in January 1988 (Fearnley Construction Co. Ltd, of Salford). The roof was encased in scaffolding and plastic sheeting during the period the work was in progress. It was completed in early May 1988. The rafters and slates were removed and replaced by new ones. The nave roof formed part of the original building and was about 140 years old, prior to replacement. A further scheme to reroof the chancel and transepts was started in October 1988. The work was carried out by a different firm of contractors and was completed in early 1989.

15. According to an item in *The Builder* reprinted in *Manchester Courier*, 1st November, 1851.

16. Both chancel and vestry of this original building were taken down to accommodate transepts in a later extension scheme (see p.158).

17. The compass positions denoted on the plans are wrong. They are based on the assumption that the Church has an east-west axis; in fact it has a north-south axis. Accordingly, the orientations given should be amended as follows: for *north* read *east*; for *south* read *west*; for *west* read *south*; and for *east* read *north*.

18. This work necessitated the removal of four mural monuments from the nave and resiting them in the transepts. The church was closed from 1st April to 24th June, 1888.

19. Installed in 1908.

20. Pre-1865 organ was sited in the nave gallery.

21. Font removed to its present position in 1865. It was presented to the church as a memorial to Maud Dowling '... from her sorrowing parents', the then vicar and his wife.

22. Full descriptions of the faculties listed are recorded in the Bishop's Registers.

23. Sir Thomas Bosdin Leech helped in the building of the Manchester Ship Canal.

24. An access path to the market garden. It ceased production and in 1981 the site was developed for housing. The access path is now permanently closed.

25. The author was able to inspect the weathercock which had surmounted the spire since 1849. Made of copper and in excellent condition, each arm was about 18 inches long and the cock (gilded) was about 12 to 15 inches high.

26. See local newspaper reports in *The Sale and Altrincham Messenger*, dated 21st February, 1992 and *The Timperley Independent*, 30th October, 1992.

27. 1841 Census lists 35% of population as residing in the Deansgate Lane area.

28. At that time the trustees were involved in raising finance for Stockport Road School.

29. Replaced by contemporary St. Andrews.

30. Pamphlet No.239 deposited in Altrincham Reference Library.

31. All references inspected by the author, with the exception of this one, label it 'Roaring Gate Lane'.

32. Now demolished. A garage on Bancroft Road is located, approximately, on its site.

33. Perfectly sited.

34. For example, Well Green estate, council housing, Delahays and adjacent roads, etc.

35. This wall is still extant and its western and eastern sides are contiguous with the lines of Riddings and Acresfield Roads respectively.

36. The dates of opening and closure of this school have not been established due to the limited amount of archive material available. It was probably established post-1930.

TRANSCRIPTION OF THE INSTRUMENT DELINEATING THE DISTRICT COMPRISING THE ECCLESIASTICAL PARISH OF CHRIST CHURCH, TIMPERLEY

'An Act of Parliament... the reign of his late Majesty William the fourth Chapter Thirty Eight and subsequent Acts relating thereto it appears to us expedient in pursuance of the provisions of the said Act and all other Acts in that behalf to assign to a particular District of the said Church for the Visitation of the Sick and other pastoral and Ecclesiastical duties. WE therefore by these Presents do assign and declare that the said District shall comprise and consist of such parts of the said Parish of Bowdon as lies within the following boundary that is to say, a line drawn from a point in Long Lane, Hale, at the junction of the townships of Hale and Altrincham, from thence following the course of the Long Lane until it reaches a farm at present known as 'Warburtons', from thence turning to the left by Shaw Lane to Davenport Green, from thence again turning to the left passing the farm known as the 'Roaring Gate' and proceeding onwards to the junction of the road with White Carr Lane, there turning to the right to Newall Green Hall and then again turning to the right to the Old Wood Farm and from the Old Wood Farm by a fence to Baguley Brook, from thence taking the course of the brook to Black Carr Wood, from thence turning to the left it pursues the boundary which separates that part of the township of Baguley paying Tithe and Church Rate to Northen [Northenden], from that part paying Church Tithe and Church Rate to Bowdon until it again reaches Baguley Brook, from thence pursuing the course of the Brook until the Brook passes under the Bridgewater Canal, from thence turning to the left it takes the course of the canal to Timperley Brook near Deansgate Lane from thence again turning to the left it proceeds up the Brook and across the Warrington and Stockport Turnpike Road taking the course of the boundary between the township of Timperley and Altrincham until it arrives at the Foot Path leading from Wood Lane in Timperley to Hale Moss, from thence turning to the right down the Foot Path to Hale Moss, from thence passing to the right down the side of the Moss to the stream which separates the townships of Altrincham and Hale, from thence turning to the left it takes the boundary of the last named two townships across the Moss and through the fields adjoining until it reaches the first named point in Long Lane, Hale aforesaid and which said District is more particularly delineated set out and shown on the plan hereto annexed [see map on p.153] and bounded thereon by and included in a Red line. And we hereby declare that the same shall be a District of the said Church called Christ Church, Timperley aforesaid so far only as regards the Visitation of the Sick and other pastoral and Ecclesiastical duties Reserving nevertheless to ourselves and our successors all power to assign any part of the District hereby assigned to Christ Church, Timperley aforesaid to any other Church new or thought to be built and erected within the said Parish of Bowdon. GIVEN under our hand and Episcopal Seal – the Seventh day of May – in the year of our Lord One Thousand Eight Hundred and Fifty Two and of our Consecration the Fourth.'

Note: Some of the place names used in the instrument have changed over the years.

Long Lane	–	Hale Road
Shaw Lane	–	Shay Lane
Warburton's Farm	–	junction of Hale Road and Shay Lane
close	–	field with a hedge
Hale Moss	–	now Stamford Park (mostly)
Newall Green Hall	–	Newall Green Farm.

13

NON-CONFORMISM IN TIMPERLEY
'...All protestantism, even the most cold and passive, is a sort of dissent...'

Edmund Burke

Introduction

Dissent outside the Church of England really began in the 1640s, after the end of the Civil War. It was tolerated until the Restoration. Then Charles II and his government brought in the Act of Uniformity, the Test Acts and the Conventicle Acts in 1662/3, which ejected puritan ministers and tried to make sure that neither they nor their supporters could meet or take office.[1] The 1673 Toleration Act licensed some meeting places, but restrictions such as the Act of Uniformity and the Conventicle Acts were largely removed by the Toleration Act in 1689:

'... An Act for exempting their Majesties Protestant Subjects dissenting from Church of England from the penalties of certain laws...'

It gave dissenters the freedom to worship in their own chapels subject to the proviso that:

'... Dissenting Places of Worship are required to be registered at the Diocesan Registry or Quarter Sessions...'

This provision was repeated by an Act of 52 Geo. III (1812) which further required:

'... The Registrar and Clerk of the Peace to notify each other of the places so registered...'

An Act 32 Geo. III (1791) extended some of the provisions of the Toleration Act to Roman Catholics.

Non-conformism, which was falling into decline in the early eighteenth century, found its position eased by these Acts, but it was given an additional boost by the arrival of Methodism between 1750 and 1850. Timperley reflected this trend and the burgeoning of non-conformism in the township is predominantly the story of the growth of Methodism.

When considering the development of non-conformism in the township it is useful to keep in mind the population figures during the period 1750-1971 as revealed principally by the Censuses.[2]

1750	–	450[3]	1800	–	588
1851	–	1008	1901	–	3215
1951	–	19,232	1971	–	24,343

The Methodist Church in Timperley

During the period 1691-1735 no dissenting places of worship were registered for Timperley, although at least nine such places are registered for townships bordering Timperley, including four in Hale. The first such registration for Timperley was formally recorded at the Diocesan Episcopal Registry at Chester on 13th November, 1786.[4]

Residence:	Dwelling House of John Potts (husbandman)[5]
Denomination:	Not stated
Person Certifying:	John Potts X (his mark)
Signed:	Jeremiah Brundrett, David Matley, Johnathan Goulden and Samuel Palpryman.

The lack of documentary evidence before 1786, and the initial registration (on the previous page) possibly means that non-conformism was first established in the township c.1785. Although the religious denomination of the place of worship is not listed on the certificate, it is almost certain that it was registered by members of a Timperley Methodist society, as the subsequent non-conformist evidence available for the nineteenth century is exclusively Methodist.

In 1803 a membership register lists thirteen members, with one William Greenwood as their leader.[6] By 1808 membership had increased to nineteen. No membership registers are extant for the years 1809-14 and it may well be that, during that period, Timperley Methodists worshipped at the meeting house of the Altrincham Society as, on 13th March, 1815, Samuel Holt, a prominent Timperley resident,[7] and a member of the Altrincham Society and a Sunday School teacher there, made the following application to the Altrincham Sunday School:

> '... for the forms belonging to the Timperley teaching house and which *for some time past* have been used for the purposes of the School...'

This would appear to be fairly conclusive evidence that Timperley Methodists had, for a period, ceased to use their Timperley premises and worshipped at Altrincham. Samuel Holt was intent on revitalising Methodism in Timperley. A Manchester Circuit Preaching Plan shows that, in 1816, fortnightly Sunday Evening Services, at 6pm, were held in Timperley, and around this date Samuel Holt was appointed leader of the Timperley Methodist group, an office he held for over twenty years. His cottage, in Thorley Lane (long demolished), was used as the Preaching House. At the outset of the nineteenth century, in addition to the Holts, some long established Timperley families including Marslands, Lucases, Chorltons and Hankinsons were members of the Society.

Heyes Lane Chapel

In 1825 John Marsland[8] joined Samuel Holt and, under their joint leadership, Methodism in the township burgeoned with membership increasing to thirty[9] within five years. The fortnightly Sunday service was now supplemented by a monthly Monday evening meeting at 7pm and the society was financially able to subscribe £10 per annum, no mean sum in those days, to circuit funds.

The Thorley Lane Preaching House accommodation facilities were, by 1830, inadequate and the erection of a purpose-built chapel was proposed and approved. John Marsland offered a plot of

67. Heyes Lane Chapel dates from 1833 and had a frontage to Wash Lane. Following the opening of the 'New Chapel', in 1847, the building was converted into a terrace of three cottages in 1850 called 'Chapel Cottages'. The terrace was demolished in the early 1980s and the site redeveloped: part of the site is unused but the rest was redeveloped with a block of two storey local authority town-houses. (Photograph, c.1960-70, is reproduced here by kind permission of Guardian Newspapers.)

his land for sale, situated at the corner of Heyes and Wash Lanes, which was obtained and building commenced in the latter half of 1832.

A number of tradesmen were engaged in the work. Some of the labour appears to have been voluntary (for example, it is recorded: 'John Marsland carted the bricks...').

Some of the accounts have been preserved. The bill presented by Thomas Aimson (joiner), whose workshop stood at the corner of Stockport Road and Moss Lane, is the most imposing. Presented on an unruled sheet of foolscap, it is faultlessly written. The total amount of the bill is £47 3s 0d. The items listed include planks, boards, nails and also records the making of a gate, doors and forms. It also records workmen's day rates of pay and that joiners were paid 3s 6d per day. Amongst the other accounts there is listed a payment to:

'John Starkey' – 'For making a book-rest – 3s 6d.'

Another of the accounts is quoted verbatim below:

		s	d
'John Barrow			
to			
James Shigley			
To white washing Timperley Chappel		s	d
1. Day & Half Thos. Garner, 3/8d pr. Day	–	5	6
2. Do. To Thos. Sheldon 2/6d Do.	–	6	3
		11	9
Altringham			
19 July, 1833.	Settled July 20, 1833		
	James X Shigley's Mark.'[10]		

The cost of the project was financed through a loan from John Barrow, a prominent Altrincham Methodist. For a number of years, following completion of the building, a sum of £124 remained owing to him. A number of Altrincham Methodists, together with a number of Timperley Methodists, served as trustees of the new Heyes Lane Chapel which was opened for worship early in 1833, as the entry in Quarter Sessions and also the Diocesan Registry proves:

Date:	8th January 1833
Residence:	A certain house erected at Timperley in Bowdon Parish
Denomination:	(Not stated)
Person Certifying:	Nathaniel Pass[11]

Following the building of the Stockport Road Chapel, in 1847, the Heyes Lane Chapel was converted into a block of three cottages which were called 'Chapel Cottages'. They were occupied until c.1980 when they were demolished and the site redeveloped with a block of small, two-storey terraced houses, each accommodating two purpose-built flats.

The purpose-built chapel served Methodism in the township for fourteen years and laid the foundations for its future expansion in the second half of the nineteenth and onwards into the twentieth century; the scale of that development would have amazed its founder members.[12]

By 1845 the Heyes Lane Chapel was found to be inadequate for the needs of the congregation which, in addition to members, attracted a number of 'hearers', about sixty, for whom accommodation needed to be provided. It was now started that:

'... the application for pews is such as to justify the expectation of raising £20 per annum in pew rents...'

68. Victorian shop built pre-1876. It is known colloquially, at least since c.1930, as 'Constable's', the name of its quondam proprietor for many decades. It stands adjacent to the site of the Methodist 'Chapel Cottages' which were demolished c.1980-82 and the site redeveloped with a block of modern cottages. Note the end elevations of the 'new' cottages. (Compare with the photograph on p.177.) (Photograph taken by the author, February 1993)

The Timperley chapel had now been a constituent part of the Altrincham Methodist Circuit for some years and at the Circuit quarterly meeting, in June 1845, the following resolution occurs in its Minute Book:

> '... Resolved that as increased accommodation is required at the Timperley Chapel, the Trustees be recommended to consult together as to which is most desirable, viz., alter or rebuild our Chapel there or procure a new site and erect a new Chapel, applying to the Conference, through the Building Committee, for power to dispose of the present erection...'

Following consultation the chapel was declared to be:

> '... small and incapable for being improved; site also bad...'

Subsequently, John Chorlton[13] secured a plot of land on Stockport Road[14] on a lease for 1,000 years which he later assigned to the trustees. On 14th September, 1846 the foundation stone was laid and building commenced. The Heyes Lane Chapel was sold for £153; after paying off the debt of £124 still owing to John Barrow, and other minor expenses, the trustees were left with a balance of £24. The total cost of the chapel was £600, of which £420 was raised through subscriptions and collections,[15] leaving a debt of £180. The builder was Charles Holt.

Extracts from building accounts:
The principal account was submitted by Charles Holt (builder) for the sum of £446 10s 0d. It was paid in cash.

Some of the minor accounts are most revealing as regards contemporary labour, building materials and refreshment costs:

Item: '... Five Barrels of Beer –	10s 6d.'
Item: '... Provisions –	11s 6d.'
Item: '... Paid Wm. Pearson for Tenant's right of land –	£4 0s 0d.'
Item: '... Five Hundred Bricks –	£1 7s 6d.'
Item: '... Philip Renshaw for two days work –	5s 6d.'

A number of entries record wages paid to journeymen (possibly bricklayers and/or labourers) which suggest that they earned less than £1 per week.

The bills were paid by Jeremiah Rogerson (trustee) and in total amounted to £579 18s 5½d. It exhausted the building fund and resulted in a debit balance of £183 4s 2½d. Mr William Ackroyd then donated the odd £3 4s 2½d, leaving the fund exactly £180 in debt.[16]

The new chapel opened for worship on Whit Sunday, 23rd May, 1847, but apart from the amount of the collections no details of the opening services are known.

The external and internal features of the chapel building are described in E.H. Wright's book, *The Story of Timperley Methodism: 1833-1933.*

'The appearance of the chapel was exceedingly plain. It was a square shaped building with a low pitched roof. There was no porch or entrance at the front, but only a very ordinary doorway at the side – on the left hand. A small schoolroom was built at the back and was covered by a roof which sloped away from the end of the main building. Although a considerable portion of the chapel still remains in the fabric of the present church, it has been since altered and improved out of all recognition of its former appearance.

On entering the chapel, the visitor found the same simplicity. In the centre of the floor there was a stove, the chimney of which ascended to the ceiling. Here, also in the centre, were the forms on which the children sat. Behind the forms, uninviting wooden pews rose in tiers to the wall where the plain windows overlooked the Stockport Road. Thus, the late comer, entering by the door at the side, found it impossible to reach his seat without being observed by the whole congregation. Facing the stove, the forms and the rising pews, there was a pulpit and above the pulpit, a small gallery. 'The singing gallery', as it was called, contained sufficient room for the man who played the double bass fiddle and a few chosen people who led the singing, and it was entered by steps from the school-room behind...'

The building was registered at the Chester Diocesan Registry a fortnight before the opening service:

Date:	10th May, 1847
Residence:	Altrincham
Person Certifying:	William Elton[17]
Denomination:	Wesleyan
Building Certified for:	A certain building called a chapel recently erected by the side of the highway leading from Altrincham to Stockport in the township of Timperley, parish of Bowdon, county of Chester.

The Timperley Methodists appear to have acted unilaterally in the sale of the Heyes Lane Chapel as, following official enquiries, it was stated there had been:

'... considerable irregularity', but that '... no blame attached to superintendent...'

Shortly before the building of the new chapel, Samuel Holt had relinquished the leadership and his office was filled by George Fletcher who lived at Riddings Hall Farm. He occupied the post for twenty years and also served as Trustee, Society Steward and Sunday School Superintendent; in this latter position he was ably assisted by his nephew, Christopher Webster. George Fletcher was a highly respected member of the community and proved a worth successor to Samuel Holt.

In the Methodist tradition most services were conducted by local preachers; hymn singing was an integral part of the services, the tunes being played by one James Potts on the double bass and the singing led by his 'singers'. They were all accommodated in the small Singing Gallery sited at the rear of the pulpit. It was not until 1860 that a small organ was installed when William Potts[18] was appointed organist.

The Trustees' Accounts and Records Book covering the period 1847-1900 is preserved,[19] although in poor condition and the records section has many gaps[20] which makes it difficult to date precisely the completion of subsequent modifications and extensions to the building.

Following the opening of the railway to Altrincham, in 1849, the influx of new residents into

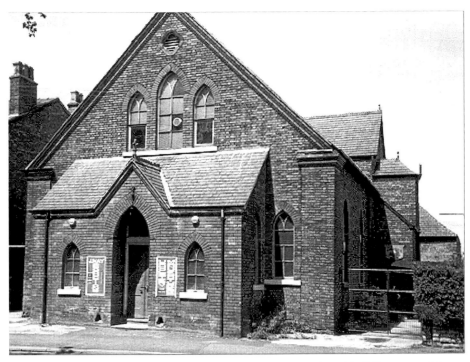

69. Methodist Chapel, Stockport Road, erected 1847. The chapel building was sold c.1958-59. In the 1980s, when this photograph was taken, it was being utilised for industrial purposes as a small clothing factory. Note the noticeboards – possibly the original chapel noticeboards – advertising the company's name.

In 1989 the building was in a poor state of repair and its future uncertain.
(Photograph taken by the author, 1989.)

Timperley, although slow initially, began the metamorphosis of the township into a dormitory suburb. These new residents brought a new dynamism to the village and were responsible for the active development of Methodism in Timperley from 1850 and on into the twentieth century.

Following the loss of George Fletcher as Leader, in 1865, the affairs of the Society languished for some years. This is revealed by a question posed at the Circuit quarterly meeting in September 1867:

'What leaders have we at Timperley and have they any Leaders' Meeting?'

In his reply we are told only that the Superintendent:

'... explained how peculiarly the Society there [Timperley] was situated...'

This may well be coded language for internal disagreements between the members. The Society by this time may well have been augmented with nouveaux residents who desired to change the established scheme of things, causing factional differences. It would appear any such problems had been largely resolved when in September 1870:

'... Mr Jackson of Timperley reported that there appeared to be more unity in the Society...'

This was followed, in March 1871, by a resolution to draw up a new trust deed which was duly constituted[21] and recorded in the Minutes in rhyme by Samuel Warren, a man noted for his humour:

> *'Unanimously Agreed – That there be a New Trust Deed –*
> *The Chapel painted outside – And also beautified –*
> *To spend all we get – But not increase the Debt...'*

This marked the end of the period of disunity and the beginning of a long period of continuous development of the Methodist Church in the township.

Obviously, the internal problems of the past had been resolved as, in 1872, the trustees agreed to proceed with a scheme involving the entire remodelling of the church[22] and in May of that year plans, specifications and an estimate for the work had been accepted. Due to the gaps in the records, one cannot establish precisely when the work was completed but it was certainly finished before the end of 1873 or early 1874, since in 1874 the trustees were discussing further improvement of the property and the 'comfort and convenience it afforded', viz:

'... cushioning of chapel seats... lamp for the front door for week night Services during the Winter months...'

Estimates were also called for:

'... framing round chapel walls and,... boarding and treating walls of Schoolroom and adjoining vestry... expenses to be met by "Trust Sermons" being preached and collections made...'

The 1872 scheme of internal modifications to the chapel involved a complete remodelling of the interior and some redesign of the porch:

Removal of tiered pews.
Levelling of church floor.
Redesigning of pews to make them shorter in height and their (originally) straight backs to be sloped, followed by staining and vanishing and replacing on the level floor.
The side entrance to the chapel being bricked up and a centre doorway made at the front with an outside and inside porch.
The Singing Gallery at the rear of the pulpit to be removed and a large archway made with folding doors made in the wall to unite the school and chapel when occasion demanded.

The cost was defrayed by the proceeds of collections at the opening services and various fundraising events such as 'A Christmas Tea Meeting' and 'A Sewing Meeting Bazaar'.

In April 1878 the small schoolroom was extended and the pulpit end of the chapel rearranged.[23] Following the appointment of the Revd. J. Bush as Superintendent of the Altrincham Circuit, he initiated a number of improvements at Timperley, one of which was the formation of a new trust. Its influential membership included prominent Timperley Methodists.[24]

During the period 1882-3 a further major building project was put in hand, which, on completion in September 1883, gave the chapel its contemporary appearance.[25] It involved:

'Removal of roof... raising walls ten feet... installing new roof and ceiling;... building outside vestibule with staircases and installing a gallery.'

The work was carried out by Cross and Bell and cost £325.

A circular in the Methodist Archives gives the following details of the opening services after completion of the modifications:

Services	Preachers
4th October, 1883	Revd. W. Barlow Sarjeant of Manchester, Cheetham Hill Circuit. (followed by a public tea served in the schoolroom and evening meeting in the chapel, presided over by Mr Edward Potts of Bowdon.) At the meeting a lecture given by Revd. Joseph Bush, by 'special request', entitled 'Marriage Before and After'
7th October, 1883	1. Revd. Allen Rees, Minister of Circuit 2. Revd. F.C. Stuart of Manchester, Oxford Road Circuit
14th October, 1883	1. Revd. F. Luke Wiseman, Assistant Tutor, Didsbury College 2. Revd. Alfred Roebuck of Sale. 3. After service of song, conductor Mr John Lambert

Enlargements were made later following a Sunday School initiative in 1893 when a deputation of that body conveyed to the trustees:

'... the wishes of the Teachers' meeting for an enlargement of the School' and promising '... extensive help on condition that the Sunday School be represented on the Trust...'[26]
The reply they received is a model of diplomacy:

'The Trustees say... while they appreciate the zeal shown for this important branch of Church work they cannot sanction the principle that different departments... should be separately and specifically represented on the Trust... gratefully recognise number of gentlemen have settled in the neighbourhood... doing good work for God in different departments of Church... desirable to attach these workers more fully to the cause... willing to take steps for enlargement of Trust by those who have qualified themselves, according to Model Deed, by Church Membership...'

As far back as 1882 the trustees had appreciated that increased accommodation was needed and had discussed the possibility of obtaining a strip of land at the rear of the chapel, but the landowner (when interviewed by a trust member, Mr Blackwell) stated, 'he would not part with it at any price'. Not until 1895 were the trustees able to purchase a plot of land from Mr William Jackson. It was located between the rear of the chapel and Grove Lane, which included a four foot wide strip on the east side of the chapel.[27]

Shortly afterwards a scheme was put in hand which involved the demolition of the old school premises, extending the chapel and the erection of a, then, new school room on the newly acquired land. Work commenced in September 1896 and the new school room opened on 14th March and the extended chapel on 30th June, 1897. The cost was £1,380. As usual, it was largely defrayed by voluntary contributions[28] and the outstanding balance of £200 was cleared in 1900 by the generosity of Mr John Lambert.[29]

The chapel continued to serve the community until superseded by the new Methodist church in 1937 (see next section). The chapel continued to house the Sunday School, except during the war years,[30] until 1959 when the building was sold for the sum of £3,250. Since then it has been utilised for various commercial activities, not perhaps the fate one would have wished for a building which had served Methodism in the township for over a century. Apart from the addition of two small classrooms above the vestry, the building has not changed since 1897.

The trustees, foreseeing the acute need for more accommodation provision, occasioned by the post-1920 population explosion, acquired an excellent building site fronting Stockport Road and adjacent to Grove Lane, in about 1930, which was subsequently destined to become the hub of the next and most recent phase of Timperley Methodism. (See next section.)

Methodism in Timperley in the Twentieth Century

The most recent phase of Methodism in Timperley may be said to have commenced in 1937 when the present church building opened for worship. It is the third purpose-built Methodist church in the township and reflects and caters for the phenomenal population growth in Timperley post-1920.[31]

The detailed history of the church during the half century c.1930-1980 is dealt with meticulously in a recent publication[32] and thus it is only necessary, in the interests of continuity, to cover the period in general terms in this chapter. The site of the building of about 4,000 square yards was purchased for the sum of £650 and initially was largely financed by a bank loan of £450. Com-

70. *Methodist Church and Sunday School building, Stockport Road, built 1959. (Photograph taken by author, 1990.)*

mencing in 1931, following the purchase in May 1930, fundraising initiatives were organised with the aim of extinguishing the debt by the date of the centenary celebrations in April 1933; they were so successful that by May 1933 a sum of £610 plus had been raised, sufficient to clear the bank loan and incidental expenses and leave a sum of £100 to start a building fund. By November 1933, following active discussions, the consensus was for two separate buildings, church and Sunday School, each with a seating capacity of 400 at an estimated total cost of £10,000. Of four architects invited to submit plans, those of Chippendale and Needham were chosen and an application for a 50% grant submitted to the Chapel Department. In the event a 33% grant was offered and the trustees calculated that the shortfall of £3,000 precluded them from proceeding with the project at that time. Following intensive fundraising initiatives in 1935-6, the building fund stood at £1,350 plus and it was resolved to proceed with a modified scheme for a church only, seating 350, at a cost of £5,000. Tenders were put out in April 1837 and within six months, on 24th November, 1937, the new church was opened.

The wartime requisitioning of the old chapel highlighted the urgent need to acquire premises for the use of church organisations, especially youth activities. In 1943 an ideal opportunity arose to satisfy that need when a large dwelling house, with land attached, adjacent to the church was offered for sale.[33] Following negotiations, the property and land was purchased by the trustees for the sum of £1,630. The conveyance was signed in August 1944 and the premises were opened on 9th September, 1944 as the Belmont Youth Centre. The Belmont premises, managed by an executive committee, served the needs of the youth centre and other church organisations, in association with the old chapel premises, until 1960 when it was superseded by the present schoolroom. It was then demolished and the grounds developed as a car park and lawns, giving the site its present day aspect.

The need for a purpose-built Sunday School had been appreciated since 1930 but the 1930s' building programme, due to lack of funds, was restricted to the construction of the present church. The war years had effectively quashed further building for the foreseeable future. Not until 1953 was a committee formed to reactivate the project. It estimated the capital needed would be about £15,000 plus an additional £8,000 if a second storey over the main halls was to be included in the plan. A fundraising scheme was launched on 9th January, 1954 which flourished and by September 1955 stood at £2,000 plus. At this juncture various building plans were considered and by August 1956 the siting of the proposed building had been determined. In 1957 the building fund exceeded £5,000 and with grants totalling £6,000 promised (i.e. Rank Trust £5,000;[34] Chapel Committee £1,000) funding was adequate for building work to be put in hand. After careful consideration the committee decided to err on the side of caution and delay a start until the building fund had been augmented further; accordingly they determined that building should commence in early Spring 1959. In that year the sale of the old chapel for £3,250 augmented the fund. Building went ahead as planned and the chapel was officially opened, following completion, on 12th December, 1959, by Mr Albert Walsh. The cost of the project was £20,199 5s 6d, leaving the building fund with a credit balance of £2 13s 10d. From its initial conception in the early 1930s over two decades had elapsed for the project to be brought to fruition. The sums raised voluntarily reflect great credit on the efforts of all the subscribers to the fund whose names are recorded for posterity in a record book.

Some fourteen years later a further building project was undertaken. It involved the construction of a covered link connecting the church and schoolroom and certain modifications to the chancel area of the church. The principal works were undertaken in late 1974 and the church was reopened on 14th December, 1974 by Mr Arthur Marsland,[35] doyen of the trustees and the oldest member. These modifications were the final responsibility of the Timperley trustees as, from 16th April, 1977, the provisions of the Methodist Church Act came into force and managing trusteeship was vested in the Church Council. The post-1938 activities of the Church Community is well documented[36] and is not duplicated in these pages. Suffice it to say that a Timperley Methodist community has been extant for over 150 years, is an integral part of the village community and continues to flourish.

Ministers of Timperley Methodist Church, Part of Altrincham Circuit	
1920-1923	Revd. J. Allan Fletcher
1923-1924	Revd. Harold Roberts
1924-1928	Revd. Ernest H. Wright
1928-1931	Revd. A. Reginald Todd
1931-1935	Revd. Donald G. Brook
1935-1940	Revd. William J.D. Evans
1940-1948	Revd. Cyril J. Thomas
1948-1952	Revd. Edward W.H. Herron
1952-1959	Revd. John Stacey, B.D.
1959-1964	Revd. Austin J. Rees
1964-1970	Revd. James Wright
1970-1973	Revd. John Harris
1973-1978	Revd. J.G. Alan Williams
1978-1986	Revd. Malcolm L. Braddy
1986- ?	Revd. I. Johnson

Although the Protestant non-conformist tradition in the township is predominantly Methodist, a number of other non-conformist denominations have a presence – albeit they have not been established as long.

A paucity of documentary evidence appertaining to them limits their treatment in these pages to brief details only.

Heyes Lane Congregational Church

Heyes Lane Congregational Church has been established in Timperley for over half a century, probably c.1930-5 and possibly earlier than that. Following a 1949 application, sanction was obtained for a new church building which was subsequently built in 1954 at a cost of £16,500 to plans drawn up by Mr F. Barber, MBE, A.R.I.B.A. The official opening of the new church took place on 27th November, 1954.[37] The minister at that time was the Revd. J.H.E. Hull, BD. The old church building was then utilised for general church purposes.

Woodlands United Reformed Church

This was originally a Broadheath-sited foundation. Having sold the church and site in Broadheath, the trustees applied the proceeds to the building of this new church on a site in Woodlands

71. Heyes Lane Congregational Church, built c.1930-5, now used as a church hall. (Photograph taken by author, February 1993.)

72. Modern Congregational Church and Sunday School building, Heyes Lane, built 1954. (Photograph taken by author, February 1993.)

Parkway. The opening ceremony and dedication service[38] was held on 7th October, 1972 and was conducted by the Revd. John White, Moderator of the East Midland U.R. Church. The minister in 1980 was the Revd. Graham Carling.

Other Churches

These include Newstead Evangelical Church, Newstead Terrace and the Jehovah's Witnesses Church on Wellington Road.

73. St. Hugh of Lincoln, Roman Catholic Church, Manchester Road. (Photograph taken by author, February 1993.)

74. St. John the Baptist, Roman Catholic Church, Thorley Lane. (Photograph taken by author, February 1993.)

Roman Catholic Churches

After 1925, housing development occasioned a great increase in the population of the village. The new residents included Catholic families who initially needed to travel to Altrincham or Sale to worship. This difficulty was resolved when a new Catholic church, St. Hugh of Lincoln, was built on a site fronting Manchester Road, close to its junction with Park Road. Building commenced in 1931 and, following completion, opened for worship in 1932. A presbytery and church hall were added later. This church served the local Catholic community until the late 1950s. By this time extensive housing development in the south-eastern part of the township had generated an urgent need for a Catholic church in the same area. This need was catered for when, c.1958, a site was acquired on the west side of Thorley Lane which comprised a large detached house[39] and its associated land. The house was converted into a presbytery and a fine new church built, adjacent and connected to the presbytery by a covered corridor. The church is called St. John the Baptist and recently celebrated its twenty-fifth anniversary (c.1985).

Notes

1. For more details on the complex history of non-conformity in North-east Cheshire, especially Ringway Chapel, see *Hale: Domesday to Dormitory* edited by R.N. Dore, *Cheshire 1660-1760: Restoration to Industrial Revolution* by J.H. Hodson, *V.C.H. Cheshire*, Vol.II.

2. See also the statistical chart in Chapter 16 for more detailed figures for the intervening years.

3. Interpolated from 1800 figure.

4. Register of places certified for worship under the Toleration Act (1689).

5. It may well be that this house was situated in what is now Grove Lane as there is a cottage, still extant, built in 1834 sited there. Possibly it replaced the residence of John Potts (1786) as a plaque in the wall names it as 'Potts Cottage'.

6. See Appendix 1 for the list of members.

7. Samuel Holt is listed in the 1799 Land Tax Survey for Timperley township and was assessed at £2 per annum rateable value.

8. John Marsland was a prominent landowner, owning lands between Heyes Lane and Riddings Hall.

9. A 50% increase in five years. If only heads of families are listed it may well be that their wives and families would suggest a membership total well in excess of thirty.

10. Thomas Aimson's account, Parish Chest.

11. Nathaniel Pass was the Sheriff's Officer in Altrincham at that date and a prominent Altrincham Methodist and Circuit Steward of the Altrincham Circuit when it was formed in 1838.

12. See *The Story of Timperley Methodism: 1833-1933* by E.H. Wright, pp.16-18 for details of chapel organisation and anecdotes concerning John Marsland, William Davenport and the influence of the Jackson family on Methodism in the township.

13. He assigned the lease to the trustees and received £5 for his expenses.

14. Between Grove and Bloomsbury Lanes – the rear of the chapel has a frontage on Grove Lane.

15. See *The Story of Timperley Methodism*, pp.20-21 for details of collections.

16. The building accounts are deposited in Manchester Central Library. Assuming the retail price of beer was c.1d per pint it would indicate that they were small barrels of approximately three gallons capacity. Mr Holt's gross account was for £535 18s 3d, but he deducted: '... £89 8s 3d Price of Bricks as per Contract.'

17. The Revd. William Elton resided on The Downs, Altrincham and was, at that time, a Methodist minister in Altrincham. He moved to Manchester in 1850.

18. William Potts was the son of James Potts. Some interesting comments regarding prominent members of the congregation are to be found in *The Story of Timperley Methodism*, pp.22-23.

19. They are deposited in Manchester Central Library Archives.

20. The minutes for the following years in the Records Section of the book are missing: 1847 to 1854; 1856 to 1870; 1875 and 1876; and 1884 to 1900 inclusive.

21. See Appendix 1 for details of members.

22. See Appendix 1 for details of scheme.

23. The cost was £232 and Mr T. Lomas (businessman) defrayed half the cost.

24. See Appendix 1 for details of members. Bush was a fine organiser and administrator.

25. See Appendix 2 for a selection of Trustees' Minutes contained in extant Accounts and Records' Books, 1870-1900.

26. The deputation was led by three gentlemen, Messrs Lambert, Simpson and Hilton; they gave many years of sterling service to the Sunday School. See *The Story of Timperley Methodism*, pp.34-37 for description of their service and backgrounds.

27. Presumably a different landowner to the one who refused to sell in 1882.

28. At bricklaying ceremonies over 170 bricks were laid by trustees, Sunday School members and scholars. The Archive contains a document giving details of their names, positions and number of bricks.

29. In memory of his wife, who had died shortly before he made the gift.

30. It was requisitioned in 1939 for civil defence purposes and derequisitioned in July 1946. The arrangements made for carrying on the work of the Sunday School and other church activities is described in Part I: 'Wartime' of *Methodism in Timperley 1933-1983* by M. Farnworth. Following derequisitioning it continued in use for church activities: see *Methodism in Timperley 1933-1983*, pp.13-16.

31. Population: 1921 – 4,263; 1971 – 24,343 (Census).

32. *Methodism in Timperley* by M. Farnworth.

33. 'Belmont' was the home of the late Mrs Arnold. The Arnolds were a prominent Timperley family whose ancestors had resided in the township since, at least, the beginning of the nineteenth century.

34. In the event, they only received a grant of £3,000 from the Rank Trust.

    The Sunday School Building Fund accounts are deposited in Manchester Central Library (also other records). They show that the fund stood at £12,453 in 1969 (inclusive of sale proceeds of the old chapel). They also show that Mr P. Rowles (builder) was paid a total of £12,410 in four instalments.

35. *Methodism in Timperley: 1933-1983*, p.20. Mr Marsland was a member of a long established Timperley family who owned extensive lands in the township during the nineteenth century.

36. *Methodism in Timperley: 1933-1983*, Part 2.

37. A copy of the order of service is deposited at the Cheshire Record Office (Ref: ECU 5/43).

38. A copy of the order of service is deposited at the Cheshire Record Office. A manuscript annotation on the copy states: 'The first new United Reform Church formerly Broadheath'.

39. The house was called 'Glendarvel'.

APPENDIX 1
MEMBERS AND TRUSTEES OF METHODIST CONGREGATIONS IN TIMPERLEY

Members of Timperley Methodists in 1803

This is a list of the names of members of the small Methodist Society in Timperley, which met in a house or cottage. The list is contained in a membership register[1] under the date June 1803 and is probably one of a number of lists in the register detailing various Methodist Societies and members' names in the vicinity of Manchester.

William Greenwood (Leader)	Mary Lucas
Richard Sandbach	Ellen Massey
Elizabeth Sandbach	Ellen Worthington
Thomas Lucas	William Warrington
Thomas Lucas, junior	Joseph Owen
William Hughes	Alice Chorlton
John Hankinson	

Trustees of Heyes Lane Chapel

Altrincham Methodists	**Timperley Members**
William Worsley (grocer)	James Whitelegge (farmer)
Robert Worsley (grocer)	William Davenport (farmer)
Nathaniel Pass (Sheriff's Officer)	Amos Rogerson (farmer
George Stuart (tailor)	John Chorlton (farmer)
Charles Dean (overlooker)	Thomas Chorlton (grocer)
Thomas Potter (solicitor)	Peter Heywood (farmer)
John Barrow	

List of Members: 1871 Trust Deed

It consisted of ten members. Eight of them were from Altrincham and included several prominent Manchester businessmen (for example, Richard and Edward Boyer and John Lees Barker). The two Timperley members were John Jackson[2] and David Cross.

List of Members: The 1882 Trust

William Champness, Woodlands	George Cooper, Timperley Hall
Thomas Cundill, Quarry Bank	Thomas England
James A. Moss, Bloomsbury Lane	William Jackson, Bridge Farm
Robert Rogerson, Fir Tree Farm	William Rogerson, Deansgate Lane

Notes

1. Circa 1933 the register was deposited in the Methodist Chapel Committee's Office in Manchester.
2. The extended Jackson family were stalwarts of the Methodist Church in Timperley and for a number of years the chapel was known, colloquially, as 'Jackson's Chapel'.

A SELECTION OF MINUTES EXTRACTED FROM TIMPERLEY METHODISTS' TRUSTEES' ACCOUNTS AND RECORDS' BOOKS, 1870-1900[1]

March 1871

Chapel to be painted outside from current income – debt *not* to be increased.

February 1872

Resolved: Chapel keeper's salary to be increased from £4 4s 0d to £5 5s 0d conditional on satisfactory performance of duties.

March 1874

Resolved: Chapel keeper's salary be increased to £10 p.a. with request to light fire on Saturdays am – anticipated it would improve state of organ.
Note read from Young and Sons re removal of organ.
Discussion of changes in choir to '... secure more efficient singing...'

February 1877

Resolved: Sanction be given to have 'Town's water laid on...'

February 1878

Resolved: Chapel keeper's salary be increased by £1 for each of two Winter quarters – Summer payments to remain same.
Resolved: Alteration to be carried out as per plan to rearrange pulpit and extend schoolroom.
Resolved: Present organ be removed and an American organ procured as a replacement.

February 1879

Resolved: Consent be given for laying of new 6 inch drain from cellar to new main sewer now being laid.
Insurance cover increased from £600 to £1,000.
Letter requesting increase of £3 p.a. in his salary by organist – no decision taken.

December 1879

John Perrin (organist) resigned. Mr W. Dunkerley appointed in his place. 'Appointment approved at Feb. 1880 meeting at salary of £5 5s 0d p.a.'

January 1883

Letter from organist requesting increase in salary.
Resolved: To give 25% increase (i.e. to £6 10s 0d p.a.)
Note adds: 'majority present thought it possible to get member(s) of congregation to play gratis.'

February 1883

Records opening of chapel at Cross Green, Baguley – taking away some of the old Methodist families living locally who had previously worshipped at Timperley.

Note
1. Deposited in Manchester Central Library, St. Peter's Square, Manchester.

14

EDUCATION PROVISION
IN
TIMPERLEY ECCLESIASTICAL PARISH, 1788 TO 1985

'... I hold it for indisputable that the first duty of a State is to see that every child
born therein shall be well housed, clothed, fed and educated till it attains years of
discretion...'

John Ruskin

Introduction

An essential prerequisite of any study of the English education system is an appreciation of the
fact that society in England is arranged on the basis of what is usually termed social class. Basically, society is divided into three separate and distinct social classes usually defined by the terms
Lower, Middle and Upper – although within each category there are subtle gradations. Education
provision has always reflected these basic divisions and until at least the end of the nineteenth
century such class divisions were rigid. During the twentieth century, and especially since 1945,
their boundaries have become less clear cut, albeit they still operate, and upward mobility between the classes, especially for the economically successful, has become much easier to achieve.

Education provision today splits into two distinct categories: private and public.

The Private Sector

This embraces all the independent schools (i.e. self-governing and fee charging). They range from
the large public schools (a misleading term) down through the ancient *grammar schools* to small
private schools catering for only a handful of pupils. They may be boarding and/or day schools.
The quality of the tuition offered could, and often did, vary tremendously, especially during the
nineteenth century. They catered, almost exclusively, for children of middle and upper class
families. The boarding school regimes were then often harsh and spartan and the curriculum principally confined to the classics and thus narrow in content.[1] The twentieth century has witnessed a
revolution in the breadth of curriculum and standards of teaching offered. The continuing pressure of demand for places at these establishments, despite the high fees charged, pays tribute to the
excellent standard of education most of them provide.

The Public Sector

Includes all those schools offering a free education to children (today from the ages of five to sixteen). Initially, they were usually founded and funded by public spirited benefactors who, in the
locality in which they resided, were concerned at the abysmal lack of educational provision for
children of poor parents. They subscribed funds to build and finance the on-going costs of a
school, sufficient to cater for at least some of the children in their parish. Such initiatives began in
the sixteenth and seventeenth centuries but greatly increased in the last two decades of the eighteenth. Prior to that the educational opportunities for a child belonging to the lower class were vir-
tually nil. Even those fortunate enough to obtain a place in such a school could only expect to be
taught the basics of the Three Rs. The establishments were usually called *charity schools*. State involvement in the public sector did not materialise until the middle of the nineteenth century and
was a slow process.

One of the first ventures into mass public education was undertaken by Robert Raikes,[2] who
founded the first Sunday School in 1780. His idea flourished and by 1795 approximately 250,000
children across the country were receiving a modicum of mental and moral training – albeit only
for an hour or two per week. There were various kinds of day schools, including the so-called
dames' schools, largely child-minding establishments for the children of working parents.[3] Later
other schools were provided throughout the country by two distinct organisations supported by

the church authorities:

- *The National Society for the Education of the Poor* (founded 1811): which was supported by the established church. Teachers had to be communicants of that church.
- *The British and Foreign School Society* (founded 1808): which had non-conformist support. Teachers could be either non-conformist or Anglican.

Colloquially they were referred to as National Schools and British Schools respectively. The curriculum offered was restricted to the Three Rs.

Public sector education, as we know it today, has evolved from these early nineteenth century initiatives. It was not until the middle of the nineteenth century, approximately, that the state actively involved itself in the public sector. From then on it gradually extended its influence and eventually assumed, in association with the local authorities, complete control of the finance and administration of public education in the, then new, state schools and also, by its control of the purse strings, partial control of the church-supported schools.

It is against this background, only sketched briefly here, that educational provision in Timperley is now discussed.

Education in Timperley from 1788

The Charity School

The story begins in 1788 when a group of residents[4] were appointed trustees for monies raised by voluntary subscriptions, purchased a plot of land and erected a 'Charity School and Schoolhouse' on the site.

'By an Indenture[5] between Thos. Warburton (Gent.) (of 1st Part) George Johnson[6] (and eleven other persons) (of 2nd Part)'... 'Inhabitants have raised money by voluntary subscriptions'... 'and lately erected an Edifice or Building for a School and Schoolhouse on a plot of land... hereby granted enfeoffed... to said Trustees... in consideration of the sum of 5s – 0d hereby grants enfeoffs etc. all that plot of land part of a close field... commonly called "Colley Croft"... which said plot contains on its East and West sides 6⅔rds yards and on its North and South sides 14½ yards... to use of said Trustees for ever to be used as a Schoolhouse and School and for a Schoolmaster to be appointed for the purpose of teaching and instructing children therein subject to... such rules... hereinafter declared... and to permit so much of said plot not covered by Edifice to be used as a yard... or for erecting other buildings for the better accommodation of said Master... nomination of Schoolmaster to be by majority vote of Trustees... will full power of remove and discharge... validity of Trustees' meetings determined by Public Notice of a meeting... signed by at least four trustees being given in Parish Church of Bowdon at least one Sunday preceding such meeting... also at least ten days previous thereto upon outside of door of said school and in some other public place in Timperley... Lastly it is agreed that all Privy dung to be made in necessary house... shall belong to and be received by the Occupier of the field called "Colley Croft" for ever.'[7]

This indenture was dated 6th November, 1788, so it is probable that the school actually opened in 1789 or 1790. In 1802 Miss Jane Houghton, a resident of Baguley township, executed a Deed of Gift for the sum of £200 which provided for the interest thereon to be paid to:

'the... schoolmaster of the Public School in Timperley... as the perpetual curate of St. George's chapel, Altringham [*sic*] should direct...'[8] and specified that the curate should... 'nominate the children who should attend and elect them from out of the families of poor persons resident in the townships of Baguley and Timperley... in equal numbers out of each township...' (See also Appendix 1.)

Subsequently, in her will dated 1803,[9] she bequeathed two further sums, each of £100, specifying that the interest earned should be applied to

'... the purchase of Bibles and prayerbooks to be given annually to the poor children taught at Timperley school...'

The school functioned efficiently for over seventy years until, in 1861, radical changes were deemed necessary. The causal factors were:

The population had more than doubled.[10]

Timperley Church had been built in 1849 and in 1852 Timperley township, most of Baguley town-

By Mr. HENRY BALSHAW.

On Wednesday, February Twenty-fifth.
In the Matter of the Charity, comprising the BUILD-
ING and PREMISES, known as "The Charity
School," in the parish of Christ Church, Timperley,
in the county of Chester.

TO BE SOLD BY AUCTION,
By Mr. HENRY BALSHAW,
by order of the Trustees of the said Charity, selling
with the consent and under the authority of the
Charity Commissioners for England and Wales, at
the Axe and Cleaver Inn, Altrincham, Cheshire, on
Wednesday, the 25th day of February, 1874, at Six
o'clock in the evening, subject to such conditions as
will be then produced :—
All that Plot of LAND, situate in Timperley
aforesaid, containing, by admeasurement, 234 square
yards or thereabouts, together with the BUILDING
there, recently used as a school, and the Outoffices
thereto belonging.
The Plot is freehold of inheritance, and free from
chief rent, and has a frontage of about 17 yards 7
inches to the turnpike road leading from Altrincham
to Stockport.
Further particulars may be obtained from the
AUCTIONEER, Springfield-road, Altrincham, and 61,
Princess-street, Manchester ; or from Mr. SOUTHERN,
Solicitor, Altrincham. [a

Notice of the sale of the Charity School in the Altrincham and Bowdon Guardian, 21st February, 1874.

ship and part of Hale township were carved out of Bowdon parish to constitute the new ecclesiastical parish of Christ Church, Timperley.

A National School had been built in Thorley Lane, in 1856. (See section on the National School.)

Responding to these developments the trustees resolved to effect certain alterations at the charity school.

Conversion of the upper room of the building into a library for the use of '... Inhabitants of Timperley and Baguley and to be used for Town's [sic] meetings as heretofore...'

Erection of a wall round the playground and some general repairs to the building.

Restricting the classes to infant pupils and a decision to '... accept children of any denomination if other than free scholars...'

The incumbent of St. George's church[11] ceding his rights – apropos Timperley Charity school – in favour of the vicar of Timperley parish church.

To appoint an Infant schoolmistress.[12]

The resolutions were processed and the school continued as an Infants' school until 1870 when the Trustees resolved:

'... that the premises are inadequate and it is not practical to make them adequate for the requirements of neighbourhood...' power was sought and obtained to '... sell the same at Auction or Private Contract and proceeds be applied to a new Infants school on a more eligible site...'[13]

Accordingly, on 27th February, 1874, the premises were sold. So ended the township's first school, following eighty-five years of service to the community.

To maintain a chronological sequence, the then relatively new National School will be discussed.

The National School

In response to the factors listed in the above section this school was built in 1855, to the designs of Mr R. Lane (architect) of Manchester, at a cost of c.£1,000. The site, donated by the landowner, Lord Stamford, occupied about 4/10ths of an acre and previously formed part of a 4 acre field called Higher Carr. The buildings, consisting of school and schoolhouse, had a frontage on the east side of Thorley Lane. At that time, and even in 1876, the site was completely rural.[14] Only six private houses, fronting on to Thorley Lane and standing in their own grounds, were between the parish church and the village centre. A half-timbered black and white cottage adjoined the northern boundary of the school site[15] and, by 1876, the private house 'Heightside' stood opposite the school. Designed to accommodate 250 pupils, the school opened on 4th February, 1856 with about eighty children on the roll. A Miss Betsy Kingsnorth was appointed its first Mistress (see list of headteachers on p.195). It served the children in the parish for over a century prior to its closure in 1960. After demolition, the present parish hall was built on the site.

The 'New' Infant School

The building, still extant, was built, at a cost of £1,534, to the designs of E.J. Thompson (architect) of 90 King Street, Manchester[16] and occupies a site of c.1200 square yards, with a frontage of 20 yards to the south side of Stockport Road, adjacent to the Village Hall. It opened in May 1873 with about fifty children on the roll. The land was conveyed, for a consideration of £225, from the trustees of Samuel Brooks (deceased)[17] to the Revd. Edward Dowling and the churchwardens of the parish church under the authority of an Act dated 8 Victoria. The conveyance stipulated that the site was:

'... to be ever used for a school for the Education of Children and Adults of general manufacturing or Poorer Classes in the District and no other purpose...'

75. In 1988 the building closed and was unoccupied for over three years. (Photograph taken by the author, 1987.)

also

'... school to be managed by the Incumbent, Curate (if Appointed), Churchwardens and four other persons...'

also

'... school to be a Public Elementary School within the meaning of the Education Act, 1870...'

The following clauses contained in the indenture[18] are of interest.

'... Committee to be elected annually from amongst subscribers to the school who shall have subscribed at least ten shillings during the current year...'

'... Secretary to be elected... who shall keep... minutes in a book...'

'... instruction shall comprise at least... Reading, Writing, Arithmetic, Geography, Scripture, History and in case of Girls – Needlework...'

'... all provisions of Elementary Education Act, 1870... shall apply to school...'

'... If Committee pass a resolution... to repay any Grant in Aid, paid out of Parliamentary Grant for Education the aforesaid declaration, whereby this school shall be a Public Elementary School, within meaning of the 1870 Education Act shall be void...'

There were also clauses prohibiting any industrial or factory buildings on the site. The school was closed in 1981 and the last headmistress, Mrs P. Noble, retired at the same time, following twenty-one years' service.

St. Andrew's Day School and Mission House

By 1841 and probably at least until the end of the nineteenth century the Deansgate Lane/Brook Lane sector of the township was the most heavily populated.[20] It is also distanced from the parish church and the two schools then extant. By the late 1860s[21] it was apparent that the child popula-

76. Following closure in 1981, the building was (apart from the occasional jumble sale, etc) unoccupied for a decade. Following renovation in 1991-2 (such as new windows, repainting, removal of old entrance gates, renovation extension and recapping of wall abutting pavement) and installation of double gates at the eastern end, the building began a new phase in its history on 2nd March, 1992 when it re-opened as the kindergarten for Bowdon Preparatory School. Thus it continues as an education establishment in conformity with the restrictive covenants contained in the original deeds. (Photograph taken by the author, 1990.)

tion warranted additional school provision. The new Infant School (see previous section) partially met this problem.

The school trustees, realising this shortcoming, had purchased a second site, in Deansgate Lane,[22] in 1873, for a consideration of £133 with the intention of building a school on it immediately. Unfortunately only the Stockport Road school was built as the then available funds were insufficient to finance two school developments. Not until 1882 did building commence (see Chapter 12, section on St. Andrew's Day School and Mission House). The building had a dual function as it served also as a Church Mission School.[23] It was licensed to conduct divine service on 7th March, 1885 and so continued until 1932. It educated Timperley children for almost a century before it was closed, simultaneously with its counterpart on Stockport Road, in July 1981 (see newspaper reports in Appendix 1, p.207). During the 1920s a hut of galvanised iron construction, was erected on the site and served as a social club for local parishioners.[24] The site and buildings were offered for sale by tender in April 1986. Subsequently the sale was completed, the site cleared and four residential houses built on the site in 1987.

Valedictory Comments, 1988

The Stockport Road School, the sole remaining edifice with c.200 years of voluntary supported education in the township, now stands empty and largely unnoticed by the bustling throngs of shoppers patronising the adjacent supermarkets and shops. Observing it, one senses a faint air of neglect surrounding the building (i.e. last autumn's leaves still cluttering the base of its walls; discarded litter bestrewing its paths; windows boarded up, etc.). One opines that it has, sadly, become an anachronism – having more of an affinity with the slower tempo of life associated with its vintage years pre-1920 – than the brash, automobile clogged lifestyle of Stockport Road, in the 1980s. The writer trusts it will escape the attention of the property developers and be found a useful role to play in the future, thus preserving the historic building for many years to come.

Postscript 1992
One is delighted to record that the building, following a hiatus, again functions as a school. Following renovation, it is now utilised as a private kindergarten. The Fates have been kind.

Educational Development in the Late Nineteenth Century in Timperley

With the opening of St. Andrews, the township had three church supported schools, largely financed by voluntary contributions, offering a basic education to children in the age range five to ten. They were mostly attended by children who belonged to Church of England families and so the curriculum provided Anglican religious instruction. Less than three years prior to the opening of the Stockport Road school a watershed in the history of English education was reached when the 1870 Education Act became law. By virtue of this Act the Government, through its newly created Board of Education, made itself responsible for the control and development of public education provision. In co-operation with local authorities and voluntary organisations, its role from then on, increased inexorably with each year that passed. The reforms it initiated over the years have culminated in the sophisticated system of public education, financed by the state and local authorities which we have today.

The principal provisions of the 1870 Act ensured that:

- A school was provided within reach of every house in the country to which children *could be sent* (author's italics) to receive primary education.
  (NB. Attendance at a school was not necessarily free to parents at this stage.)
- Local Government Boards[25] were established with powers to acquire land, build new schools on such land and levy a local rate to finance the costs incurred in any area where under-provision of schools was identified, thus ensuring the first provision was achieved.
- Gave all children, regardless of religious denomination, the right to attend a school of their parents' choice coupled with a conscience clause allowing them to opt out of any religious instruction given in such school.

Further Acts, listed on the next page, followed:

1876

Sandon's Act, created School Attendance Boards in areas where there was no local school board.

1880

Mundella's Act made schooling compulsory by obliging local government boards and school attendance boards to make attendance bye-laws.

1891

Parents given the right to demand free education.

1893

School leaving age fixed at eleven.

1899

School leaving age raised to twelve.

77. St. Andrew's School and Mission House ceased to function as mission house when St. Andrew's Church was opened in 1832. The building was demolished 1986 and the site re-developed for housing. (Photograph taken by the author, 1985.)

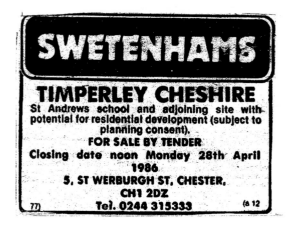

Advertisement for the sale of the St. Andrew's school site in the Altrincham and Bowdon Guardian, dated 18th January, 1986. (Reproduced here by permission by Guardian Newspapers.)

The brief outline above sketches the framework which controlled the development of public education in Timperley into the first decade of the twentieth century. Up to that time all the children who received public education attended at least one of the three schools (some would attend two if they moved on from the Infants to Navigation Road School) and received instruction in the Three Rs, plus geography, history and, for girls, needlework. As was the norm during these three decades, the teachers appointed usually gave many years of dedicated service (see List of Headteachers on p.197), a tradition which seems to have continued up to the final closure of the schools. Some of the past members of staff were prominent local citizens with a distinguished family record of service to the schools and local government.[26]

List of Headteachers

Charity School, 1789-1874
1838-1860 John Richardson
1861-1864 Ann Rawlinson
1864-1866 Mary Hansford
1866-1874 Miss Frances Cubbin[27]
Average length of headship 11.25 years

The National School, Thorley Lane, 1856-1937
1856-1858 Miss Betsy A. Kingsnorth
1858-1860 The Misses Macleod
1860-1871 Henry Stanley
1871-1874 Charles Shaw
1874-1917 Charles Fitton
1917-1922 Miss Edith Fitton
1923-1937 Harry Litherland
Average length of headship 12.8 years

New Infant School, Stockport Road, 1874-1981
1874-1883 Miss Frances Cubbin
1883-1918 Miss Sarah Anderson
1918-1929 Miss Carrie Pickston
1929-1932 Miss Annie Clark
1932-1956 Miss Olive Longworth
1956-1974 Mrs Nora Cornall
1974-1981 Mrs Patricia C. Noble
(Average length of headships = 15.43 years.)

St. Andrew's Mission School, 1883-1981
1883-1890 Miss Emma E. Roulson
1890-1897 Miss Ellen Macaulay
1897-1902 Miss Helena M. Robinson
1902-1914 Miss Mary Ann Bridge
1914-1938 Miss Frances M. Ryder
1938-1940 Miss Grace H. Mollart
1940-1946 Miss Gwendoline M. Poole
1946-1981 Mrs Laura M. Shaw
(Average length of headships = 12.25 years.)

Education in the Twentieth Century in Timperley

By 1900 primary education to age twelve was generally available, not necessarily free, and provided by two types of establishment: Board of Education and Voluntary Schools. From 1902 free public education for all, coupled with expanding educational opportunities gradually evolved, culminating in the three tier system of primary, secondary and further education from five to eighteen plus. Conceived as a continuous process, it is now compulsory to age sixteen.

The principal legislation and official reports which have brought this about are:

1902 Education Act
Established local education authorities (LEAs) which replaced the local school boards; gave rate financed support to the voluntary schools;[28] extended the syllabus of subjects taught.

1910
School leaving age raised to fourteen.

1926 to 1943
Hadow (1926); Spens (1938); and Norwood (1943) Reports.

1944 Education Act
Raised school leaving age to fifteen; created secondary modern schools (replaced elementary schools).

1970 Plus
LEAs given power to close LEA, grammar and secondary modern schools and replace them with a comprehensive school system for the eleven plus to eighteen plus age range.[29]

How did this period of educational development effect education in Timperley? Firstly, administrative and financial control was partially transferred from the voluntary schools (now designated 'non-provided schools' by the 1944 Act)[30] and the major running costs of such schools (i.e. salaries, books, teaching materials, etc.) were met by a general rate charge.[31] The Timperley schools thus became 'non-provided schools'. As yet the township had no schools provided directly by the LEA; however, in 1906 the first LEA 'provided school' opened in Altrincham (Navigation Road Council School) offering an elementary education from the age of five to thirteen,[32] and some Timperley children became pupils – the first of many who attended this type of school.

Secondly, from c.1910 pupils could compete for free places (scholarships) at local independent grammar schools and/or LEA central schools. Thus Timperley children, awarded a free place, obtained a secondary education at Altrincham High Schools for Boys or Girls[33] or Bradbury Central School.

The system outlined above formed the pattern of local education provision until the early 1930s, as regards primary, and the 1950s, as regards secondary provision. The two decades between the First and Second World Wars marked the commencement of a period of intensive housing development in Timperley which, apart from a necessary break during the 1940-1945 war years, is still not completed.[34] Its causes and effects are discussed in Chapter 9; its effect on education provision is now discussed.

The population graphs show that the population increased from 4,263 in 1921 to 7,080 in 1931 and 19,232 in 1951. A concomitant of these figures was a significant increase in demand for primary school places which the church schools could not satisfy and this additional primary school provision became an imperative. The demand was located, principally, in the area bordering the railway and canal on both sides of Park Road, where, in the 1930s, intensive housing development had taken place. The LEA (Cheshire County Council then) resolved to build a primary school in this locale.[35] Land between Leys and Frieston Roads was purchased and Park Road County Primary School, initially an Infants' School, built on it. When it opened in 1936 it became the first LEA provided primary school in the township. During the 'Birth Rate Bulge' years, post-1945, its capacity was stretched to the limit (some infants were compelled to attend Altrincham schools).[36] To meet this continuing pressure for places the LEA, in 1951, built a second school on land between Crofton Avenue and Heyes Lane.[37] It opened in 1952 as a two-form entry Infants' School but was subsequently extended in 1953-4 by the addition of a two-form entry Junior department. The two developments constituted Heyes Lane County Primary. This satisfied the demand until the development of the Broomwood council housing estate, during the period 1952-7, created a new demand. It was met by the LEA building a two-form entry Junior school on the estate[38] which opened in 1954. Initially it had to accommodate Infants as well as Junior pupils. Subsequently, an Infants' School was built, which opened in 1959. The two departments constitute Broomwood County Primary School.[39]

To cater for the children of Roman Catholic families a voluntary aided Roman Catholic Junior school was built in 1962 on a site in Park Road, which the Roman Catholic authorities had actually purchased in 1937.[40] The school, St. Hugh's Roman Catholic Voluntary Aided Junior School, opened in 1963.

Further primary provision became necessary in the middle 1960s, which the LEA provided by building two additional primary schools: the Willows and Cloverlea Primary schools[41] in Alexander Drive and Green Lane North respectively. Cloverlea School incorporates a partial hearing unit, catering for children from other parts of Trafford.

Due to various factors, such as variation in birth rate trends, primary provision in the civil parish today exceeds demand for places. This situation led the LEA,[42] despite much local opposition, to close the two Church schools still extant. They finally closed their doors in 1981. Timperley now has six primary schools each with excellent facilities, including spacious playing fields, serving the community (i.e. five LEA maintained and one Roman Catholic voluntary aided). This scale of provision appears to be more than adequate for the foreseeable future.

Prior to the middle 1930s there were no LEA schools educating children of secondary age in the township. Children aged eleven plus attended the Thorley Lane Church School, Stamford Park, or Navigation Road Council schools. Children proceeding to selective secondary education were catered for by the grammar and central schools in Altrincham and Sale. This shortage of post-primary provision occasioned much parental concern at the time.[43] Their lobbying of the appropriate authorities was effective. In 1933 the LEA acquired a plot of land upon which Wellington Road Boys' and Girls' Schools were built, both of which opened in 1937/8. After the 1944 Education Act they became secondary modern schools educating children from eleven plus to fifteen; two decades later the leaving age was raised to sixteen. In 1989 the two schools were officially closed and re-organised as one co-education school. The 'new' school is named Wellington Road High School and occupies the same buildings. Its first headmaster, Mr J. Knowles, was previously head of the 'old' Boys' school. The only other secondary modern school in the township, built in 1962, occupies a site on Green Lane: initially it was a Girls' school and opened in 1963. Its first intake of pupils were girls transferred from Bradbury Central Co-educational School in Queens Road, Hale from which it took its name (i.e. Bradbury Central School for Girls). Following the closure and demolition of Bradbury Central School, in Queens Road, its pupils were transferred to the Green Lane premises which school was re-organised as a co-educational school[44] and renamed Delahays Secondary Modern School.[45]

During the period 1986-88 the borough's secondary schools were the subject of much council debate with one faction opting for a comprehensive system and another advocating preservation of the proven grammar school tradition in Altrincham and Sale. In 1988 the Council put forward proposals for secondary education to the Secretary of State for Education.[46]

The only other LEA schools in Timperley are two special schools: Brentwood and the Grove Schools, which opened in 1972 and cater for pupils with special educational needs.

Private Education in Timperley

This chapter has been predominantly concerned with public education provision, but it should be noted that the private sector has had a presence in the township for over a century. Before 1920 the evidence is fragmentary and largely confined to entries in local directories and some photographic records.[47] It is axiomatic that for a private school to be viable a demand must exist: this in turn necessitates a sufficient number of families able to meet the school fees. These prerequisites materialised locally post-1850 when numbers of professional families took up residence in the township and its environs. A demand thus burgeoned and schools were established to meet it. The following private schools are listed in Cheshire Directories.[48]

1855
Day School: Proprietor, Revd. W.J. Read, Ellesmere House, one of a pair of mid-Victorian villas sited in what is now Brookfield Avenue.

1883
Ladies' School: Proprietor, Fanny Cox, The Grange, a mansion standing in its own grounds on a site close to what is now Stelfox Avenue. It was located about 100 yards from Stockport Road and was approached by a drive. It has been long since demolished. There is no record of how long the school was extant.[49]

1903
A *'Ladies' Preparatory School*: Proprietor, William Valentine Reid Crawford. It specialised in elocution. It was housed at 2 Egerton Terrace, one of an elegant terrace of mid-Victorian houses, sited at the corner of Wash Lane (now Park Road) and, what is now, Brookfield Avenue.[50] It probably functioned for at least twenty-two years prior to closing down in about 1925 as it is listed in all the directories from 1902 to 1923 inclusive but not in the 1928 Directory.

78. *Ellesmere House, built c.1850 on a site in Brookfield Avenue (then called The Avenue), off Park Road. It was one of a pair of large Victorian semi-detached house. It is still occupied. In 1855 the premises were used as private day school. (Photograph taken by the author, 1990.)*

79. Egerton Terrace, built in 1852 at the junction of Park Road and Brookfield Avenue. In the early years of the twentieth century it was a Ladies' Preparatory School specialising in elocution. The school closed in c.1925. (Photograph taken by the author, 1990.)

1902

A Mixed School: Proprietress, Miss J. Bond. It was probably extant for at least fifteen years at its premises, 6 Richmond Terrace, Stockport Road[51] as it is listed in all the directories up to and including 1914, but not in the 1923 Directory.

1914

Larkhill School: Proprietress, Miss Mary Adshead. Housed in an early Victorian mansion fronting on Thorley Lane and standing in its own grounds. It probably catered for girls in the eight to thirteen plus age range. First listed in the directories in 1914, it appears to have closed down c.1920 following the demise of the proprietress.[52]

1924

Forest School: founded by its first Proprietress Miss Clegg and initially housed in a large late Victorian or Edwardian semi-detached house named The Laurels, one of a row of such houses situated in Moss Lane, close to its junction with Brook Lane.[53] A few years later the school was transferred across the road to Oak Cottage which had many advantages as a school site including outbuildings and almost an acre of land. An increasing demand for places was satisfied by converting the stable block into additional classroom accommodation initially and subsequently by the addition of a pre-fabricated classroom block in the grounds. It celebrated its Diamond Jubilee in 1984 when it had approximately 100 pupils on the roll (see next page). Indubitably, it has an excellent scholastic reputation in the district. It prepares children of primary school age for entry into LEA and independent grammar schools. It continues to flourish.

80. The Laurels, built c.1890, is one of a row of large semi-detached houses on Moss Lane, close to its junction with Brook Lane. Forest School was founded here by a Miss Clegg in 1924. The school moved to its present site, opposite the Laurels c.1930. (Photograph taken by the author, 1990.)

Forest School's Diamond Jubilee, 1984
Extracts from the *Sale and Altrincham Messenger* and *Altrincham and Bowdon Guardian*.

Sale and Altrincham Messenger, 23rd June, 1984
'With its anniversary coming up... Forest School is preparing for much celebration. For it was just sixty years ago that a young trainee teacher, Miss Clegg, from a small school in Lancashire, stepped off the train at Timperley Station and asked a taxi driver for "The Laurels". He had replied, "Oh you mean the Forest houses", and that is how Forest School was first established in 1924. Later it moved across the road to a larger building where it remains still... Another of the Clegg sisters came to help and the reading was done in two classrooms... Attached to the school were the stables where ponies used to give the children riding lessons. These stables made possible further expansion as parts of them were converted to create more classrooms. Nothing... than the outbreak of war. Old photographs show the children assembling with gas masks... Even more strange was that the school was camouflaged and it even boasted its own air raid shelter which now looks like a bandstand surrounded by flower beds and graces the front lawn... The girls' winter dresses, once a proud purple, changed to grey as a country's supply of purple dye was exhausted. Their purple and white checked summer dresses became maroon and white stripes and the boy's grey pullovers, edged in purple experienced a similar change... It is hard to believe that the school was surrounded by open land where market gardens prided themselves on their "Timperley Early" rhubarb...

To commemorate its Diamond Jubilee the Parents' Association is to hold a grand fete in the school grounds on Saturday, 30th June. This will include pony rides and a barbecue in the evening.'

(NB. A photograph featuring members of staff and pupils, vintage 1938, accompanies the article.)

Altrincham and Bowdon Guardian, 28th June, 1984
'Forest School, Timperley, celebrates its diamond jubilee with a fete in the school grounds on Saturday.

Founded in 1924 by Miss Clegg, a teacher from Kersal in Lancashire, the school started life in The Laurels cottage[54] [*sic*] on Moss Lane, Timperley. But as the number of pupils rose a bigger build-

81. *Forest School. These premises were built pre-1840. The Tithe Schedule of 1840 lists them as 'Farmhouse Appurtenances and Orchard' and names the farmer as Thomas Hulme. Later the house was named as Oak Cottage. It is sited at the junction of Moss and Brook Lanes. The school, founded in 1924, moved into these premises c.1930 from its original premises the Laurels, a very large semi-detached house sited opposite Oak Cottage. (Photograph taken by the author, 1990.)*

ing was needed and the school moved a few years later to its present home, at what was then known as Oak Cottage, also on Moss Lane.

The school now has a register of 100 pupils, aged between three and eleven, with the assembly hall and some classrooms housed in a converted stable block. And headmaster, Mr. Stephen Jobling, who took over from Mr. Knapp last Christmas, is proud of his new school. "We have a very good academic reputation," he told the *Guardian*, "and are extremely lucky to have a school set in such beautiful grounds right in the middle of a built-up area."

Mr Jobling, who was born in Lincoln, previously taught at an English school near Benidorm in Spain before returning to England to take charge of Forest School.

And one former headmaster can claim an unusual distinction – for Mr. Hoogewerf, who took charge of the school in 1954, introduced Rugby Union to the American city of St. Louis, where teams still compete every year for the Hoogewerf Rose Bowl.

Pupils also recently held their own event to celebrate the school's jubilee, with a sponsored walk around Dunham Massey Park which, with more money still to come in, has raised more than £500 for School funds...'

(NB. A photograph featuring pupils in attendance at the school in 1942 accompanied the article.)

Conclusion

It had been the intention to describe how the Church Schools adapted to the changes in educational practice and organisation down the years as revealed by their written records. Such archive material, especially post-1870, is essential for that exercise. Unfortunately, despite meticulous searches in the parish chest, Altrincham Reference Library and Cheshire County Record Office no records appertaining to Timperley Church Schools appear to be deposited in those repositories. Log books, at least, were certainly kept by the school staffs but where they were deposited, following closure of the schools, appears to be an enigma.[55] Possibly they may turn up at some future date and be deposited in Greater Manchester Record Office or Trafford Local Studies Centre for the benefit of posterity.

Notes

1. Dotheboys Hall, featured in *Nicholas Nickleby* by Charles Dickens, exemplifies the worst type of private school of the early nineteenth century.
2. A master printer in Gloucester.
3. Strictly speaking they were not 'free' as parents paid a few pence for services offered by the dames' schools.
   An item in the *Altrincham and Bowdon Guardian* of 19th August, 1982 comments on a booklet entitled *Church Schools in Timperley 1851 to 1981* by Hazel Prior contains the following '... a Timperley school existed between Orchard Place and Baker Street as far back as 1799... she found a bill for 2s 0d for coals for the school...'. This could possibly have been such a dame school. The two streets mentioned had not been built in 1799.
4. They included a brewer, an innkeeper, and a grocer and a number of farmers. For information on the education facilities available to Timperley children in other nearby townships prior to 1788 see *A History of Sale* by N.V. Swain; *Some Aspects of Education in Eighteenth Century Cheshire* by D. Robson; *VCH Cheshire*, Vol.II.
5. Deposited in the Parish Chest.
6. George Johnson was the owner of Timperley Hall. Another trustee was his son Croxton, Rector of Wilmslow. The innkeeper was William Goulden of the Hare and Hounds.
7. An interesting sidelight on the Victorian 'Waste Not Want Not' mentality. The field, Colley Croft, had a frontage on the north side of Stockport Road. The school site was approximately opposite the present site of Vantage Garages. At least until 1838 the school building and school house were the last buildings in the village, at its eastern edge, on Stockport Road.
8. The gift of £200 purchased £380 1s 0d of 3% Consols in 1803.
9. Miss Jane Houghton's will, dated May 1803, bequeathed £100 on her demise and a further £100 following the demise of her two sisters. In fact, they predeceased her and so the total £200 became available in October 1813 following her death. It also was applied to the purchase of £291 1s 0d of 3% Consols. In 1832, the old stock certificates were consolidated into one certificate for £672 of Stock.
10. See population graph in chapter 16 dealing with statistics.
11. When St. George's parish was created in 1868 this chapel-of-ease became the parish church for Altrincham.
12. The schoolmaster at that time, Mr. J. Richardson, left at Christmas 1860.
13. See transcriptions of relevant documents in Appendix 1.
14. See O.S. 25 inch plan, 1876.
15. The cottage was demolished in about 1970. The pear tree which stood in its front garden has now been felled and the site, at the corner of Thorley Lane and Mainwood Road, redeveloped.
16. The actual plans of the site and buildings are deposited in C.C.R.O., dated respectively April and August 1871.
17. Samuel Brooks, banker, was the largest landowner in the township at that time.
18. Deposited in the parish chest.
19. See article in *Timperley Independent* dated 1993.
20. The 1841 Census proves this.

21. The township population was 2,112.

22. Quote in *Altrincham and Bowdon Guardian*, dated 23rd July, 1981: located opposite Batemans' Nursery. It formed part of a field designated Canal Field in 1838 Tithe Schedules.

23. After 1945 it was an Infants school only. In its early years it is probable that children up to the age of eleven or twelve attended.

24. Known colloquially as 'The Tin School', it was previously a gymnasium owned by a Miss Balmer and stood on Grove Lane. It was acquired, dismantled and re-erected on the St. Andrew's site in Deansgate Lane. (Ref. *Altrincham and Bowdon Guardian*, dated 17th January, 1985.)

25. Colloquially called 'School Boards'.

26. The Fitton family: a plaque to one member of this family records his service to the community and is fixed to the east wall of the nave of Christ Church.

27. Served in both schools.

28. Financial provision by trustees limited principally to maintenance of fabric of building.

29. Trafford Council did not decide to apply to Department of Education for approval to introduce a comprehensive system until 1985/6, not yet approved (1987).

30. Timperley's church schools, prior to closure, were 'non-provided schools'.

31. LEA (pre-1974) Cheshire County Council; (post-1974) Trafford Borough Council.

32. To fourteen (post-1910).

33. Fee-paying schools at that time, now LEA grammar schools.

34. No census taken in 1941.

35. See Appendix 2.

36. Only with the greatest difficulty was the author able to obtain places for his two sons at Park Road County Primary in 1952/3.

37. See Appendix 2.

38. In the publication *Cheshire Education* (in Altrincham Reference Library) it is designated as a 'two-form infants' (*sic*). This is probably an error and should read 'Junior' as in the 1951 development it is described as 'Infant school'.

39. See Appendix 2.

40. See *Cheshire Education*.

41. Ibid.

42. The *Altrincham and Bowdon Guardian* carried a number of reports, in the months preceding the closures, of local reaction to the closure proposals.

43. Timperley electors and property owners lobbied (see Parish Council Minutes, 29th September, 1933).

44. It opened on 1st September 1984 as a mixed school (see Pamphlet No.542, Altrincham Reference Library).

45. It has now been renamed 'Green Lane High School'.

46. Following the debate, the Council resolved to retain the existing grammar school system in the borough. Subsequently, following government legislation, schools were permitted to apply for grant maintained status. If granted they could opt out of LEA control giving a school total autonomy in its administration. At the same time local school management gave all schools autonomy over finances.

When this chapter was written in 1989 the Secretary of State's decision on the proposals was still awaited.

47. See *Looking Back at Timperley* by Hazel Pryor.

48. Slater's, Balshaw's and Kelly's Directories.

49. In 1883 the approach was called The Avenue. Two large Victorian semis are still extant and occupied in Stelfox Avenue.

50. The terrace, built in 1852, is still extant and occupied for residential purposes.

51. This terrace is also still extant and occupied. It stands between the old Methodist Chapel and the corner of Bloomsbury Lane.

52. *Looking Back at Timperley* contains a photograph of Larkhill with pupils playing in school grounds.

53. The Laurels, still occupied residentially, is approximately in the centre of this row of large houses; all the houses are named after trees.

54. The word 'cottage' does not accurately describe The Laurels. It is in fact a very large semi-detached house in its own grounds.

55. *Church Schools in Timperley* contains some material extracted from school log books which suggests that such archive material is deposited somewhere.

Timperley Village School.

At a Meeting of the owners of Property in the Township of Timperley, duly convened in accordance with the Trusts of the above School, it was resolved, that an application should be made to the Charity Commissioners, for liberty to effect certain desirable changes in connection with this School.

The sanction of the Charity Board having been obtained, and the Incumbent of St. George's, Altrincham, having kindly ceded his rights in favor of the Clergyman of the District:—it is now proposed that the Building itself be put into an efficient state of Repair, and that a Wall be built around the Play-ground,—that the Upper Room be fitted up as a Reading Room and Library for the benefit of the Inhabitants of Timperley and the adjoining Townships,—and that the same be used for Towns' Meetings as heretofore—that the lower room be converted into an Infant School, and that a Mistress be appointed thereto,—and that some few other arrangements be made for the more useful employment of the Building.

The Promoters of this Plan earnestly request the kind co-operation of all persons who are interested in the well being of the neighbourhood. A sum of £50. at the least, will be required for carrying out the proposed alterations. The names of all parties who may be willing to assist—by annual subscriptions—grants of money or of books; and especially of young men prepared to take an active Interest in the management and working of the Library and News-room, will be thankfully received by the REV. EDWARD DOWLING, Chairman of the Meeting, or by MESSRS CHARLES MOORE, and WILLIAM BINKS, Members of the Sub-Committee for Building.

Timperley, Nov. 1861.

The following contributions have been already promised,

Mr. Skelton,	.. ..	£5	0	0
" Lyon,	.. ..	5	0	0
" Nickson,	.. ..	5	0	0
" Moore,	.. ..	3	0	0
Rev. E. Dowling,	.. .. ..	2	0	0
Mr. J. R. White,	.. .. ..	2	0	0
" Rycroft	.. ..	2	0	0
" Fletcher,	.. ..	1	0	0
" Hollinpriest,	.. .. ..	1	0	0
" Atkins,	.. ..	1	0	0
" Ambler,	.. ..	1	0	0

Cimperley Village School.

~~~≈⊙⊱⊰⊙≈~~~

The Sub-Committee for Building, having completed the work entrusted to them, in connection with this School, have now to present their account, and to report progress.

All the subscriptions promised have been paid except one; the debts have all been discharged; and a balance of £2. 2s. 10d. remains due to the Treasurer.

The School Building is now in an efficient state of repair and safety, and the Play-ground has been enclosed with a substantial wall.

The School itself has more than realised the expectations of the Projectors. An Infant Mistress has been appointed, and on some occasions there have been more than 100 children in attendance.

The Upper Room is ready for use as a Reading Room and Library :— A Working Committee of the most intelligent and active young men in the neighbourhood has been formed; and it is hoped that by October next the entire will be in full operation.

Assistance is now respectfully and earnestly invited towards the formation of the Library and the annual support of the Reading Room. Those Gentlemen who take an interest in the well-being of the district, are especially requested to help on the good work, by donations of suitable Books, and by subscriptions in Money. Two Members of the working committee hope to canvass the neighbourhood shortly; and by them subscriptions and donations will be thankfully received.

EDWARD DOWLING,
Chairman and Treasurer of the Original Committee.

AUGUST 4TH. 1862.

OPENING OF TIMPERLEY PARK ROAD JUNIOR SCHOOL, 7TH APRIL, 1937
(pamphlet No.989)[1]

TIMPERLEY PARK ROAD
COUNCIL JUNIOR AND INFANTS' SCHOOL.

SITE.

The site adjoins Leys Road and Frieston Road, and was purchased in 1934. It has an area of approximately 3¼ acres.

THE BUILDINGS.

The buildings have been erected as a Junior and Infants' School, accommodating 400 scholars. The accommodation comprises six Classrooms, one Practical Subjects Room, and one Infants' Room. together with an Assembly Hall of 1,800 feet superficial area, and the usual Staff Rooms, Cloakrooms and offices. There are two Playgrounds at the rear.

The external facings are of sand faced bricks, and the roof is covered with hand made sand faced tiles.

Internally the floors to the Classrooms, Hall, etc., are beech wood block with tiles and granolithic elsewhere. The lighting is by electricity, and the leating by low pressure hot water.

The general contractors were Messrs. Edwin Marshall & Sons Ltd., of Ashton-under-Lyne, and the contract price, excluding furnishings £9,585.

The sub-contractors include the following:-

Heating	Messrs. Caldwells Ltd.
Patent Glazing	Messrs. Williams Gamon & Co. Ltd.
Sanitary Fittings	Messrs. Rowe Bros. & Co. Ltd.
Electric Light	Messrs. E. Feneley & Co. Ltd.

CHESHIRE COUNTY COUNCIL
Altrincham Bowdon, Hale and District Administrative Sub-Committee.

OPENING

OF THE

TIMPERLEY PARK ROAD JUNIOR SCHOOL,

ALTRINCHAM,

ON

WEDNESDAY, APRIL 7TH, 1937,

at 3-0 p.m.

Stockport Road Infants' School Centenary

(From *Altrincham and Bowdon Guardian*, dated 17th May, 1973.)

'Timperley Village School... which educates about sixty children at the moment celebrates its centenary this year. The premises were opened in May 1873 and cost £1534, most of which came from Timperley people interested in education.

This school, however, was not the first in Timperley. It was the third. First was an "endowed" school sponsored by local Christian families and by 1855 this was deemed inadequate and the Church built a second school in Thorley Lane at a cost of £1000 which opened in 1856.

However, more extensive school provision was needed and the church started the new school for infants in Stockport Road. Land was purchased from the estate of Samuel Brooks for £225 and Mr Edward James Thompson of Timperley was appointed Architect.

Many hundreds of children have gone through the... village school during the past 100 years and three of them in that time served the local community as Mayor.

Present Headmistress is Mrs N. Cornall... but within the next two years the village school is to be replaced by a new County Primary School in Mayfield Road. It could mean the end of the school as most people know it.

Last weekend was Centenary Weekend. A special committee organised a birthday tea last week for present pupils and on Saturday afternoon a reunion for ex-pupils and friends was held at Christ Church Hall followed by a celebration dance... special Centenary Mugs have been made to mark the occasion and each pupil has received one.'[2]

Closure of Church Schools in Timperley, 1981

(From *Altrincham and Bowdon Guardian*, dated 23rd July, 1981.)

'Two Timperley Headmistresses close the door on more than 200 years of village education tomorrow (Friday) when they leave the Village and St. Andrew's Infant Schools for the last time. The buildings are too old and there aren't enough children to go round any more, say the local council, so teachers and pupils have to find somewhere new to read and write and count and paint. Or, like headmistress Mrs Patricia Noble, with twenty-one years' service at the village school behind her, and Mrs Laura Shaw, after thirty-five years at St. Andrews, they might retire along with the schools.

The village school was built by the Church of England and opened in 1873, opposite the Church's other Thorley Lane [*sic*] school.[3] A year later an appeal for funds to build a third began and after buying land for £133 the new "Mission School", which doubled as a church on Sundays, was opened in Deansgate Lane on 8th April, 1883.

For many years they were the only sources of education in Timperley. They became focal points of local attention when epidemics claimed large numbers of pupils, and they "did their bit" during the Second World War when young evacuees joined the registers.

Miss Hazel Pryor, of Thorley Lane, has been researching their histories for a pamphlet to be published later this year.[4] She found that holidays used to vary with the weather to take account of the main local industry, market gardening – if the strawberries were late so were the holidays.

And in the old days schoolchildren could always look forward to a piece of ginger cake and a halfpenny on Shrove Tuesday.

There were cakes for them all on Friday, too, when both schools held parties to mark the closures'.

Notes

1. Deposited in Altrincham Reference Library.

2. Alderman Miss Edith Fitton, then aged eighty-seven, the daughter of a noted headmaster of the Thorley Lane School, attended and appears on a photograph accompanying the item.

3. The 1873 school was built on Stockport Road, *not* Thorley Lane. Group photographs of children and staff of both schools accompany the above article.

4. See booklet *Church Schools in Timperley 1851 to 1981* by Hazel Pryor, copy available at Altrincham Reference Library and/or Trafford Local Studies Centre, Sale Library.

APPENDIX 2
LOCAL EDUCATION AUTHORITY SCHOOLS, VOLUNTARY SCHOOLS AND SPECIAL SCHOOLS

NAME	ADDRESS	SITE; LOCATION; TITLE	BUILDING COST	DATE
Broomwood CP	Mainwood Road	Little Oaks Field or Higher Riddings Field – possibly part of both (TM Schedule 556/7)	£49,280	1954
Cloverlea CP	Green Lane North	Part of Big Meadow field (TM Schedule 442)		1968
Heyes Lane CP	Crofton Avenue	Two-form entry Infants a) Part of Spint field: Two-form entry Infants b) (TM Schedule 135)	£55,529 £39,400	1950 1954
Park Road CP	Frieston Road	Whitegate Field or Harlequin Field – possibly part of (TM Schedule 23/24)	£9585	1937
The Willows CP	Victoria Road	Map designation 'Field' (TM Schedule 226)		1968
St. Hugh's RC Primary	Park Road	Map designation 'Field' (TM Schedule 81 or 82) (NB. Land acquired 1937)		1963
Wellington Road (Secondary)[1] (Girls) Wellington Road (Secondary) (Boys)	Wellington Road Moss Lane	(See TPC Minute dated 14.2.1935) Part of two fields marked 'Intake' and 'Field' respectively (TM Schedules 231 and 248) (NB. Land acquired 1933)	£31,782 *(estimated)	1938 1938
Delahays Secondary (mixed) (NB. Girls only until 1984)	Green Lane	Part of a field designated Black Field (TM Schedule 425)	£117,645	1963
Brentwood Special	Brentwood Avenue	Part of Canal Field (TM Schedule 62)		1972
Grove School	Grove Lane	Part of field called Big Bradley or one designed 'Field' (TM Schedule 258 or 259)		1972

Key

CP – County Primary School; SEC: – Secondary Modern; RC – Roman Catholic;
TM – Tithe Map 1838

Note

1. Both schools were formally closed in 1989. A new school, Wellington Road High School (co-educational), was formally opened in September 1989, on the same site, catering for the pupils from the 'old' schools. Mr J. Knowles became its first Headmaster.

15

PRINCIPAL LEISURE FACILITIES PROVIDED IN TOWNSHIP

'... Increased Means and increased Leisure are the two civilizers of Man...'
Benjamin Disraeli, 1872

Leisure facilities stem from two sources: public provision and private provision.

Public Provision

Prior to c.1850 it was effectively nil in rural parishes. After 1850 and onwards to the turn of the century such provision was minuscule by contemporary standards. Parish councillors were notoriously parsimonious in the disbursement of public monies and levied ratepayers, of which ilk they were members, at a rate in the pound tailored precisely to meet their statutory obligations. Any scheme of public provision was invariably financed by inviting public subscriptions and largely depended for its success on the philanthropy of the wealthier residents. Timperley Parish Council was no exception to this nineteenth century convention. The first public leisure facility to be provided in the township was a library and reading room which materialised as a concomitant of building modifications to the 1788 Charity School. In 1861 the school trustees' building project include the following clause:

'... that the upper room of the building be fitted up as a Reading Room and Library for the benefit of the inhabitants of Timperley and adjoining townships...'

'... The Upper room is ready for use as a Reading Room and Library:- A Working Committee of the most intelligent and active young men in the neighbourhood has been formed; and it is hoped that by October next the entire will be in full operation...'

Edward Dowling, Chairman and Treasurer, August 4, 1862

82. Timperley Recreation Ground, opened 1901. (Photograph taken by author, February 1993.)

A number of prominent residents subscribed the necessary funds and, following completion of the work, local people enjoyed the facility until 1874 when the building was demolished.

Timperley Recreation Ground

In response to a letter from London, circulated to all local authorities, inviting them to commemorate Queen Victoria's Jubilee by:

'... obtaining parks or similar amenities for the use of local children...',

the parish council, at its meeting on 15th January, 1897, appointed a committee to study the feasibility of such a project and report back. At the parish council's 20th April meeting it was proposed that a new recreation ground should be provided and that negotiations were in progress to purchase a plot of land, c.3½ acres,[1] from the trustees of Samuel Brooks[2] and that over £300 in public subscriptions had been promised. On 10th June copies of a circular letter were forwarded to prominent residents outlining the progress made and canvassing additional subscriptions.[3] Subsequently, on 2nd July, 1898, the ground, then called Jubilee Field, was formally opened at a public ceremony held on the site. The initiation, organisation and completion of the project is recorded in the Parish Council Minutes.[4]

In 1901 the Parish Council resolved to rail off a portion of the ground as the minute below shows:

'With unclimbable Hurdles...' and '... to erect two sets of swings, one for boys and one for girls with iron railings between them and separate entrances... and some cheap trees and shrubs to be planted inside the plot to make it more private ... at an estimated cost of £70...'

The project was completed and the contractors paid by November 1901.[5]

The initial resolution of the Parish Council was to restrict the use of the facility to the '... Children and young people of the Parish' but it did not take long for this decision to be breached. In September 1903 the local YMCA Club was granted permission to use the ground for cricket and football the only proviso being that the club '... should be open to all eligible young men in the Parish...'. The ground continues to be widely used and over the years, especially post-1945, has been developed extensively. It is now, in addition to a children's playground, a first-rate sports ground, boasting an all-weather floodlit football pitch with associated athletics' tracks and purpose-built changing facilities.

The Golf Links in Timperley

In April 1934 an initiative by the Timperley Electors and Property Owners' Association advocated the preservation of Timperley Golf Links[6] as a public open space or municipal golf links. The Parish Council agreed but opined the best method of achieving that aim was by negotiation with the owner. In the following May, in association with Altrincham Urban District Council,[7] the joint councils' negotiators met the owner, Mr Tomlinson, and his agent[8] to discuss the purchase of the Golf Club lands and lands adjoining, in all c.143 acres. It was offered for sale for a consideration of £38,000. In July 1934, following Ministry of Housing approval and borrowing sanction, the joint councils purchased the land which included the Timperley Golf Links land, Timperley Hall, Timperley Hall Farm and associated outbuildings and Timperley Cricket and Hockey Club field. In September 1934, at a joint Altrincham Urban District Council and Timperley Parish Council Committee meeting a scale of charges was approved, and also the arrangements for terminating the tenancy of Timperley Golf Club and ancillary matters were discussed. This provision was the final leisure provision with which the Parish Council was associated prior to the township's amalgamation with Altrincham Urban District Council in 1936.

Pickering Lodge Open Space or Park

Was originally a small private estate with a frontage on what is now Grove Lane. The residence was approached by an entrance drive leading from a lodge gate sited at the junction of Grove and Moss Lanes.[9] From c.1845 to c.1865 it was owned by a prominent Timperley resident Mr John Skelton, gentleman. The house and land is described thus in *White's Directory of Cheshire*, 1850:

'... a handsome stuccoed residence pleasantly situated and beautified with extensive pleasure grounds...'[10]

83. The Homestead, sited on Park Road. It was acquired by Altrincham Borough Council in 1936 and utilised as a branch library until 1981. (Photograph taken by the author, 1990.)

Post-1864 he left the district and subsequently it was owned and resided in by Mr S. Hardy, brewer. The reference book to the 1877 O.S. 25 inch plan of Bowdon parish lists the fields on the estate as arable which suggests the land was then being farmed. In 1951 the owner, Mr Garner, farmer, offered the land and outbuildings[11] for sale at public auction[12] on 14th November, 1951. It was purchased by Altrincham Borough Council for a consideration of £2,372 the sale being completed on 31st March, 1952 when the conveyance was signed. Subsequently, some land adjoining that purchased was acquired by the council c.1954, which then proceeded to develop the combined parcels of land as a public open space containing a children's play area, tennis courts and bowling greens, together with a pavilion. The grounds were officially opened by the Mayor of the borough on 28th April, 1956.

Branch Library
Following the establishment of Altrincham Borough Council in 1936, the council acquired a large Victorian house, The Homestead,[13] standing in its own grounds and sited on the east side of Park Road. Subsequently, they converted the premises into a branch library for the use and convenience of Timperley residents. Opened in late 1937, or early 1938, it served the local community for over forty years. Following its replacement in 1981 by a purpose-built library, the building was modified to serve as a community centre called the Timperley Community Centre.[14] It now provides accommodation for various local voluntary organisations and societies.

Watling Gate Art Gallery and Museum and Newton Park
Prior to coming into public ownership, Watling Gate[15] was the residence of the Newton family.[16] The house occupies a site on what was originally the family estate, of c.25 acres, called Timperley Park. Most of the land was sold for housing development in the 1920s, only the house and a small plot of land surrounding it being retained by the family. Shortly after the township amalgamated with Altrincham Urban District Council, Lt. Col. C.E. Newton, last male member of the family, bequeathed the house and land to the newly created Altrincham Borough Council, c.1937.[17] In 1938 Altrincham Borough Council resolved to utilise the premises as a public art gallery and museum with separate, self-contained, living accommodation units for the use of the chief librarian and a resident caretaker and also to develop the grounds as a public park to be called 'Newton Park. Following internal modification, the art collection and museum exhibits of the old Altrincham Urban District Council were transferred from Altrincham and housed, together with the 'Newton Collection' of museum exhibits, in the new Watling Gate Art Gallery and Museum. The building was officially opened on 23rd August, 1939, by the Mayor of the new borough, Alderman W. Waterhouse.[18]

The following quotation comes from an article in the *Altrincham and Bowdon Guardian*, 20th August, 1939:

'Altrincham's New Public Art Gallery and Museum
Many Pictures of Cheshire Scenes
How Local Painters Are Being Encouraged
From our Special Correspondent

Altrincham, Sunday

The Mayor of Altrincham is to open on Wednesday Watling Gate, a new art gallery and museum, the latest addition to the town's cultural amenities. This gallery, though officially a branch, will, it is hoped, be used by people from the whole borough, not merely by those who live near it and it will be open on Sundays as well as week days.

Watling Gate is in Leys Road, Timperley and was left to the town by the late Lt. Col. Charles Edward Newton who in 1923 gave over £1000 towards the cost of library extensions and in 1936 gave the town its first permanent art gallery. Colonel Newton also gave the land in Timperley now known as Newton Park, and in many other ways helped to provide constructive pleasures for a rapidly growing population. Not the least of the additions he made in the district was the house itself, which lies only a couple of hundred yards from the line of Watling Street. Col. Newton designed it himself, and it was built in 1904, after he had visited many Cheshire mansions gathering ideas and impressions for a home which was to be representative of the County's distinctive domestic architecture.

It is a low building surrounded by lawns and gardens, roofed with thick creamy stone and colour washed in a rich comfortable shade. The grounds contain a lily pond and a large vegetable patch which is to be laid out soon as an 'old English' garden. The panelled rooms radiate from a large lofty hall or 'house part' with a gallery running round it and so far as possible they are being left in their original state.

History of Cheshire

The gallery contains almost 300 pictures, over a third of them Cheshire scenes by fourteen local or county painters. There are also 72 'old Altrincham' items – prints, photographs, and the original drawings Roger Oldham used to illustrate T.A. Coward's *Picturesque Cheshire*. The museum, too, gives a good picture of Cheshire's history generally, and Altrincham's in particular. There is a reproduction of the Charter granted in 1290, the Hillkirk collection of British birds' eggs and the Cunliffe-Brook collection of Greek and Roman antiquities.

This gallery represents another stage in a development which has had amazing public support. After two years in temporary premises, the town's art collection was moved to a fine permanent building three years ago and since then there has sprung up a dynamic local art movement centring on the gallery.

Encouraging Local Artists

It would have been gratifying if the public had merely used and appreciated the gallery, but what is more remarkable and less intangible is the way in which local painters have been encouraged. The first exhibition of work by local artists attracted twenty exhibitors. The last contained work by over seventy all of them living within five miles of Altrincham. So great has been the practical interest that a local society of artists, of which Lord Stamford is president, was founded and is now flourishing. If development of technique comes as freely as growth of interest there should be before long a distinctive 'Altrincham School' of painters. In a wider sphere the central gallery has done much to improve local knowledge and appreciation of art by its frequent visiting exhibitions. There will be more space for these, since so much of the permanent collection has been moved to Watling Gate.

The town's library system is in an equally healthy state. Particular local conditions – the building of many new houses with young inhabitants, the tendency of previously rural districts to be built up and the blend of rural and urban life – are well represented in the services offered. In addition to the central library there are three branches – at Bowdon Vale, Oldfield Brow and Park Road, Timperley, which is also used for other purposes and may soon be replaced.

The Taste in Books

The inhabitants... seem voracious readers... There is a great demand for books on the theatre, stagecraft and musical scores and libretti... Children are particularly well catered for, two special features being the 'story telling' groups...'

84. Beech Playing Fields, off Heyes Lane. (Photograph taken by author, February 1993.)

Beech Playing Fields

These playing fields of c. 12 acres are bordered by the Fairywell Brook on the north with access from either Beech Avenue or Stelfox Avenue. In 1838[19] they constituted a part of the landholding of William Stelfox and consisted of two large fields,[20] which were part of a c.60 acre farm tenanted by John and Amos Rogerson. By 1877[21] the fields were part of the Hollins Farm and were put to arable use. Ownership was now in the hands of Samuel Brooks, banker.[22] Following his demise, ownership was vested in his trustees until at least 1895 and probably into the early years of the

85. The New Library, Timperley's first purpose-built library, is sited on Stockport Road at its junction with Baker Street. It was built by Trafford Metropolitan Borough Council and opened on 14th December 1981. (Photograph taken by the author, 1990.)

86. Timperley Village Hall, sited on Stockport Road, close to its junction with Bedford Drive. It was originally called the 'Parish Rooms'. (NB. The history of Timperley Village Club is described in an article printed in a free local newspaper, Timperley Independent, dated 23rd February, 1990.) It was built in 1910. (Photograph taken by author, 1990.)

twentieth century. In 1948 ownership was vested in the executors of L.F. Harvey deceased, from whom Altrincham Borough Council purchased the land[23] for a consideration of c.£650. At least up to 1955 the council let out the land to tenants who utilised the land for market gardening. Subsequently, the tenancies were terminated, the land sown to grass and used exclusively as a public open space. It is easily the largest open space in the township and offers facilities for sporting activities and public events (for example, the Altrincham Festival).

The New Public Library

The township's first purpose-built public library was opened on 14th December, 1981. It was officially opened by the Mayor of Trafford, Councillor Stan Brownhill on 24th March, 1982. It occupies a site at the junction of Stockport Road and Baker Street,[24] previously occupied by the village smithy. Provided by Trafford Metropolitan Borough Council, it replaced the Altrincham Borough Council Branch Library sited at the Homestead, Park Road,[25] which had served the township from 1938.

The front section of the building is of two storeys: the ground floor accommodates the book issuing and receiving counters and the children's library whilst the first floor provides staff offices. The public entrance is via a diagonal glass panelled portico, located in the south-west angle of the ground floor. A single storey rear section is attached, with large panelled windows, c. 8 feet high, piercing the west and north walls at intervals. It houses the adult library and tables and chairs for the convenience of the public. The whole of the ground floor is of open plan design.

Private Provision

Timperley Cricket Club

This is the oldest sports' club in Timperley and celebrated its centenary in 1977.[26] It enjoys the use of a first class field, ideally sited – adjacent to the Trafford Metropolitan Borough Golf Links – which easily accommodates two large cricket grounds and tennis courts. During the winter months the fields are used as hockey and lacrosse pitches. The pavilion sited between, and separating, the two cricket grounds has been extensively enlarged, particularly during the post-1930 decades, and provides excellent changing accommodation and ancillary facilities for members. In 1934 the land was owned by the then Club President, Mr F.A. Tomlinson. He sold the whole of the lands comprising the golf links and cricket ground to Altrincham Urban District Council[27] in the same year. Subsequently, the Altrincham Urban District Council agreed to lease to the Cricket Club its field, together with a meadow on the west side of it, subject to the club providing net facilities for local schoolboys, for an initial period of fifteenth years at a rent of £25 a year with an option to renew for a further fifteen years. The club continues to flourish and has extended its activities into other sports. Currently, it offers members, in addition to the men's cricket teams the following facilities:

Activity	From
Cricket (Ladies' Team)	1920s (Early years of)
Hockey	Men 1888, Ladies 1921
Tennis	1922
Lacrosse	1971
Netball Section	1976

These additional sports have occasioned a modification to the club's nomenclature which is now Timperley Cricket, Hockey, Squash and Lawn Tennis Club.

Timperley Golf Club

Prior to 1934 this private club leased the golf course land and clubhouse premises at Timperley Hall from the landowner, Mr F.A. Tomlinson. It was formed c.1890.[28] In 1903 it had a membership of 294, each of whom paid an entrance fee of £4 and an annual subscription of two guineas. It was licensed to sell alcohol on the premises.[29] Following the purchase of the golf course lands by Altrincham Urban District Council in 1934, Timperley Golf Club's tenancy was terminated on 31st December, 1934, but then the Council gave the club the opportunity to continue, subject to the following terms:

- Temporary tenancy of clubhouse for twelve months at a rent of £20.
- Club to provide visitor facilities on premises.
- Altrincham Urban District Council to have two representatives on the club committee.
- Altrincham Urban District Council to take over personnel of the club for twelve months.

This interim arrangement was occasioned because Altrincham Urban District Council's amalgamation with Timperley had not been finalised. On the amalgamation coming into effect in 1936, the golf course became a municipal golf club and Timperley Golf Club was wound up.

87. Timperley Cricket, Lawn Tennis and Hockey Club – cricket grounds and pavilions. (Photograph taken by the author, October 1990.)

Notes

1. Bounded by the Cheshire Lines Railway and Wash Lane (now Park Road).

2. One of the largest landowners in the township.

3. See copy of the letter in Appendix 1.

4. See copies of the relevant minutes in Appendix 2.

5. Charles Marston and Sons' (village joiners) tender of £31 for the swings was accepted and T. Steele's tender of 6s 4d per yard for railings was accepted.

6. At that time a private club. Timperley Hall opened on 8th July, 1896 as its new clubhouse.

7. At this time the two councils were finalising plans for the subsequent amalgamation of the two authorities to form a municipal borough.

8. Earle and Co. of Manchester.

9. The lodgekeeper's cottage is still extant and used residentially.

10. An excellent photograph of the house is contained in *Looking Back at Timperley* by Hazel Pryor.

11. Outbuildings, consisting of eight greenhouses, suggests the land was by now a market garden.

12. By John Arnold, auctioneers, Altrincham.

13. See Altrincham Borough Council Libraries Committee Minute, dated 26th April, 1937.

14. Formerly the Riddings Community Association. The name was changed on moving to The Homestead, when it opened in November 1983 in its new premises.

15. The internal design of Watling Gate was inspired by the traditional plan of a mediaeval hall. See Appendix 3 for description.

16. Lt. Col. Newton, civil engineer, played an active part in the parish local government, being a member of the Parish Council and Overseer of the Poor in the township for many years. See Appendix 3.

17. The estate was bounded by the Baguley Brook, the Bridgewater Canal and Park Road and its northern boundary was within 100 yards of the Manchester Road.

18. See Pamphlet No. 575 (Altrincham Reference Librarian) contains a number of interesting documents germane to the bequest.

19. Ref. Tithe Awards and Tithe Map.

20. Each of c. 6 acres, nos. 331 and 332 on the Tithe Map.

21. See O.S. 25 inch plan of Bowdon Parish, dated 1877, and associated book of reference to the plan.

22. At that time the largest landholder in the township.

23. At c. £55 per acre, an exceptional bargain.

24. On the 1876 O.S. 25 inch plan it is called Woodall's Terrace.

25. Now Timperley Community Centre.

26. See the club's *Centenary Souvenir Book* which contains a wealth of information reminiscences and anecdotes on its activities and personalities down the years.

27. They acted in conjunction with Timperley Parish Council in the transaction shortly before the two authorities amalgamated in 1936.

28. There is a reference to it in the *Altrincham and Bowdon Guardian* of 8th July, 1896.

29. Ref. Return of Licensed Premises in the township for the year 1903, deposited at CCRO.

𝕮ommemoration of t𝕳e 60t𝕳 year of

𝕳er 𝕸ajesty's 𝕽eign.

TIMPERLEY,

JUNE 10TH, 1897.

DEAR SIR,

This question was some time ago brought before the Parish Council who found their powers limited to the purchase or taking over of a Recreation Ground. As they could not burden the rates with the former, they appointed a Sub-Committee to consider the wants of the District and the possibility of acquiring a Recreation Ground by gift or subscription.

The Sub-Committee were impressed by the fact that the Children had no play-ground but the streets and roads, fraught with physical and moral dangers, and that many of the lads were loiterers at street corners, and trespassers, because they had no means of expending their youthful energies in ways suited to their age, such as Cricket, Hockey, Drilling, &c., which would afford health, and help to develop manly and generous qualities. They decided therefore to recommend the provision of a Recreation Ground to be placed under proper rules and restrictions.

Their search for a suitable spot was not, however, very encouraging; when they reported to a Parish Meeting they had only two sites before them and one of them was rejected as too small. The Meeting passed a resolution, that, whilst approving of a Recreation Ground, any under two acres would be inadmissable and they asked the Sub-Committee to continue their efforts.

Mr. Thos. Brooks was again approached and he has agreed to reduce the price of a most eligible site behind the Infant's School from £1200 to £500. The Sub-Committee have also another very suitable site under offer and for one of the two they hope to come to terms.

Under these circumstances and as the time is short, they decided at once to canvass for subscriptions and so far have met with a generous response, over £300 having been promised in sums of £50 and under. When purchased it is proposed to hand the land over in trust to the Parish Council who will see to its maintenance and that proper regulations are enforced. In addition to the cost of purchase, a sum will be required for fencing, entrance gates, &c. The intention is to leave the land in a state of nature and not to lay it out.

As it will be impossible before the 22nd inst., to call on all the inhabitants, it is specially requested that ladies and gentlemen who desire to show their loyalty and gratitude by providing a lasting memorial in Timperley of the Queen's long and beneficient reign will at once send their subscriptions to any member of the Committee whose names are given below.

BOSDIN T. LEECH,

Chairman of the Parish Council.

COMMITTEE:—

SIR BOSDIN T. LEECH, (*Chairman*) Oakmount, Timperley.

ROBERT ASHTON, ESQ., Charlecote, Timperley.

WM. BELL, ESQ., Addison Villas, Timperley.

W. L. GALLOWAY, ESQ., The Lawn, Timperley.

217

APPENDIX 2
EXTRACT FROM REPORT OF CHARITY SCHOOL BUILDING SUB COMMITTEE:-

Items from Parish Council Minutes 1897-1898 and report of a meeting of Subscribers to Jubilee Commemoration Fund:-

20th April, 1897
'Queen Victoria's Diamond Jubilee Commemoration: Subscriptions of over £300 raised and negotiations in progress with Earle[1] for purchase of land in village of c. 3½ Acres.'

2nd July, 1897
Meeting of Subscribers to Rec. Ground Fund at Infants School:-

Resolved:-
a) To purchase field of 3 Acres from Trustees of Samuel Brooks, adjoining Wash Lane and bounded on one side by Leigh's Nursery and on the other by C.L.C. Railway for £500.
b) Appointed a Committee to complete purchase, Conveyance and fixing up the ground and to collect balance of funds required.
c) That field should be handed over in Trust to Parish Council for use of inhabitants of Timperley on terms to be arranged by Committee.
d) To open a Timperley Rec. Ground Account at Cunliffe-Brook and Co.'

24th July, 1897
'Resolved:- 'That the offer of the field for a consideration of £500 by Mr. Earle, Agent for Brook's Trustees, be accepted on terms arranged on 20th July. 1897.' Secretary asked to write to Mr. Earle at Hertford requesting a meeting on 27th July, 1897.'

4th May, 1898
'Resolved: – 'To complete Conveyance after consideration of Draft Copy; also to arrange the Opening Proceedings.'

10th June, 1898
1) Rec. Ground Committee reported Conveyance ready for signing within two weeks.
2) Chairman and Clerk instructed to see Mr. Daniel, tenant of field to arrange for its pasturage until 2 February, 1899.'

2nd July, 1898
Resolved: 'Conveyance dd. 20th June, 1898 be executed on behalf of Parish Council by three named Officials and memo. of agreement signed with Mr. T. Algernon Earle (For Brooks' Trustees). Chairman authorised to accept on behalf of Parish Council gift of Jubilee Field and to convey Council's thanks to Subscriber's for their provision of a Recreation Ground.'

'Petition signed by twelve ratepayers objecting to Parish Council taking over Rec. Ground in present condition. Clerk instructed to reply in suitable terms.'

(NB: Afterwards members joined in a procession to Rec. Ground where in the presence of a large number of the Public Sir Thomas Bosdin Leech, at the close of an able speech, handed over the Deeds to Major Ashton as Chairman of Parish Council who accepted the Deeds in an appropriate speech.)

15th July, 1898
Rec. Ground Deeds deposited in Parish Safe, in Clerk's Office.

11th August, 1898
Rec. Fund Committee: Accounts of Opening of Ground Submitted and approved. Resolved: Charges connected with Opening to be paid by Treasurer from General Fund.

Notes
1. Land agent for Brooks' Estate.

DESCRIPTION AND PLAN OF 'WATLING GATE', LEYS ROAD, TIMPERLEY

Preamble

After visiting and photographing many Cheshire halls, Lt. Col. Newton drew up his own plans for this house. The article below appeared in a journal called *The Studio* in an issue dated 5th March, 1910 and was most probably written from facts supplied by the colonel himself. A visitor to the house would immediately realise that the archetypal Saxon hall provided the inspiration for the design of the main room of the house and from which all the ancillary rooms, on both levels, are accessible.

A copy of the article is deposited in Altrincham Reference Library (Pamphlet No.575).

*

Built 1904; *Cost*: £2500; *Contractor*: Robert Carlyle, Manchester; *Architects*: Newton and Bailey, Manchester.

'Recent Designs in Domestic Architecture

"Watling Gate", Timperley, Cheshire, is built in a rural setting, immediately to the south of that portion of the famous Roman highway, the Watling Street. Simplicity is the keynote to the design, and homely comfort with an entire absence of bijou residence "prettiness" has been the aim of the architects from first to last. Based upon the general lines suggested by many an old Cheshire homestead, the plain colour-wash of the walls, and the soft toned, grey flag-slates of the roof combine to produce a home which harmonises admirably with its landscape environment. A conspicuous feature of the interior is the large hall or "house place", with its open timber roof and cosy chimney corner. The withdrawing-room opens out of this chamber on the same level, and the dining-room is also reached by a set of some five or six steps down, with the kitchen offices on the same level. The main staircase heads up to the bedchamber gallery, bounding two sides of the hall and only 6 feet above floor level. The illustration of the hall on page 136 gives a very fair idea of the ample proportions and homely character of this interior. Another feature of the house is a large roof-garden or sun-bath, approached only by a staircase from the bathroom. The architects, Messrs. Newton and Bayley, of Manchester, have, in this as in other country homes designed by them in Cheshire and Oxfordshire, studiously avoided the importation of outside materials, and relied entirely on local materials and, as already mentioned, they have, as regards design, made a point of following local traditions.'

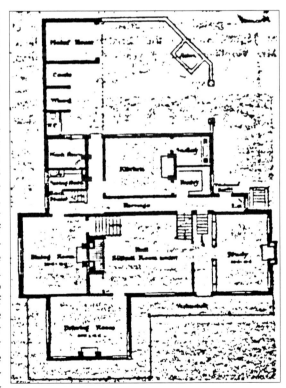

Watling Gate, Timperley, ground plan. Newton and Bayley, Architects.

NB. Two photographs accompany the text but their poor definition precludes their reproduction here.

Newton. — CHARLES EDWARD NEWTON, M.Inst.C.E., F.G.S., The Leys, Timperley, Cheshire, and 17, Cooper Street, Manchester. Son of the late John Newton, Esq., M.Inst.C.E., J.P., of High Legh and Altrincham, Cheshire. Born at Moor House, Preston, September 5th, 1859; educated at Windermere College, Manchester Grammar School, and Owens College; Member of the Institution of Civil Engineers; Fellow of the Geological Society of London and various kindred bodies; engineer to many corporations and local authorities in England and Ireland, in respect to water supply, drainage, tramways, etc.; Hon. Secretary of the Manchester and District Society of Surveyors, Land Agents and Valuers; takes an interest in antiquarian, historical and geological research; author of papers relating to these subjects.

Mr. C. E. Newton.

This curriculum vitae, with associated photograph, is a copy of a document deposited in Altrincham Reference Library, Pamphlet No.575. It appeared in a publication entitled Manchester and Salford at the close of the Nineteenth Century: Contemporary Biographies, published in Brighton by W.T. Pike, in 1899. Lt. Col. Newton held the office of Overseer of Timperley parish continuously from 1909 to 1936. He died in 1937.

Responding to a request for information, Frank Bell wrote the letter, a transcript of which appears below. He was the Assistant Overseer and Parish Clerk until Timperley amalgamated with Altrincham in 1936. This document is deposited in Altrincham Reference Library, Pamphlet No.753.

Ellisland,
Timperley,
Cheshire.
28 7, 39

Dear Mr Bosworth,

Watling Gate

I am pleased to hear that Watling Gate is to be used as an Art Gallery and am sure this would have pleased the late Colonel Newton.

I have gone through the papers remaining in my possession but am afraid I cannot find much to assist you in compiling a souvenir catalogue.

The house was built by Robert Carlyle, Contractor, of Manchester, at a cost of £2500. The Colonel drew his own plans after visiting and photographing many Cheshire halls, before designing the house.

On clearing Watling Gate I retained the plans and anything likely to be useful to the Council and handed them to Mr. Brown but I do not remember anything of especial interest amongst such papers.

A note left by the Colonel stated that a photograph and description of the house appeared in the issue of *The Studio* dated March 5th, 1910. If this is in file it might be useful as the description would no doubt be given by the Colonel himself.

Kind regards,
Yours sincerely,

F. Bell.

NB. Mr W.G. Bosworth was the then Chief Librarian of Altrincham.

APPENDIX 4
BOROUGH OF ALTRINCHAM
LIBRARIES, MUSEUM AND ART GALLERY
RE: WATLING GATE, LEYS ROAD

The report below was submitted to the appropriate committee of the Borough Council in response to the committee's request to assess Watling Gate's suitability as a branch library and as a depository for the 'Cheshire Collection'.

'This detached residence has been bequeathed to the Council in the following terms: 'shall hold the said dwelling-house upon trust to use the same or permit the same to be used for any civic purpose such as a branch library and/or welfare centre and that part of the house may if the Council so desires be used as an official residence for one or more of the Council's employees, and the said dwelling-house shall not be sold, let or occupied by a private individual or private individuals...' Land situated in Leys Road is also bequeathed 'in case the Council shall sell the said plot of land (which they shall be at liberty to do if they so desire) the proceeds of the sale thereof shall be applied at the discretion of the Council:–

(a) In adapting and maintaining the dwelling-house known as Watling Gate for the civic purposes for which it is by my said will directed to be devoted,

and/or

(b) In improving the usefulness of the Altrincham Public Library by the purchase of books or in improving the said Library in any other manner the Council or its Library Committee may think fit."

I have duly examined Watling Gate and the plans thereof and am of the opinion that without structural alterations whatever it is well adapted for the purpose of a Branch Library, and for some time ahead additional rooms might be used for art gallery purposes for which the necessary pictures are available. There is also ample separate accommodation for living purposes.

I have reason to believe that it would serve a public of at least 5000 living in the immediate vicinity. In summer months it would be a most popular place of resort, and the making up and lighting of Leys Road would render it accessible in winter.

The cost of the scheme would lie chiefly in the necessary works of decorations, lighting, provision of shelving and furniture. The room referred to as 'Study' on the plan is already equipped to hold the Cheshire Collection bequeathed by Col. Newton, and to serve as Reference Library.

The present branch library in use in Timperley has for some months been acutely congested, and there is no room for expansion.

(Signed) W.G. BOSWORTH
Chief Librarian and Curator
20th January, 1938

(NB: The recommendation that Watling Gate should be used as a library was not accepted. Despite the remarks of the Chief Librarian in the last paragraph of his report, the branch library, located at The Homestead, Park Road, continued to serve Timperley residents until 1981 when its library function was taken over by the new purpose-built library on Stockport Road.)

16

DEMOGRAPHIC STATISTICS OF TIMPERLEY, 1800 TO 1985

'I have often... admired the secret magic of numbers.'

Sir Thomas Browne (1605-1682)

The graphs contained in this chapter purport to illustrate the radical topographical, social and economic developments which have occurred, inexorably, in Timperley – especially during the twentieth century. They provide a visual supplement to the facts contained in the chapters treating the socio-economic trends in the township. A description of the graphs is set out below.

Ref.	Civil Parish	Period
A	Population Statistics	1801-1971
B	Population Distribution	1841
C	Population: Occupation Classifications	1841
D	Residents: Places of Birth	1851, 1871, 1881
E	Houses: Growth in Number	1801-1971

Ref.	Baptisms, Marriages, Burials, Timperley Residents	Period
F	Bowdon Parish Church (excluding 1641-59)	1600-1900
F	Statistical Summary of B.M. & B. for Parish and Non-conformist Churches	
G	Timperley Parish Church – Baptisms	1850-1985
H	Timperley Parish Church – Marriages	1850-1985
I	Timperley Parish Church – Burials	1850-1985
J	Timperley Non-conformist – Baptisms	1841-1979
K	Timperley Non-conformist – Marriages	1905-1985

Explanatory Notes

Prior to 1849 Timperley was one of a number of townships which, in aggregate, constituted the vast ecclesiastical parish of Bowdon. Prior to the opening of St. George's Chapelry, Altrincham, in the 1760s, Bowdon Church was the only one available to Timperley residents.[1] From 1841 a Methodist community in the township baptised children and, from 1905, solemnised marriages.[2] In 1931 a Roman Catholic church was opened in the township and was followed by a second in 1959/60. From 1933 a Congregational Church (Heyes Lane) conducted baptisms and marriages.

The statistics following are not exhaustive for the township. They *do not* include figures for baptisms, marriages and burials of Timperley residents registered at the following places.

Bowdon, St Georges, Altrincham, and St. Albans, Broadheath, Parish Churches *post 1900*.
St. Hugh of Lincoln and St. John the Baptist, Timperley and St Vincent's, Altrincham Roman Catholic Churches.
Non-conformist churches other than Methodist and Congregational.
Timperley residents buried at Altrincham Cemetery (opened 1894).
Timperley residents cremated at Altrincham Crematorium (opened 1959).[3]

Bowdon Parish Church Registers

Entries for Timperley residents have been collected for 1600 to 1700 inclusive and 1705 to 1900 at five year intervals.

The figures have been extracted from the Bishop's Transcripts.[4] Gaps occur in the records occasioned by one or more of the factors listed below.

Clerk omits township of residence of a person.
Documents illegible or damaged or missing.
1642-1659 Civil Wars – no transcripts returned.

Notes

1. See Chapter 12 on Timperley Parish Church.
2. See Chapter 13 on Non-conformism in Timperley.
3. Ref. booklet describing the building of the crematorium, deposited in Hale Library.
4. The Bishop's Transcript runs from 1st May to 30th April, 1600 to c.1768.

Marriage entries for the period 1628-1699 have been extracted from a typewritten copy of the actual parish register, compiled by C. Rogers of Sale (deposited CCRO, document no. 173, dated 23rd August, 1966).

A
TIMPERLEY CIVIL PARISH
Population Statistics 1801-1971

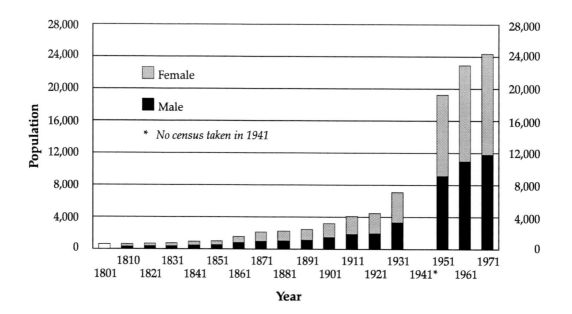

Population Figures									
Year	**1801**	**1810**	**1821**	**1831**	**1841**	**1851**	**1861**	**1871**	**1881**
Males	-	323	357	386	480	509	809	969	1,035
Females	-	301	326	366	467	499	763	1,143	1,206
Total	588	624	683	752	947	1,008	1,572	2,112	2,241
Increase[†]	-	6.1%	9.5%	10.1%	25.9%	6.4%	56.0%	34.4%	6.1%
Year	**1891**	**1901**	**1911**	**1921**	**1931**	**1941**	**1951**	**1961**	**1971**
Males	1,120	1,467	1,855	1,942	3,324	-	9,097	10,948	11,794
Females	1,341	1,728	2,235	2,521	3,756	-	10,135	11,964	12,549
Total	2,461	3,195	4,090	4,463	7,080	-	19,232	22,912	24,343
Increase[†]	9.8%	29.8%	28.0%	9.1%	58.6%	-	171.6%	19.1%	6.2%

† Percentage increase in total population since previous census

Notes
1. The figures for 1801 and 1810 are extracted from 'Returns to Parliament' (51 Geo. III)
2. The figures for 1821 and 1831 are extracted from 'Pigot and Slater Directory of Manchester and Salford', 1841 and 'White's Directory of Cheshire', 1850.
3. The figures for 1841-1971 inclusive are from 'National Census Reports for Cheshire'.
4. In the 1801 Return no breakdown of figures was given below Ecclesiastical Parish Level. This was also the case in the 1861 Return so in the above data the figures for males and females for that year have been interpolated.

B

TIMPERLEY CIVIL PARISH

Distribution of Population

(According to 1841 Census)

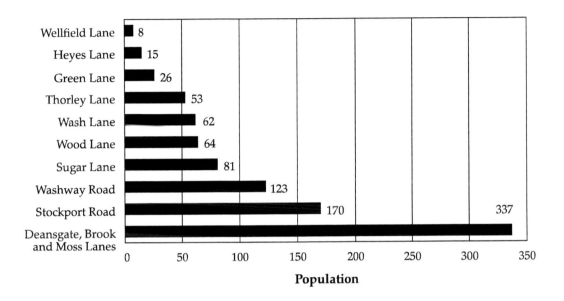

Notes
1. Figures list the total number of persons in each road.
2. Total population 939 plus 4 transients residing overnight in Parish. N.B. Census gives population as 947.
3. Wash Lane now re-named Park Road.
4. Sugar Lane now re-named Ridgeway Road.

C
TIMPERLEY CIVIL PARISH
Occupations of Residents
(According to 1841 Census)

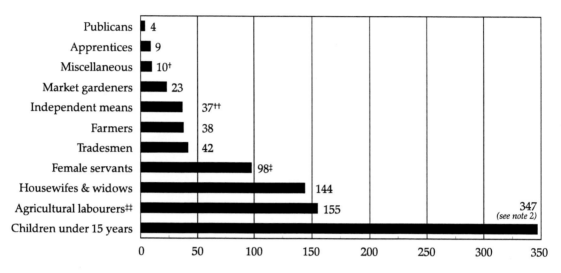

Key
†   Includes 2 teachers and 4 transients
†† Excluding children under 15 years of age of such families
‡   Includes 41 daughters over 15 years of age living at home
‡‡ Agricultural labourers and/or male servants over 15 years of age.

Notes
1. Data shows occupations of 907 persons designated out of a total population of 947.
2. Compulsory registration of births, marriages and deaths was introduced in 1837. Accordingly the accuracy of the age of any child over four years old in 1841 cannot be officially verified. A child's age as supplied by a parent to the Census Enumerator may not necessarily have been accurate, e.g. it could be understated. Although the total of 347 is accurate according to the Census Return it should be treated with caution.

D
TIMPERLEY CIVIL PARISH
Residents' Places of Birth
(As listed in National Censuses of 1851, 1871 and 1881)

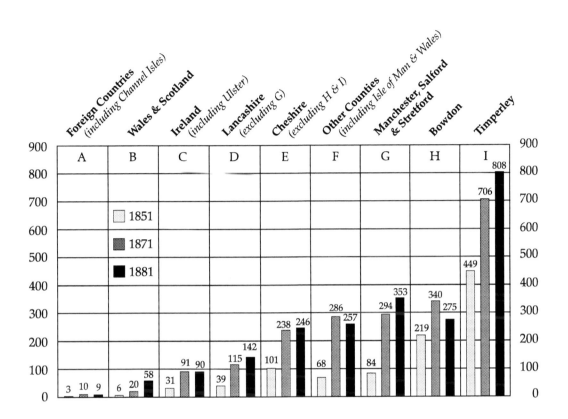

Note
1.   Total population: 1,008 in 1851; 2,112 in 1871 and 2,241 in 1881.

227

E

TIMPERLEY CIVIL PARISH
Growth in number of houses 1801-1971

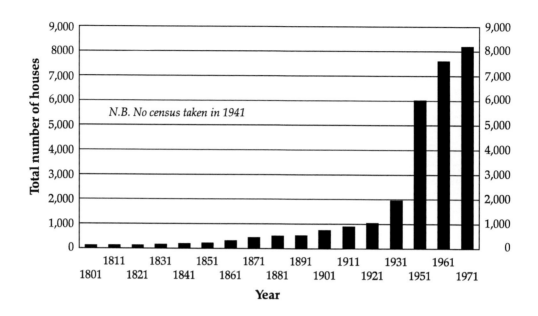

N.B. No census taken in 1941

Total number of houses (y-axis)

Year (x-axis)

Total number of houses at the end of each decade

1801	1811	1821	1831	1841	1851	1861	1871	1881	1891	1901	1911	1921	1931	1951	1961	1971
119*	127	129	155	188	219	312*	438	507	528	740	892*	1,044	1,957	6,020	7,607	8,200

Number of uninhabited houses

1801	1811	1821	1831	1841	1851	1861	1871	1881	1891	1901	1911	1921	1931	1951	1961	1971
4*	6	1	4	4	18	15*	13	63	28	29						

Percentage increase in number of dwellings over the previous decade

1801	1811	1821	1831	1841	1851	1861	1871	1881	1891	1901	1911	1921	1931	1951	1961	1971
†	†	1.6	20.1	21.3	16.5	42.6	40.4	15.8	4.1	40.2	20.5	17	87.5	207	20.9	7.8

* Interpolated figures, Nataional Census returns incomplete.
† No breakdown of figures below Ecclesiastical Parish level.

Notes

1. The figures for the period 1801-1831 are extracted from the Returns to Parliament under the authority of Act 41 Geo. III.
2. The figures for the period 1841-1971 are extracted from National Census returns. N.B. No census taken in 1941.

Table A Statistics of Timperley Residents' Baptisms, Marriages and Burials conducted in Bowdon Parish Church, 1600 to 1700 (inclusive)			
Year	Baptisms	Marriages	Burials
1626	0	1	3
1646	0	1	0
1654	0	0	3
1655	0	2	0
1660	5	0	3
1663	7	*	1
1666	2	0	4
1668	4	0	3
1669	3	0	3
1670	7	0	1
1671	4	0	5
1672	7	0	4
1673	7	1	3
1676	1	0	1
1678	3	0	3
1679	1	0	4
1680	2*	1	4
1681	6*	0	4*
1682	2	0	3
1683	8	0	9
1684	4	0	2
1685	7	0	2
1689	0	0	5
1690	2	0	5
1691	1	@	3
1692	8	0	3
1694	5	0	2
1695	2	0	5
1696	5	0	1
1697	0	0	5
1698	1	0	4
1699	3	1	4
1700	10	0	4

NB: * document damaged; @ document of poor legibility.

In a number of the missing years Timperley marriages cannot be identified as the clerk does not record township of residence.

In this seventy-five year period the total baptisms and burials for the thirty-three years actually quoted are as below.

Baptisms – 117 (an average of 3.55 a year); burials – 106 (an average of 3.21 a year).

Assuming an average life expectancy of forty-five years, this would suggest an approximate population of 150 to 175 in the seventeenth century. This correlates very closely with the estimate of approximately 200 population in the mid-seventeenth century, interpolated from the Hearth Tax Returns for the township of 1663 and 1673/4.

On the basis of these evidences, it is justifiable to state that the township population was in fact between 150 and 200 in the latter half of the seventeenth century.

Table B Statistics of Timperley Residents' Baptisms and Burials only 1705 to 1900 (at intervals of five years)		
Year	Baptisms	Burials
1705	6	1
1710	4	3
1715	5	2
1720	6	5
1725	6	2
1730	5	5
1735	4	3
1740	@	@
1745	6	0
1750	6*	5*
1755	9	2
1760	6	2
1765	11	3
1770	8	7
1775	16	4
1780	12	6
1785	17	6
1790	18	6
1795	14*	7*
1800	15+6	10
1805	13+2	14
1810	12+2	9+1
1815	16+1	15+1
1820	12	9
1825	11+3	9+1
1830	18+4	15+1
1835	19+4	11
1840	20+1	13
1845	16+7	16+3
1850	28+2	4
1855	10+6	9+1
1860	4+1	13
1865	4	1
1870	12+7	22
1875	3+5	10
1880	4+1	6
1885	3	12
1890	–	–
1895	2+6	2+2
1900	0	3

NB: for example, 1855: 10+6: 9+1 denotes ten baptisms at Bowdon and six at St. George's, Altrincham and nine burials at Bowdon and one at St. George's.

A Summary of the figures in Table B

(They illustrate clearly that the period 1705-1900 witnessed a steady natural increase in population; it was much more pronounced in the period 1800-1900 than it was in the period 1705-1795, i.e. in pure percentage terms.)

Period	Baptisms		Burials	
	Total	Average p.a.	Total	Average p.a.
1705-1795 (18 sample years)	159	8.83	69	3.83
1800-1900 (20 sample years)	270	13.5	231	11.55

(NB: During the period 1855-1900 twenty-three of the baptisms were of infants who died before attaining the age of two years, i.e. in the entries for those particular sample years.)

A Statistical Summary of Baptisms, Marriages and Burials in Timperley Parish Church, Timperley Methodist Church and Timperley Congregational Churches

Church 1850-1985	Baptisms			Marriages			Burials		+
	C.P. Residents	Others	Total	C.P. Residents	Others	Total	C.P. Residents	Others	Total
Christ Church	7946	2308	10254	3412	589	4001	2356	1836	4192
Methodist	*1640	*1290	*350	565	119	684	Nil	Nil	Nil
Congregational	@915	@825	@90	232	15	247	Nil	Nil	Nil
Grand Total	10061	2748	12809	4209	723	4932	2356	1836	4192

* Covers the period 1841-1979
@ Covers the period 1933-1985
(NB. Refer to the appropriate graph for a detailed breakdown of the figures listed in the table above.)
C.P. – Civil Parish

TIMPERLEY PARISH CHURCH
Baptismal Register Statistics, 1850-1905

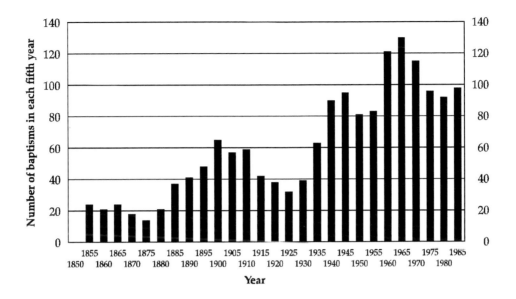

Number of baptisms in each year

1850	0	1870	18	1890	41	1910	59	1930	39	1950	81	1970	115
1851	2	1871	34	1891	32	1911	49	1931	48	1951	66	1971	116
1852	12	1872	21	1892	44	1912	37	1932	44	1952	73	1972	89
1853	15	1873	25	1893	41	1913	42	1933	26	1953	79	1973	106
1854	13	1874	20	1894	46	1914	43	1934	44	1954	74	1974	84
1855	24	1875	14	1895	48	1915	42	1935	63	1955	83	1975	96
1856	20	1876	22	1896	42	1916	92	1936	92	1956	119	1976	87
1857	22	1877	16	1897	49	1917	37	1937	75	1957	133	1977	182
1858	22	1878	19	1898	30	1918	36	1938	90	1958	137	1978	123
1859	36	1879	20	1899	47	1919	38	1939	97	1959	122	1979	115
1860	21	1880	21	1900	65	1920	38	1940	90	1960	121	1980	92
1861	26	1881	43	1901	40	1921	50	1941	64	1961	111	1981	121
1862	23	1882	19	1902	51	1922	41	1942	90	1962	130	1982	114
1863	31	1883	20	1903	55	1923	35	1943	81	1963	106	1983	105
1864	42	1884	41	1904	50	1924	39	1944	108	1964	116	1984	99
1865	24	1885	37	1905	57	1925	32	1945	95	1965	130	1985	98
1866	27	1886	36	1906	55	1926	30	1946	92	1966	134		
1867	26	1887	35	1907	45	1927	38	1947	107	1967	142		
1868	28	1888	35	1908	47	1928	50	1948	79	1968	111		
1869	28	1889	55	1909	48	1929	46	1949	78	1969	117		

The first entry in the register was in 1851

Date	Baptismal name	Parents	Surname	Abode	Occupation	Vicar
29 October	Charlotte	James and Anna	Renshaw	Baguley	Farmer	R. Dowling

Notes

1. Breakdown of figures: residents of Timperley 7,946; remainder of parish (i.e. parts of Hale and Baguley) 1,256; non-residents 1,052; total 10,254.

2. It is interesting to note that of the total number of baptisms 25.19% occurred in the twenty-five year period 1961-1985. (N.B. On the basis of the evidence of the entries the illegitimacy rate averaged 1.5 per annum or an annual rate of 1.97%. The rate for the twenty-five years 1961-1985 is 1.33 per annum or 1.29% per annum.)

H
TIMPERLEY PARISH CHURCH
Marriage Regsister Statistics, 1850-1985

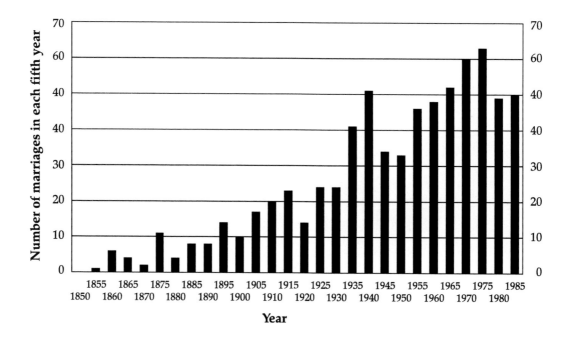

Number of marriages in each year

1850	0	1873	4	1896	12	1919	16	1942	47	1965	52
1851	0	1874	9	1897	11	1920	14	1943	29	1966	63
1852	0	1875	11	1898	16	1921	19	1944	34	1967	54
1853	3	1876	11	1899	18	1922	14	1945	59	1968	57
1854	6	1877	10	1900	10	1923	24	1946	49	1969	62
1855	1	1878	9	1901	20	1924	12	1947	51	1970	60
1856	2	1879	8	1902	17	1925	24	1948	49	1971	46
1857	6	1880	4	1903	17	1926	21	1949	31	1972	42
1858	1	1881	12	1904	17	1927	26	1950	33	1973	58
1859	3	1882	11	1905	17	1928	23	1951	32	1974	50
1860	6	1883	10	1906	21	1929	17	1952	41	1975	63
1861	5	1884	13	1907	20	1930	24	1953	35	1976	46
1862	2	1885	8	1908	23	1931	23	1954	34	1977	51
1863	1	1886	9	1909	16	1932	25	1955	46	1978	44
1864	3	1887	11	1910	20	1933	20	1956	39	1979	53
1865	4	1888	9	1911	19	1934	32	1957	49	1980	49
1866	6	1889	8	1912	16	1935	41	1958	54	1981	58
1867	5	1890	8	1913	18	1936	34	1959	38	1982	45
1868	7	1891	14	1914	20	1937	36	1960	48	1983	49
1869	8	1892	10	1915	23	1938	50	1961	49	1984	71
1870	2	1893	11	1916	16	1939	45	1962	45	1985	50
1871	5	1894	15	1917	13	1940	51	1963	52		
1872	9	1895	14	1918	12	1941	41	1964	56		

Notes
1. Marriages in which at least one of the contracting parties is a resident of Timperley Civil Parish account for 85.3% of all marriages in the register.
2. Breakdown of figures: at least one of contracting parties a resident of Timperley civil parish 3,412; both parties residing in the Hale or Baguley parts of ecclesiastical parish or non-residents of civil parish 589; total 4,001.

I
TIMPERLEY PARISH CHURCH
Burial Register Statistics, 1850-1985

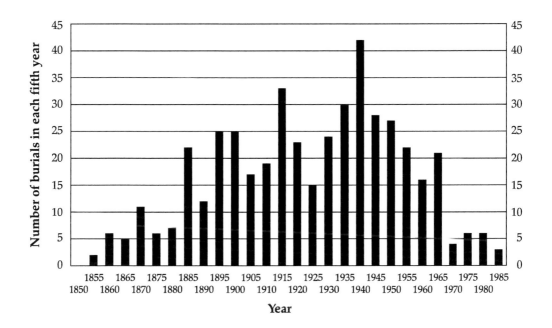

Number of burials* in each year											
1850	0	1873	7	1896	15	1919	39	1942	25	1965	21
1851	0	1874	7	1897	16	1920	23	1943	31	1966	17
1852	0	1875	6	1898	27	1921	12	1944	34	1967	16
1853	0	1876	9	1899	27	1922	21	1945	28	1968	7
1854	0	1877	5	1900	25	1923	20	1946	19	1969	13
1855	2	1878	7	1901	20	1924	19	1947	22	1970	4
1856	2	1879	11	1902	28	1925	15	1948	25	1971	10
1857	2	1880	7	1903	24	1926	16	1949	20	1972	15
1858	6	1881	12	1904	27	1927	26	1950	27	1973	11
1859	4	1882	14	1905	17	1928	34	1951	20	1974	6
1860	6	1883	12	1906	25	1929	35	1952	19	1975	6
1861	4	1884	20	1907	18	1930	24	1953	17	1976	5
1862	5	1885	22	1908	24	1931	34	1954	20	1977	10
1863	2	1886	15	1909	17	1932	53	1955	22	1978	4
1864	13	1887	24	1910	19	1933	31	1956	17	1979	8
1865	5	1888	12	1911	32	1934	36	1957	23	1980	6
1866	5	1889	12	1912	18	1935	30	1958	14	1981	12
1867	7	1890	12	1913	23	1936	42	1959	18	1982	10
1868	5	1891	19	1914	35	1937	39	1960	16	1983	5
1869	13	1892	21	1915	33	1938	29	1961	21	1984	6
1870	11	1893	34	1916	32	1939	32	1962	12	1985	3
1871	10	1894	29	1917	20	1940	42	1963	11		
1872	7	1895	25	1918	45	1941	30	1964	5		

* Timperley civil parish residents

Notes
1. Breakdown of figures: residents of Timperley civil parish 2,356; residents of the Hale and Baguley parts of ecclesiastical parish 795; non-residents of parish 1,041; total 4,192.
2. The first internment was in 1854, viz. Name: Mary Anne Packer, Address: Altrincham, Age: 30 years.
3. Altrincham cemetery opened in 1894.
4. Altrincham crematorium opened in April 1959.
5. The number of internments declined steeply from the 1930's in spite of a rapid increase in population occasioned by housing development in the parish. This reflects the much wider use of the Altrincham cemetery and crematorium facilities by residents of the parish.

J
TIMPERLEY NON-CONFORMIST CHURCHES
Baptism Register Statistics, 1840-1985
(Congregational statistics commence in 1933)

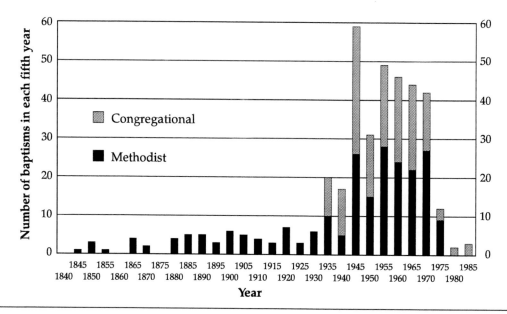

Number of baptisms in each year *(Methodist*/Congregational*)*

Year	M/C	Year	M/C	Year	M/C	Year	M/C	Year	M/C	Year	M/C	Year	M/C
1840	0/-	1861	0/-	1882	8/-	1903	6/-	1924	5/-	1945	26/33	1966	21/18
1841	3/-	1862	0/-	1883	8/-	1904	5/-	1925	3/-	1946	22/22	1967	32/26
1842	1/-	1863	2/-	1884	6/-	1905	5/-	1926	3/-	1947	19/32	1968	17/10
1843	1/-	1864	0/-	1885	5/-	1906	7/-	1927	13/-	1948	21/29	1969	25/17
1844	3/-	1865	4/-	1886	4/-	1907		1928	3/-	1949	18/22	1970	27/15
1845	1/-	1866	3/-	1887	2/-	1908	2/-	1929	10/-	1950	15/16	1971	26/18
1846	3/-	1867	5/-	1888	1/-	1909	6/-	1930	6/-	1951	15/24	1972	20/9
1847	1/-	1868	3/-	1889	6/-	1910	4/-	1931	12/-	1952	21/21	1973	13/4
1848	3/-	1869	7/-	1890	5/-	1911	7/-	1932	2/-	1953	24/18	1974	18/2
1849	2/-	1870	2/-	1891	2/-	1912	7/-	1933	13/1	1954	15/18	1975	9/3
1850	3/-	1871	7/-	1892	3/-	1913	3/-	1934	3/4	1955	28/21	1976	14/3
1851	3/-	1872	3/-	1893	3/-	1914	3/-	1935	10/10	1956	29/27	1977	3/2
1852	3/-	1873	7/-	1894	1/-	1915	3/-	1936	7/9	1957	25/28	1978	8/10
1853	4/-	1874	5/-	1895	3/-	1916	3/-	1937	7/5	1958	34/26	1979	13/8
1854	2/-	1875	0/-	1896	6/-	1917	4/-	1938	16/15	1959	26/21	1980	†/2
1855	1/-	1876	4/-	1897	5/-	1918	6/-	1939	12/15	1960	24/22	1981	†/3
1856	1/-	1877	7/-	1898	5/-	1919	8/-	1940	5/12	1961	46/24	1982	†/4
1857	0/-	1878	1/-	1899	5/-	1920	7/-	1941	8/18	1962	53/22	1983	†/6
1858	0/-	1879	9/-	1900	6/-	1921	0/-	1942	11/21	1963	44/27	1984	†/4
1859	1/-	1880	4/-	1901	2/-	1922	7/-	1943	18/27	1964	39/19	1985	†/3
1860	0/-	1881	8/-	1902	8/-	1923	6/-	1944	19/25	1965	22/22		

* Baptisms of infants resident in the civil parish - extracted from the total baptisms at the church that year.
† Figures not available at time of survey.

First entries in Methodist[1] and Congregational[2] registers

	Year	Month	Child's Name	Parents	Abode	Age	Minister
(1)	1841	17 June	Hannah	Samual & Mary Jackson	Baguley	-	Isaac Woodcock
(2)	19??	9 October	Barbara Joan	? & ? Davies	-	-	Arthur Burgess

(Congregational entry imprecise - registers not maintained carefully)

Notes
1. Breakdown of Methodist figures 1841-1979 inclusive: residents of civil parish 1,290; non-residents 350; total 1,640.
2. Breakdown of Congregational figures 1933-1985 inclusive: residents of civil parish 825; non-residents 90; total 915.

TIMPERLEY NON-CONFORMIST CHURCHES
Marriage Register Statistics, 1905-1985
(Congregational statistics commence in 1933)

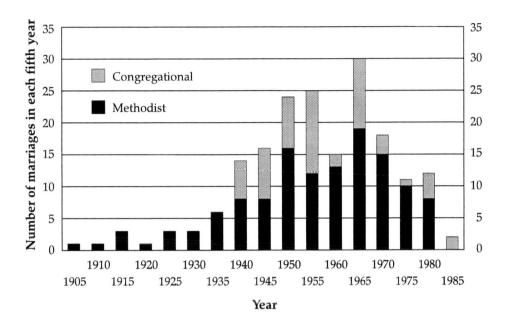

Number of marriages in each year *(Methodist/Congregational)*												
1905	1/-	1919	2/-	1933	4/0	1947	12/6	1961	15/5	1975	10/1
1906	1/-	1920	1/-	1934	2/1	1948	9/11	1962	13/7	1976	10/5
1907	2/-	1921	2/-	1935	6/0	1949	9/9	1963	12/12	1977	7/1
1908	1/-	1922	2/-	1936	3/1	1950	16/8	1964	14/8	1978	10/1
1909	1/-	1923	1/-	1937	0/2	1951	13/5	1965	19/11	1979	16/5
1910	1/-	1924	4/-	1938	8/1	1952	9/3	1966	15/8	1980	8/4
1911	3/-	1925	3/-	1939	6/1	1953	13/6	1967	16/3	1981	6/1
1912	3/-	1926	2/-	1940	8/6	1954	11/5	1968	10/9	1982	6/1
1913	1/-	1927	5/-	1941	4/3	1955	12/13	1969	11/2	1983	11/1
1914	3/-	1928	1/-	1942	3/4	1956	8/8	1970	15/3	1984	7/1
1915	3/-	1929	1/-	1943	4/6	1957	13/12	1971	11/9	1985	/2
1916	0/-	1930	3/-	1944	5/1	1958	13/5	1972	9/2		
1917	1/-	1931	1/-	1945	8/8	1959	16/7	1973	9/1		
1918	3/-	1932	1/-	1946	8/3	1960	13/2	1974	15/7		

Notes
1. Total number of marriages at Methodist Church (1841-1985) was 684 of which 565 (82.6%) were of residents of Civil Parish.
2. Total number of marriages at Congregational Church (1933-1985) was 247 of which 232 (93.9%) were of residents of Civil Parish.

SCHEDULE OF SOURCES

Primary Sources

Manuscript Sources

Altrincham Reference Library

Pamphlets:

No. 171	Mr. H. Hulme: Manuscript, unpublished, re Place Name
No. 209	
No. 239	Leaflet: Appeal for £600 to build St. David's Church
No. 343	Collection of Several Acts pertaining to canals of late Duke of Bridgewater
No. 542	Opening of Delahays Secondary Modern School
No. 575	Magazine article re Lt. Col. C.E. Newton, 1899
No. 753	Mr Frank Bell: Letter to W.G. Bosworth

Frank Bell Collection (Miscellaneous Papers)

Trafford Local Studies Centre

Altrincham Borough Council minutes	1934 to 1974
Timperley Parish Accounts	1895 to 1910
Timperley Parish Council Allotments – Cash Book	1914 to 1936
Timperley Parish Council Minutes Book	1895 to 1936
Timperley Parish Council Postage Book	1926 to 1936
Timperley Select Vestry Minutes	
Timperley Township Book	1770-1833

Cheshire County Record Office

Census Returns for Timperley, 1841 and 1851

Alehouse and Alesellers Licence Registers: 1743-57; 1774-1787; 1799-1821; 1828

Alehouse Keepers Register, 1629-1650

Altrincham and District Out Relief Order Books, 1928 to 34

Altrincham District Return of Licensed Houses, 1891

Altrincham Poor Law Union Minutes, 1844 to 1928

Bowdon Parish Registers: Bishops' Transcripts

Bowdon Parish Register: Typescript copy by Dr Colin Rogers, document no. 173

Bucklow Hundred Poor Law Union Ledgers, Document LRB 38/2, 1897

Bucklow Rural District Council Minutes, 1896 to 1915

Constables' Accounts for the Township of Timperley, 1798 to 1801

Electoral Roll, October 1778

Grant of Free Warren in his Demesne Lands to Robert Masci of Tatton by Edward I, 1294

Heyes Lane Congregational Church, Order of Service, Official Opening 27th November, document ECU5/43, 1954

Hearth Tax Returns, document P.R.O. E179\86\145), 1664 and 1673-4

Land Tax Assessment for Timperley, 1798 to 1842

Leicester-Warren Archive: Subsidy Rolls for Timperley and Ashley 1667

Local Government Board Assistance Committee Minutes, 1904 to 1929

Newton, Lieutenant Colonel C.E., paper delivered by himself to Altrincham Mutual Improvement Society entitled 'The Geology of Altrincham and District', in Frank Bell Collection, 'Papers of C.E. Newton', Document no. DDX 131/28, c.1890 undated

Overseers' Accounts for the Township of Timperley, 1798 to 1838

Plea Rolls, dating from 1194

Poor Rate Returns for the Township of Timperley, 1800-1817 and 1821-1834

Recognizance Rolls, 1397 and 1402

Records of Removal to Workhouse, 1915 to 1929

Records of Non Poor Law Duties, 1862 onwards

Register of Licensed Houses, document QAL/5, Licensing Act, 1904

Return of Licensed Premises, Licensing Act 1902

Timperley Tithe Awards, 1838

Timperley Tithe Map, 1838
Will of John Higginson of the Brook, Timperley, yeoman, 1727
Woodlands United Reformed Church, Order of Service, Official Opening, 7th October, 1972

Greenall Whitley plc (The owner in 1984)
Original deeds of the Pelican Hotel, dating from 1680

Manchester Central Library Archives
Methodist Archives: Altrincham Circuit quarterly meetings minutes
Methodist Archives: Trustees' Accounts and Record Books, 1847-1910, for Timperley Methodist Chapel
Methodist Archives: Methodist Sunday School Building Fund Accounts

Public Record Office
Census for Timperley, statistics only: 1921, 1971 and 1981
Hargrave v. Thompson, Probate Court, 1904
Hargrave v. Hargrave, Lancashire Chancery Court, Liverpool District, Letter H, No.1819
Palatine of Chester: Eyre Rolls of Justice of Chester
Plea Rolls of the City of Chester

Timperley Parish Chest
Documents relating to Christ Church, Timperley from 1850
Indenture: Infant School, Stockport Road, Timperley 1788

Printed Sources

Altrincham Crematorium, Building of (copy in Hale Library)
Accounts of the Chamberlains of Chester, 1350-1363, Record Society of Lancashire and Cheshire, Vol.59, 1916
Altrincham Crematorium (building of) (copy in Hale Library)
Calendar of Charter Rolls, Cheshire, Public Record Office, London
Calendar of Cheshire Recognisance Rolls, Public Record Office, London
Calendar of Close Rolls, Public Record Office, London
Calendar of County Court, City Court and Eyre Rolls of Chester, Public Record Office, London
Calendar of Patent Rolls, Public Record Office, London, 1901
Catalogue of Ancient Deeds, Public Record Office, London, 1890
Charters of the Anglo-Norman Earls of Chester c.1071-1237, edited by Geoffrey Barraclough, Record Society of Lancashire and Cheshire, 1988
Cheshire Antiquities, Sir Peter Leycester, 1670
Cheshire Education, Cheshire Local Education Authority (copy in Altrincham Reference Library)
Cheshire in the Pipe Rolls, Mills and Brown, Record Society of Lancashire and Cheshire, 1938.
Distraint for Knighthood, Vol.12, Record Society of Lancashire and Cheshire
Domesday Book, edited by James Tait, Chetham Society, 1916
Domesday Monachorum
Pudsey Deeds, Yorkshire Archaeological Society, Record Series, 56
Recognizance Rolls, Public Record Office, London
Register of the Black Prince, Public Record Office, London, 1930-33
Reports of the Deputy Keeper of Public Records, Public Record Office
Rotuli Chartorum, London, 1837

Directories

Cheshire Directory	1850
Kelly's *Directories of Cheshire*	1892, 1896, 1906 and 1914
Kelly's *Directory for Altrincham and District*	1860 to 1864
Morris's *Directory of Cheshire*	1874
Pigot's *Directories of Manchester and Salford District*	1822, 1834, 1836 and 1838
Pigot and Slater's *Directory of Manchester and Salford District*	1841
Slater's *Directory for Altrincham*	1848 to 1858

White's *Directory of Cheshire* 1850 and 1860
Maps and plans
Ordnance Survey plan, 25.344 inches to 1 mile, sheet nos.: 9/14, 9/15, 18/2, 18/3, 18/6 and 18/7, 1876
Ordnance Survey plan, Timperley, 6 inches to 1 mile, sheet nos.: 9 S.W., 9 S.E., 18 N.W. and 18 N.E., Cheshire 2nd edition, 1899
Ordnance Survey, Geographical Survey of Great Britain, map sheets 198 Solid and 99 Drift, 1962
Plan: Estate of F.A. Tomlinson Esq., 1934
Plan: Riddings Hall Estate Development, 1933

Newspapers and Magazines
Manchester Courier   1st November, 1851
Altrincham and Bowdon Guardian   8th July, 1896
The Studio (a fine art magazine)   5th March, 1910

History Society Journals
Bulletin of John Rylands Library
Journals of the Chester Archaeological Society

Newspaper Articles
Altrincham and Bowdon Guardian   23rd July, 1981
Altrincham and Bowdon Guardian   19th August, 1982
Altrincham and Bowdon Guardian   17th January, 1985
Sale and Altrincham Messenger   21st February, 1982
Sale and Altrincham Messenger   28th June, 1984
Timperley Independent   30th October, 1982
Timperley Independent   25th June, 1983

BIBLIOGRAPHY

AUTHOR	TITLE	PUBLISHER
Arnold, Horace	*'Memories of Timperley Village – 1877 to 1952'	monograph unpublished
Armstrong, A.M.	*Place Names of Cumberland*, Vols. 20 and 21	English Place Name Society, Cambridge University Press
Balshaw, Charles	*Stranger's Guide to Altrincham*	Charles Balshaw, 1858, reprinted 1973 E.J. Morten
Borer, M.C.	*The British Hotel through the Ages,*	Lutterworth Press, 1972
Cameron, Kenneth	*English Place Names*	Methuen, 1969
Dickens, Charles	*Nicholas Nickleby*	Odhams Press Ltd
Dodgson, J. McNeill	*The Place Names of Cheshire,* Volumes 44 and 45, Part 2	English Place Name Society: Cambridge University Press, 1970
Ekwall, Eilert	*Concise Oxford Dictionary of English Place Names, Introduction to the Survey of English Place Names*, Volume I, 4th edition	Oxford University Press, 1960
Farnworth, M.	*Methodism in Timperley 1933-1983*	Douglas Printers, Wigan, 1984
Hadfield, Charles, and Biddle, Gordon	*The Canals of North West England.* Volume 1	David and Charles, 1970
Holt, G.O.	*A Regional History of Railways in Great Britain: Volume 10 – North West*	David and Charles, 1978
Hoskins, W.G.	*Local History in England*	Longmans, 1984
Ingham, Alfred	*History of Altrincham and Bowdon*	Cartwright and Rattray, 1879
Murray, P.H.,	*A New English Dictionary* *Dictionary of British Surnames*	Clarendon Press, 1935 Routledge, Kegan and Paul, 1958
Nickson, Charles	*Bygone Altrincham – Traditions and History*	Mackie and Co. Ltd, 1935
Ormerod, Dr George	*A History of the County Palatine of Chester,* Volumes I, II and III	T. Helsby edition, London, 1892
Pryor, Hazel	*Looking Back at Timperley* *'Church Schools in Timperley 1851 to 1981'	Willow Press, 1982 unpublished
Timperley Cricket, Hockey and Lawn Tennis Club	*Timperley Cricket, Hockey and Lawn Tennis Club Centenary Souvenir*, 1977	
Toller, T.N.	*An Anglo-Saxon Directory*	Oxford University Press, 1890
Valline, G.H.	*English Spelling Dictionary*	Andre Deutsch, revised edition, 1965
Whitney, W.D.	*Concise Dictionary and Cyclopaedia,*	publisher unknown, 1914
Wright, E.H.	*Story of Timperley Methodism, 1833-1933*	Mackie and Co., 1934

* Publications referring to Timperley specifically.

Index

Tulip Drive, Timperley, 137
Tyrrell & Westlake, 132

Udeman, 15-16
Unicorn Hotel, Altrincham, 87
Union Fever Receiving House, Timperley (proposed), 65-66
Upton Drive, Timperley, 132, 137
Urban and Rural Sanitary Districts, 36
Urban District Councils, 45, 47
Urmston, 75

Vale Cottage, Stockport Road, 118
Vale House, Timperley, 134
Vale Road, Timperley, 137
Valery, William de, 51
Vaudrey Drive, Timperley, 137
Vawdrey family, 34, 54; Alice (née Alice, widow of Ralph Brereton of Wettenhall), 31; Alice (née Barton), 31; Anne (née Newton), 31; Edward, 30-31; Robert, 29-31, 34, 53-55; Thomas, 31, 53-54
Vawdrey family of Bank Hall, Hale, John, 34; Richard, 30, 34; Thomas, 29
Vawdrey of Bowdon, Robert, 34
Vawdrey family of Riddings, 55; Vawdrey, Edward, of Riddings, 55; Vawdrey, Jane (née Hyde), 31; Vawdrey, Margaret, 29; Vawdrey, Margaret (née Mosley), 30-31, 54
Venables of Bollin, William, 27; Gilbert, 15
Victoria Avenue, Timperley, 137
Victoria Close, Timperley, 137
Victoria Road, Timperley, 137, 208
Voluntary Schools, 197

Wales, 22
Walker, James, 39; Sarah, 63
Wallwork, Mrs, 80
Walsh, Albert, 184; Ralph, 149
Walton, George, 149; Mrs M.A., 149
Warburton family, 50; Ellen, 58; George, 149; Hannah, 64; Isaac, 149; J., 39; James, 92; John, 103; Joseph, 149; Thomas, 39, 43, 149, 192; Thomas, of Altrincham, 141
Warburton of Arley, Peter, 26; Piers, 26
Warburton's Farm, Shay Lane, Hale Barns, 175
Ward, George, 55; Mary, 58
Warren, Samuel, 181; William, 39
Warrington, 11, 92
Warrington and Stockport Railway Company, 92-93, 96
Warrington and Stockport Turnpike Road, 175
Warrington, Richard, 58-59, 63; William, 189
Wash Lane (Park Road), Timperley, 12, 30, 34, 44, 64-65, 68-69, 72-73, 78, 83-85, 89, 96-97, 104, 108, 137-138, 145, 166, 172, 177, 199, 216, 218
Washway Road, Timperley, 9-10, 12-14
Waterhouse, W., 211
Watling Gate Art Gallery and Museum, 146, 211
Watling Gate, Leys Road, 14, 33, 129, 146, 211-212, 216, 219, 221
Watling Street, 219
Webb, Edgar, 45
Webster, Christopher, 180; J., 105, 108
Well Green council estate, Timperley, 174
Wellfield Lane, Timperley, 10, 12-13, 66, 72-74, 78, 124-125, 128, 138
Wellington Road High School, Timperley, 126, 198, 208
Wellington Road, Timperley, 10, 13, 115, 138, 186, 208
Wemyss, Earl of, 27
Wentworth Avenue, Timperley, 138
West Timperley Station, 10, 85, 93
West Vale Road, Timperley, 132, 138

Westmead Drive, Timperley, 138
Westwood Avenue, Timperley, 131, 138
Whalley Close, Timperley, 133, 138
Whatcroft, near Northwich, 22-23
Wheatfield, Timperley, 53
Wheatley, 4
Wheeler, Mary (née Tatton), 28
White Carr Lane, Timperley, 9-10, 13, 122, 154, 171, 175
White, Revd. John, 186
Whitegate Field, Timperley, 208
Whitegates Close, Timperley, 131, 138
Whitehead, William, 39
Whitelegg(e), J., 65; James, 189; Mr, 108; Sam, 44; Thomas, 42; William, 39, 103
Whiteley, Frank, 132
Whitley Gardens, Timperley, 138
Whitley Place, Timperley, 138
Whittaker, Amelia, 149; Charles, 149; Hannah, 149; Mrs Ann, 149
Wilkinson, Revd. C., 160, 165; Revd. Samuelus, 167
William III, 27
Williams, Revd. J.G. Alan, 185
Williamson, J., 39; John, 149
Willow House, Moss Lane, 131
Willowbank, Moss Lane, 126
Willows Primary School, Timperley, 198, 208
Windmill Field, Timperley, 90
Windsor Bridge, 155
Windsor Drive, Timperley, 132, 138
Windsor Gardens, Timperley, 138
Windsor Grove, Timperley, 132
Wingate Drive, Timperley, 132, 138
Winstanley, Leonard, 149
Wirral, 16, 19, 28
Wiseman, Revd. F. Luke, 182
Withington, Mary, 108
Wood Lane, Timperley, 4, 9-11, 13, 21, 38, 50, 64, 68, 72, 78, 104, 108, 110, 115-116, 129, 131, 133, 135, 144, 175
Wood Mount, Timperley, 138
Wood Road, Timperley, 138
Wood, Edgar, 165; J., 108; James, 25-26, 102; Mary, 165; Richard of the, 51
Woodall's Terrace, Stockport Road, 216
Woodall, Robert, 103
Woodcote Farm, Timperley, 76
Woodhouse Lane East, Timperley, 34, 132, 138
Woodhouse Lane, Timperley, 9
Woodlands Hotel, Timperley, 147
Woodlands Lane, Timperley, 138
Woodlands Parkway, Timperley, 4, 10, 50, 71, 74, 110, 115, 138, 185
Woodlands United Reformed Church, Timperley, 185
Woodlands, Timperley, 189
Woodlea, Park Road, 82
Woodleigh, Stockport Road, 45
Woolnough, Revd. Edward, M.A., Northenden, 154
Worsencroft, Robert, 149
Worsley, Lancashire, 83, 85
Worsley, Robert, 189; William, 189
Worthington, Ellen, 189; Isaac, 58; Jonathan, 141; Mary, 102; William, 59
Wray, Captain K.C.G., 166; Revd. G.D., 167
Wright, Revd. Ernest H., 185; Revd. James, 185
Wyatt, J., 63; Mrs, 63
Wythenshawe, Cheshire, 47, 59
Wyvern Cottage, Deansgate Lane, 91, 95, 119

Yearsley, William, 145
Yorkshire, 93, 129